ISBN 978-1-334-73490-8
PIBN 10758348

English
Français
Deutsche
Italiano
Español
Português

www.forgottenbooks.com

Mythology Photography **Fiction**
Fishing Christianity **Art** Cooking
Essays Buddhism Freemasonry
Medicine **Biology** Music **Ancient
Egypt** Evolution Carpentry Physics
Dance Geology **Mathematics** Fitness
Shakespeare **Folklore** Yoga Marketing
Confidence Immortality Biographies
Poetry **Psychology** Witchcraft
Electronics Chemistry History **Law**
Accounting **Philosophy** Anthropology
Alchemy Drama Quantum Mechanics
Atheism Sexual Health **Ancient History**
Entrepreneurship Languages Sport
Paleontology Needlework Islam
Metaphysics Investment Archaeology
Parenting Statistics Criminology
Motivational

THE PREVENTION OF MALARIA IN THE FEDERATED MALAY STATES

THE SILENT WAR.

Somewhere in Malaya—the ruins of a coffee store on an estate abandoned on account of Malaria. The jungle is beginning to take possession (see p. 293).

(see p. 293).

[*Frontispiece.*

THE
PREVENTION OF MALARIA
IN THE FEDERATED MALAY STATES
A RECORD OF TWENTY YEARS' PROGRESS

BY

MALCOLM WATSON, M.D., C.M., D.P.H.

Chief Medical Officer, Estate Hospital's Association, Klang, F.M.S. ;
late Senior District Surgeon, F.M.S. Medical Service ; author of
" Rural Sanitation in the Tropics," etc.

WITH CONTRIBUTIONS BY

P. S. HUNTER, M.A., M.B., D.P.H.

Deputy Health Officer, Singapore

AND

A. R. WELLINGTON, M.R.C.S., L.R.C.P., D.P.H., D.T.M.& H.

Senior Health Officer, Federated Malay States

AND A PREFACE BY

SIR RONALD ROSS, K.C.B., K.C.M.G.

F.R.C.S., D.P.H., M.D., LL.D., D.Sc., F.R.S., Nobel Laureate

SECOND EDITION—REVISED AND ENLARGED

LONDON
JOHN MURRAY, ALBEMARLE STREET, LONDON, W.
1921

DEDICATED

BY PERMISSION

TO

SIR FRANK ATHELSTANE SWETTENHAM

G. C. M. G.

LIST OF CONTRIBUTORS TO THE PUBLICATION OF THE FIRST EDITION OF THIS BOOK

THE ANGLO-MALAY RUBBER COMPANY, 11 Idol Lane, London, E.C.

THE HIGHLANDS AND LOWLANDS RUBBER COMPANY, Ceylon House, Eastcheap, E C.

THE CHERSONESE RUBBER COMPANY, Ceylon House, Eastcheap, London, E C.

THE LINGGI RUBBER COMPANY, 5 Whittington Avenue, London, E.C.

THE SELANGOR RUBBER COMPANY, 124 St Vincent Street, Glasgow.

THE PENANG SUGAR ESTATES, LIMITED, E. L. Hamilton, Esq., 27 Austin Friars, London.

THE RUBBER ESTATES OF JOHORE, 11 Idol Lane, London, E.C.

THE JOHORE RUBBER LANDS, 16 Philpot Lane, London, E.C.

THE RUBBER PLANTATIONS INVESTMENT TRUST, 11 Idol Lane, London, E.C.

THE GOLCONDA RUBBER COMPANY, 2 Fenchurch Avenue, London, E.C.

MESSRS GOW, WILSON, AND STANTON, 13 Rood Lane, London, E.C.

PREFACE TO THE FIRST EDITION

By SIR RONALD ROSS

TOWARDS the end of last year, I asked Dr Malcolm Watson to contribute an article to my book on the Prevention of Malaria regarding his work in the Federated Malay States. Unfortunately, the article which he sent to me, though interesting from beginning to end, was too long to be inserted with the contributions furnished by nineteen other workers in various parts of the world: and I therefore determined to try to publish his paper as a separate book. We are greatly indebted to Sir Frank Swettenham, G.C.M.G., the distinguished organiser of Federal Administration in the Protected Malay States, for the assistance which he gave us in this respect. Mr H. J. Read, C.M.G., of the Colonial Office, was kind enough to approach him on my behalf regarding the matter; and the result was that the various Companies mentioned on a previous page generously provided the necessary funds. Not only Dr Watson and myself owe our thanks to Sir Frank Swettenham and to these Companies for the help given to us, but I think that the Governments and peoples of many malarious countries will be not less grateful.

The time is one of change and advancement in our ideas of colonial development. We are passing away from the older period of incessant wars and of great military or civil dictatorships into one of more minute and scientific administration in which the question always held before us is: What can best be done for increasing the prosperity of the people? Sanitation is almost the first word in the answer. Prosperity is impossible in the face of widespread disease, and perhaps the very first effort which must be made in new countries is to render them reasonably safe, not only from human enemies, but from those small or invisible ones which in the end are so much more injurious. As one example of this new theorem I can quote that of Panama, where the Americans began their great work by laborious sanitary preparations. Another example will be found in this book.

The author describes the origin of the Federated Malay States and the great sanitary problem which remained when that Federation was completed. It is a picture of a great work and of a great difficulty beyond it. Political adjustments are not everything, and for additional successes the statesman must be followed by the man of science and the scientific adminis-trator. Possessed of great natural riches, of an intelligent population, and of neighbouring sources of intelligent labour, the States appeared from the first to have been designed for wealth and success. Within them, however, there lived a relentless enemy—a disease which hampers all human work, especially that of the pioneer and the planter, to a degree which will scarcely be believed in this country; and the task before the Government was to subdue this enemy if possible. I have said elsewhere that the Panama Canal is being dug with a microscope, and I believe that the same instrument will double the wealth of the Federated Malay States.

Technically, Dr Watson's book is of the utmost value to all workers against malaria. He has laboured at his campaign for eight years; he has studied the disease from every point of view, and its prevention by every method. He has attacked it in towns, in villages, and in plantations; and has thrown into the work a degree of energy and enthusiasm which has not been exceeded in any anti-malaria campaign which has been carried out since we learned the manner in which it is carried from man to man. This book contains the details of his methods and the lessons which he has to teach. I may, perhaps, be allowed the privilege of considering it to be a part of my own work mentioned above.

More than ten years have now elapsed since we learned how the disease is carried. This has been a period of probation, during which many methods of prevention have been tentatively investigated. We have had great examples of success by various methods in the Panama Canal Zone, in Italy, in Ismailia, and in many other places; but I trust that this book, which describes the no less brilliant campaign of the Federated Malay States, will furnish the Governments, the health departments, and the planters of every malarious country with detailed information which they can always use for similar work ; and we may now hope that progress will become still more rapid and complete in the future.

RONALD ROSS.

UNIVERSITY OF LIVERPOOL,
    1st December 1910.

AUTHOR'S PREFACE TO THE
SECOND EDITION

WITHIN a few months of its publication by the Liverpool School of Tropical Medicine in 1911, the first edition of this book was sold out. A reprint was suggested, but as our knowledge at that time was increasing rapidly, I felt the book should be re-written.

Visits to Sumatra, Panama, and British Guiana, the writing of *Rural Sanitation in the Tropics,* and the war, have all served to delay the issue of a new edition; but another, and perhaps the chief cause, was a disinclination to write during the progress of many anti-malaria schemes, and before they had reached fruition—in other words, a dislike to write of uncompleted work.

Whatever hesitation there may be elsewhere, mosquito reduction, as the method of stamping out malaria, has been so widely adopted throughout Malaya that each year always leaves work unfinished, as it also initiates new work, and sees the completion of what was begun in former years. But, however fascinating it is to gather in one harvest, and to look forward to the next, the need of the new workers for guidance is too great to allow of further delay in publishing.

Sir Ronald Ross pointed out in the first chapter of his *Prevention of Malaria,* that the work described in the first edition of this book recorded a new phase in anti-malarial work, namely the control of malaria by anopheline reduction in rural areas. From small beginnings in towns, the work has spread in ever-widening circles, and, I might add, in spite of an apparently ever-deepening complexity of the problem.

So far from the map of Malaya being evenly washed with the malarial taint, violent contrasts have been found in different parts, and widely different, often diametrically opposed, methods have been found necessary for its control. Some land, when covered with jungle, has been found to be malarial, and some non-malarial; some land has become healthy when cleared of jungle, and some has become intensely malarial when so treated; drainage frees some land from malaria, but some remains malarial; some land is malarial whether drained or undrained, whether under jungle or cleared of jungle; some rice fields are malarial, and some are non-malarial; while in a single ravine, the various insect inhabitants may come and go in the wondrous fashion of a fairy tale. In their stories of the little Mouse-deer, the Malays have invented a "Puck," who plays endless tricks on the other creatures of the forest. Sometimes I suspect he has been working his wiles on men and mosquitoes, and, uninvited, been taking an elfish interest in mosquito control, which we could gladly have excused.

Through the maze, however, the great truth discovered by Sir Ronald Ross has been an unfailing guide. But for that discovery no progress would have been possible; we would have been absolutely baffled and utterly lost; because of it, tens of thousands are alive to-day in Malaya who would have been dead, while the suffering from which the children have been saved is almost beyond belief.

From the mass of material available, it has been necessary to make some selection. Examples of the control of malaria in mangrove swamps, on plains, and on hills have been given, with plans and illustrations. It is hoped these will assist medical officers to control malaria under most conditions, and to suggest means of overcoming difficulties, even if a replica of the place and problem is not to be found in these pages. And I would forcibly impress on the beginner not to be daunted by apparent failure. The destruction of anopheles always bears fruit, although, as this book shows, the full benefits may not be reaped for months or years.

Some readers may be interested in the development of our present ideas of malaria. For them portions of the previous edition have been retained and marked thus (1909). Although the record is of unbroken progress, scientific and practical, there are problems ahead. Yet in looking into the future, I can see—not far distant—the extension of the present methods, the evolution of new ones, and triumphs in averting death, in promoting happiness, prosperity and joy, more brilliant than any hitherto recorded in the history of medicine in the tropics.

I wish to acknowledge my indebtedness to Mr C. Ward-Jackson for valued assistance, and for revising and correcting the proof sheets.

MALCOLM WATSON.

KLANG,
FEDERATED MALAY STATES,
23rd July 1921.

CONTENTS

CHAPTER I

INTRODUCTION

xvii   B

CHAPTER V

THE STORY OF A COAST ROAD

CHAPTER VI

KAPAR DRAINAGE SCHEME

CHAPTER VII

A MALARIAL SURVEY

CHAPTER VIII

THE MALARIA OF THE COASTAL PLAIN AND *ANOPHELES UMBROSUS*

CHAPTER IX

THE MALARIA OF MANGROVE SWAMPS AND *ANOPHELES LUDLOWI*

CHAPTER X

THE COASTAL⁷ HILLS

CHAPTER XI

THE EFFECTS OF MALARIA

CHAPTER XII

ON QUININE

CHAPTER XIII

SEAFIELD ESTATE AND SUBSOIL DRAINAGE

CHAPTER XIV

SEAFIELD ESTATE (*continued*)

CHAPTER XV

SEAFIELD ESTATE (*continued*)

CHAPTER XVI

ON THE BORDER OF THE HILL LAND

CHAPTER XVII

OILING

CHAPTER XVIII

SOME OTHER EXAMPLES OF HILL CAMPAIGNS

CHAPTER XIX

ON THE POSSIBILITY OF ALTERING THE COMPOSITION OF WATER AND THE ANOPHELINES BREEDING IN IT

CHAPTER XX

THE INLAND HILLS

CHAPTER XXI

THE MALARIA OF RIVERS

CHAPTER XXII

THE REAPPEARANCE OF MALARIA

CHAPTER XXIII

SCREENING

CHAPTER XXIV

ON DRAINAGE

CHAPTER XXV

ON MOSQUITOES

CHAPTER XXVI

THE MALARIA OF KUALA LUMPUR

Measures taken to bring about its Abatement, showing the Failure of Empiricism and the Success of a Scheme based on the Findings of Entomological research. By Dr A. R. WELLINGTON, M.R.C.S., L.R.C.P., D.P.H., D.T.M. and H., Cantab., Senior Health Officer, F.M.S.

CHAPTER XXVII

ANTI-MALARIAL WORK IN SINGAPORE

By P. S. HUNTER, M.A., M.B., D.P.H., Deputy Health Officer, Singapore.

CHAPTER XXVIII

ON STATISTICS

CHAPTER XXIX

RESULTS

CHAPTER XXX

CONCLUSIONS

LIST OF ILLUSTRATIONS

xxv

" Life is a warfare and a stranger's sojourn."

M. AURELIUS ANTONINUS.

THE PREVENTION OF MALARIA IN THE FEDERATED MALAY STATES

CHAPTER I

INTRODUCTION

British Administration in the Federated Malay States.—Only a generation ago a small band of Britons was sent to Malaya. Utterly insignificant in number, backed by no armed force to give weight to their words, they had strict orders only to advise the native chiefs, and not to rule. Civil war raged in the land. To take one step from the beaten track was to be lost in a forest, which had held men in check from the beginning of time. They were expected to create order from jungle, and turn strife to peace.

A hopeless task it might appear; but they brought with them those qualities which have spread the power and influence of Britain throughout the world. In the work of these men will be found the highest examples of the tact, of the scrupulous dealing with the native rulers, and of the sound administration which have built up the British Empire; and the progress they made is almost too great to grasp. They found it a land deep in the gloom of an evergreen forest whose darkness covered even darker deeds; for man fought with man, and almost every man's hand was against his fellow's. During the course of a generation, thousands of acres were wrested from jungle; thousands of people now live in peace and plenty; a railway stretches from end to end of the lands; roads, second to none, bear motors of every kind; while chiefs, who had never entered each other's country except with sword in hand, met in harmony in conference with the man whose genius had made Federation possible.

In Swettenham's *History of British Malaya* will be found the record of this marvellous change; and, with scientific instinct, the author contrasts the condition of the Federated States under British control with that of the other Malay States which were still under Siam and their native rulers. These form a "control" to the British experiment. To the Federated Malay States, British administration has brought wealth and prosperity to a degree to which can be found no parallel.

And with wealth has come health. From hundreds of square miles malaria, which formerly exacted a heavy toll from Malay and foreigner alike, has been driven out.

Day by day it is being pushed back. Strong as its position now is in the hills, that too is being undermined, and it is my object to record the victories of the past and indicate the line of attack for the future.

Position and Climate.—The following observations have been made in portions of the Malay Peninsula lying between the 2nd and 6th degrees of North Latitude. The Peninsula itself lies between the 100th and 107th degrees of East Longitude. The climate is, therefore, to be described as equatorial; that is, it is equable, hot, moist, and without extremes either of heat or cold. Than such a climate none could be conceived more suitable for the propagation of the mosquito, and both in number of species and number of individuals, the Culicidæ are well represented.

The rainfall is large, and is, on the whole, fairly evenly distributed throughout the year. In those parts of the States where a difference is noticeable, the wettest period is from September to March. The rainfall is always considerably heavier in localities near hills than on flat land near the coast.

The average rainfall in the hilly inland districts varies between 100 and 200 inches, while in the drier parts of the States it is usually recorded at from 70 to 100 inches per annum.

The general meteorological condition is as represented by the official return given in the medical report of Selangor for the year 1908.[1] There are differences from year to year and between different places in the Peninsula, but these will be referred to later where necessary.

FIG. 2.—VIRGIN JUNGLE IN MALAYA.

[*To face page* 2.

Meteorological Return of Kuala Lumpur for the year 1908.

	Temperature.						Rainfall.		Winds.	
	Solar Maximum.	Minimum on Grass.	Shade Maximum.	Shade Minimum.	Range.	Mean.	Amount in inches.	Degree of Humidity.	General Direction.	Average Force.
January . .	147·2	53·1						79	N.-W.	
February . .	149·6	52·5					·	77	Calm	
March . . .	143·9	52·6					·	79	S.-W.	
April . . .	144·2	52·3					·	75	,,	Not recorded.
May . . .	147·7	51·9					·	78	,,	
June . . .	146·4	52·4						78	,,	
July . . .	146·4	52·6						80	,,	
August . .	147·8	51·6						79	,,	
September .	142·8	52·8						81	,,	
October . .	142·5	52·9						80	,,	
November .	140·5	53·2						81	S.-E.	
December .	147·7	52·8						78	Calm	
Mean . .	145·5	52·5						78	S.-W.	...

Under such conditions it is not surprising that malaria should, in certain places, be a veritable scourge; and it has been and is so.

The former residence of the British Resident of the State of Perak, built on one of the finest sites in the capital, had to be abandoned on account of malaria; and when recently I visited it the fine drive up the hill was so overgrown that I was unable to force my way to the top. Proposals for the abandonment of the town of Jugra at one time were made.

Orders were actually given by telegraph by the High Commissioner to close Port Swettenham, within two months of its being opened, on account of the disease. A coffee estate was abandoned a few years ago on account of the impossibility of living on it, and at the present moment on many estates this disease is the cause of the gravest anxiety.

Since the disease is essentially a local one, it will be preferable if I first deal with my observations of various localities, and afterwards treat of their relationship with one another.

Before doing so, however, it will be worth while glancing back for a moment at a brief history of our knowledge of malaria. We will then be better able to appreciate the position in 1900.

A Short History of Malaria.[2]—A disease which appears every day, every other day, or every fourth day, with a punctuality rivalling a railway schedule, and one, too, which goes through such definite phases as shivering, burning fever, sweating, and rapid recovery all within a few hours, is a phenomenon not readily to be overlooked. We find it referred to by both Greek and Latin writers. Though recognised when the attack was a regular quotidian, tertian, or quartan fever, it was not until cinchona came into use that the irregular forms of malaria were distinguished from other diseases accompanied by fever. Cinchona was brought to Europe about 1640 by the Countess D'El Cinchona, wife of the Viceroy of Peru, who had been cured of fever by the drug in that country. Its use soon spread through Europe and other continents with benefit to millions of unhappy beings.

By giving quinine the physician had a fairly certain test for a malarial fever. If the fever was checked by the drug it was malaria; if not, the fever was not malaria. This was a long step forward, yet it still gave no clue to the cause of the disease. Already its association with marshes had suggested a miasma, or an effluvium, or bad air, rising from the swamps, a theory which has given us two of the names for the disease, namely paludism and malaria (the Italian *mal aria*, or bad air). Later, when the disease was found to be associated with disturbances of soil, quite apart from marshes, the theory of a telluric miasma was invented.

At an early date drainage was seen to drive out malaria from certain areas, and there were even suggestions that the mosquito might be the means of infection.

On 6th November 1880, A. Laveran, when working at Constantine in Algeria, discovered malaria parasites in human blood. The Italians, notably Golgi, Canalis, Marchia-fava, Celli, and Bignami, soon took up this discovery and worked out the details of the three human malaria parasites. They showed how the quotidian, tertian, and quartan fevers were due to different and easily recognisable parasites; how the parasites multiplied in the blood by breaking up into spores; and how the fever paroxysm commences at the time when the spores are set free in the blood. Although by these discoveries we passed from the hypothesis that malaria is due to a miasma to the theory that it is due to a living organism, not unnaturally it was many years before the miasma hypothesis, which had held the field for centuries against all comers, was given up by the public.

The problem then was how these parasites passed from one human being to another; if they lived outside of man, where and in what condition? Failure attended every effort to discover the exit of the germs from the human body; the most exhaustive search for them in swamps and soil was fruitless. Manson, who had already traced a blood worm, the *Filaria nocturna*, into the mosquito, then suggested that certain forms of the malaria parasite, the motile filaments given off by the crescents, were for the purpose of infecting the mosquito; and that, when the infected mosquito died, the parasites escaped from its body into water, which when drunk by man infected him.

By a series of brilliant researches the genius of Ross dispelled the mystery. The parasites were taken up by certain mosquitoes (the anopheles) when they sucked blood from a fever patient; male and female parasites were taken up; they conjugated to form a new parasite in the mosquito's stomach wall; this sub-divided into many new fine threads or young parasites, which were injected into man when the mosquito took its next meal of blood. This wonderful development within the mosquito is completed in about ten days in a tropical climate.

Such a discovery, pregnant with so much good for humanity, at once attracted widespread attention in every country where malaria existed; unfortunately there are few countries from which it is absent. Commissions were despatched from European countries to the tropics; in a few months the discovery was confirmed in every detail. The years which have passed have still further confirmed the work completed by Ross between 21st August 1897 and August 1898.

Ross left India, in February 1899, to join the newly-formed Liverpool School of Tropical Medicine. A few months later he set out for West Africa to continue his studies, particularly the prevention of malaria and the habits of mosquitoes. The policy he adopted was that of mosquito reduction; arguing that by eliminating the mosquito, where this was practicable, and it seemed to be so in towns, the disease would soon be stamped out. Koch, who had gone to Java to study the problem, advocated the use of quinine, hoping to kill the parasites in man, thus preventing mosquitoes from becoming infected, and conveying the disease to a new host.   The Italians also adopted this method on a large scale, combining with it, in many places, the screening of houses with wire-gauze in order to prevent mosquitoes from biting the inhabitants. To bring the subject dramatically home to the public, Manson in 1900 carried out two experiments.   A mosquito-proof house was built in a notoriously malarious spot in the Italian Campagna, and occupied by Drs Sambon and Low throughout the most malarious months of the year.   They worked in the fields during the day, but retired within the house before sunset.   Neither observer contracted malaria.   The other experiment was to bring anopheles mosquitoes, which had fed on fever patients in Rome, to London, and there to make them bite two people, who had not previously suffered from malaria. Both men—one was Manson's son—developed malaria, and parasites were demonstrated in their blood.

Such was the state of our knowledge when early in January 1901 I found myself in Klang, in the Federated Malay States.

CHAPTER II

In 1901.—This town, the headquarters of the district of the same name, is situated on the Klang River, some twelve miles from its mouth, and five miles as the crow flies. In 1901 the census of the population showed there were 3576 inhabitants, occupying 293 houses. Since then the town has greatly increased in density of population as well as in area. Within the old town limits of 1901 the number of houses has increased from 293 to 468, which would give an estimated population of 5745. This, I believe, will be found to be less than the actual increase of the population. In all subsequent statistics when comparison is made between the figures of different years it is to be understood that these figures refer only to the population within the town limits of 1901, and not to those of the present town limits. The old town limit was practically the Jalan Raya, except where for three-quarters of a mile this road ran parallel with the river, and the river was the boundary.

The area of the town was in 1901 approximately 290 acres. Of this 22 acres was swamp, 25 acres virgin jungle, 60 acres dense secondary growth in many places 30 to 40 feet high. The distribution of these undesirable portions will be seen from the map. The whole town was permeated with their influence, and it is hardly surprising that malaria was a scourge.

Assuming duty early in January 1901, as Government Surgeon of the Districts of Klang, Kuala Selangor, and Kuala Langat of the State of Selangor, one of the Federated Malay States, I found the hospital at Klang full of malaria. It appeared to me that my duty consisted in doing more than remaining in hospital all day treating patients, since to this there could be no end, if steps were not taken to

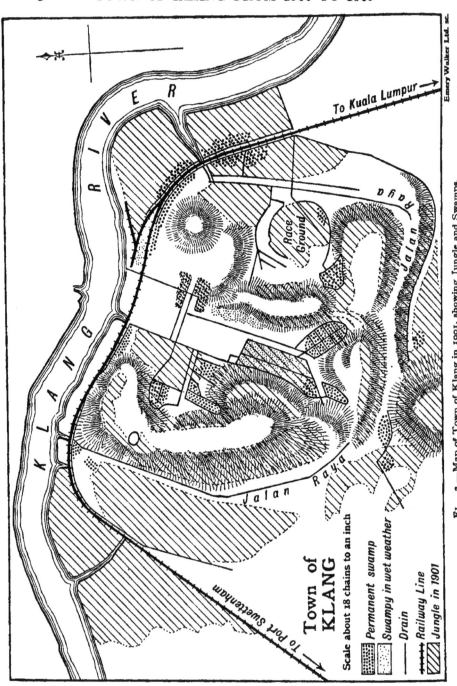

Fɪ 3.—Map of Town of Klang in 1901, showing Jungle and Swamps.

prevent infection of the population. At that time, Ross's brilliant discovery had been fully confirmed by the Italians and others. Manson's[3] dramatic proof at Ostia and at London left no doubt of what could be done under certain conditions. Ross himself had favoured mosquito reduction, and was actively engaged in West Africa in putting this method to the test. The Italians[4] were rather in favour of mechanical prophylaxis by mosquito netting, and by the use of quinine; and Koch[5] had already reported a success in a small community by the regular use of this drug.

At this time nothing was known about the species of anophelines, and the valuable reports[6] of the Commissioners of the Malaria Committee of the Royal Society bearing on the importance of species were not published until the year after the work at Klang had been begun.

Choice of Anti-malarial Method.—At Klang the work of eradicating malaria seemed well-nigh hopeless. No hot or cold season even temporarily stopped the mosquito pest; and every well, ditch, and swamp teemed with larvæ. The active co-operation of the native community could not be expected; and active resistance, especially from the Chinese, was certain if any attempt was made to enforce the use of quinine. Then enforcement of mosquito nets was, of course, impossible; since this would have meant constant house visitation at night. Compulsory screening of the whole of every house was equally impossible for financial reasons; nor would people have remained within mosquito-proof houses in the evening, which is so pleasantly cool after the heat of a tropical day. Again, with an area so extensive, subsoil water so high as to form permanent swamps, and aquatic vegetation so dense, the sweeping out or dealing with the individual collections of water in any continuous manner was impossible. As surgeon of a district fully 100 miles long, I felt that the time I could devote to any anti-malarial measures would be limited, and I also felt that no other member of the community was at all likely to be willing or able to give more time than myself to the supervision of measures which would keep down mosquitoes only as long as they were constantly applied. And to be quite candid, knowing that the burden would fall on myself, I did not quite appreciate the idea of having constantly to stand in the sun supervising coolies and insisting on the thoroughness on which alone success would depend.

Considering all these elements of the problem, I rejected as impossible Koch's quinine method, and the Italian mechanical prophylaxis, and decided to recommend Ross's method of mosquito reduction. To suit the local conditions, I determined that any expenditure should be on works of a permanent nature. By draining and filling, there would be a large and permanent reduction of the breeding-places of mosquitoes; and presumably malaria would be correspondingly reduced.

As time has shown, it was indeed a fortunate choice. It has been successful far beyond our expectations. No other method would have been of any real value; nor would any of them, or even several of them combined, have given anything like the results obtained by this. It is easy to see, too, that some of the failures to control malaria in other countries, reported in later years, were due to those in charge not adopting the radical method; or, where it was attempted, not carrying it out with sufficient energy and on a large enough scale.

It was a fortunate choice from another point of view. Although our first efforts were on a small scale in a town, its immediate success induced me to consider the possibility of extending the method to rural areas; and in these, too, the results have been not less successful in many places, as this volume will show. Although the details have required modification to suit the particular habits of the species of anopheles we have encountered, the radical method of mosquito reduction has everywhere given results superior to any other, even among the small populations to be found in plantations and villages.

Although the success was due to a fortunate choice of the method adopted, as it turned out, there was a real stroke of luck, not recognised until many years after. It was this: Had the hills of Klang been higher, or had Klang been situated in the main range of hills, instead of being practically an island in the coastal plains, the clearing away of jungle from the hills and the draining of the valleys and swamps would have led to the introduction of a new malaria - carrying anopheles, certainly not less terrible than the one we got rid of by our drainage. Instead of success there would have been complete failure; and there can be little doubt anti-malarial work would have been set back for years in the Federated Malay States. Indeed we escaped very narrowly from this peril. For at the very moment my scheme for the drainage of Klang reached Government, a proposal to test Ross's new theory was received from the then State Surgeon of Negri Sembilan. He suggested that if he were given the requisite staff, he would make full inquiries into the incidence of malaria in the town of Seremban and the mosquitoes there. After the records were complete, an attempt would be made to eradicate the mosquitoes, and the results recorded. Now Seremban is a town among the hills of the main range; so there is every reason to believe from my own experiences in similar places the experiment would have been a complete failure. Fortunately my scheme was sent in with full details of the incidence of malaria in Klang, of the houses infected, of the mosquito breeding-places, and of the urgent need for action. The case for carrying out an experiment in Klang was overwhelming. It won the day; and much more than that, as the years were to show.

Finally I must confess that I by no means expected the success, which as a fact followed the works. I had the feeling that perhaps a 20 per cent. or 30 per cent. reduction might be obtained in the hospital returns. At times a feeling of despair came over me. Although I can afford to laugh at it now, one portion of the railway line between Klang and Port Swettenham always recalls to my mind the feeling of despair which came over me there one day, at the height of the outbreak of 1901. How was it possible to eradicate a disease like malaria, when those infected were liable to relapses for years, and at each relapse be capable of infecting others if any anopheles at all were present? Then there was the danger of infected people coming from other parts keeping up a constant supply of malaria. Indeed I was prepared for a total failure of the works, and had my answer already prepared should I be called to account by Government. It was that Ross had proved anophelines did carry malaria; that to remain doing nothing was to remain to die; and that it was at least worth spending money to try whether such a scourge could be removed or even reduced. I record these feelings that they may encourage others who may be dissuaded by the apparent magnitude of the task from attempting to combat this disease.

Preliminary Steps.—Although the extreme prevalence of the disease was apparent to me from seeing so much of it in the hospital, some definite statistics were required if Government were to be justified in spending money. And as a business transaction it was also necessary to obtain some knowledge of the then condition of the town for comparison with subsequent periods after the works had been undertaken, to determine whether the results were worth the expenditure. Unfortunately, although there were many cases of malaria in the hospital (they had in fact formed 24·9 per cent. of the total admissions for the previous year) there was no record of the residence of the patients beyond the district in which they lived. And, although there had been much sickness among the Government officers, no record existed of the disease from which they had suffered, although numerous prescriptions for quinine probably supplied a very significant hint. From the death register little help could be obtained since the only qualified practitioner in the district was the Government surgeon, and only such deaths as were certified by him could be advanced as being assigned to their true cause.

My first care was, therefore, to put the record on a more satisfactory footing. The exact residence of every case of malaria admitted to hospital was carefully and personally inquired into by me. This was very essential, since the patients, if casually asked where they lived, generally answered Klang, although in fact they might have lived miles beyond the town limits. But for these precautions the returns would have exaggerated considerably the actual amount of malaria in the town. To widen the basis of the statistics, I had new returns prepared showing the number of out-patients treated for malaria. The disease for which an officer obtained sick leave was recorded; and for some months I personally kept a register of the houses within the town which were infected with malaria, at the same time recording the number of cases which occurred in each as they came to my knowledge.

These precautions I maintained until I went on leave early in 1908. Subsequent changes in the staff led to these being overlooked, and only recently I discovered that it was so.   The record has again been put on a satisfactory basis; but unfortunately the returns for the years 1908 and 1909 on this account are not available for comparison with previous years. Fortunately the blood and spleen census of the children is a record of the condition of the town not affected by hospital statistics.

*Anopheline Breeding-places.**—These were found everywhere within the town, and a plan was prepared showing their distribution.   In the very centre of the town a swamp existed, with houses close up to it.   People have told me they shot snipe on it from the Rest House.   As will be seen from the map the town is situated within, upon, and around, a somewhat semicircular group of small hills.   At the foot of the hills, especially where they bend to form small valleys, the ground water was so high as to form permanent swamps.   In the absence of a town water-supply, wells innumerable were found, mostly teeming with anopheline larvæ.

The exact species were not determined for some time after the works had been started, but even then some of the original swamps had been completely drained.   In December 1903 and January 1904, Dr G. F. Leicester investigated the anophelines of Klang and reported as follows in his *Culicidæ of Malaya*:[7]—

" Caught in houses—

> *Myzomyia rossii.*
> *Cellia kochii.*
> *Myzorhynchus karwari.*

" Caught in jungle—

> *Myzorhynchus umbrosus.*
>   „   *sinensis.*

" The larvæ of the following mosquitoes were taken :—

" (*a*) In mud holes, *i.e.*, small holes made by the feet of a heavy animal or a wagon rut in a road—

> *Myzomyia rossii.*
> *Cellia kochii.*

---

* [1920.—I have left this section as it appeared in the previous edition, since it will be more convenient to discuss the anopheles of the F.M.S. in a later chapter (see Chapter XXV.).—M. W.]

"(*b*) In stagnant shallow water supplied by rain and liable to dry up—

>*Cellia kochii.*

"(*c*) In swamps—

>*Myzorhynchus barbirostris.*
>„   *sinensis.*
>„   *umbrosus.*
>*Cellia kochii.*

"(*d*) In marshy ground fed by a stream—

>*Cellia kochii.*
>*Nyssorhynchus nivipes.*

"The jungle on the hill range running parallel with the Langat Road was entered at several points to ascertain what mosquitoes were common there. On the first occasion *Myzorhynchus (Anopheles) barbirostris* and *Mansonia annulipes* were obtained in very large numbers during the day, but on the hill marked M on the map, no anopheles were obtained in the evening though they were abundant in the day. Later on the jungle was visited on two other occasions, and the number of anopheles present had considerably diminished.

"There is evidence that great seasonal variation of the number of anopheles in the jungle occurs, as on an unknown date last year Mr E. V. Carey observed anopheles in great numbers in the jungle at the third mile; on a later occasion he, with Drs H. E. Durham and Watson, visited this jungle, and they were unable to find a single anopheles."

The disappearance of the mosquitoes does not seem to have any relation to the rainfall, nor should I expect this, as the swamps at the foot of these hills where larvæ were found are permanent, and therefore the breeding-places would not dry up during the season.

I think there is a possible mistake with regard to the *Myzorhynchus* which was found by Dr Leicester on the hill. My recollection is that he called it at the time *umbrosus*. In his *Culicidæ* he calls it *barbirostris*. I think the explanation is to be found in the existence of another *Myzorhynchus* so closely allied to *umbrosus* as to be possibly only a variety. It differs from *M. umbrosus* in having two costal spots, the basal of which is very small. I think, therefore, that Dr Leicester when he came to go over his specimens in Kuala Lumpur rejected it as *umbrosus* on account of the two costal spots, and so called it *barbirostris*. I call this variety in the meantime *Myzorhynchus umbrosus x*. I am the more disposed to think this is the true explanation of the change of name, as *Myzorhynchus umbrosus x*. is the common jungle anopheles, and I have found it universally in jungle here. Not only so, but I have found it in enormous numbers. On the occasion when Dr Leicester visited the hill, the mosquito was in such numbers that simply by slipping a test-tube from one part of our clothes to another, six or seven mosquitoes could be obtained in perhaps about two minutes. Dr Leicester, myself, and an attendant caught something like two hundred anophelines in a quarter of an hour, and simply could not stand the biting further. I may mention that *Mansonia annulipes, Desvoidæ jugrænsis*, and *Verallina butleri* were present in considerably greater numbers than the anopheline, so it can be imagined a quarter of an hour in that jungle was unpleasant. It is of sufficient interest to record, that although *Myzorhynchus umbrosus x*. was swarming in the jungle and attacking during the day, in a rubber estate separated only by a 20-feet road, but, of course, free from undergrowth, we were entirely free from attack, and no adults could be seen.

The point of the presence of this anopheline is important, as I have found it to be a natural malaria carrier.

Of ten adults taken from coolie lines on Estate " T," one was found with numerous zygotes and sporozoites.

The anophelines found in Klang Town in 1909 have been :—

> *Pseudo-myzomyia rossii* ? var. *indefinita.*
> *Cellia kochii.*
> *Myzorhynchus barbirostris.*
> „ *sinensis.*
> *separatus.*

The last of the breeding-places where *N. nivipes* and *N. karwari* were found was destroyed about 1904, and except for the renewal of a small piece of one of the swamps in 1908 through a brick drain being put at too high a level, there is now, 1909, in Klang no breeding-place suitable for these mosquitoes. It is still impossible to say exactly what mosquitoes were carrying malaria in 1901, but I think *Myzorhynchus umbrosus x*. was probably the most important one. Only two miles from the centre of Klang there is now, 1909, a spot in which this mosquito abounds, and in which 50 to 100 per cent. of the children suffer from enlargement of the spleen, the percentages varying universally with the distance they actually live from the mosquito's breeding-place.

In the earth drains and such wells as remain, there has been a great reduction in the number of larvæ. The number of adults which can be caught varies very greatly. In the month of August 1909, during a period when the weather was dry, not an adult could be caught, although the most careful search was made. Yet two months later specimens of the above-mentioned species, particularly of *M. separatus*, were caught with great facility, and in fact for about a week rarely a night passed without my being attacked as I sat reading.

Proposals made to Government for Drainage Scheme.— Having made definite observations, which convinced me of the necessity of striking at the disease, I laid the facts before the Klang Sanitary Board in May 1901, with proposals for a drainage scheme. The proposals were accepted by the Board and were included in the proposed estimates submitted to the Government by the Board for 1902. This was entirely due to the strong support given to them by the Chairman, Mr H. B. Ellerton; and I wish to record my grateful thanks to him not only for his support, but for many valuable suggestions in connection with the proposals. When it is borne in mind that I personally had no experience of either the tropics or of the methods of presenting proposals to the Government, those who have had experience of both will realise how much Klang owes to Mr Ellerton.

The support of the State Surgeon of Selangor, Dr E. A. O. Travers, was then sought; and in July 1901, I forwarded a report to him asking for support for the Board's proposal. In it I pointed out that :—

(a) While the total number of cases treated at the hospital during the first half of 1901 showed an increase of 3·25 per cent. over the corresponding period of 1900, the increase in the number of malaria cases amounted to no less than 69 per cent.; (b) of these malaria cases 55 per cent. came from the town, while the estates, which were better drained, sent in only 11 per cent.; (c) to my personal knowledge 60 houses out of 293 within the town boundary had been infected within the previous three and a half months; (*d*) the prevailing type of parasite was the tropical or malignant form; (*e*) a water-supply was shortly to be introduced, and it would be unwise to bring increased moisture into a town already suffering from malaria without previously providing proper drainage; and (*f*) since in the returns from 1896 onwards 'Malaria has been more prevalent in the latter part of the year, the marked increase of fever in the first six months of 1901 is a matter for serious consideration, and some action in the way of drainage is clearly indicated.'"

This report was accompanied by a plan of the town showing the general distribution of the swamps, the breeding-places of anopheles, and the houses infected by malaria. The proposals received from Dr Travers the strongest support, and the Government not only indicated that the proposal would be favourably considered, but ultimately *doubled the sum asked for by the Board.*

The Outbreak of 1901.—It was soon evident that the end of the year was to make good our worst fears. The outbreak reached terrible proportions. The inhabitants of house after house went down before the disease in the months of September, October, November, and December, which period, incidentally I may mention, coincided with a marked rise in the level of the ground water of the town. It is difficult to convey any proper conception of such an outbreak and the misery it involves; but the following extracts from my note-book will show how much Government officers and their families suffered.

In the clerks' new quarters there were 11 cases with one death; clerks' old quarters, 4 cases; clerk of works' quarters, 7 cases; adjoining quarters, 2 cases; post office, 2 cases; railway quarters, 16 cases; rest house, 5 cases; inspector of police's quarters, 6 cases; police constables, 21 cases; in the district officer's quarters the servants were attacked; in the surveyor's quarters all the Europeans were attacked, the family consisting of the husband, wife, and two children. In my household all my servants were attacked (three in number). My wife and I escaped, I believe because the servants were sent to hospital at once and were kept there until their blood was found to be free from parasites, and they were dosed with quinine on their return to work. In addition we used citronella oil lavishly on our persons and clothing in the evenings, and our mosquito curtains were thoroughly searched and cleared of anophelines each night.

In addition to those occupying Government quarters, many Government officers were attacked who did not live in Government quarters; and I think two clerks' quarters and the dresser's quarters at the hospital were the only ones to escape. I may mention these had been attacked in the earlier part of the year.

In the lower lying town, the condition was more terrible. Hardly a house escaped. In many cases I found five and six persons attacked, and the observations I then made have left an indelible impression on my mind. Night after night I was called to see the sick in houses and found men in all stages of the disease. Many and many a time it was only to find the patient in the last stage of collapse or in burning fever. The whole population was demoralised; and when in November the death-rate rose to the rate of 300 per mille, the Chinese suspended business entirely for three days, and devoted their energies to elaborate processions and other religious rites calculated to drive away the evil spirit.

Work done in Klang. — Although the money voted by Government did not become available until 1st January 1902, the Board was by no means idle in 1901. All the available Sanitary Board Staff was occupied in felling jungle, and clearing undergrowth, and doing some minor draining. Owners of private land were, under one of the Board's laws, compelled to drain and clear their land. The section reads as follows and had been in force since 1890, although its power had been little invoked in Klang :—

"When any private tank or low marshy ground or any waste or stagnant water being within any private enclosure appears to the Board to be injurious to health or to be offensive to the neighbourhood, the Board shall by notice in writing require the owner of the said premises to cleanse or fill up such tank or marshy ground or to drain off or remove such marshy water." (Section 45, Conservancy of Towns and Villages Enactment, 1890.)

This section gave the fullest powers to the Board, and it was freely used.

During 1902 the sums seen below were expended by the

FIG. 4.—SMALL HILLS OF TOWN OF KLANG.

The swamps were situated at the foot of the hills, especially where they bend to form cavities.

FIG. 5.—HILL-FOOT DRAIN, TOWN OF KLANG.

Hill-foot Drain, encircling what was formerly a swamp, with water knee-deep in places. The drains have rendered this so dry that a part of it is used for the racecourse and part for a golf green. No filling was used to obtain this result. On other swamps in Klang of exactly the same nature much money was spent in "filling," with absolutely no result, as the springs from the hills poured water out over the new surface.

[To face page 18.

Board on draining and filling. The work was not, however finished all at once, and even in 1904 some small swamps were still in existence.

It was not until Mr E. V. Carey pointed out that the only way of draining the swamps effectively was by contour drains at the foot of the hills, the method universally employed by planters, that these became really dry.

The actual expenditure was as follows :—

		Dollars.*
1901.	Extension of Brick Drains	750
1902.	Extension of Brick Drains	1925
	Filling in Swamps .	8579
	Main Sewer	3856
1903.	Extension of Existing Drains	368
	Extension of Brick Drains	2340
	Filling in Swamps .	1303
	Main Sewer	6142
1904.	Rebuilding another Main Sewer .	4000
	Extension of Brick Drains	2500
	Lowering of Railway Culverts	1500
1905.	Brick Drains	2554

* The value of the dollar was fixed at two shillings and four pence of British money on 29th January 1906. Before that it fluctuated with, and was of equal value to, the Mexican dollar.

This work included the drainage of swamps just outside the old town limits, some 16 acres in extent.

I am indebted to Government for information regarding the actual expenditure. This expenditure may appear to be very great, but local circumstances are responsible for much of it.

Our Mistakes.—In the first place most of the houses of the town were situated close to the river, and connecting them with the river were several brick drains, or more correctly, open sewers. In order to drain the swamps of the town, which were further from the river than the houses, as will be seen from the plan, it was necessary to bring the water down these sewers. Unfortunately these sewers were at much too high a level to allow of this ; and consequently they had to be pulled up and rebuilt before the swamps could be effectively drained. In some places efforts were made to avoid this, but, in reviewing the result, l am convinced that had the original drains been entirely discarded better results would have been obtained for the money spent. The drainage system of the town is bricked

D

practically only where house sewage flows into it, and nine-tenths of the system (1909) is open earth drain. As will be seen from the sections relating to rural anti-malarial sanitation, an open earth drainage system is sufficient in land such as Klang. Brick drains (the most expensive part of the works) were, as far as a malaria was concerned, unnecessary, and that they should properly be debited to ordinary sanitation.

Much money was spent on filling which could have been avoided had the town not been burdened by the legacy of its old brick drains.* In some places where no fall could be obtained because a brick drain was too high, the land was raised by filling. This was very expensive work, and work to which I should be strongly opposed now.

Until Mr Carey pointed out the mistake, much money had been spent on filling in at the foot of the hills where our drains had proved ineffective.

I speak plainly of our mistakes, in order that others may benefit and avoid similar errors and extravagances. But for the necessity of constructing part of the system as a sewage system, and but for this unnecessary and expensive filling, there is no reason why the works at Klang should have cost more than the cost of draining the land, i.e., about £2 an acre; or in other words, about £100 instead of £3000. Thousands of acres have been cleared of malaria in the neighbourhood at this cost; and I can see no reason why Klang should not have been similarly dealt with at a similar cost.

Results.—These can be more conveniently dealt with when we come to consider the results of the works at Port Swettenham.

* See Chapter XXIV.

FIG. 6.

A Main Drain at K ang, with concrete invert and turf top sides, made in 902.

[To face page 20.

THE origin of this port was the necessity of having a port for the State to which ocean-going steamers could come. It was impossible for large steamers to come up the winding Klang River in which, at spring tides, a current of 5 or 6 knots runs. It was, therefore, decided to make a port at the mouth of the river, and work was begun on 1st January 1896. The port was to be called Port Swettenham; it permitted of the entry of ocean-going vessels.

The land at the spot chosen was very low-lying mangrove swamp, which was covered at all spring tides to a depth of 2 or 3 feet by the sea. In the higher tides, especially at the September equinox, the tide floods the land for a distance of a mile inland.

The railway was carried along the fore-shore on an embankment, and wharfs were built connected with the embankment. No attempt was made to reclaim the land; and the workmen, during the construction, lived in huts raised on posts above the swamps after the Malay fashion.

Port Swettenham in 1901.—When I assumed duty at Klang in January 1901 the wharfs were practically completed, and only the finishing touches were being given to the station buildings. There were few inhabitants in the place, and there were few cases of malaria; but I observed that new arrivals quickly became affected. I also heard there had been a considerable amount of malaria among the workmen formerly employed there. The place was practically a mangrove swamp in which about fifteen acres had been cleared. No attempt had been made to reclaim or drain it, and it was full of anopheline breeding-places.

It was obvious what should be done. In February 1901, at the suggestion of the Klang Sanitary Board, the resident

21

engineer began to clear the land, fill in holes, and generally improve the land as far as his votes permitted. There was, however, no money available for a proper scheme.

On the 20th April 1901, at the request of the Acting State Surgeon, Dr Lucy, I forwarded a report with recommendations. These included, in addition to ordinary sanitary measures:—

(1) Clearing and levelling the Government Reserve and putting it under grass.

(2) The filling in of abandoned drains.

(3) A complete scheme of drainage.

(4) The notification and, if considered necessary, the removal to hospital of cases of malaria.

(5) Experiments with mosquito netting and quinine on certain sections of the population.

In urging these recommendations, I expressed the opinion that the "Government Staff shortly to be stationed there will be seriously affected and their services much impaired."

That such was necessary was obvious; and Government put $10,000 on the estimates for 1902.

Opening of the Port.—On 15th September 1901 the port was opened; and the Government population and the coolies connected with the shipping were transferred from Klang to Port Swettenham.

Fearing an outbreak of malaria, and desiring to have a record if such occurred, I had a register started of the Government population, showing for each person, name, age, previous history of malaria, date of arrival at Port Swettenham, date of attack, date seen, nature of parasite, if sent to hospital or not, date of return to duty, remarks. Each house had a separate page. This was completed within a few days of the opening of the port by Mr R. W. B. Lazaroo, the Deputy Health Officer; and in order that I might have as complete a record as possible, this officer visited each of the Government quarters. This registration was continued for some years, and by this means cases were properly treated from the beginning and removed, if necessary, to hospital.

As far as possible all officers were sent to hospital, and to remove one of their objections to this, Government allowed at my request the recovery of travelling expenses on the certificate of the Medical Officer. These precautions had the happiest results in the saving of lives, as will be shown hereafter.

The Outbreak.—Immediately after the port was opened malaria assumed an epidemic character. In less than a month the 180 leading coolies were so decimated by disease that the remnant refused to live any longer at the port, and returned to Klang. Two other batches (about seventy each) were imported on the 10th and 20th October respectively, and were lodged in separate houses in Klang. Klang, however, was then in the throes of the epidemic foreshadowed by the great sickness in the early part of the year, and these coolies suffered so much that the majority left within a month. The leading contractor had then to employ Tamil coolies from a coffee estate. The Government population also suffered severely; out of 176 persons, including the crews of the Government yachts and launches, no fewer than 118 were attacked between 10th September and 31st December.

Table showing the Number of Persons living in Government Quarters prior to 31st October 1901, attacked by Malaria within Certain Periods after arrival.

Days after Arrival.	9-18.	19-28.	29-38.	39-48.	49-58.	59-68.	69-78.	79-88.
No. of persons attacked	13	12	20	20	16	20	8	1

Two months after the port was opened I visited the native houses which had been built; of the 127 inhabitants 78 were said to have been attacked, and 25 of the 27 houses were infected.

The effect of the disease on the business of the port was very serious. Ships came in and could not unload. Those on fixed runs had to overcarry cargo. The crews contracted malaria, and after a month or so it was impossible to obtain a crew willing to trade to the port. The Harbour and Railway Departments were so crippled that they could only imperfectly do their duties, and so utterly demoralised did the port become that the High Commissioner ordered the closure of the port until it could be made more sanitary. To go back to Klang was out of the question, and Government advised the trial of the recommendations of a Commission,* which in the meantime had been appointed.

The Commission advised the measures which I had recommended in the previous April, and within six weeks the work of the port was proceeding without great difficulty.

An area of about 100 acres was bunded, drained, and freed from jungle. All possible mosquito-breeding places were oiled freely. Quinine was systematically given to all who would take it, and most did. The outbreak had so much diminished by the time information about wire gauze was received, that none was ever required.

Cost of the Works at Port Swettenham.

1901.   Jungle clearing, drain cutting, forming bunds
1902.   Filling in, tide flaps   .   .   .   .
1903.   Felling and clearing jungle   .   .   .
        Brick drains   .   .   .   .   .
1904.   Felling jungle, filling in, etc.   .   .   .
        Brick drains   .   .   .   .   .
1905.   Clearing scrub, etc.   .   .   .   .
        Brick drains   .   .   .   .   .
        Concrete drains   .   .   .   .   .

                                    Total   .

---

* Consisting of the Director of the Institute for Medical Research (H. Wright), the State Surgeon (E. A. O. Travers), the District Surgeon, Klang (M. Watson), the General Manager for Railways (C. E. Spooner), the State Engineer (B. P. M'Glashan), and the Resident Engineer for Railways (A. P. Watkins and later D. J. Highet).

FIG. 7.—FLOODING OF PORT SWETTENHAM IN OCTOBER 1909.

In October 1909, for the first time since 1901, exceptionally high tides overflowed the bunds and flooded the town to a depth of three to four feet. The bunds were about one foot above the ordinary spring tides. But for the bunds the town would be flooded every fortnight by the spring tides.

FIG. 8.—TIDAL VALVE IN SOUTH BUND AT PORT SWETTENHAM.

The photograph shows the original tide valve which opens outwards only.

[To face page 24.

CHAPTER IV

RESULTS OF DRAINAGE OF KLANG TOWN AND
PORT SWETTENHAM, 1901 TO 1909

Two definite experiments were thus carried out on a considerable scale. The experiments were in areas quite different in physical characters: the one being a mangrove swamp which was reclaimed from the sea by bunds; and the other on and about low hills with swampy ground at the hill foot. Further, the two places were five miles apart. In 1901 they were probably the most malarial localities in the district.

It was not until December 1902 that a water-supply was laid on to the towns; so this factor cannot have influenced the public health. That the improvement was not due to any general improvement is clearly shown by the continuance of malaria in the surrounding district, which thus acts as a control. The final proof, an undesirable one, is to be found in the recurrence of malaria, after a considerable period of freedom from the disease, in one of the places, when its drainage suffered interference and its inhabitants spread beyond the drained area; while in other places where the drainage was efficiently upkept no such recurrence has taken place.

Malaria treated at the Klang Hospital.—From 1901 to 1904 the number of cases treated has greatly diminished. There was a subsequent increase owing to the increasing rural population.

	1894.	1895.	1896.	1897.	1898.	1899.	1900.	1901.	1902.	1903.	1904.
Outdoor	172	479	730	554	694	668	737	965	364	245	240
Indoor .	91	112	158	128	163	251	467	807	403	219	298
Total . . .	263	591	888	682	857	919	1204	1772	767	464	538
Percentage .	20·4	28·9	25·0	19·7	25·2	20·2	24·9	38·8	20·4	12·1	11·1

25

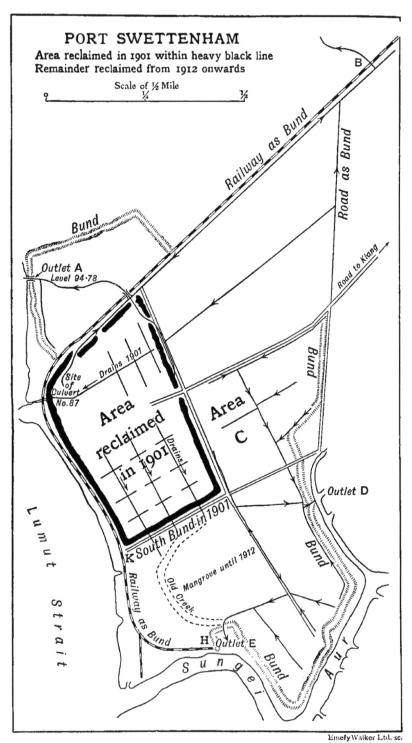

FIG. 9.—Drainage Plan of Port Swethenham.

The table on page 25 shows the number of cases of malaria treated at the Klang Hospital, and their percentage to the number treated for all diseases.

The incidence of the disease shown is striking, and the following table enables one to appreciate its cause ·—

Table showing the Number of Cases of Malaria admitted to the Klang Hospital from Klang Town and Port Swettenham, as compared with the Number of Cases admitted from Other Parts of the District.

Residence.	1901.	1902.	1908.	1904.	1905.
Klang	334	129	48	28	12
Klang and Port Swettenham	88*	...	...	...	...
Port Swettenham . .	188	70	21	4	11
Other parts of district . .	197	204	150	266	353
Total . .	807	403	219	298	376

* Certain persons lived some nights in Klang and some in Port Swettenham.

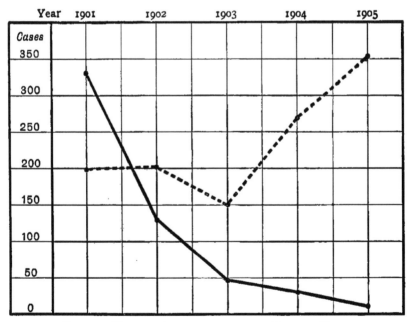

FIG. 10.—Chart showing the Admissions for Malaria to Klang Hospital, 1901 to 1905.
▬▬▬ From towns.   ▬ ▬ ▬ From other parts.

Situated as Klang and Port Swettenham are in a malarious country, their inhabitants are liable to infection should they spend a night away from home in the neighbourhood; and, on the other hand, imported cases of malaria are frequent in both towns. A difficulty arises in connection with the classification of the residence of new arrivals, who, giving a history of malaria shortly before coming to the Town or Port, develop symptoms again after they have been in residence over eight days, which length of time is generally regarded as the minimum incubation period of naturally acquired malaria. Such attacks are probably relapses; yet they might be the result of fresh infection acquired after arrival. Consequently,

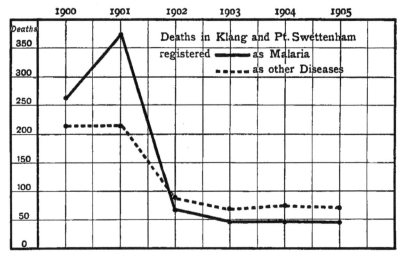

FIG. 11.—Chart of Deaths in Klang and Port Swettenham, 1900 to 1905.

so as neither to underestimate the number of cases contracted in Klang and Port Swettenham, nor to overestimate the benefits derived from the anti-malarial works in the table on page 27, a residence of eight days free from symptoms brings the case under the heading " Klang and Port Swettenham." In the light of these remarks, it is not uninteresting to note that of the thirty-two cases recorded from the two towns in 1904, eight were probably imported cases having definite histories of malaria before arrival, three* were Klang residents, who

* One was my servant. On 28th October 1904, I found the man in charge of the Resthouse at Jugra had malignant malaria, a severe crescent infection. Despite a warning my servant slept in the man's room. From 6th November to the 9th, he had headache; on the 10th and 11th his temperatures were 103·8° and 104° F. respectively, and on the 12th malignant parasites were found in his blood.

nine to twelve days before admission had slept out of the town, and eight were rickshaw pullers who frequently sleep away from home after a long journey instead of returning to town. In 1905 similar deductions have to be made.

Reduction in Number of Deaths Registered.—The reduction in the number of cases of malaria from Klang and Port Swettenham was accompanied by a remarkable fall in the number of deaths registered in the same places, while there was no similar reduction in the number from the surrounding district.

Table A shows the Deaths in Klang and Port Swettenham corrected for Deaths occurring in Hospital.

	1900.	1901.	1902.	1908.	1904.	1905.
Fever . .	259	368	59	46	48	45
Other diseases .	215	214	85	69	74	68
Total .	474	582	144	115	122	113

It will be noted that the remarkable improvement in the health of the inhabitants occurred in 1902, immediately after the anti-malarial works had been undertaken.

Table B shows the Number of Deaths in Klang District, excluding those occurring in Klang Town and Port Swettenham.

	1900.	1901.	1902.	1908.	1904.	1905.
Fever . .	173	266	227	230	286	351
Other diseases .	133	150	176	198	204	271
Total .	306	416	403	428	490	622

The above tables show convincingly that subsequent to the anti-malarial works there has been a great reduction in the number of deaths, while in the district outside of the towns the number of deaths still increases. And it is evident, too, from Table A, that the improvement is due mainly to the great reduction in the prevalence of malaria. Striking as this appears from the tables, the actual reduction has been, I believe, still greater, for among the deaths recorded as due to "other diseases" many were doubtless due to malaria. For in a malarious country the native informant is prone to report deaths, really due to malaria, as due to diarrhœa, dysentery, convulsions in children, or other terminal complications of malaria. Indeed, natives so frequently fail to recognise that their illnesses are connected with malaria that it has been found necessary to examine microscopically for malaria parasites the blood of all cases of diarrhœa, dysentery, anæmia, cardiac and renal diseases admitted to Klang Hospital, quite irrespective of whether or not the patient says he has had fever. That the native informant of death should make a mistake can, therefore, easily be understood. At the same time, the eradication of malaria to the extent that has occurred has undoubtedly improved the health of many of the town inhabitants; so that individuals, who in former years would have increased the mortality under "other diseases," simply because they were in a low state of health consequent on malaria, are now able to resist the attack of such "other diseases," or if attacked to overcome them and recover.

Although a good water-supply was brought into the town in December 1902, and greater attention was being paid to general sanitation, I could not help believing that the improvement was due mainly to the diminution of malaria. As all deaths, with the exception of those certified by myself (up to 1907 the only qualified practitioner within twenty miles of Klang), are registered in accordance with the report of the friends, I regard the above tables as an "unsolicited testimonial" unconsciously given by the native community to the efficacy of the anti-malarial works in Klang and Port Swettenham.

The following table shows how much Government and its officers have benefited :—

Table showing Number of Sick Certificates and Number of Days'
Leave granted on account of Malaria.

	1901.	1902.	1903.	1904.	1905.
Certificates . .	236	40	23	14	4
Days of Leave . .	1026	198	73	71	30

From 12th July 1904 until December 1906 no officer in Port Swettenham suffered from malaria.

The results of the anti-malaria measures also resulted in financial loss to me from diminution of my private practice, from patients suffering from malaria contracted in Klang or Port Swettenham. In 1901 my private practice brought in $734 from patients suffering from malaria contracted in Klang and Port Swettenham. In 1904 it was nil, and it remained at this cipher until 1909 when cases were seen from Port Swettenham.

Children Infected with Malaria, Klang.—Unfortunately in 1901 no examination of the children was made to ascertain the percentage affected. I had, however, abundant evidence, both in my official and private practice, that they suffered severely. The disease frequently ran through a household. As an example I may mention that on one occasion (15th April 1901), when called to the Astana, the official residence of H.H. The Sultan of Selangor, to see a child with malaria, I asked if there were any others, and I found no fewer than 15 suffering from malaria.

Since 1904 I have made a series of examinations, at first of the blood, and latterly of the spleen and blood of children under the age of ten, differentiating according to the age. For the sake of simplicity I give only the totals. The examinations were made in the months of November, December, and January, but mainly in November and December. In Klang the children were examined both in the centre of the town and at its periphery.

Table showing the Number of Children in Klang Town giving Evidence of Malaria on Blood and Spleen Examination.

	1904.	1905.	1906.	1907.	1909.
Blood—					
Number examined . .	173	119	91	...	...
Number with Malaria .	1	1	1	...	...
Per cent. with Malaria .	0·5	0·8	10	...	...
Spleen—					
Number examined . .	...	...	142	71	455
Number with Malaria .	...	...	1	3	13
Per cent. with Malaria .	...	...	0·7	42	2.8

Convincing as these figures are of the absence of malaria in Klang Town, further inquiry showed that cases with evidence of malaria had only recently come to the town, and had contracted the disease previously to coming. For example, in 1904 the child with malaria belonged to a company of travelling players, and had had malaria in Kuala Lumpur; in 1905 the child with malaria was an inhabitant of Klang who two months previously had gone to Malacca for a month and, when there, contracted malaria; in 1906 the child with malaria had arrived only three days previously from Port Dickson; and in 1907 the examinations were made not by me personally as the others had been, but by a dresser, and no history is recorded of those with enlarged spleen.

In 1909, desiring to have the fullest evidence possible of the condition of the town, *I personally went to every house in it, and also to all the schools, examining in all 463 children.** Of the 308 examined in the schools five had enlarged spleen, giving a percentage of 3·8 of the school children; four were not residents of Klang, but came in daily; one from Kampong Quantan; one from 2nd mile Langat Road; one from Padang Jawa (by train); one from 2½ mile Kapar Road.

Thirteen resided in the town; I give notes of their previous history:—Seven were in the police barracks, four of whom had been transferred from Sepang, two from Jugra, and one had just arrived from Malacca: all gave a history of malaria before coming to Klang. Jugra and Sepang are notoriously malarious; two were in Government coolie lines, one having previously been in Batu Tiga—a very unhealthy place; and one had come from Kuala Lumpur where it had had malaria; two were children of an old watchman known to me for years who told me he had gone to an estate for three months, and when there both he and his two children had contracted malaria— the estate he referred to has a spleen rate of about 50 per cent. One child had come to Klang only ten days previously from 2½ mile Kapar Road; the mother informed me the child had fever before coming to Klang. One child came from an estate 20 miles from Klang known to me to be malarious.

It is to be remembered that Klang is constantly receiving people who are capable of infecting others with malaria if the connecting link be present. In Klang Hospital in the years 1906, 1907, 1908 respectively, 789, 1901, and 1537 cases of malaria were treated without any special precautions to prevent

---

* The children examined were under an estimated age of ten, in all places, unless expressly stated otherwise.

the spread of infection.   One ward had been enclosed by wire netting, but when this decayed it was not replaced as there was no evidence that malaria was being spread from the !hospital ; for four years I had used mosquito nets in the hospital, but had given these up for Tamil patients as they would not use them unless compelled to do so ; so that in 1907 when the maximum number of cases was treated there was the fullest opportunity for the infection spreading.   No more severe test of the absence of malaria-carrying anophelines could be devised.

That the whole child population of Klang, except that known to have contracted malaria outside, should be com- pletely free from all symptoms of the disease, is conclusive evidence of the value of drainage, and *I would add here that not one single grain of quinine was given to any of the population except to patients actually suffering from malaria in hospital and in my official or private practice.*

Children at Port Swettenham.—In 1901 there were thirteen children under the age of ten living in Government quarters. Of these nine contracted malaria within three and a half months of their arrival.

Table showing the Number of Children with Evidence of Malaria at Port Swettenham.

	1904.	1905.	1906.	1907.	1909.
Blood examination—					
Number examined . .	187	76	100	...	...
Number with parasites .	1	0	5	...	...
Per cent. with parasites .	1·14	0	5	...	...
Spleen examination—					
Number examined . .	...	...	100	41	109
Number with enlargement	...	...	2	9	9
Per cent. with enlargement	...	...	2	21·9	8·9

In 1904 the child who showed infection was found in the Police Station, and had only recently been transferred from Cheras, where she had fever.   In 1906 I found evidence in the children of the recrudescence of the disease, simultaneous with its reappearance among the adults, as I shall relate.

For subsequent history see Chapter XXII.

CHAPTER V

A Wave of Malaria.—Under the District Surgeon of Klang
are two other districts, namely Kuala Langat and Kuala
Selangor; the three are commonly known as the Coast
Districts of Selangor. At the time I assumed duty, the
populations of Kuala Langat and Kuala Selangor, like that
of Klang, were suffering from malaria. In the annual *Medical
Report of the State of Selangor* for the year 1899 it is thus
described :—

" During the last two years the Coast Districts have been
visited by severe outbreaks of malarial fever. All nationalities
have been affected by it, and Government clerks, Tamils and
Chinese coolies, and Malay settlers have been equally attacked.
. . . It is difficult to assign a cause for these outbreaks of
malarial fever. It was thought at one time that the earth
work in connection with road-making, granite quarrying and
spreading, might account for the increase of the fever at Jugra
in the Kuala Langat District; but it has been found to be
equally prevalent on the sea-beach in the Jeram and Kuala
Selangor Districts, among Chinese fishermen, where no road
work or quarrying operations had been undertaken."

Two years later, writing in his annual report for 1901, the
State Surgeon says :—

" By far the greatest number of cases of malaria were
admitted to hospital in the coast districts, which have during
the last two and a half to three years been attacked with what
may be called a wave of malaria, principally of a malignant
type."

The reader will have gathered from the previous chapters
some impressions of what this wave of malaria meant to the
towns of Klang and Port Swettenham, and of the results
obtained in our attempts to control it. It is now time to

turn to the wave as it affected the district of Kuala Selangor. Its study there threw a flood of light on the whole malarial problem, broadened the outlook, and had a profound influence on the subsequent anti-malarial policy which I adopted. It convinced me that controlling malaria over wide rural areas, even in low-lying localities with high ground water, and in a tropical country with heavy rainfall, was within the range of practical politics.

Malaria in the District of Kuala Selangor.—North of the district of Klang, etc., lies that of Kuala Selangor. It stretches away towards the N.N.W. for about sixty miles, and is, like Klang district, flat for some miles inland from the sea.

When I assumed duty as District Surgeon of Kuala Selangor district in addition to that of Klang, I found malaria was very severe. In 1902, being desirous of obtaining as much information as possible about it, I went through the hospital registers for the previous years, and obtained the following figures—as far as then possible:—

	1895.	1896.	1897.	1898.	1899.	1900.	1901.	1902.	1908.
Total treated	433	524	782	836	1837	2115	2061	2297	1880
Number with Malaria . .	103	136	222	336	1086	1007	512	528	268
Per cent. with Malaria . .	23·7	25·9	28·3	40·1	59·0	50·1	33·4	23·0	14·1
Number of Deaths in district .	170	193	163	168	278	317	290	287	248

These figures could be no mere statistical vagary. A definite rise in the percentage of the malaria treated at the hospitals during a series of years appeared to me to represent the existence of some definite fact—a phenomenon, the investigation of which was of urgent importance.

The census had shown an increase of 30·7 per cent. in the population of the district, and while the increasing population might have accounted for the rise in the malaria wave, it could hardly account for the remarkable subsequent fall. I had no idea to what to attribute the phenomenon, but I thought some explanation might be found in the history of the district. Accordingly I read up all the Annual Reports of the District Officers, and also those of the State Engineers for the previous ten years. The explanation was soon forthcoming. In order to open up the country, to which access hitherto had been possible only by rivers and creeks, Government had constructed a road

E

and bridle tract for a distance of some sixty miles from Klang to Sabak Bernam on the Perak boundary. The road passes through the villages and mukims (sub-districts) of Kapar (10th mile), Jeram (20th mile), and Kuala Selangor (28th mile).

Before the construction of the road the inhabitants had opened up the land at certain places, and malaria was not present to any serious extent. The road interfered with drainage, as there is abundant evidence to show, and it was followed by the outbreak of malaria. The road was put through in the early years of the nineties, and complaints were soon found in the reports of the District Officers, who in no uncertain terms accused it of doing serious damage. Mr A. Hale in his Annual Report for 1897 says :—

" Javanese who took up land on the Bukit Rotan road and planted it with coffee which was destroyed by flood water, the drain having been dammed by the Public Works Department to use as a canal for transport of metal, have now most of them planted cocoanuts, as also have many others who hold land on the inland side of the coast road, which, as my predecessor pointed out, acts like a long dam from Sabak to Kapar, as if built purposely to prevent the water getting to the sea."

Stronger evidence could hardly be obtained, but if it was required, it was to be found in an Annual Report of the then State Engineer. Referring to the Klang end of the Klang-Kuala Selangor road, he congratulated the Government on the low cost of constructing the road due to the drain on the inland side of the road having been used as a canal. There is thus evidence that from end to end the road had acted as a serious obstruction to drainage of land on its landward side, and coincident with this there appeared the remarkable increase in the malaria of the district.

Now about the end of the nineties, we find in the reports proposals for a great irrigation scheme for the cultivation of rice in the same district. The first step in irrigation is the provision of drains to carry off water, so that the amount of water on the land may be properly regulated. In 1898 a start was made with the Jeram drainage scheme, but before it was completed all idea of rice cultivation had been given up by the natives in favour of the more remunerative dry cultivation of cocoanuts and coffee, made possible by means of drainage. More and more land came under this cultivation; the drainage begun in 1898 has steadily proceeded; European cultivation of rubber had spread over the district, and with it the district has become populated by the Tamil coolie, who is non-immune to malaria. Yet the health has improved steadily. Malaria in serious extent is to be found only in the hilly land as in the Klang district. On the same Bukit Rotan road, where Mr Hale said the Javanese coffee was destroyed by flood, a large population is now living practically free from malaria. Dr J. Lang Niven, who was in charge of the estates there, kindly informed me that of seventy-five children whom he examined, only 4 or 6·1 per cent. had splenic enlargement, and three of the four children had been on estates in Southern India before coming to Kuala Selangor.

The parts of this district which are drained are now as healthy as any to be found in the country; while the parts still undrained and the hilly land, where *A. maculatus* is still present, are unhealthy. I think, therefore, we may reasonably conclude that the rise of the malaria epidemic which coincided with the obstruction of the land drainage by the road, and the fall in the epidemic which coincided with the more efficient drainage of the land, were respectively due to obstruction and to drainage.

(1919).—The preceding was written in 1909. Another ten years have served to prove the correctness of the conclusions reached in 1903. The following extract published in that year [8] seems worth reprinting:—

"This sudden decrease in the amount of malaria, as a result of draining comparatively small areas (I was writing about Klang and Port Swettenham), is in striking contrast to the gradual decrease, the result of the draining of Kuala Selangor district. In that district the population is scattered along the coast for many miles. The road runs parallel to the coast about a mile inland, and when first constructed acted according to the official reports of the district officers, as a dam preventing the land from being drained." After giving the table of malaria treated from 1895 to 1902 inclusive, I continue. "In 1898 a start with extensive drainage works was made. The first result of the introduction of the labour force was further to increase the amount of malaria. The work has, however, been steadily pushed on, and the result has been a steady fall in the amount of malaria as the drainage works became effective. This, I think, forms an interesting contrast to the results obtained in Klang and Port Swettenham."

The next chapter will show how soon the idea of controlling rural malaria was to bear fruit.

CHAPTER VI

KAPAR DRAINAGE SCHEME

In my first published report of the anti-malarial measures of Klang, I referred to the gradual improvement in the health of Kuala Selangor district, as the result of draining large areas, in contrast with the more rapid improvement, which had occurred in Klang and Port Swettenham, as the result of measures carried out in a shorter period. These facts came to the notice of the late Mr W. W. Bailey, who wrote to Government, complaining that the Klang end of the road still obstructed the drainage of the land, making it impossible to drain the estates efficiently; and attributing the malaria, which then existed on the estates, to the road. In support of his proposals he quoted my investigations in Kuala Selangor, and referred the Government to me for further information.

On 29th April 1904, at the request of Government, I forwarded a report which was published,[9] and from which the following are extracts:—

"Roads and other public works, by producing breeding-places for mosquitoes, are important agents in spreading malaria and filaria. Roads in flat country, especially when parallel to the coast, are injurious in two ways: (1) During their construction borrow pits are formed, and these remain afterwards as mosquito breeding-places; (2) when completed, roads may interfere with drainage of land on the inland side of the road."

I quoted such figures as were available, which showed that from 55 to 65 per cent. of the deaths registered among residents on the Kapar road were attributed to fever, and up to 35 per cent. of the admissions to hospital were from malaria—and said, "Without straining these figures, there is little doubt that malaria is an important cause of sickness and death among the people living along the road."

Not being a civil engineer I declined to say that the drains were insufficient to drain the land, or that the openings through the road were insufficient to allow the water to find its way to the sea, although in wet weather the whole inland side of the road was flooded and the water came to within a short distance of the level of the road. I, however, wrote :—

"It would be going beyond my province to express an opinion as to whether or not the Klang-Kuala Selangor road is still preventing the drainage of the estates and the land on the inland side, but the unanimity of the planters on the point and the sight of water standing often many feet higher on the landward than seaward side of the road, seem evidence sufficient to justify a thorough inquiry. . . . When it can be proved that a road interferes with the drainage of the land on which any considerable population live (such as on the Klang-Kuala Selangor road), then expenditure on drainage is advisable from every point of view." I then made some remarks on the construction of drains from the point of view of anti-malaria sanitation, and the necessity of engineers remembering that "work which without excuse leaves a trail of malaria behind it is bad engineering. . . ." "Finally, I would express the opinion that the stamping-out of malaria, or at least reducing it to a negligible quantity, is a much more hopeful affair than has hitherto been anticipated. . . . The experience of Klang and Port Swettenham, taken with the knowledge that malaria has died out of the Fen Country in England, while anopheles still flourish in considerable numbers, all point in the same direction. I would, therefore, urge upon Government that to abolish malaria it is not necessary to abolish mosquitoes completely, and that measures intelligently directed at the disease may at once cost little and be strikingly effective."

As a result of the representations made, the Resident-General, Sir W. Hood Treacher, K.C.M.G., the acting British Resident, Mr Douglas Campbell, the Director of the Institute of Medical Research, Dr C. W. Daniels, the Government Engineers, Mr W. W. Bailey and other planters, visited the Kapar sub-district and held an inquiry into the condition of the road and land. The necessity for improved drainage was recognised, and a scheme involving the expenditure of $110,000 was approved. The outlets through the road were enlarged,

FIG. 12.—KAPAR DRAINAGE SCHEME.
One of the main drains, with rubber trees on both sides.

FIG. 13.
Photograph showing sites for Coolie Lines selected in the centre of a clearing
to be at the maximum distance from undrained jungle and hill streams.

[To face page 40

necessitating in some places bridges double the length of the previous ones; and the scheme provided 37 miles of main drains sufficient for the drainage of 24,000 acres upon which the estates now pay drainage assessment. Some of the drains constructed are 20 feet wide (Fig. 12, p. 40). The effect of this drainage will be shown further on.

CHAPTER VII

A MALARIAL SURVEY

ABOUT the time when the Kapar drainage scheme was sanctioned, namely in 1904, the pioneers of the rubber plantation industry, who had started about 1898 in a small way in the coast districts of Selangor, began to obtain some tangible reward from their enterprise. Coming from Ceylon after the coffee debacle, when that prosperous industry had been almost completely wiped out of the island within a few months by disease, they had planted Liberian coffee in the State of Selangor in the F.M.S. By 1901, however, this coffee had ceased to pay. It could not compete with Brazilian coffee; and the price of the local product dropped in the course of two or three years from $44 to $12 and $15 a picul, at which figure it did not pay. Casting round for some alternative crop, a few men interplanted their coffee with rubber about 1898. From the first the young trees throve so well and grew so sturdily that the coffee was soon overshadowed and was cut out. By 1904 the new industry was firmly established. Planters were confident in its ultimate success. Large areas of land for its cultivation were taken up, and labour began to come in freely from India.

If the history of other tropical enterprises was to be taken as a guide, the opening up· of the land, especially when done with imported labour, was likely to produce virulent outbreaks of malaria, and to be costly in lives, both of Europeans and Asiatics. My hospital returns showed how severely the existing estates were suffering already, and I determined to study the matter in more detail.

From one point of view this great agricultural development presented a unique opportunity for the study of tropical malaria. From small areas like Klang and Port Swettenham, malaria had almost been completely eradicated by the

42

draining of swamps, and the clearing of jungle; and from Kuala Selangor malaria, I gathered the idea that the disease could be controlled over wider areas. The great agricultural development, which was to be assisted by the Kapar drainage scheme, was now to put the idea to the test. It was, indeed, from my point of view a great experiment in the prevention of malaria; that it was to be on a scale infinitely larger than any experiment, which would have been undertaken as such, was no disadvantage; while the fact that it would be carried out by planters, on practical and commercial lines, added to its fascination.

Arriving in the middle of the epidemic of malaria in the coast districts in 1901, I commenced work at once on the control of the disease, but I always felt that I was handicapped by the absence of information which would have been available had the records of previous years been more complete. In the new developments, I was in a much more favourable position. I was witnessing the "birth," so to speak, of many new estates. The opportunity was afforded me of examining and recording the conditions which existed on them from their earliest days, and, as it has happened, I have since been able to watch their development for many years. Further, by 1904 I had acquired a considerable knowledge of what malaria was, and how it affected a community —a knowledge which I did not possess in 1901. Between 1901 and 1903 I had devoted considerable time to microscopic work on the blood of patients admitted to hospital, and to the clinical aspects of malaria. It soon became evident that many patients were really suffering from malaria, who when admitted, complained of symptoms other than pyrexia. Some of these observations were published in 1905 in a paper entitled "Some Clinical Aspects of Quartan Malaria."[10] In it I showed that in 18·18 per cent. of the cases pyrexia was absent for periods averaging 6·4 days; and in 18·18 per cent. of the cases the rise in temperature was at so much longer intervals as to lead to little, if any, importance being attached to it by the patient. A considerable experience of labour convinces me that 1 or 2 per cent. of coolies working on malarious estates have pyrexia of which they are unconscious; and which they deny, even when the thermometer shows a temperature of 102° F. The same will often be seen in hospital. I was led to the conclusion that while there might be much pyrexia and few, if any, parasites to be found in the peripheral blood during the first few days of the illness, the later stages might show large numbers of parasites and no pyrexia, as immunity was becoming established. It appeared to me that sufferers from malaria might be divided into two classes, those with pyrexia and those without, the latter being neither fewer in number nor less in importance. And the more I see of malaria the more I find to support this conclusion. It supplied an explanation of the extraordinary fall in the number of deaths registered in Klang in 1902 as due to diseases other than malaria; and the observations on coolies on large doses of quinine and apparently in good health referred to on p. 112 further bears it out.

It is sometimes said that the native registers everything as malarial fever, and that the returns grossly exaggerate the amount of the disease. This may be so where there is little malaria. I am convinced, however, that where there is any considerable amount of malaria the error is entirely the other way, and that many deaths from malaria are recorded as due to its complications instead of to the disease to which they are really due. In confirmation of this view, there is the great fall in the number of deaths recorded as due to diseases other than malaria when malaria was reduced in Klang, as shown in the table on p. 29.

The result of my microscopic work in hospital convinced me of the enormous amount of malaria on the estates of the district; and, in 1904, I determined to carry out as complete a survey as my official work would permit.

Choosing the most unhealthy months of the year, November and December, I visited a number of estates in different parts of the district, and made examinations of the fresh blood of the children. The work was laborious, but the specimens were taken by an assistant; and I examined about eight to ten an hour. Out of the 298 children under the age of ten examined in 1904, no fewer than 101, or 33.89 per cent., were infected. During the same months, 1905, 1906, and 1907, either blood or spleen examinations were made, and in 1909 and the early part of January 1910, examinations of the children on every estate of Klang and Kuala Langat districts were made either by

Dr Macaulay or myself, and blood examinations were also made by Dr Macaulay on some estates. The species and breeding-places of the anopheline have also been determined.

These observations have been continued by my medical officers and myself year by year until the present date (1919), as the subsequent pages will show. It is probably rare for one man to have the opportunity of making so long a series of observations under the conditions which obtain here. If so, they must have an added interest, even if they are not a unique record.

CHAPTER VIII

THE MALARIA OF THE COASTAL PLAIN AND
ANOPHELES UMBROSUS

PERHAPS the word "Plain" is not altogether apt. If it conveys to the reader the notion of an open treeless plain, something akin to a prairie, it certainly has misled him. No such thing as a treeless acre of land exists in Malaya. The country is naturally and permanently covered with a heavy jungle; only where this is felled, burned off, and cleared of all weeds every three weeks or less, does open land exist.

The land to which I allude is the alluvial land between high-tide level and the nearest lower or Coastal Hills. In the course of our inquiry, it will be found convenient to consider malaria as it is found in the different zones of land existing in the Peninsula. The zone nearest the sea I propose to call the Mangrove zone. Next will come the Coastal Plains; then the Coastal Hills. Still farther inland we come to areas of flat or relatively flat land which may be conveniently called the Inland Plains. Finally we come to the main range of hills forming the backbone of the Peninsula which I propose to call the Inland Hills. When opened up and inhabited, each of these areas presents special problems. It must not, however, be forgotten that in nature all are clothed in primeval forest; and that when inhabited they are in an unnatural, indeed a highly artificial, state. The Coastal Plain, in nature, is an alluvial flat composed of a heavy clay covered by dense, almost impenetrable, jungle. The ground water is almost permanently above the surface level; during the wetter months it may be waist deep. In some places the clay is covered with a coarse peat, formed from slowly decaying vegetable matter. Its depth varies from a few inches to many feet.

Many mosquitoes have their home in this jungle; but practically the only anopheles is *A. umbrosus*, which I found to be

46

an efficient natural carrier of malaria. I use the word practically, for only on one occasion have I found another anopheles in this virgin jungle. It was *A. aurirostris.* There may, of course, be others yet to be discovered.

A. umbrosus, as we saw (Chapter II.), may be present in enormous numbers. Generally speaking, it is so abundant in houses situated near to this jungle, that it may be obtained without difficulty ; for, being a large black mosquito, it is easily seen. Sometimes, however, it disappears temporarily even from places where it is the rule to find it in abundance.

As we pass away from the jungle the number of the mosquitoes decreases, and at half a mile (or 40 chains) the number has so decreased that malaria, as indicated by the spleen rate, has disappeared, although occasionally cases of malaria do occur. For many years this mosquito has been under observation, and its association with malaria studied. The sum of these observations is that malaria, in certain portions of the district, namely the flat land, is exclusively carried by *A. umbrosus,* which breeds in pools in undrained jungle ; and when the jungle is felled and the pools drained, this mosquito is exterminated completely ; and with its extermination malaria disappears. It has been found, too, that the spleen rate in the children decreases with the distance they live from the breeding-places of the mosquito ; and that the death rate of an estate varies as the spleen rate. Finally these facts have enabled me to forecast with considerable accuracy the probable health or unhealthiness of a proposed site for coolie lines, and to give advice which has borne fruit. *A theory which will provide a sound working rule is one of considerable value.*

In order to make good these statements, I must now refer to the individual estates, the positions of which will be seen from the maps. In these are seen the parts under cultivation and the parts still (1909) undrained jungle. Coolie lines or houses are shown by the number, which is the spleen rate for the lines or group of lines at that part of the estate.

Estate " A."—This was opened in 1906, and the coolies were housed within 100 yards of the jungle. In 1907 malaria was very prevalent among them, and it became necessary to administer quinine daily. Rapid progress, however, was made in opening up the land ; and within a year there was an extraordinary improvement in the health of the estate. The most striking evidence is to be found in the reports of the Indian Immigration Department, from which the following figures are taken:—

Year.	No. on 1st January.	Additions to Labour.	Died.	Deserted.	Discharged.	Sent to India.	Total Deductions.	No. on 31st Dec. 1907.	Average Population.	Deaths per mille.
1907	132	261	12	34	125	12	183	78	120	100
1908	60	173	2	7	19	...	28	100	101	20

These figures demonstrate the economic importance of malaria. The whole success and, in fact, the very existence of tropical agriculture depends on a healthy and contented labour force. The severe prevalence of malaria in 1907 led not only to a high death rate, but to the unnecessary loss, in other ways, of about 150 coolies. Coolies will not remain on an unhealthy estate; therefore, 34 deserted, 125 gave the legal month's notice and left. Instead of having a fine labour force of close on 300 coolies, the estate had to begin the year with considerably fewer than it had the previous year.

In 1907 the manager, and a friend who had lived with him for some time, both suffered severely from malaria. On 23rd July 1907, only 167 out of 245 coolies were working, and of those not at work 10 had high temperatures. Three months later, after much loss of labour, I found on one occasion 8 per cent. of the labour force with fever, with œdematous feet, and the other sequelæ of malaria.

The present manager has been on the estate for nearly two years. He has been off work for one day only and that not as a result of malaria, a disease from which he has not suffered. On 10th January 1910 I examined all the children on the estate (it is to be understood that practically every child on estates is examined: and that where a spleen rate is shown, it is based on the examination of the child population, and not merely calculated from an examination of a proportion of the children), and out of the fifty-one examined, I found one with enlarged spleen, who, inquiry elicited, had come from an estate in another district, the death rate of which in 1908 was 108 per mille, and which I knew suffered severely from malaria. The child had malaria when it came to estate " A."

I regret I have no figure referring to the children in 1907, but I consider the figures I have given demonstrate in the most striking way how malaria has disappeared with the draining and opening up of the land. Undrained jungle is now about half a mile distant from the lines. For its subsequent history see Chapter XXI.

Estate " B."—I first examined this estate in 1904, when all the nine children were found free from parasites. There was only a small labour force, about sixty in all, and only occasionally was there a case of fever. The jungle was comparatively near ; but the land immediately behind the coolie lines was drained. I find, however, that a small labour force often escapes when a larger one is seriously affected. This estate has continued to enjoy good health throughout, and on 10th January 1910 none of the thirty children on the estate had enlarged spleen, and the conductor, who had been there for one and a half years, told me he had not had fever.

The death rates during 1906, 1907, and 1908 have been 22, 28, and 9 per mille respectively.

Since I came to know it, this estate has shown continued good health, although in 1907 its neighbour, only half a mile away, had suffered severely from malaria.

(1919).—The history of this estate during the subsequent ten years has been uneventful, except for an outbreak of cholera in 1911. The following table shows the spleen rates :—

Year.			No. of Children.	Spleen Rates.
1912	.	.	30	6·6
1915	.	.	64	7·5
1916	.	.	70	8·5

In 1912 two children had come from India two months before ; both looked healthy and had not been ill.

The death rates have been :—

	1909.	1910.	1911.	1912.	1913.	1914.	1915.	1916·	1917.	1918.
Rate per mille	14	17	65	25	2	12	3	6	9	52

In 1918 there was influenza.

The next four estates, " C," " E," " F," and " G," illustrate clearly the association of malaria with undrained jungle. In

1909 they were being developed from virgin jungle, of which, of course, only a portion could be opened each year. During this period of development the labour forces were necessarily housed in varying proximity to the jungle; and all four suffered from malaria. It will be noted that at any time the incidence of malaria was greater the nearer a labour force was to the jungle; and that as the years passed it decreased *pari passu* with the disappearance of the jungle. The years in which the various blocks of land were cleared are marked on the plan.

Only part of the story could be told when the first edition of this book was written in 1909. Malaria had not yet disappeared from the upper division of estate " C "; estate " E " was only half-way out of the wood ; the labour forces of estates "F" and "G" were still living close to jungle, and still suffering from intense malaria. But development was proceeding rapidly. It was a period of transition, which can best be recalled by reprinting what was written in 1909. Afterwards I will bring the story up to date.

(1909). *Estate " C."*—This estate began operations in 1904, when its labour force was placed on land already opened a year or two before by Malays. They were thus placed on drained land from the beginning, and accordingly were healthy. Its death rate shows this, and was as follows :—

	1904.	1905.	1906.	1907.	1908.
D. R.	25		34	37	13

An experiment was carried out on this estate in 1906 and 1907, which bore out the extraordinary limitation of the flight of the mosquito, the relation of malaria to undrained jungle, the importance of selecting the best site for the housing of a labour force, and the certainty with which one could predict the health or otherwise of a site on the flat land.

It is an estate of about 3000 acres, and, with the healthy labour force it possessed, such rapid progress was made that within three years of starting 1000 acres were already opened ; and it was proposed to open still more. In 1906 much of the work of the coolies was one to two miles distant from their lines, and it was obviously an economy, both to the estate and the coolie, to house him nearer to his work. I was informed in 1906 that it was proposed to remove most of the force to what would ultimately be the centre of the estate, which at that time was still on the edge of undrained jungle. Knowing from experience that the site would probably be very unhealthy, I strongly advised that only a few coolies should be removed until the land had been further opened up. However, four sets of lines were built, three about 25 chains, *i.e.*, quarter of a mile from jungle; and the other about 100 yards. The removal took place in October 1906, and on 22nd November there were 120 coolies in the lines marked Spleen Rate 16, and 80 in a set of lines near to the jungle at quarter of a mile from the place marked 80.* The result was disastrous. The coolies were overwhelmed with malaria, and soon had to be removed. I am indebted to the manager for the following :—

" *Re* abandoning lines : You ask me my reason for abandoning four sets of coolie lines in March 1907. They are as follows : I found that amongst the coolies living near EE drain (place marked 16, about twenty-five chains from the jungle) I had 28 per cent. down ill with fever every day, and amongst those living near to my bungalow, marked 80 about ten chains from —— jungle, the rate was 33 per cent. daily. On that account I removed that portion of my labour force to the south-western end of the estate, which had previously been healthy, and I abandoned the top lines altogether; but about the beginning of 1909 I put a portion of my labour force back again near EE drain, the jungle being then forty chains away; and I am glad to say the fever rate has been very small, and of very little consequence. E. H. KING-HARMAN."

On 22nd November 1906, there were fifteen children in the lines marked 16, of whom only one had enlargement of the spleen. On 17th February 1907, there were twelve children, of whom seven, or 58 per cent., had enlarged spleens.

As these were the same children, it shows how malarious the place had become.

On 4th January 1909, there were fifteen children living in the same place, of whom three had enlargement (very small in the case of two), equal to 20 per cent. A portion of the force had only recently been removed to the edge of the

* The place marked 80 on estate " C " does not represent a spleen rate, but only the number of coolies there in 1906. Coolies no longer live on this site as it was so unhealthy, and the lines were destroyed.

F

drained jungle on block II, so that the figures for the whole division were thirty children, of which five, or 16 per cent., had enlarged spleens.

Now on the south-western portion of the estate, that is the portion of the estate first occupied in 1904, I examined, on 5th January 1910, the children—in all 109. Of these, four had enlarged spleen, giving a spleen rate of 3·6. They were recent arrivals. I recognised two sisters as being the only two children who had been found with enlargement on an estate in the neighbourhood; one other had come two months previously from an estate in another district; and one had come from an estate where the spleen rate was 100. The corrected spleen rate should therefore be *nil.*

The bungalow to which the manager refers is still in occupation, and malaria is far from unknown to its occupants; while the bungalow on the south-western division has never been infected with malaria.

The medical history of this estate has been practically that of a series of experiments of the most convincing character. If any doubt remained, a glance at the map showing the condition of the estates marked " E," " F," and " G," the coolie lines of which at the present moment vary in distance from jungle which has been drained for about one year only. The lines marked 23 had undrained jungle to within 200 yards about a year ago. Jungle is now about 500 yards distant, and it has been drained for about four months. The lines marked 59 on estate " F " are opposite and within fifty yards of jungle, which, however, has been drained for some months. The percentage of children with abnormal spleens was 59, based on the examination of thirty-two children. Of the thirteen with no enlargement, one has been one and a half years on the estate, three had been only fourteen days, while the others had been less than six months. It is interesting to note that the jungle opposite had been drained for about the same period, and this probably accounted for these children having escaped. Dr T. S. Macaulay kindly examined the blood of twenty children on this estate, and found parasites in seven, or 31·9 per cent. These children got about 5 grains of quinine daily.

On 6th December 1906 I examined three children on this estate, and of these two had considerable enlargement of the

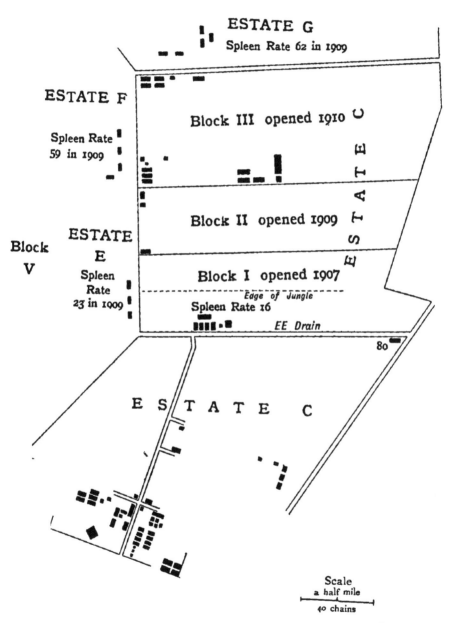

FIG. 14.—Plan of Estate "C."

Emery Walker Ltd. sc

spleen. The death rate of the estate in 1908 was 41 per mille.

Estate "G" has been unhealthy since it was opened, as undrained jungle has always been within less than 100 yards of all the coolie lines.

On 5th January 1910, I examined twenty-four children on this estate, and of these fifteen had enlarged spleen, equal to 62 per cent. Of the nine with no enlargement, two had been only fourteen days on it; and one had a high temperature at the time of my examination.

Dr Macaulay examined the blood of eleven of the children on this estate, but did not find parasites. All were on quinine, about 5 grains daily.

On 6th December 1906, I examined eight children on this estate and found three, or 37 per cent., with enlarged spleen. The death rate given in the Indian Immigration Return is 69, but this does not represent the exact death rate, since estate "M," which belongs to the same Company, had an estate hospital, to which the sick from this estate were sent. Those who died there were not accredited to "G," but swelled the death rate of estate "M," to an unnatural degree. I will draw attention to this later.

From these figures it is evident that the opening up of the estates "F" and "G" did not lead to any improvement in their health; and the reason was obviously that the lines were still as near to the jungle as when the estates were first opened. This is in marked contrast to the improvement to be seen where the opening of the estates pushes the jungle away from the lines.

(1919).—Such were the conclusions reached in 1909. If they were correct, and if jungle swamp was the cause of the malaria, then the health of estates "F" and "G" could not be expected to improve until they moved their labour forces away from the block of jungle marked III or until the jungle was opened up. Time proved the conclusions to be correct. In due course the jungle was opened: so too were the blocks marked I, II, IV, and V. Then, and not till then, the high spleen rates fell, as the following records show. Jungle Block I was opened in 1907, block II in 1909, and blocks III, IV, and V in 1910.

Spleen Rates of Estate " C."

Lower Division. Lines never near to jungle :—

Year.			No. of Children.	Spleen Rates.
1910	.	..	109	3·6
1913			237	1·2
1915	.	..	223	1·7
1917	.	..	306	2·2

Upper Division. Line 100 to 400 yards from jungle in 1909 :—

Year.			No. of Children.	Spleen Rates.
1909	.	.	. 30	16
1913	.	.	. 109	2·7
1917	.	.	. 138	3·6

The death rates of Estate " C " from 1906 onwards have been as follows :—34, 37, 13, 3, 11, 13, 15, 7, 5, 8, 13, 23, 31, 12.

Spleen Rates of Estate " E."

Lines 200 yards from jungle in 1908 :—

Year.			No. of Children.	Spleen Rates.
1909	.	.	. 13	23
1911	.	.	. 18	11·1
1913	.	.	. 20	15
1915	.	.	. 31	10·7
1917	.	.	. 39	2·5

Spleen Rates of Estate " F."

Jungle next to lines drained in 1909 :—

Year.			No. of Children.	Spleen Rates.
1906	.	.	. 3	66
1910	.	.	. 32	39
1912	.	.	. 32	24
1913	.	.	. 92	2·1
1915	.	.	. 76	14·4 *
1917	.	.	. 83	4·8

* Included eight children from malarious estate.

Spleen Rates of Estate " G."

Jungle next to lines drained in 1909, and planted in 1910 :—

Year.				No. of Children.	Spleen Rates.
1906	.	.	.	8	37
1910	.	.	.	24	62
1911	.	.	.	62	6
1913	.	.	.	110	1·8
1915	.	.	.	76	11
1917 { February				118	
1917 { September				111	10

So we see how hundreds of healthy children now live on places which only a few years ago were most malarious. Further comment on the figures is superfluous, beyond a reminder that just as the labourer is free to leave a healthy estate when attracted by the higher wages of an unhealthy one, so he often returns when ill, and he and his sickly children raise the death rate and spleen rate of the healthy estate. For example, eight of the eleven children with enlarged spleen found on estate "F" in 1915 had recently come from an unhealthy estate. It is easy to ascertain a fact like that, and so the correction of spleen rates is easy. In the course of this book, many such instances occur. As it would merely burden the narrative unnecessarily to give details in every instance, it will be done only in some.

Estate "H."—The medical history of this estate can be found from the subjoined table.

	1904.	1905.	1906.	1907.	1908.	1909.
Blood examination—						
Number examined	25	13	27	...	...	26
Percentage infected	28	48	0	...	...	0
Spleen examination—						
Number examined	...	...	27	...	...	58
Percentage enlarged	...	...	0	...	...	1·6
Death rate	...	...	30	30	22	...

Now from these figures it is obvious that a marked improvement occurred in the health of this estate in 1906. I give in the manager's own words the explanation :—

"In answer to your inquiry with regard to the health of this estate : In 1904 only 160 acres were opened and jungle came comparatively close to the lines. There was so much fever that coolies had to be dosed with quinine daily at muster. Little opening was done during 1905, and the state of health among coolies remained much the same: in 1906 jungle was carried back by opening to a distance of one and a quarter miles on one side and about half a mile on the other, and from that date there has been practically no fever on the estate and the out-turn of coolies daily has improved to a marked extent.   Dated 5/1/10.   N. C. S. BOSANQUET."

Comment on this is hardly necessary, but I might mention that the lines were distant from the jungle in 1904 about a quarter of a mile. The extra quarter of a mile made all the difference. Being a quarter of a mile away to begin with the estate was not suffering so severely from malaria as would have been the case had the lines been closer, but I think the lesson can hardly be missed.

(1919.)—The health on this estate has continued good. Malaria has never returned.

Spleen Rates of Children.

Year.	No. Examined.	Spleen Enlarged.	Spleen Rates.
1911	73	3	3·7
1912	83	2	2·4
1914	66	2	2·7

The death rates per mille have been equally satisfactory; from 1906 inclusive they have been:—30, 30, 22, 5, 13, 24, 14, 10, 2, 8, 23, 20, 15.

Estate "I." — Opened in 1904, this estate suffered very severely from malaria, more so than the percentage of children infected in 1905 would lead one to suppose. It was so severe that not a child below the age of one year was to be found on the estate; although the adult labour force was then about 250. The manager suffered so severely from the disease that he had to be sent on three months' leave of absence. In December 1905, I saw no fewer than seventeen coolies, or 6·8 per cent., of the whole labour force ill with malaria fever, while diarrhœa and dysentery, the common terminal sequelæ of malaria, were far from uncommon. Then, in 1906, opening up having been continued, improvement took place. The present manager had been on the estate for over three years and had not had malaria.

Table giving Particulars of Estate "I."

	1905.	1906.	1907.	1908.	1909.
Blood—					
Number examined	15	16	...	...	59
Percentage infected	26	0	...	...	1·6
Spleen—					
Number examined	...	...	...	...	58
Percentage enlarged	...	...	...	...	1·4
Death rate	...	68	...	54	...

The jungle is now (1909) rather less than half a mile from the lines.

(1919).—In subsequent years the jungle was pushed back still farther, and the good health was maintained. In 1913 there were eight children with enlarged spleen out of 129 (6·2 per cent.); in 1915, two children out of 177 (1·1 per cent.). Further comment is superfluous.

(1909).—We have thus seen that, on the same road on two different estates, the lines, which were near to the undrained jungle, were unhealthy; and that when the jungle was pushed back, the lines became healthy. Yet there has been no general change in the country; for we find that, at the present date (1909), we have only to go to the lines still on the jungle edge to find malaria. Immediately inland from estate " I," we come to estate " J "; and here of the nine children, four, or 44 per cent., have enlarged spleens. Quinine was given systematically on the estate, and doubtless this kept the death rate comparatively low. It was thirty-four per mille in 1908, and 120 in 1907.

(1919).—The jungle next to the coolie lines on estate " J " is still there. It is now reduced to a strip 80 chains wide; on both sides and at the ends, the land has been opened, drained, and cultivated for long distances. The jungle grows on a clay, covered by a deep layer of peat; in very wet weather, water stands on the surface, so only during a short period of the year is it a breeding-place for anopheles. The result is that the health of estate " J " has materially improved; sometimes, in the wet months of the year, a few malaria cases appear; but the low spleen rates show how little there is.

Spleen Rates of Estate " J."

Year			
1909	.	.	.
1913	.	.	.
1915	.	.	.
1917	.	.	.
1919	.	.	.

A similar condition of health exists on another estate close to estate " J " and similarly close to jungle. Out of twenty children examined not one had an enlarged spleen; but malaria does occur at times in the wet months.

(1909).—The story of how malaria has disappeared from estates on flat land, as the jungle has been pushed back to about half a mile, little short of miraculous as it is, becomes monotonous as we trace it north up to Kuala Selangor, and down south through Klang to Kuala Langat, over a distance of some fifty miles. The maps, indeed, tell the tale. I would gladly leave it at that, but the subject is of such economic importance that I must make the proof of the improvement as full as possible. For, marvellous as the disappearance of malaria has been with the opening up of the flat land, just as striking has been the total failures of similar opening to affect malaria on the hilly land. The explanation of the difference is to be found in the mosquito theorem; that alone can explain it. On the flat land the carrier of malaria is the mosquito, *A. umbrosus*, which, breeding in pools in the jungle, is exterminated when these pools are drained even by open drains; while on the hill land, the chief carrier is *A. maculatus*, a mosquito which cannot be exterminated in the ravines by open drainage, however quick the current, since its proper breeding-place is the running water of springs and hill streams.

My object, therefore, even at the risk of being tedious, is to show that on flat land the manager of an estate can put his coolie lines, in almost every instance, beyond the reach of the malaria carrier, and so save his labour from malaria; and I maintain that, since over thousands of acres of flat land malaria has been abolished by extermination of the mosquito which carries the disease, so the manager of the hill estate can also abolish the disease if he abolishes the breeding-places of the hill-carrier by putting the water of the ravines underground.

Estate "K" is small, and I have few figures referring to it. Its coolie lines have always been at a distance from jungle, and have always been healthy. I am indebted to Dr Macaulay for examining the fourteen children on this estate. Of the fourteen he fo nd one with an enlarged spleen, equal to 7 per cent. This chil J, however, came from an estate on which the spleen rate is 23, and had suffered from fever before coming to estate "K." The death rate of this estate was 18 per mille in 1908.

(1919).—In 1912 and 1916 the number of children examined was 30 and 129 respectively. No enlarged spleen was found on either occasion. The health of the estate has remained uniformly good.

(1909).—*Estates* "*L*," "*M*," "*N*," "*O*," "*P*," "*Q*."—Their spleen rates, as given on the map (p. 68), show that those away from the jungle are healthy, while those close to it are more unhealthy; and that, even on the same estate, there are marked differences of health depending also on the proximity or other-wise of the lines from the jungle. Estates "L," "M," "N," "O" are all at some distance from the jungle, and all are healthy. Estate "P" has some lines near to the jungle, and these are very unhealthy; while others away from it are healthy. Estate "Q," on the other hand, had all its lines close to jungle until recently, and some remain so; and its spleen rate is high.

Dealing with these estates in detail, we find that during the course of the past few years some of those, which are now healthy, were unhealthy when the lines were closer to jungle.

Estate "L."—This estate, begun in 1902, had already a considerable area opened and drained by November 1904, when I first made an examination of the children.

Table showing the result of Blood and Spleen Examination of Children, and the Death Rate of Estate "L."

	1904.	1905.	1906.	1907.	1908.	1909.
Blood—						
Number examined	10	16	18	...	...	...
Percentage infected	33	6	0	...	...	...
Spleen—						
Number examined	...	...	18	...	...	39
Percentage enlarged	...	...	0	...	...	2·5
Death rate	...	...	...	20	21	...

Dr Macaulay, to whom I am indebted for the examinations in 1909, says that of the thirty-nine children, the only one with enlargement of the spleen was a child eight months old, born on the estate. The enlargement was so slight that he could hardly call it pathological.

Here again we see the improvement which has followed the abolition of the malaria carrier, for *A. umbrosus* can no longer be found on this estate.

(1919).—In 1912 there were ninety-five children on the estate, none of whom had enlarged spleens.

Estate "M" was first opened in 1898, and I cannot recall the time, since I came to the district in 1901, when it was unhealthy.   Such figures as I have show this:—

	1905.	1906.	1907.	1908.	1909.
Blood—					
Number examined	26	25	...	...	...
Percentage infected	3	4	...	...	...
Spleen—					
Number examined	...	25	...	...	202
Percentage enlarged	...	4	...	...	3·4
Death rate	...	...	15	26	35

The death rate of this estate is shown as larger than it should be since coolies sent from estate "G," who died in the estate hospital on "M," have been counted in this death rate.

That the estate is free from malaria is shown by the fact that no European has contracted malaria on it since I came to the district; and there is now, and has been for several years, a European staff of six.

(1919).—The following table shows the spleen rates:—

Year.	No. Examined.	No. Enlarged.	Spleen Rates.
1912	57	1	1·7
1914	138	6	4·3
1916	128	3	2·3

The Europeans have continued to be free from malaria.

Estates "N" and "O."—The lines of both the estates are now a considerable distance from the jungle, the nearest being the mangrove, which is 600 to 1000 yards off.

I have few figures concerning these estates. I remember on one occasion in 1905 visiting a set of lines on "N" and found many cases of fever. It was then within 100 yards of the jungle. Unfortunately, I cannot find my notes of this.

The following figures show that the estates are not by any means unhealthy. The labour force is small on each, being only 280 on "N" and 120 on "O":—

	Death Rates.			Spleen Rates, 1909.	
	1906.	1907.	1908.	No. Examined.	Percentage Enlarged.
Estate " N " . .	8	20	43	29	◡
Estate " O " . .	44	18	34	45	2·2

Estate " P " is one of the largest in the country, and stretches over several square miles.   Within its boundaries are to be found lines at varying distances from undrained jungle. These show in the most distinct manner what has been evident on all the other estates to which I have previously referred.

It will be seen from a reference to the map, that the lines 82 are close to the jungle.   They contained seventeen children, of whom fourteen had enlarged spleens.   Farther along, on the edge of the same jungle, are lines containing eleven children— of whom ten have spleens abnormal in size, giving a rate of 90·9.   Two hundred yards from these the lines containing fifteen children showed a spleen rate of 53·3, while at a distance of 300 yards from the lines marked 82 the spleen rate of twenty-two children was 59·9.

In marked contrast to these are the 109 children who live at a greater distance from the jungle and whose spleen rate is 8·2.   That it should be so high as this is due to some of the lines being near to a small belt of jungle once drained—but whose drains are not upkept.   When the lines were put there in 1906 I have notes showing that there were considerable numbers of cases of malaria on the estate, and I recollect that these were unhealthy ; but, unfortunately, I have not recorded the exact number of cases found in each of the different sets of lines. There is no doubt, however, that these lines next to the belt of jungle have improved in health to a very considerable extent.

In tabular form these facts become more evident :—

Distance from Undrained Jungle.

	Within 100 yards.	200 to 300 yards.	Beyond 300 yards.
No. Children examined . . .	28	37	109
No. with enlarged spleen . .	24	17	9
Percentage with enlarged spleen .	85·7	45·9	8·9

For the subsequent history of estate " P," see Chapter XVI.

Estate " Q."—The lines on this estate also vary in distance from one hundred yards to a quarter of a mile from the jungle. I found, however, that the coolies had been moving from the lines nearest to the jungle to others farther away. I, therefore, cannot determine with accuracy the spleen rate of the different lines. The lines a quarter of a mile from jungle have a spleen rate of 28; while that of those within 100 yards is 59·3.

The other rates are 55·5, 42·9 and 60, and that for the whole estate is 53·6.

The death rate was 60 per 1000 in 1908. For the later history see Chapter XVI.

Estate " R."—Within 150 yards of the lines on this estate is a small swamp about half an acre in extent. There is no other swamp within half a mile.

Of nineteen children examined in 1910, 10·5 per cent. had enlarged spleen. The death rate of the estate has been 40, 56, and 45 in the years 1906, 1907, and 1908 respectively.

(1919).—There are other two records of the spleen rate of this estate. In 1915 and 1916 there were 32 children; on each occasion one child had enlarged spleen, giving a rate of 3·2. The child had returned to estate " R " after having bolted to an unhealthy estate.

Passing south across the Klang River we come to *estate* " *S* " which has been opened for some years. Although extensive in area, the opening has not been such as to decrease the distance of the lines from the nearest jungle. The following table gives the facts:—

Distance of the Various Lines from Jungle.

	200 yards.	300 yards.	350 yards.	300 yards.	200 yards.
No. examined .	4	7	13	8	20
Spleen rates . .	50	28·5	23·0	37·5	20

There has been a great improvement in the health of this estate during 1909 due to the extensive use of quinine. It is an example of how quinine may appear of greater value in a place where malaria is not very severe than where the disease is intense.

The estate has always been unhealthy, but not intensely malarious, the spleen rate of the whole estate being only 23; still the disease has caused considerable trouble. There are no official figures for 1907, but in that year the manager was invalided to Europe on account of malaria. In the same year a large gang of coolies also left on account of the disease. In 1908 there was great sickness; and I saw many cases of chronic and acute malaria on the estate. In the months of November and December, no fewer than sixteen coolies died from malaria and its complications. The whole labour force was then put on to quinine—ten grains daily, and the death rate at once came down. Of the six deaths in 1909, none was due to malaria either directly or indirectly. The figures are interesting:—

Year.	Average Population.	Deaths.	Desertions.	Discharges.	Total Loss.
1908	362	42	137	230	409
1909	373	6	46	172	224

This is the only estate on which quinine is given systematically, the spleen rate of which is below 40. I refer to the subject of the dose of quinine in relation to the intensity of the disease on p. 119.

(1919).—The subsequent history of this estate is of great interest, as is that of another estate subsequently opened beside it. It will be found in Chapter XXII. on the Reappearance of Malaria.

(1909).—The next two estates, " T " and " U," I deal with together, as they form practically one clearing in the middle of jungle.

On *Estate " T "* one set of lines is close to jungle, about 50 feet from it, and of three children all have enlarged spleens; while, in the set of lines 100 yards from jungle, nine out of ten have enlargement. The spleen rate of these two sets of lines is therefore 92·3.

The other lines on the two estates are close to each other, and about one-third of a mile from jungle. Of the fifty-four children twenty-one suffer from enlargement, giving a spleen rate of 38·8.

The rate of the whole sixty-seven children on the two

estates in 1909 is thus 49·2. On the 16th January 1907, I examined forty-four children on these same estates and found twenty-six with enlarged spleens, giving a rate of 59. It will thus be seen that here again the lines near to the jungle are the more unhealthy, and that during the last three years, because the nearest jungle is still at the same distance from the lines, there has practically been no improvement in the health. The death rates bear this out.

	1906.	1907.	1908.
Estate "T" .	72	33	107
Estate "U". .	37	64	75

(1919).—Development has proceeded rapidly since that was written in 1909. Except for a small area of perhaps 5 or 6 acres, no jungle exists within three-quarters of a mile of the lines: in many directions it is over a mile away. The health has improved according to rule. In 1919 the spleen rate of 177 children on estate "T" was 1·6 per cent.

(1909).—*Estate* "*SSS*," a small clearing in the jungle, follows the usual rule. No coolies can be kept on it, *as it is so unhealthy*.

Turning back towards the coast we come to the estates "V," "X," "Y," "AA," "BB," "CC," which are among the oldest in the district, and have large areas opened up. On all, with one exception, the lines are at a distance from jungle, and the health of all is good. It was not, however, always so. I remember, when District Surgeon, that cases of malaria were not infrequently admitted from estate "V"; while in the first half of 1906 I find from my notes that malaria was constantly seen in the lines of estate "X," which are marked 7, and which were then on the edge of the jungle. I have, however, no figures referring to the children.

The following table shows their present condition :—

	"V."	"X."	"Y."	"AA."	"BB."	"CC."
Number examined . .	32	85	145	26	25	82
Spleen rate . .	9·6	7·0	4·8	0	4	3·6
Death rate, 1908 . .	11	30	29	22	22	9
" 1907 . .	6	25	35	...	20	30
" 1906 . .	0	67	23	38	20	30

It is hardly necessary to comment on these figures. But on estate " V," of the three coolies with enlarged spleens, one came from a set of lines on another estate the spleen rate of which is over 50. In April 1909, Dr Stanton, of the Institute for Medical Research, examined 160 unselected coolies on this estate, and found only two, or 1·3 per cent., with malaria parasites in the blood.

Although the estate is classed among those of the flat land, it is not entirely flat. Part of it is hilly. The absence of malaria is due to the valleys between the hills being of such a formation that no proper hill streams are found, and *A. maculatus* cannot be found either in the drains or in the lines of the estate. Klang Town is also hilly, but here again there are no hill streams in which *A. maculatus* breeds.* Hence open drains sufficed to eradicate malaria. An idea was prevalent among medical men at one time that malaria was due to a disturbance of hill soil, the exposure and excavation of red earth, and the quarrying of laterite.

The absence of malaria from estate " V," where red earth and laterite are abundant, from the town of Klang where the constant quarrying of laterite and the excavation of red earth have gone on for years, from the midst of the town and at the hospital, shows that malaria is not due to the presence or disturbance of these soils. The one constant condition which I have found associated with malaria is the presence of certain species of anopheles. It is true that, in some of the most malarious places, it is said by the layman that there are no mosquitoes. On one such place, an estate where the spleen rate is 100 and the death rate in 1908 was 300 per mille, the manager, a man of more than ordinary intelligence, assured me that mosquitoes were never seen except on a wet night, and then only in small numbers. My experience was that, whereas the man who helps me to catch mosquitoes usually earns 20 or 30 cents in a couple of hours, being paid at the rate of 3 cents for each anopheline, on this estate he earned 3 dollars and 12 cents in the same time, and at the same rate; having thus caught 104 anophelines. When I went to the lines I found the mosquitoes, mostly *A. maculatus*, in great abundance. *A. maculatus* is a small mosquito; it makes little noise and causes little, if any, pain when it bites. This is

* In 1913 *A. maculatus* appeared in the hill-foot drains. (See Chapter XXII.)

different from *A. umbrosus*, which gives a painful bite something like a sharp hot needle.

(1919).—The town of Klang and estates "V" and "X" remained free from *A. maculatus* until 1913. Fortunately for estate "V" they came mainly to a small ravine more than half a mile from the coolie lines of the estate; unfortunately for estate "X" they were within 100 yards of its lines, in which they produced a serious outbreak of malaria. (See Chapter XXII.)

Estate "V" continues to be healthy as the spleen rate shows.

Spleen Rates of Estate "V."

Year.	No. Examined.	No. Enlarged.	Spleen Rates.
1915	73		6.8
1918	79		2.5

(1909).—Of the six children on estate "X" with enlarged spleen, three had been on the estate only fourteen days, having come from India. The presumption is that these children had malaria before their arrival on the estate. The high death rate of this estate in 1908 was due to the return to the estate of a gang of coolies, eighty in number, who had gone to an estate whose spleen rate is 100. They suffered so severely from malaria there that they returned at the end of six weeks.

The manager of estate "X" was afraid these coolies might infect the others, but this did not occur since there was no anopheline to act as carriers.

On *Estate "Y"* seven of the lines were close to jungle, which, although drained on the two sides which are close to the lines, could not be called properly drained. Three years ago, however, I was unable to find anophelines in it on one single occasion. Of the ninety children in these lines 5.2 per cent. had enlarged spleen, while in another set of lines close to drained jungle twenty-two children showed a spleen rate of 8.3. The spleen rate of the remaining thirty-three children who were housed about half a mile from the jungle was *nil*.

This is the only estate which even appears to be an exception to the rule that lines within 200 yards of the jungle should have a spleen rate of about 50, but the presence of a large 15-foot drain along one side of the jungle and a 6-foot

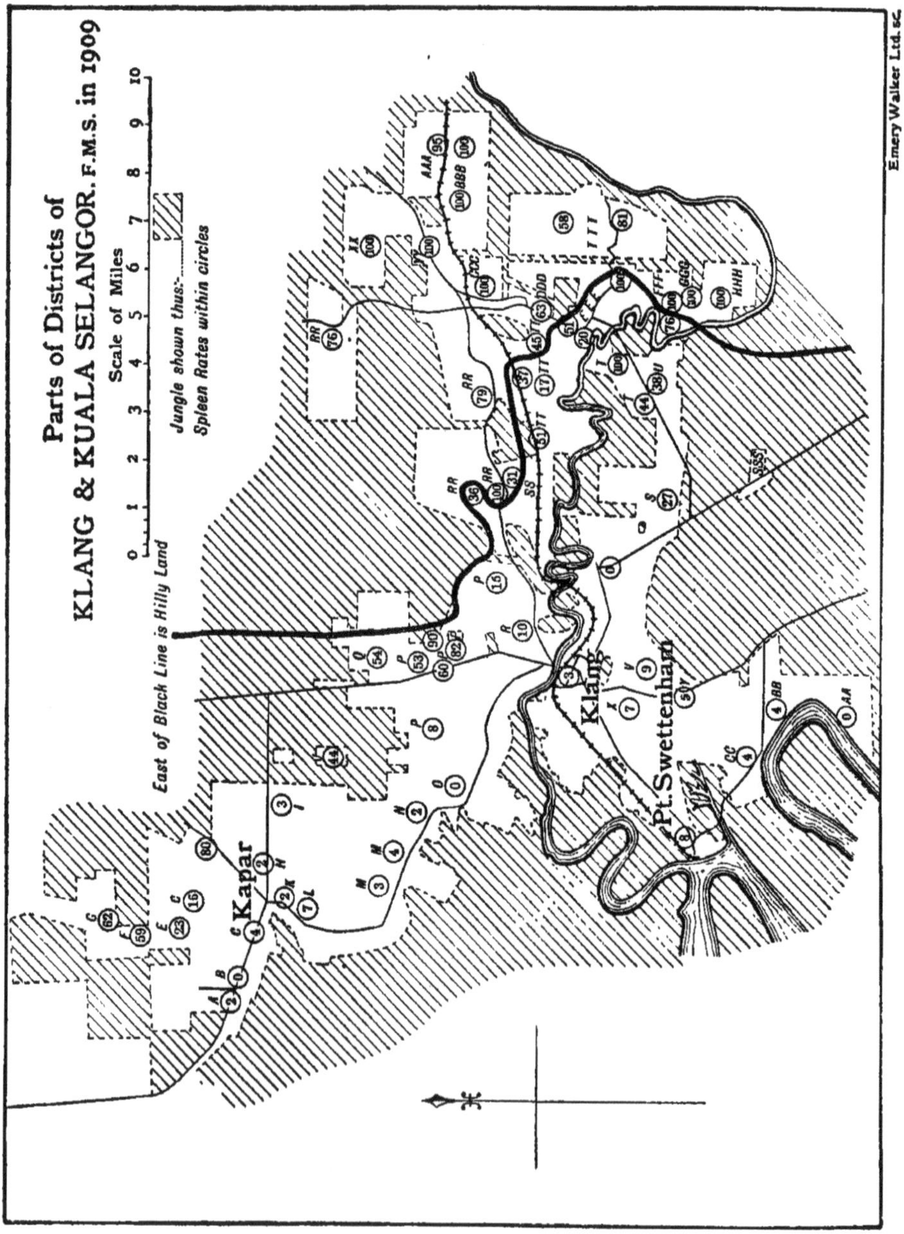
Parts of Districts of
KLANG & KUALA SELANGOR. F.M.S. in 1909
Scale of Miles
0 1 2 3 4 5 6 7 8 9 10
Jungle shown thus:-
Spleen Rates within circles
East of Black Line is Hilly Land
Kapar
Klang
Pt. Swettenham
Emery Walker Ltd. sc.

drain along the other side, as well as the fact that the jungle here is peaty, probably explains the freedom from sickness.

(1919).—At times large numbers of *A. umbrosus* temporarily appear in the lines and bungalows of this estate.

Estate "EE," see Chapter IX. *Estate "CC,"* see Chapter XXII.

(1919).—The health of *Estate "BB"* has continued to be excellent; the spleen rate in 1915 was 1·36 (– 2·8 per cent.). The death rates from 1907 to 1918 inclusive have been 20 to 23, 19, 21, 25, 7, 8, 0, 3, 16, 8, and 19.

(1909).—Passing on to the Langat District again, we come to a small estate, "*JJJ*," the lines of which are a little over a quarter of a mile from jungle. The spleen rate of the twenty-one children is 14. The death rate in 1908 was 19 per mille.

(1909).—The next estate is "FF," and in the lines next to the jungle the rate is 33, while in the more distant lines it is *nil.* For the whole estate it is 23·7, and the death rate for 1908 was 53 per mille.

(1919).—As years passed the estate grew in size; the labour force was housed in three different areas or divisions, the latest still farther from the jungle than the other two. I shall call them Divisions I., II., and III.

Division I. next to the jungle maintained its high spleen rate; and each wet season saw a number of malaria cases, with rarely a death; for more than ordinary care is taken with this labour force. The chief difficulties in making the estate healthy were a special jungle reserve for "Sakais," one of the native races of the Peninsula; and the prohibitive prices the surrounding natives placed on patches of swampy kampongs.

In 1915, however, the kampongs were cleaned up and drained, and by 1917 the estate had reaped the benefit of these measures as the following figures show.

Spleen Rates of Estate "FF."

Year.	No. Examined.	No. Enlarged.	Spleen Rates.
1909	13	3	23
1915	56	18	32
1917	99	5	5

These figures are for the whole estate. It is not necessary to go into details : they simply show that as long as the spleen rate of the estate was high, it resulted from the children living next to the jungle. Division III. was from the first free from the disease.

(1909).—Farther on, *Estate "GG"* has a spleen rate of 2·2 (fifty-nine examined), although the lines are a quarter of a mile from jungle and separated from it by a river. On this estate were eighteen children, of whom ten had enlarged spleen. These came from an estate whose rate is about fifty. By deducting these children the corrected rate of the estate would be 7·3.

The death rate of the estate in 1908 was 31. It has been healthy from the beginning as it began on open land.

(1919).—Nothing much of note has to be recorded : the health has continued to be good. The spleen rates have been :—

Spleen Rates of Estate "GG."

Year.	No. Examined.	No. Enlarged.	Spleen Rates.
1914 (May)	32	4	12·5
1914 (Dec.)	113	3	2·6
1917	138	0	0

Of the four children found with enlarged spleen in 1914, three belonged to a family which had left the estate for a time to live at Jugra Hill, a very malarious place (see p. 183); there the father died of malaria; the widow and children then returned to the estate.

At the muster in 1917, I was interested to see three of the eighteen children, mentioned as having come from a malarious estate in 1909, now mothers with healthy babies in their arms.

(1909).—In marked contrast to this is the next *Estate "HH"* only half a mile farther on ; where all the lines are within a hundred yards of jungle. Of forty-six children 54·3 per cent. had enlargement of the spleen, and in 1908 the death rate of the estate was correspondingly high, namely 60 per mille.

(1919).—In 1909 "HH" was an estate of only a few hundred acres; to-day there are over 4000 acres, except for a narrow strip of swampy jungle on the stiff clay soil of the river bank, jungle is everywhere distant from the lines.

Spleen Rates.

Year.	No. Examined.	No. Enlarged.	Spleen Rates.
1909	46	25	54·3
1915	200	6	3·0
1917	257	9	3·3

Five out of the nine children with enlarged spleen were among 42 on the division nearest the strip of jungle on the river bank.

(1909).—*Estate " TT "* has a spleen rate of only 13 in the fifteen children examined. The lines are about 200 yards from jungle, but are separated from it by a river. Its death rate in 1908 was 47.

(1919).—The jungle on both sides of the river is now opened ; in fact, a portion of the labour force now lives on the opposite bank.

Spleen Rates.

Year.	No. Examined.	Spleen Rates.
1915	80	0·0
1917	126	1·5

Both children with enlarged spleen in 1917 were on the old division.

(1909).—The following three estates again corroborate the evidence which we have been so steadily accumulating. *Estate " JJ "* has lines within a quarter of a mile of jungle and the spleen rate of fifty-three children is 26·3. Its death rate was 39. The figures tell their own tale.

	Distance Lines are from Jungle.	Spleen Examination.		Death Rate, 1908.
		No. Examined.	Percentage Enlarged.	
Estate "JJ" .	400 yards	53	26·3	39
„ "KK" .	Over 1000 yards	48	0·0	12
„ "LL" .	„ „	70	1·4	17

The only child found on estate " LL " with enlarged spleen had come from an estate whose spleen rate was between 30 and 40.

(1919).—All three are now free from malaria; no jungle is near to any of them.

Year.	Estate "JJ."		Estate "KK."		Estate "LL."	
	No. Examined.	Rate.	No. Examined.	Rate.	No. Examined.	Rate.
1914	...	...	135	0·7	209	1·4
1917 (Jan.)	112	0.8	135	0·0	226	0.8
1917 (Oct.)	165	1·2	155	0·0	246	0·0

The examinations in 1917 were by different European observers.

(1909).—Adjoining estate " KK " are two estates illustrating the same rule. *Estate " PP"* is a small one, but the manager and his coolies suffer considerably from fever. The two children on it had both enlarged spleens. They all live within a hundred yards of jungle.

In due course the jungle was opened up and health improved.

Spleen Rates.

Year.	No. Examined.	No. Enlarged.	Spleen Rates.
1915	41		7·3
1917	63		0·0

The three children with enlarged spleen belonged to one family, which had arrived from India only 1½ months previously.

(1909).—*Estate " OO"* has lines in two places. One set of lines is now half a mile from jungle, but until recently the jungle was only a quarter of a mile away. The other set of lines are, and have been, half a mile from jungle for about two years. The result is very striking; for, whereas in the lines which were until recently a quarter of a mile from jungle, 60 per cent. of the twenty-eight children examined suffered from splenic enlargement; of the seventeen in the other lines, the spleen rate was *nil.*

(1919).—Here, too, with the development of the estate, the jungle was pushed farther from the lines and the health improved.

Spleen Rates.

Year.	No. Examined.	Spleen Rates.
1915	177	0·5
1917	130	0·7

The only child with enlarged spleen in 1917 had come from Seremban (an unhealthy district) one month before.

The death rates from 1907 to 1918 inclusive have been :— 40, 40, 21, 29, 27, 15, 14, 13, 2, 7, 12, 17, the last being the year of the influenza pandemic.

(1909).—Until recently the lines on *Estate "NN"* were one third of a mile from jungle. The spleen rate of the thirty-five children is 11·4; while the lines of *Estate "MM"* are over 1000 yards from jungle and none of the twelve children have abnormality of the spleen.

(1919).—Estate "MM" continued healthy—the spleen rates being :—

Year.	No. Examined.	Spleen Rates.
1915	121	2·4
1917	131	0·7

Estate "NN" is now one of the largest in the district; it is divided into two divisions a few miles apart. The spleen rates have been :—

Year.	No. Examined.	No. Enlarged.	Spleen Rates.
1909	35	...	11·4
1917 (Jan.)	238	1	0·4
1917 (Dec.)	190	2	1·0

The girl with enlarged spleen in January 1917 had recently come from India. She had not suffered from fever on the estate, and had worked regularly without missing a day. At

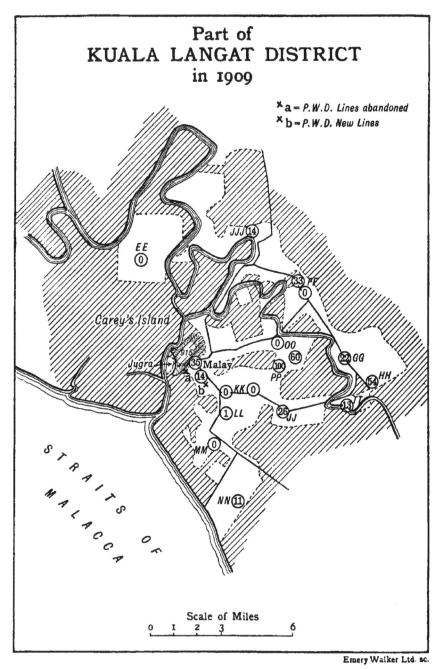

FIG. 16.—Map of a Part of Kuala Langat District, showing Spleen Rates in 1909.

the November examination, her spleen could not be palpitated, nor was splenic dullness enlarged to percussion. Of the two with enlarged spleen in November, one was a returned bolter, the other had suffered from fever on the estate a month previously.

(1909).—It is sometimes argued that malaria is never as severe on flat land as it is on hilly land. This is generally so, for the conditions from the first are different. On hill land, the coolies are housed on the side of a ravine so that water may be conveniently to hand. They are, therefore, placed as close as possible to the breeding-places of the malaria carrier, that is on the most unhealthy spots on an estate, and there they remain. No further opening of the estate alters the distance they are from the breeding-place.

In the case of flat land estates the conditions are entirely different. Before a Tamil coolie is brought to an estate, at least fifty acres are felled, drained, and burned by Javanese, people who are, as we shall see, generally immune to malaria.

The Tamil on the flat, therefore, starts with the breeding-place of the malaria carrier at a distance of some hundreds of yards, and every few months further openings put the breeding-places farther off. He starts, therefore, under better conditions as a rule, and the conditions improve with every additional opening.

That there is no essential difference is seen if a non-immune population is placed on undrained flat land. The conditions are then the same as on hill land, and the results are the same. It is not often, of course, that we see a population under such circumstances; but it occurred at Port Swettenham in 1901, and there malaria was as severe as it ever was on any hill estate.

We have seen, too, that lines close to the jungle have 90 to 100 per cent. of the children suffering from enlarged spleen, and the occurrence of a case of Blackwater fever in a European, who lived within 100 yards of the jungle on the flat land, supplies a further proof, if the history of Port Swettenham has failed to convince.

Summary of Examination of Children on Flat Land Estates.— On the flat land estates altogether 2,295 children were examined in 1909.

Tabulating the results, we find that the health of the lines bears a very definite relationship to their distance from the jungle, and the following is the table :—

Table showing the Spleen Rates of Children living at Different Distances from Undrained Jungle on Flat Lands.

	Distance from Jungle.				
	Within 300 yards.	300 to 600 yards.	600 to 1000 yards.	Over 1000 yards.	Total.
Number of Children examined . .	325	396	532	1042	2295
Spleen Rates per cent. . . .	47	21·9	11	2·6	14·2

It is clear from these figures that malaria can be avoided on the flat land by housing coolies about 1000 yards from the nearest undrained jungle, and that every yard the coolies are removed from jungle improves their health.

In a later table it will be seen that the death rate of estates in Malaya is largely due to malaria, and that were malaria abolished the death rate would be about 10 per mille of the coolie population as at present constituted.

Over an area of the Selangor coast, some fifty miles long, I have traced how malaria, affecting a population of many thousands, has been driven back, year by year, as the land has been drained and opened by agricultural operations.

At the towns of Klang and Port Swettenham, deliberate attempts were made to deal with the disease; and they were successful in the highest degree.

But of infinitely more importance have been the results of the agricultural operations. Although malaria may affect a town, it is essentially a disease of the country. The capital of the peasant is his health, and if this be destroyed by malaria, poor, indeed, is he. The planters in Malaya have carried out unconsciously it is true, what really form an extensive series, of rural anti-malarial and anti-mosquito experiments. I have watched, over a number of years now, experiment after experiment, with control after control, which have proved that the pool-breeding anopheline, which carries malaria on the coastal plain of Malaya, can be exterminated by open drainage at a very low cost; and that with the extermination of the anopheline, malaria has disappeared. Anti-mosquito measures have, therefore, been proved on the coast of Malaya to be not only entirely suitable to rural districts, but have greatly improved the value of the land.

CHAPTER IX

THE MALARIA OF MANGROVE SWAMPS AND
ANOPHELES LUDLOWI

" BEING in Manila early in 1901," wrote [11] Dr Clara S. Ludlow, B.Sc., Ph.D., " it was repeatedly suggested by some of the medical officers of the United States army stationed there that I should take up the study of mosquitoes, and the thought strongly emphasised that the study of mosquitoes was likely to be of real benefit to mankind, especially if carried out in connection with the occurrence of certain diseases, notably malaria." It was a period when the mosquitoes of tropical countries were being studied in detail for the first time. Miss Ludlow, who had accompanied her brother, a colonel in the army, to Manila, was a student of science, well qualified for the task; and the work was regarded as so important that it was put under the jurisdiction of the Surgeon-General. Thus began a research, which was continued for many years in the Philippines, and is still carried on by Dr Ludlow at the Army Medical Museum, Washington, where I had the pleasure of meeting her in 1913.

Dr Ludlow soon found that [12] " . . . the mosquitoes taken were not described in the books available, and in a little while it became evident that no one knew the mosquitoes of the Philippine Islands." She worked, however, in conjunction with Mr Theobald of the British Museum, and rapid progress was made in describing the species taken. At quite an early date (1903) she differentiated the three members of the *Rossii Group* of anopheles, although for many years to follow this interesting and important group remained a puzzle to most workers. The group consists of three mosquitoes, *A. rossii*, Giles, *A. indefinita* and *A. ludlowi;* the interest lies in the fact that they are so much alike that for long many workers did not regard them as separate species: the importance, in that only *A. ludlowi*

77

is an important natural carrier of malaria, while the innocence of the other two has been generally accepted. Another point of interest is that *A. ludlowi* breeds mainly along the coast and in brackish water. Our knowledge of these mosquitoes has come slowly, and even now is probably incomplete.

Anopheles rossii (type Giles), the first member of the group to be recognised, was described by Giles from specimens taken in India. It was studied by the Commissioners sent to India by the Royal Society; and their conclusion was that, although it could be infected with malaria experimentally, it played practically no part in propagating the disease in nature. They showed there were wide areas where it existed in which the spleen index was low; if found in malarious places, there was also present another anopheles, in which alone malaria parasites were to be found.

Anopheles indefinita is common in the Malay Peninsula. It differs from *A. rossii* (Giles) in minor details. The evidence is against it being a carrier of malaria, for it is regularly found in large quantity where the spleen rate is low. Its larvæ are to be found in small muddy pools and puddles, especially when polluted by the presence of animals or man.

Anopheles ludlowi.—The story has been more involved. Dr Ludlow found it to be the species of anopheles most frequently taken in the Philippines, and it was associated with malaria in such a way as to give her the impression that it was an important carrier of malaria—although this was not actually proved by dissection. She noted that it was found, not only along the coast, but also in inland valleys, far from brackish water.

In Java in 1902 Dr De Vogel[13] found an anopheles breeding in salt marshes, often in large numbers in the water of sun-cracked mangrove mud. He noted the prevalence of this anopheles along the coast, and the existence of high spleen rates "60 per cent. to 100 in the native villages (kampongs) situated along the coast, and in the two overflow canals which carry brackish water far into the land and contain innumerable pools between their banks. Among the rice-fields and fresh water marshes farther in the interior, the numbers vary between 5 per cent. and 25 per cent." Dr De Vogel also experimented with this mosquito and was able to infect it easily; but he was unable to keep the insects alive long enough

Photograph showi   t Swettenham, with   ps outside the Bund.
Anopheles fo   even during spring ti   the land, 906.

Fig. 17.

[*To face page* 78.

FIG. 18A.

FIG. 18B.
BREEDING-PLACES OF *Anopheles ludlowi*.

[*To face page* 78.

to trace the parasites to the salivary glands. Specimens were sent to Mr Theobald, who declared them to be *A. rossii*, but there can be little doubt, in the light of our present knowledge, that Dr De Vogel was working really with *A. ludlowi*. That Mr Theobald should have made the mistake shows how close the resemblance between *A. rossii* and *A. ludlowi* is. To distinguish the two is at times difficult indeed; for in dried specimens the leg spots of *A. ludlowi* may have faded, and in some *A. rossii* there are stripes not unlike spots. Mr R. M. M. Mangkoe-winoto[14] has drawn attention to the value of the wing spots when the leg markings are doubtful.

It was not until 1912 that the question was practically settled by Christophers[15] in the Andaman Islands, where the convict settlement has been notoriously malarious. On investigation he found that "malaria in the settlement is confined to a belt around the margins of the harbour, and is absent or nearly so from villages more than half a mile from the sea-coast or the salt swamps associated with this. This freedom from malaria is seen even in inland villages situated on the margins of swamps amidst rice-fields and near jungle."

He ascribed this peculiar distribution of malaria to the "distribution of *Anopheles ludlowi*," and he found malaria developing in the stomach wall of two mosquitoes out of fifty-three dissected.

It is of interest that *A. umbrosus* was not found in the Andamans. In 1913 Dr De Vogel,[16] investigating malaria at Sibolga in Sumatra, found it associated with *A. ludlowi* and described how the spleen rate decreases the farther the kampong is in from the sea.

Finally in 1919 Dr N. H. Swellengrebel[17] and others published an exhaustive study of the association of *A. ludlowi* with malaria. It is printed in Dutch and English in parallel columns, and so is available for those who cannot read it in the original. The authors are to be congratulated on their investigation, which is a model of what a scientific inquiry should be; and the moderation of their conclusions is altogether admirable. It should be read by every student of malaria.

They found *A. ludlowi* to be the most important carrier of malaria in the parts of Java and Sumatra in which they worked. They not only infected it experimentally, but also determined its natural index of infectibility for successive months; in each set of observations *A. ludlowi* is compared with other species of anopheles. They compare the malarial infection of man and mosquito; and show that, although *A. ludlowi* is usually confined to the brackish waters of the coast, nevertheless it is found in some fish ponds in inland valleys in which there is alga; that in mangrove forests regularly covered by the tides it does not occur; while it breeds freely in the portions submerged only during spring tides. A picture of sun-cracked mud, which is almost a replica of that published by De Vogel years before, is given.

Now Java and Sumatra are volcanic islands, and the conclusions of these authors support the observations originally made by Dr Ludlow working in the Philippine Islands—which are also volcanic. In the Malay Peninsula, which is not volcanic, *A. ludlowi* has never been found away from the coast by either Strickland, Hacker, or myself; and other species are responsible for the inland malaria. When visiting Sumatra in 1913 I was struck with certain differences between that island and the Malay Peninsula; in particular the freedom from malaria of some of their opened hill land. These differences, and the importance of studying the species of anopheles of a country, I discussed with Dr Swellengrebel and Dr Schuffner; and it was this discussion, the authors say, which induced them to begin their research. The impressions I then gathered have been confirmed, and there can be no doubt that important differences exist between the two countries, although they are separated by only a narrow strait.

In towns and villages on the sea-coast or mangrove belt of the Malay Peninsula which I have examined, malaria produced by *A. ludlowi* alone is rare. *A. ludlowi* is usually found in association with *A. umbrosus;* and as good drainage clears away the two insects and the malaria produced by them, the prevention of malaria has in practice presented little or no difficulty in these places.[18]

The mangrove forest consists of a number of species of trees which can live only in salt or brackish water; hence they are not found away from the sea-coast or tidal rivers. The forest can be divided roughly into two zones: one nearest the sea, which is covered twice daily and by every tide; the other, farther inland, covered only by spring tides for a few hours

FIG. 19A.

FIG. 19B.
BREEDING-PLACES OF *Anopheles ludlowi.*

[*To face page* 80.

in perhaps three days of every fortnight. When the forest is intact, in other words in virgin mangrove forest, no anopheles breed in the outer zone; and houses built on the sea edge of the mangrove have the reputation generally of being free from malaria. It is otherwise with the inner zone, even in the virgin mangrove. In this inner zone there are, as I [18] wrote in 1903, "vast numbers of breeding-places among mangrove trees and stumps. Here crabs raise mounds, and between these small pools of water are found. Certain of the pools, situated on the zone of land covered by spring tides only, become as the result of heavy rain comparatively fresh-water pools, and at times I have found these at Port Swettenham to be teeming with the larvæ of anopheles. This I regard as the real danger of a mangrove swamp—and there were large tracts of this at Port Swettenham." Two anopheles are found here —namely *A. umbrosus* and *A. albotæniatus*.

To put it briefly, the outer zone of the virgin mangrove forest is harmless—because no anopheles breed there; on the other hand the inner zone is malarious because *A. umbrosus* and *A. albotæniatus* live in it; and the former is a known carrier of malaria. As far as I am aware *A. ludlowi* has never been found in virgin mangrove; and, as Strickland has pointed out, the larvæ appear to require sunshine.

When man destroys the forest, and more particularly when he carries out engineering operations in it, one thing certainly happens, he lets sunlight into the land; another thing may happen, he may prevent the tide from covering and flushing the outer zone twice a day as it naturally does. A railway line along the foreshore is an example of an engineering work which might create extensive areas of stagnant brackish water in the lower zone. In such pools *A. ludlowi* may breed in enormous numbers; indeed, I think the largest number of larvæ of any species ever seen by me in a breeding-place has been *A. ludlowi ;* at times they have appeared like a moving pellicle. *A. ludlowi* are to be found, too, in the inner zone when the forest has been felled. Yet even in felled mangrove the breeding-places of *A. ludlowi, albotæniatus*, and *ludlowi* are not identical. For while *A. ludlowi* is to be seen in large numbers in stagnant pools or blocked drains free from vegetation, the other two will be taken rarely unless there is grass, sticks, or some cover; and they may readily be missed, for they hide themselves away among the black roots of the mangrove and can be captured only by scraping these with the collecting dish.

MALARIA DUE TO *Anopheles ludlowi.*—The following is an instance of a place in which I found malaria due apparently to *A. ludlowi* unaccompanied by *A. umbrosus.** It is a coconut estate near to the mouth of a large tidal river, and is divided into three divisions. The severity of the malaria is indicated from the following spleen rates.

Division I.—Of 5 Javanese children born on the estate, 4 had enlarged spleens: of 48 Tamil children, 46 (or 95 per cent.) had enlargement; of the other two, one had been on the estate four months, and the other one year.

Division II.—Of 100 children 70 (70 per cent.) had enlarged spleen ; and of the 30 others only 1 had been on the estate over six months. It is significant that, out of the 100, only 3 were under two years old.

Division III.— Twenty-three out of 25 (or 95 per cent.) children, who had been on the estate over six months, had enlarged spleen. Of 32 under six months on the place—many of them only about one month—no fewer than 14 (or 43 per cent.) had enlarged spleen.

A. ludlowi, adult insects, were present in numbers. Immediately on entering my room, I saw two on my mosquito net. In the evening my assistant exposed his arm for about a minute in the open air, was promptly attacked, and captured four.

At daylight on the following morning my assistant searched the twenty-six occupied mosquito nets in the hospital, with the exception of four which were searched by the dresser; my assistant caught anopheles, the dresser took all mosquitoes present. In only two nets anopheles were not found. The total catch was 164 mosquitoes, of which 124 were *A. ludlowi ;* the other 40 were Culicines and were almost exclusively *Culex sitiens*, which, like *A. ludlowi*, breeds in brackish water.

The estate stretches along the river bank, and is protected from tidal flooding by an embankment. At certain times the tide gates are opened to admit sea water into the drains, so that the nuts may be transported cheaply by floating them down the drains. Larvæ were found wherever the water was stagnant or vegetation existed. In some shallow drains,

* *A. umbrosus* has since been found, but is probably not important.

FIG. 20A.

FIG. 20B.
Anopheles ludlowi does not breed in these Drains.

[*To face page* 82.

FIG. 21.—A SLUICE GA

[To face page 82.

free from vegetation, crab holes had formed little land-locked harbours; in these larvæ were abundant. The larvæ were particularly abundant where grass, weeds, or small sticks were present in a pool or stagnant drain.

In contrast to these, larvæ were not found in the main drains where the edges were free from weeds, clean cut and deep, and where there was current.

THE CONTROL OF *A. Ludlowi.* — Since Carey Island became an estate in 1906 it has been under my care. The island is surrounded by large rivers or arms of the sea containing practically pure salt water. The shores of the island were originally covered by the usual Mangrove zone; and as these portions of the land are below high-tide level, the whole is protected by bunds and sluice gates. Beyond the tidal zone the island is flat alluvial soil like the "coastal plain" and contains *A. umbrosus.*

The land and general situation of the island is, indeed, similar to that of the estate previously described. But whereas the estate is and has been intensely malarious, the island has been as consistently free from the disease since the first year it was opened. And the freedom is due to the following simple precautions taken, and the excellent drainage system which exists. On the island full advantage has been taken of the 16-foot rise and fall of the tide; and by means of low-level tide gates, a system of deep drainage has been created far superior to that of the majority of estates on the coastal plain of the mainland.

Opening up was begun at a small clearing in the mangrove occupied by Sakais, one of the aboriginal races of the Peninsula. When the island was taken over by the company, 100 acres were reserved for Sakais; but it was bunded and drained by the company; and, until a part of the estate was opened, it formed the company's headquarters. Drainage, felling, and clearing of the estate land was pushed on rapidly, so that within the first year (1907) 144 acres were planted, and within the second year no fewer than 1828 acres. Each succeeding year saw an increase in the planted area, until by 1917 there were some 10,000 acres opened altogether in two estates.

Now in opening up land, the common, I might almost say, the invariable mistake was to house the labour near to jungle, either temporarily or permanently. This was never done on

H

the island, the definite policy having been adopted, and followed of never housing coolies within half a mile of jungle; and the policy has paid handsomely. In 1909 I wrote of Estate "EE":—

"This estate commenced operations at the end of 1906. The labour was at first housed on land originally opened by natives, and drains were at once put through a considerable area by Javanese. So that when the Tamil labour force was introduced later, it was on opened land. The Tamils have accordingly never suffered from malaria, and now one of the finest labour forces in the country is there, consisting in all of about 2000 coolies of whom 1200 are Tamils.

"The death rate of the estate was 22 per mille in 1908, and in 1909 was only 11.

"Owing to the good health of the labour force, over 4000 acres are now drained and opened, and no set of lines is closer than half a mile to the jungle. On 29th December 1909, I examined 246 children on this estate, and found only one with an enlarged spleen (it was just palpable) giving a percentage of 0·4. The boy was in perfect health, and no history of malaria was obtainable. The presumption is, therefore, that he had malaria when in India.

"This estate shows that it is not necessarily the oldest estate which is the healthiest; but that old or new the state of the health is in relation to the proximity or otherwise of the jungle."

At the time that was written I was not aware that, by the draining and bunding, we had escaped danger from *A. ludlowi* in the mangrove zone, as well as the danger from *A. umbrosus* both in the mangrove zone and the more central jungle. Hence the reference only to *A. umbrosus* at that time.

Since 1909 until to-day, the island health has been consistently good; indeed, is almost proverbial here. In 1915 on one estate, out of 298 children only 13 or 4·3 per cent. had enlarged spleen; and inquiry showed that in almost every case the children with enlarged spleens had been previously employed on estates known to be malarious.

Between 1909 and 1918 the European staff numbered about seventeen, of whom only three suffered from malaria. One contracted his malaria on the mainland, and infected a companion living in his bungalow, which was about 400 yards from jungle. The other, who lived half a mile from jungle, apparently

FIG. 22.

An Automatic Vertical Tidal Gate on Carey Island, designed by Mr C. L. Gjorup.

FIG. 23.

Shows the great depth of Drainage possible by Mr Gjorup's Tide Gate.

[To face page 84.

FIG. 24.—A BUND ON CAREY ISLAND.

FIG. 25.—AN AUTOMATIC FLAP TIDE VALVE ON CAREY ISLAND.

[*To face page* 84.

contracted the disease on the island. That was in 1912, and was the last case in the period referred to.

The death rates since 1910 have been 21, 86, 26, 15, 9, 10, 9·12 and 28 in the influenza year, and 5 in 1919, when the average labour force was 2088. The other estate on the island has been equally healthy; the death rates being, since 1912, when it was opened, 0, 10, 17, 13, 22, 14 and 31 in 1918, and 7 in 1919. The spleen rate of 120 children examined in 1915 was 1·6 per cent.; one of the two children with enlarged spleen had worked on an estate in Perak, the other in Malacca.

The good health of two estates on the island stand in striking contrast to the malarious coconut estate previously described; and shows how completely the malaria of both the mangrove swamp and coastal plain can be controlled by good drainage, and the selection of good sites.

I could give other instances of estates situated on the sea, and within the reach of brackish water, where *A. ludlowi* and its malaria have been controlled. In a later chapter, however, I shall trace the recrudescence of malaria in once healthy places on the reappearance of *A. ludlowi* when breeding-places suitable for it have been created. They throw light on the mosquito and malaria from a somewhat different aspect: yet serve to confirm the conclusions already reached. (See Chapter XXII.)

CHAPTER X

The Persistence of Malaria in Certain Rural Areas. (1920).—In this chapter I deal with an area of hill land which is malarious when under jungle, or when the ravine streams are choked by weeds after the jungle has been felled. It is equally unhealthy when the jungle has been felled and the ravine streams are free from weeds, for a new malaria carrier appears, namely, *A. maculatus.* The conclusions reached ten years ago have been confirmed, and much additional evidence could be adduced were it necessary to do so. It will be sufficient, however, if I reproduce what was written in 1909, practically the only alteration being that *Nyssorhynchus willmori* now appears as *A. maculatus.*

(1909).—In the previous chapters I have shown how malaria has disappeared from certain portions of the coast districts of Malaya, as the land has been drained, and the jungle felled. That this often occurs is well known to all with tropical experience ; and it is with the hope that this will occur that the pioneer battles with his troubles. The hope is so strongly implanted that he takes it as a matter of course that the health will improve as the land is opened up.

We often hear of what a terrible place some spot was or is. We rarely hear that a place was abandoned on account of its ill-health. But we never seem to hear that a place always remains unhealthy, and never improves as time goes on. This is because after a time the population of an unhealthy place consists almost entirely of those who have acquired a certain amount of immunity. New people have practically ceased to come to it. And so the health seems to improve, and local experience seems to fall into line with the general experience

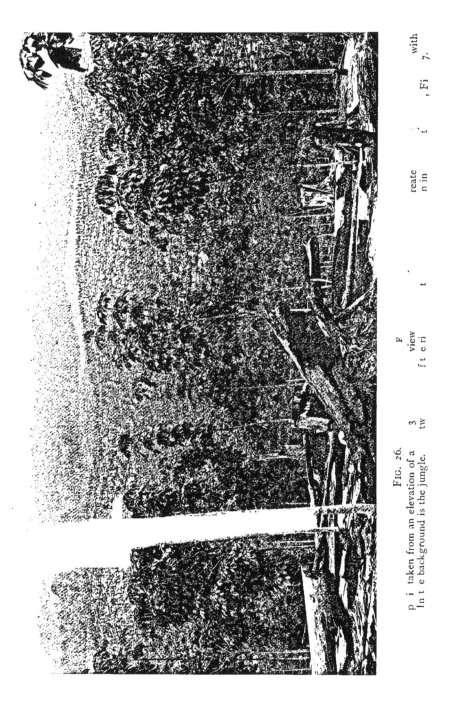

FIG. 26.

p i taken from an elevation of a
In t e background is the jungle.

F
view
ft e ri

3
tw

reate
n in

t

with
, Fi
7.

of the tropics. Yet it only wants new arrivals to come in numbers to start a severe outbreak of malaria. I have now, however, to record that in certain portions of the district, there has not been the slightest improvement in the six years during which they have been under my observation, nor have I any reason to suppose they will improve as long as the present conditions favouring the mosquito persist. The land to which I refer is the hilly land of the coast districts of Selangor, in the ravines of which run streams of water, often of very small size indeed. In this hill land the mosquitoes which are to be found are *A. umbrosus* as in the flat land, *A. maculatus* and *A. karwari.* Now the important point about these mosquitoes is that, if a ravine stream be kept free from grass and other weeds, *A. karwari* and *A. umbrosus* no longer breed in it, while *A. maculatus* will breed in streams which have been absolutely free from grass and weeds for three years to my knowledge. Extensive observation has shown *that it is not in all ravines that A. maculatus can be found, nor is it always present* in the same ravine. It is possible there may be some seasonal variation,* but of this I am not yet warranted in making any definite statement. I can say, however, that no amount of weeding or other care of a mountain stream will abolish *A. maculatus,* which I have found to be a natural carrier of malaria.

For some years malaria has formed a subject of anxiety to the managers of certain estates in the district, since their labour forces have been seriously crippled, apart from the fact that the Europeans have also suffered severely, and Blackwater fever has occurred in one instance. It was always hoped that the general experience would hold good in these estates, and that, as they were more opened up, the health would improve. In the meantime there was nothing to do but to push on with the opening programme, and give quinine to the coolies systematically. This has been done, thereby reducing the death rate and improving the general health of the coolies. The arrival of any considerable number of new coolies was, however, always the signal for an outbreak of the disease, and the older coolies who were apparently becoming acclimatised appeared occasionally to suffer with the new ones.

In the middle of 1907, when my investigations on the estates had for certain reasons suffered interruption, the

* See the *maculatus* wave, Chapter XXVIII.

position was as follows. I had determined the percentage of infected children on many of the estates of the district. I had also determined the adult mosquitoes to be found in the coolie lines, and made certain observations on their breeding-places. I had determined that the carrier of malaria on the hill land was *A. maculatus*, and that it was confined exclusively to the hill land. I had also observed on three estates that it was present when there was grass and other weeds in the drains, but not when these drains were clean. I attributed their absence to the freedom from weeds. I had also determined its absence from certain ravines altogether. I, therefore, concluded that when further opening had taken place, the health of the labour would improve on the hill land places, as it had already done on the flat land places to my knowledge.

In 1908 I was on leave in England, and on my return to Malaya was for several months fully occupied in administrative details of the hospital system, which I was organising, for the estates. During this period I came to the conclusion from what I incidentally saw, that despite the lapse of two years and despite the greater areas opened, no improvement had taken place in the hill land estates.

I accordingly determined to investigate the matter *de novo*. I determined to examine every set of coolie lines in the district and particularly those on the hill land, with the object of ascertaining the exact condition of each. I also decided to make a fuller inquiry into the breeding-places and habits of the anophelines. The result of this inquiry has been to show that *A. maculatus* cannot be exterminated as long as there is water in the ravines in which it can breed ; secondly, that malaria is as prevalent in the hill land as before ; and thirdly, that quinine in the therapeutic doses can hold in check, but cannot eradicate, malaria.

It will be unnecessary to enter into details of each of the hill land estates, but the following figures will show the general condition.

Estate "RR."—This is a large estate, work on which was begun in 1906. From the first, malaria has been prevalent. Quinine was begun in.1906 in doses of ten grains twice a week ; but as this was apparently without effect, it was increased to ten grains daily with double doses to those who did not work. The following table shows the condition :—

Fig. 27.—Stream in Hill Land.

Streams such as these run between the ridges of the Hill Land. *A. maculatus* are found in them. Large quantities of silt are dislodged in these streams, and when cleared out the silt is thrown on the banks of the stream, as will be seen from the photograph.

[To face page 88.

	1906.	1907.	1908.	1909.
Blood examination—				
Number examined .	61	...	...	...
Per cent. infected .	73	...	...	...
Spleen—				
Number examined .	61	43	...	174
Per cent. enlarged .	65	83	...	49·8
Death rate . .	...	73	165	43

It should be mentioned that one set of the most unhealthy lines was abandoned in 1908. During 1908 the amount of quinine administered was much less than had been the case in 1907, as ankylostomiasis was said to be the real cause of death in many of the coolies that year. This led to the necessity for giving quinine being questioned, and on my return from leave I found an entirely insufficient quantity was being given. The dose was at once increased and the result has been to reduce the sickness and the death rate as is seen from the above table.

From the tables on p. 92 it will be seen that the death rate in 1908 was generally higher than in the previous year. There was no special immigration in 1908; indeed it was smaller than usual; and I attribute it to the idea spread about that ankylostomiasis was the chief cause of the death rate. Quinine was consequently neglected on some estates.

The coolies on Division I. of Estate " RR " are housed in three places. The health of these varies, at least the spleen rate varies, being 90·9 per cent. in one place, 76·6 in another, and 36·6 about a quarter of a mile from the worst. The majority of the coolies are now living near the last of the three places—hence the lower spleen rate for 1909. It is possible the mosquitoes infecting the place with the low spleen rate, come from a ravine near to the place with the highest. The point is one of the greatest practical importance, but I have not yet finally determined it. In addition there has been a considerable number of new coolies lately to this division, so the spleen rate is lower than it will be when the recent immigrants have had time to become infected.

The number examined on the other two divisions on this estate were as follows :—

	No. Examined.	With Enlarged Spleens.
		Per Cent.
No. II. Division . . .	63	79·3
„ III. Division . . .	33	75·7

An idea of the amount of malaria present will be gathered from the fact that of thirteen children on the estate only two and a half months, no fewer than eight had splenic enlargement.

The death rate of this estate will be referred to later when I deal with the effect of quinine.

Estate "SS."—This estate is on the border of the hilly land, and its coolie lines are situated on the end of a ridge. The number of children examined was thirteen and the spleen rate 30·7. Five of these children had been only one month on the estate, so the corrected rate would be fifty.

Estate "TT."—This estate lies on the edge of the hills with part on the hills and part on the flat. The lines at the west end are close to jungle now being opened and on the flat; the central lines are on the flat about half a mile from the nearest jungle; while the east lines are among the ravines, but ravines which are clean. Anopheline larvæ were found only a quarter of a mile from these lines in a clean ravine. No larvæ were found in two ravines close to them. Sinniah's lines are about a quarter of a mile from rather poorly drained native holdings.

The summary of this estate is then :—

Year.	West Lines.		Central Lines.		East Lines.		Sinniah's Lines.	
	No. Examined.	Spleen Rates.	No. Examined.	Spleen Rates.	No. Examined.	Spleen Rates.	No. Examined.	Spleen Rates.
1906	14	64	28	32	5	57	17	35
1909	49	51	47	17	31	45	8	37

I should say the east lines of 1909 were on the same range of hills, but not on the same spot, as those of 1906, which had to be abandoned on account of their ill-health.

The figures are, therefore, not comparable as expressing the condition of health of the identical places, as the other figures do throughout the book. The figures, however, show that this estate is in much the same condition as it was. The central line spleen rate of 1909 was affected by four new arrivals from

an estate whose spleen rate is about 50, otherwise it would have
been 9.3, which would be in agreement with the rate generally
found for the distance the lines are from a breeding-place of
anophelines.

Table showing Spleen Rates and Death Rates of Estate " TT."

	1906.	1907.	1908	1909.
Number examined .	67	...	...	135
Spleen rate . .	41.7	...	...	37
Death rate. . .	48	86	64	...

From the figures on p. 92 it will be seen that on the other
estates in the hilly land there has been no improvement in
the amount of malaria, as indicated in the spleen rate during
the years I have been observing them. The death rate
has varied, but this, as I shall show, has been due to quinine
administration.

These figures show in the most unmistakable way that there
has been no improvement in the health of these estates. They
indeed only confirm what I had already observed from the
hospitals, from visiting the estates, and from the health of
the Europeans.

What is a Hill?—On one occasion I visited Lanadron
Estate. On the flat river bank the spleen rate was low and
the children were healthy. Further in, at the "Darat Lines,"
no fewer than 17 out of 27 children (62 per cent.) born on the
estate had enlarged spleen. The "Darat" is about 23 feet
above the general level of the surrounding flat land, and might
have been, at one time, a sand bank in the sea. Yet in the
eyes of *A. maculatus* it has found favour, and to them, at least,
it is a hill. At the time of my visit I searched for them in
vain, but Dr Rattray afterwards found them in abundance.

[TABLE.

Details of Hill Land Estates.

	1904.	1905.	1906.	1907.	1908.	1909
ESTATE.						
Blood—						
Number examined .	...	...	12	...	...	...
Per cent. infected . .	...	...	83·3	...	...	...
Spleen—						
Number examined .	...	...	12	18	...	13
Per cent. enlarged .	...	...	100	77·7	...	100
Death rate . . .	...	...	...	60	300	...
ESTATE.						
Blood—						
Number examined .	41	40	...	...	...	...
Per cent. infected .	37·8	12·5	...	...	...	...
Spleen—						
Number examined .	...	40	43	...	...	49
Per cent. enlarged .	...	17·5	30	...	...	55
Death rate . . .	...	...	95	138	176	...
ESTATE.						
Blood—						
Number examined .	6	17	18	...	...	...
Per cent. infected .	100	11·7	94	...	...	...
Spleen—						
Number examined .	...	...	...	...	...	42
Spleen rate per cent. .	...	...	...	...	...	83
Death rate . . .	...	...	...	200	...	...
ESTATE.						
Blood—						
Number examined .	6	17	26	...	...	...
Per cent. infected .	100	23	96	...	...	...
Spleen—						
Number examined .	...	...	26	...	...	13
Spleen rate per cent. .	...	...	80	...	...	100
Death rate . . .	...	...	300	178	...	...
ESTATE.						
Spleen—						
Number examined .	...	...	13	...	...	15
Spleen rate per cent. .	...	...	100	...	...	100
Death rate . . .	...	...	150	56	223	...
ESTATE.						
Spleen—						
Number examined .	...	...	14	...	...	20
Spleen rate per cent. .	...	...	71	...	...	95
Death rate . . .	...	...	...	60	90	...
ESTATE.						
Spleen—						
Number examined .	...	...	18	...	...	29
Spleen rate per cent. .	...	...	100	...	1	100
Death rate . . .	...	...	...	6	58	...
ESTATE.						
Spleen—						
Number examined .	...	...	...	...	...	15
Spleen rate per cent. .	...	...	...	...	...	100
Death rate . . .	...	...	260	93	250	...

CHAPTER XI

THE EFFECTS OF MALARIA

(1920).—The time was towards the end of July last year: Scene, the hill above Minehead in the county of Somerset: *Dramatis personæ*, the author and his two youngest sons on horseback. The school term had ended the day before; this was the start of our long-talked-of riding tour on Exmoor. The sky indicated perfect weather; it was one of the glorious mornings that England sometimes vouchsafes her long-suffering people. Below was the Bristol Channel; across it were the Welsh hills. Dunkery looked down on us from the south. The Metropole Stables had mounted us excellently, and as we settled into our saddles for the 20-mile ride through Selworthy, Porlock Weir, and Ashley Coombe to Lynton, we talked of many things—but not of malaria. That was a thing forgotten. We were living a life where it played no part. Ten thousand miles away was the Malay Peninsula, its fever and its jungle. The purple heather was under us, the horses were keen, and away we went.

And as we travelled we fell into conversation with a gentleman trying a hunter. Inadvertently I used the word "syce." As a touch to a secret spring, or the "open sesame" of the immortal tale, the doors of the East rolled open, and we talked of far-off lands. Although long retired from business, he had lived in Calcutta for many years, and he still had interests in the Malay Peninsula. One estate, to which he referred, I knew by repute as very malarious, although I had never been there; so I asked him about it, without indicating my profession. And he replied that it was just like so many other tropical ventures: "You start in gaily expecting great gain; but somehow fever strikes it in the first year, and before you know where you are, you have spent double the estimate."

A true saying, as we shall see from what I wrote ten years ago; nor need I add to it.

(1909). *Effect of Malaria on the Europeans.*—During the years I have known this district, I am talking now of hill land, only two Europeans have been known to escape the disease. They lived on a spot where the spleen rate is only 20. It is the place which is farthest from the breeding-place of anophelines, being on a point well away from any ravine or jungle. That such a spot should be found so near to very unhealthy places is of the most hopeful augury, showing that the flight of the hill-land mosquito is by no means great.

There are at the present moment twenty-nine Europeans living on ten hilly land estates. Of these twenty-five have had malaria at some time or other. Of the four who have not had the disease, two have been less than one month on the estate; one takes 15 grains of quinine daily; one has been six months on the estate without getting the disease.

As I write I have a record of the Europeans who have been on these estates during the past four years. It shows how practically all have had the disease, how from time to time they were invalided either to hospital, or off on sea-trips to recover their health, or to Europe on long leave. It shows how many have left the estate permanently, unable to withstand the disease. One man who had suffered severely from malaria had Blackwater fever, but fortunately recovered. There is only one bright spot in the record; it is, that no European has died from malaria.

So much sickness among the Europeans means that they cannot supervise their work properly; and if there be much sickness among the labour force at the same time, the absence of the controlling and directing force of the estate is, indeed, deplorable. Few native subordinates can be trusted to see that quinine is properly administered to a labour force, and one of the great troubles is that, if the manager from sickness cannot supervise it, the subordinate is very liable to do this duty in a perfunctory way. The welfare not only of the estate, but of the labour force, depends, therefore, on the well-being of the manager.

Effect of Malaria on the Coolies.—No less severely has malaria affected the coolies. In visiting estates I have always noted all cases of sickness seen in the coolie lines;

in addition I have noted on the opposite page of my book any general observations which might seem of importance. I have, therefore, a fairly complete record for some years of the health of the estates which have been under my care. From this book I will give the substance of a few notes showing the effect of malaria.

On one estate 170 coolies were recruited. They refused to take quinine at first, and were a somewhat unruly gang. Within two months of their arrival I visited the estate and found that on the day of my visit 102 out of the 170 were unfit for work. Many of these were removed to hospital. A month later I note, "Of the gang of 170 only 57 remain on the estate. Of these 29 working, and 28 off work." Practically all these coolies were lost to the estate.

Of another estate : " Have been having a bad time with malaria—turning out 170 out of 340 coolies." The following month turning out 179 out of 250 coolies. The following month again, the note is " 150 coolies.". In other words the coolies had either given notice and left or absconded. On this estate the labour force was reduced in three months from 340 to 150. I need hardly say that weeds got a firm hold of it.

Another estate: " Have been very bad with fever, practically every coolie had it, and about six deaths. Appear to be getting it in hand with quinine. 140 coolies working out of 350." The following month, "turn-out 150. Coolies looking better." A month later the manager remarked, " turn-out somewhat better but accounts not made up." The manager had been very ill. He was taking infinite pains with quinine administration. He had every room in his lines numbered and the name of every coolie who lived in each of these rooms, in a special book.

He tried to get every coolie twice daily, and ticked off in his book when each coolie had received his quinine. Only those, who, from visiting coolie lines, know how difficult it is to account for each coolie on an estate can estimate how much labour this meant.

Another estate : " 19 cases of malarial dysentery. The manager had not given quinine when complaint was dysentery. Every one gave a history of fever five to ten days previously. Are getting a considerable amount of quinine. Seventy-five out of 190 working. A month later I note, " Now only about 80 coolies on the estate. Others wish to leave, but —— and —— and —— persuaded them to stay for two months· Many have died in hospital." I promised that if they would take their quinine regularly and would report at once to the manager when ill they would not die. New lines were also built for them in another place. A month later I find less fever on the estate, and note, "old lines abandoned, coolies healthier."

Among the children malaria is no less severe. On one occasion I was asked by a manager to advise him what could be done for the children, as 15 children had died in the previous two months out of a total of 33. He told me a native clerk was giving them quinine daily. I examined the blood of the remaining 18 and found parasites in 17 of them. Such a terrible death rate among the children affects the mothers of the estates and leads to loss of labour, since the coolies naturally refuse to live in such unhealthy estates.

I have been struck by. the small birth rate of malarious estates, including those on which quinine is given. I have had no opportunity of investigating this, but inquiries are now being prosecuted. It has been said that quinine may have some injurious effect in reducing the birth rate. I am unable to express any opinion on the matter.

I am indebted to the late Mr E. V. Carey for the following :—

Notes of Fever experienced upon New Amherst Estate.

"Between the years 1892 and 1898 there were on an average over 50 Tamil women upon the check-roll each year. Yet in the whole period no living child was born. Several women became pregnant, but only in one case did the child become quick, and even in this case the woman eventually had a miscarriage. The estate was so riddled with malaria that the coolies were all miserably anæmic and lacking in strength. So anxious was the management that the stigma attached to the absence of child-birth should be removed, that every possible care was taken of the women when they became pregnant; light but regular work being provided for them, and a supply of milk, etc., being given them ; but all with no result, although a big present was offered to the woman who first brought forth a living child, and the coolies were all most anxious themselves that this reproach should be removed.

"The supply of cooked rations to all coolies under the supervision of a high caste cook worked wonders in improved health and general physique, but when the coolie insisted in returning to the system of feeding himself there was soon a relapse, and the estate had eventually to be abandoned. During the last two years, at least, all coolies were given a 5-grain pill of quinine each morning at muster, together with a cup of hot coffee."

This is very striking evidence of the effect of malaria on the birth rate, of the practical inutility of small doses of quinine in intensely malarious spots, and of the difficulty, indeed impossibility, of carrying out the most beneficent measure in the face of native opposition and prejudice.

The effect of the introduction of any large number of new coolies to estates of such an unhealthy character, as those I am describing, can be estimated from the following extract from my annual report for 1906, quoted in the Selangor Administration Report for the same year.

"The great increase in the death rate has been due to the introduction of a very large body of Tamil coolies, and the spread among these of malaria, mostly of the malignant type. These coolies came mainly from famine districts in India, and while of a fair average physique for recruits, naturally do not compare in their capacity of resistance to disease with coolies who have been well-fed and well-housed for a year on the estates here. Among these coolies malaria spreads with extraordinary rapidity, and the systematic doses of quinine, which were sufficient to maintain the older coolies in health, appeared to have little effect on these. Within two months, it is hardly an exaggeration to say that 90 per cent. of these coolies in the Batu Tiga district were infected with the disease; and the children suffered with equal or greater severity. From the new it spread to the old coolies, and also to the Chinese and others working on the estates draining and building lines. Among the Chinese, who will not take quinine, it was very fatal, and many of them were brought to the hospital in a moribund condition. The new coolies literally made no stand against the disease, and on some estates there was difficulty at first in inducing them to take quinine. Another fruitful cause of death was the bowel trouble, which so frequently supervenes on an attack of malaria. In the hospital in the month of December, out of forty-seven deaths due to malaria, no less than thirty-four were the result of bowel complications. These patients rarely complain of fever; and it is only by microscopic examination of the blood that the malaria element in the case is detected. At first the necessity of giving quinine in addition to other treatment was not recognised on estates, as the coolie made no complaint of fever, and the consequence was that many new coolies, with no stamina to spare, so to speak, were literally past hope in three or four days. As I had occasion to point out a year or two ago in a paper on quartan malaria, patients with dropsical swelling resulting from malaria are often unaware they have malaria, even when the thermometer shows they have a temperature of 102° F., and their blood is swarming with parasites. As if further to confuse the issue, many of the new coolies rapidly became anæmic and dropsical from the malaria, and attributed their illness to everything but the right thing. In some cases malignant malaria was worthy its name, and struck dead those who forty hours before had been at work. It ultimately became obvious that the only way to save the coolies was by daily administration of quinine to every coolie on the estate. This is now being done on eight estates with an aggregate labour force of about 2000 coolies, and fortunately there is some evidence that the coolies begin to appreciate the value of the drug, at least there is now no opposition to its administration." *

Variation of Death Rate with Spleen Rate.—The important influence which malaria has on the health of an estate will be more easily realised from a study of the relationship existing between the spleen rate of the estates obtained from my examination of the children and the death rates taken from the *Indian Immigration Report* for 1908.

The table on p. 99 shows the death rates of the estates arranged in accordance with their spleen rates. It shows the total population living on estates where the spleen rates varied from 0 to 100 per cent., the total number of deaths in, and the death rates of, these populations.

These figures exhibit the terrible effects of malaria, and I have exhibited them in graphic form in the chart on p. 100.

---

* Next to the anopheline the introduction of a large body of non-immune coolies is the important factor in the production of the severest outbreaks of malaria in the tropics. Captain Christophers and Dr Bentley have called the condition produced Hyper-endemicity, in a valuable paper on "The Human Factor in Malaria."[10] This is truly so called since the number of non-immune persons is greater than ever occurs in a normal population.

Spleen Rate.	Average Population.	Number of Deaths.	Death Rate per 1000.
0 to 10	7106	175	24·6
10 „ 20	492	18	36·0
20 „ 30	2291	143	62·4
30 „ 40	1121	90	82·0
40 „ 50	65	2	30·0
50 „ 60	767	35	45·6
60 „ 70	1738	232	133·4
70 „ 80	1165	189	162·2
80 „ 90	180	6	34·0
90 „ 100	933	163	167.5

From 0 to 40 the influence of malaria is unaffected by systematic quinine administration, except in the case of one estate, " S." From that onwards it is given with varying degrees of thoroughness. I think it not improbable that, although it has been possible to plot the lower values as a straight line, that from the point at which quinine begins to influence them, the values, if uninfluenced by the drug, would be represented by a curve rising to about 300 per mille. It is difficult to believe that the considerable doses of quinine given to a population of 1165 on the estates in the group 70 to 80 should have had no effect. The death rate of several estates, whose spleen rate is between 90 and 100, ranges between 200 and 300 per mille.

As will be seen from the wastage chart on p. 101, the greater the amount of malaria the greater the wastage from all causes. To maintain labour forces on the more unhealthy estates at a constant strength, larger proportions of the coolies would be new; and the death rate of these would be higher than that of the older coolies. Among the more unhealthy estates there would thus be death rates increasing at an ever-accelerating rate. I do not think 300 per mille would be the maximum in a locality of the most intense malaria were the labour non-immune.

The values which are plotted below the straight line are known definitely to be the result of quinine to a great extent. Between 40 and 50 the low death rate is due to all the coolies (65 in number) on one estate having been dosed daily with 10 grains of quinine, and once a week with castor oil. The low death rate on the estates, whose spleen rate was between 50 and 60, was due to two of the estates using quinine, one in the most thorough manner possible. The same applies to the low death rate with the spleen rate from 80 to 90.

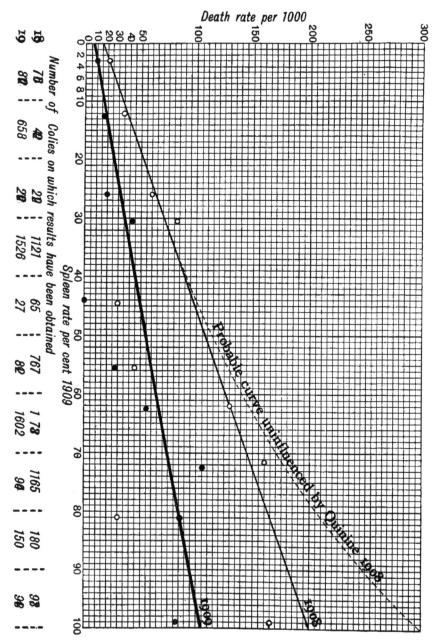

FIG. 28.—Chart showing Variation of Death Rates of 1908 and 1909, with Spleen Rate of 1909.

The plotting of the death rate values shows in a graphic manner not only how malaria is responsible for most of the deaths on the estates, but enables us by exterpolation to arrive at the conclusion that were malaria eliminated the death rate of

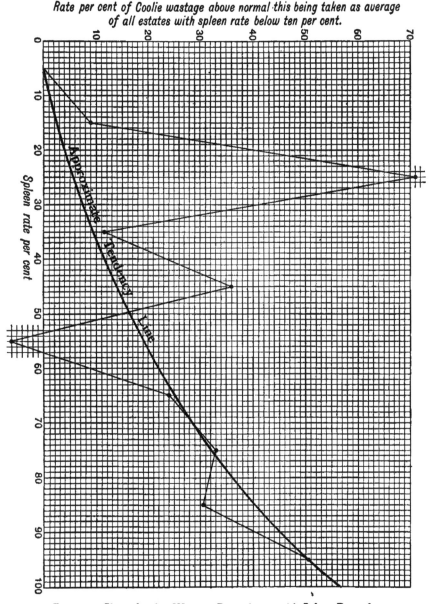

Rate per cent of Coolie wastage above normal·this being taken as average of all estates with spleen rate below ten per cent.

FIG. 29.—Chart showing Wastage Rate of 1908 with Spleen Rate of 1909.

the Tamil population on an estate would be about 15 per mille. [1919.—We now know it would be under 10 per mille.—M. W.] The line shows, too, how money can be spent with most profit and advantage in improving health on a malarious estate.

The sum of money which would be required to reduce the deaths from causes other than malaria by 3 per mille would in all probability reduce the deaths from malaria by 100 per mille, if spent on anti-malaria works. It is absurd to talk of applying to malarious estates the sanitary measures which are required in an overcrowded town, and expect them to improve its health. Expenditure on such measures would only be an obstacle to expenditure on the special sanitation required by the local conditions. As will be seen later, sanitary areas free from anophelines should be established on malarious estates, and the coolies housed on those areas.

The Death Rate uninfluenced by Quinine.—(A) *Public Works.* Those who have seen the terrible death rate on public works in the Federated Malay States, such as the Ampang and Ulu Gombak Water Works of Kuala Lumpur, the Ayer Kuning Water Works of Klang, the Changkat Jong Water Works of Teluk Anson, the Ayer Kuning railway tunnel near Taiping, will readily believe, I think, that a death rate of 300 per mille is no exaggeration. As Daniels says, "Under such circumstances in Malaya, malaria is as severe and prevalent as in bad parts of Africa."

(B) *Estates.* From what I have seen on the estates under my care, and from what I have gathered when travelling through the Federated Malay States, I have come to the conclusion that malaria is the chief factor in the death rate of estates. It is entirely in keeping with the observations I have made, that of twenty-one places of employment, whose death rate was over 200 per mille as given in the *Indian Immigration Report* for 1908, no fewer than eighteen of these should be estates in hill land, and of the three exceptions, two were estates whose coolie lines were close to jungle. I have no information as to the third. [1919.—I have since been informed the third estate suffered from a bad water-supply.—M. W.]

The average labour force employed on these places was 2130, and the average death rate was 280 per mille. On some of these places quinine was certainly given, though probably not very thoroughly; but on the majority I believe it was not given systematically to the whole labour force. Cholera, plague, and smallpox were not present to swell the death rates.

(C) *India.* Perhaps to those not acquainted with what malaria can do, the following extracts from the *Proceedings of the Imperial Malaria Conference* held at Simla in 1909 will give some idea of how great an effect this disease may have on the death rate :—

"During the two months of October and November the number of deaths recorded in the Punjab as due to fever was 307,316, as against less than 70,000 in both 1904 and 1905, and less than 100,000 in 1907.

"Studied in more detail, the ravages of the epidemic in these areas where it was most intense are more apparent. In Amritsar the mortality for many weeks was at the rate of over 200 per mille. In Palwal the mortality rose to 420 per mille, and in Bhera to 493 per mille. Curiously in Delhi, a notoriously malarious town, the death rate rose to only 149 per mille. But a closer examination of the statistics shows that parts of this town were much more seriously affected than one would judge to be the case from the statistics of the whole city; in Ward I., for example, the mortality rose to over 300 per mille.

"The death returns of Amritsar show that the densely crowded outer portions of the city were mainly affected. Again, in these the mortality was higher than the figures for the whole city would indicate. In Division IX., for example, with a population of 17,206, the death rate rose to 534 per mille, and for six weeks was over 400 per mille.

"In the district returns, with the exception of those relating to the Gurgaon district, which show among a population of 687,199 a death rate of 267 per mille, the mortality rates are not so high as those given for the towns. This might be taken as showing that the mortality was greater in towns than in rural areas, but a study of returns from individual thanas and villages modifies this conclusion, both thanas and villages frequently showing mortality rates during October and November of 300, 400, or even 500 per mille."

I think, therefore, that the curve of the death rate un-influenced by quinine as I chart it, is a close approximation to the truth. It is based on the maxima of the death rates and is certainly no exaggeration.

Wastage of a Labour Force.—Although local factors have a powerful influence on the happiness and welfare of a labour force, it can easily be understood that where an estate is unhealthy, coolies will be less contented and will be less inclined to stay. A month's notice frees a coolie on the estates of Selangor, and in many instances he leaves without giving even the legal notice. There is no indentured labour.

The chart (p. 101) illustrates how on the estates under my care the wastage of labour from all causes has a very definite relationship to the health, as exhibited by the spleen rate.

I have taken, as the base line, the wastage on the estates having the lowest spleen rate; and the other wastages have been calculated as a percentage above or below this. The chart shows that the greater the spleen rate the greater the loss of labour. There are only two exceptions. The very great loss on estates whose spleen rate was from 20 to 30 was due to practically the whole of the coolies on one estate leaving, owing to the conduct of a drunken mandor. The Government Immigration Report deals with this. Great loss was due on another estate to differences between the coolies and the manager. These are exceptional circumstances, and this group of estates showed a wastage in 1907 quite in line with that of other estates.

On the group of estates, whose spleen rate was 90 to 100, the actual loss was 507 per mille. In other words, while the coolies remain on an average three years on the healthiest estates, they remain only two years on the most unhealthy estates. The extra year means, for the healthy estates, an increase of the labour force by 50 per cent., and more than a 50 per cent. increase in the work done; for the coolie at the end of his two years is a skilled workman, especially where he is tapping. Malaria is, therefore, an economic factor of great importance.

Economic Effects of Malaria on the Estate.—In the working of an estate, a certain number of coolies are required for each class of work, and the manager must estimate some months before how many he will require, so that the necessary number may be recruited from India in time for the work. Any extension of the estate necessitates more coolies. One of the most important works of an estate is weeding. In a tropical country like this weeds grow with surprising rapidity; in less than two months they will form in many places a

FIG. : o.

...ws a young Rubber Estate invaded by jungle on accoun of shortage of ...s is practically as large as the rubber. Clearing-up ha begun : a felled ...li ...l The jungle in foreground.

complete cover to the ground, and having seeded, it will take months to eradicate them.   In addition, a grass called lalang often takes root, as its seeds are blown to great distances by the wind.   The roots of this grass grow several feet deep, and to eradicate it costs $50 an acre at least.

The most economical method of working an estate is to have a labour force of such strength that the whole estate can be weeded once in from two to three weeks.   Not a weed then has time to seed, and the cost of weeding falls to about 50 to 60 cents an acre.

If, then, there are too many coolies on an estate, the work will be insufficient for them, which will lead to dissatisfaction; while, if there are not sufficient coolies, the work gets behind, and if this work be weeding, then the whole estate may be covered with lalang.   As the cost of bringing an acre of rubber into bearing is generally estimated at about $250, it will be seen that the effect of an outbreak of malaria, which seriously cripples a labour force even for only a few months, may easily increase the original cost of an estate by 20 per cent., and on an estate of 1000 acres will actually cost about £6000 sterling.

(1920).—The foregoing was written at a time when the estates were being developed, and the chief problem was to prevent them being overgrown by weeds and ultimately smothered by the jungle.

Later, when the heavy shade of the rubber trees removed anxiety on that score, the shortage of labour made it difficult to tap the trees and collect the rubber.   Indian labour being unequal to the task, Chinese labour at a much higher rate of pay had to be employed.   How much extra the cost was will be found at the end of Chapter XV. on Seafield Estate.

CHAPTER XII

ON QUININE

Value of Quinine Administration.—During these years it must not be thought that nothing was being attempted to eradicate the disease. About 1902 I had arrived at the conclusion that once a man was infected with malaria, he should take quinine after his apparent recovery daily and not once a week, as was the custom. I made this observation first of all from one of my dressers (Lewis) in Klang Hospital, who, although he took quinine once a week with a tonic in the interval after the pyrexia had disappeared, had a return of the pyrexia about every ten days for many weeks, and only got rid of it finally by constantly taking quinine for some months.

In 1904, having determined that there was much malaria on certain estates, I advised the administration of quinine at first in weekly doses of 10 grains, and later of bi-weekly doses.*

The following tables show the result of giving quinine in the above-mentioned doses.

Table showing the Numbers of Children infected with Malaria in the months of November and December on certain Estates.

Estate Number.	1904. Quinine not given systematically.			1905. Quinine given systematically.		
	Number Examined.	Number Infected.	Percentage Infected.	Number Examined.	Number Infected.	Percentage Infected.
1	16	10	62·5	17	2	11·7
2	41	16	37·8	40	5	12·5
3	12	12	100·0	17	2	11·0
4	...	...	...	17	4	23·5
Total .	69	38	55·5	91	13	11·2

* By daily quinine administration for coolies I mean six days out of seven, namely, on the working days.

Table showing the Number of Children infected with Malaria in November and December on Estates on which Quinine was not given systematically in either 1904 *or* 1905.

Estate Number.	1904.			1905.		
	Number Examined.	Number Infected.	Percentage Infected.	Number Examined.	Number Infected.	Percentage Infected.
5	66	33	50.0	52	23	44.2
6	25	7	28.0	13	6	46.0
7	...	...	...	15	4	26.1
8	...	...	...	16	11	68.7
Total .	91	40	43.9	96	44	45.8

Table showing the Number of Coolies not at work on account of Malaria on the day of my Monthly Visit, November 1905.

A. Estates where quinine is given systematically.
B. Where it is not given.

Estate Number.	A. Quinine Given.			Estate Number.	B. Quinine not Given.		
	Number of Coolies.	Number with Malaria.	Percentage with Malaria.		Number of Coolies.	Number with Malaria.	Percentage with Malaria.
1	70	0	0.0	5	800	33	4.1
2	320	2	0.6	6	170	12	7.0
3	120	1	0.8	7	250	13	5.2
4	80	5	6.2	...	212	27	12.6
	590		1.3	...	1432	85	5.8

An estate bears the same number in all the tables. The administration of quinine is doubtful in estate No. 4. From it the manager was dismissed.

These figures appeared to me to be most encouraging, and I said of quinine administration, in a Presidential Address before the Native States Division of the British Medical Association in Ipoh in 1906 :—

" *Our Hopes.*—Although many, without thinking, consider it acts merely by curing the individual after he has been infected, and aborting threatened attacks, it is in reality much more than this. It is a real prophylaxis, for by cutting short attacks, it diminishes the chances of mosquitoes becoming infected, and thus prevents other coolies from ever becoming infected. It is by no means a case of locking the stable door after the horse has been stolen, and there need be no hesitation in advocating its use.

"Nevertheless, it is not a method which commands my unqualified approval, for the simple reason that it requires too much of the manager. He has other work to do, work which must be shown as done in his monthly report, or his directors will want to know why? Instead of spending perhaps the best and coolest time of the morning giving out quinine, he wishes to go out into the field. Again, the manager himself may fall ill, and there may be no one to see the coolies take their quinine. A new manager may come, and he has probably to learn by bitter experience, that the hours spent in giving out quinine are not only well spent, but must be so spent, if the labour force is to be kept together. Again, it is not given to every manager to have the patience to see every coolie, and especially every child, gets its quinine ration, and with new coolies more or less undisciplined, there may be great difficulty in getting down the quinine, as the coolie has little faith in it. It is a great point when a 'Kangany' realises the value of quinine, but at the same time, no native can be trusted entirely with this, and it is a considerable call on the manager's time. Then when the necessity appears to pass off, there will always be a tendency to slackness, as with all human efforts. Therefore, while I value the method, I consider the call it makes on the manager, a very serious drawback."

I hoped by giving quinine daily to those who had malaria, to prevent the formation of gametocytes which would infect mosquitoes; and that if any new coolies should chance to become infected, quinine twice a week would destroy the parasites before they had time to develop to numbers sufficient to give fever to the host. As will be seen later, neither of these hopes have been fulfilled, since it has been impossible to give the large doses which would be necessary to attain this object in people who are working. And secondly, as I shall show later, what may be a sufficient dose when malaria is not intense, is quite insufficient when it is. My advice in 1906 was as follows:—

"(1) That every coolie should get a cup of hot coffee before starting work in the morning. (2) That twice a week every coolie should get ten grains of quinine, and every child five grains. (3) That every coolie who has fever should have a mark put against his name on the check roll when he resumes work, should receive no 'Name' for his day's work until he has taken a dose of quinine, in the manager's presence."

This advice was followed on one estate which was just being opened up, and the result was a total failure of the quinine even to hold the disease in check; so that on 6th November every coolie was put on 10 grains of quinine daily, and those who were not at work on 20 grains; it being assumed that, if he did not work he might be unwell; and that the extra dose of quinine would do him good by preventing an attack of fever, even if he had no pyrexia at the time. The effect of the daily dose was to reduce sickness to a marked extent, as the following table shows.

Table showing the Number of Coolies who were unable to work from "Fever" and "Other Diseases" during certain months in 1906 and 1907.

	1906.			1907.					
	Oct.	Nov.	Dec.	Jan.	Feb.	Mar.	April.	May.	June.
Fever	136	152	50	38	19	14	14	5	8
Other diseases . . .	147	195	83	81	41	54	54	14	10
Total . . .	283	347	133	119	60	68	68	19	18
No. of Coolies on the Estate .	220	245	243	247	248	234	255	322	228

It is interesting to observe that what we saw when malaria was reduced in Klang Town, namely the reduction in diseases other than those recognised by the general population of malaria, was reduced on this estate likewise with the reduction of the amount of malaria.

The economic effect of the malaria and the effect of the quinine can also be observed from the table on p. 110.

The decrease in the out-turn of the labour of 1907 was due to unsatisfactory work of the dresser in charge, who had to be dismissed. It was found he was seriously neglecting his duties, as the coolies who did not turn out to work were not sought for and given the extra quinine. The unreliableness of native dressers will always be one of the great drawbacks to quinine administration. In this instance, the dresser, who by his hard work had helped so materially to obtain such good results in

1906 and the early part of 1907, now became lazy and mischievous for no apparent reason, and ultimately was convicted and sent to prison for six months for attempting to cause riot by setting one class of coolie against another.

Table showing the Number of Coolies on this Estate, the Number of Days which it would have been possible for these Coolies to work had they worked every working day of the month, the Number of Days they actually worked, and the Percentage this forms of the possible Working Days.

Month.	Number of Coolies.	Number of Possible Working Days.	Number of Days Actually Worked.	Percentage of Possible Days Worked.
1906.				
May . .	69	1241	1050	84·6
June . .	135	2499	2100	84·0
July . .	190	4914	3670	74·6
August .	299	8073	5590	69·2
September .	248	6200	4257	68·7
October .	220	5380	3352	62·3
November . .	245	6366	4238	66·5
December . .	243	6318	4584	72·5
1907.				
January .	247	6175	4907	
February .	248	5952	4829	
March .	248	...	...	
April . .	...	...	...	
June . . .	...	...	...	
July . . .	...	...	...	
August . .	...	...	...	
September .	...	...	...	
October . .	...	...	...	
November .	...	...	...	
December . .	...	...	...	

The best results I have obtained are shown in the following table (Seafield Estate) :—

	1905.	1906.	1907.	1908.	1909.
Average population . .	...	175	380	399	...
Blood—					
Number examined .	16	9	...	...	...
Per cent. infected . .	68·7	76	...	...	...
Spleen—					
Number examined .	16	17	23		47
Per cent. enlarged .	56	88	39		62
Deaths per 1000, Div. I. .		114	66	34	
,, ,, Div. II. .	...	...	60	27	...

Writing in 1906 I described the condition of this estate in 1905 as follows:—

" In November, out of 212 coolies I found 27 down with fever on one day (where) 5 children had died in one week: (where) coolies were bolting daily, and the work of the estate was almost paralysed. This was followed by an outbreak of dysentery, and it was in the month of February before malaria was got in hand."

In 1906 or the beginning of 1907 it was discovered that the pills which were supposed to contain 4 grains of quinine contained much less than that amount, namely about one grain. The dose was then increased with a steady improvement in the death rate each year. It is interesting that the fall held good for each division of the estate. In 1905 in the month of October 245 coolies worked 3393 days, or 58 per cent. of the possible working days. In October 1906, 260 coolies worked 2131 days, 70·9 per cent. of the possible.

The economic effect of this quinine administration has been that the present small labour force now maintains in perfect order some 2000 acres at a minimum cost. That it is not due to any improvement in the health of the estate from other causes, will be seen from the following paragraphs relating to the limitations of quinine.

The Limitations of Quinine.—In 1908 and 1909 considerable attention was being paid to the presence of the ankylostoma worm in coolies, and at the request of the Institute for Medical Research, I arranged in April 1909 for the examination of a large number of coolies. I chose for this purpose a healthy estate where no quinine was given, and the above-mentioned estate, on which quinine was being administered with such satisfactory results.

The result was to show that while ankylostoma was present in large numbers on both estates, on the healthy one (Estate " V ") 2 out of 160, or 1·3 per cent., of the coolies had parasites in their peripheral blood, and on the other estate no fewer than 56 out of 215 or 26 per cent. showed the parasite. The examinations were made by Dr A. T. Stanton of the Institute to whom I am indebted for the figures.

These results, in view of the splendid physique and work done by the force, appeared to warrant further inquiry. I accordingly visited the estate and examined all the coolies on it, paying particular attention to those who had been shown to have had parasites in their blood. I separated the 56 as follows:—

Well developed, well nourished, and apparently in perfect health   42
Less well developed and nourished, but still apparently in
    good health and fit for work   5
Anæmic   1
In hospital.   .   .   .   .   .   .
Died .   .   .   .
Deserted   1
Paid off ·   4
                                 56

In other words, 75 per cent. of the coolies with parasites in their peripheral blood were apparently in the most perfect health, while 87·5 per cent. were in good health and fit for work. Of the 48 seen 30 or 62 per cent. had enlarged spleens, and of the whole labour force of 345 I found 174 or 50·4 per cent. with enlargement.

On one division the coolies were getting 6 and on the other 8 grains, with double doses when they were ill or off work, often quinine in solution. As at this time mosquitoes were breeding freely on the estate in the ravines, close to which the coolies were living, and adult *A. maculatus* could be obtained in the lines at any time, this observation is of the greatest value in determining the effect of quinine. It clearly demonstrates that, while keeping the malaria in check, so that the coolies could carry on their work, three years' administration of the drug had entirely failed to eradicate the disease. That the estate is really as unhealthy as ever is shown by the visitors to it, who contract malaria in about ten days, and even the head kangany suffered severely from malaria on his return to the estate after a visit to India.

Finally, out of nineteen *A. maculatus* captured in the lines, four or 21 per cent. had malaria, two with zygotes, one with sporozoites, and one with both zygotes and sporozoites.

Desiring to have further information on this important point, I took the blood of every man, woman, and child on an estate on which quinine was being given in the most thorough and systematic manner. The doses being given were 10 grains daily to each adult who worked, and 20 to those who did not work, the latter being given in solution. To the children 5 grains were given daily, and double doses also to those who did not work.   Mr R. W. B. Lazaroo kindly examined the slides for me, and reported as follows:—

Of the 29 children, the results were as follows:—

			Per Cent.	
Malignant parasites (subtertian)	.	5	17·27	⎫
Benign Tertian	. . .	2	6·89	⎬ 27·58
Quartan	. . . .	1	3·44	⎭
No parasites seen	.	21		
		29		

Of the 125 adults the results were:—

			Per Cent.	
Malignant (subtertian)	.	15	12·0	⎫
Benign Tertian		3	3·4	⎬ 18·4
„ Quartan	. .	5	4·0	⎭
No parasites seen	. .	. 102		
		125		

Of the whole 154 the percentage found with parasites in the peripheral blood was 20·12.

These figures agree very closely with the ones obtained by Dr Stanton, and they at once supply the reason why no improvement has taken place in the hill land estates despite the use of quinine in what appear very large doses for constant administration.

Now this failure to eradicate malaria falls into line with our knowledge generally of quinine. I would indicate the following as the limitations of quinine:—

(1) However thorough the dosing has been, malaria is very liable to return to a patient although the possibility of re-infection is excluded.   In other words quinine does not poison the parasite outright.

(2) When a person is attacked by malignant malaria (subtertian) for the first time, even with the most thorough administration of quinine in solution, some four or five days elapse before the temperature falls, and Rogers has published figures which show that 60 grains daily have no advantage over 20 grains or less.

(3) Quinine has little if any effect on the sexual forms of the parasite in the peripheral blood.   I have watched crescents in a man's blood for three weeks during which he was taking 20 grains of quinine solution daily, and after all pyrexia had gone.*

(4) In bad epidemics I have watched cases of malaria

* [1920.—Ross and Thomson have shown there is a connection between the asexual and sexual parasites in the peripheral blood.—M. W.]

admitted to hospital, who have had no pyrexia, but rather who have been in the algid state; who despite the administration of quinine by the mouth, by the rectum, and intramuscularly to the extent of 40 grains daily, have continued for four days in this algid condition and then died. During this time the skin was in a condition of a cold clammy sweat. No diminution appeared in the number of parasites in the blood. The patient apparently failed to react any way.

(5) It is common experience that a patient, particularly if he is suffering from benign tertian malaria, must be put to bed before pyrexia will leave him, even when on full doses of quinine.

Finally, when we remember that thousands and thousands of people, who do not take nor have the opportunity of taking quinine, recover from the disease yearly, it is evident that the human subject of the disease must depend on some power within himself to save him from death. Daniels,[20] in his Presidential Address to the British Medical Association in 1909 in Belfast, appears to me to strike the right note when he insists that the protozoal diseases, of which malaria is a member, may persist for years without sexual regeneration, and despite any drugs which may be given; and that freedom from the disease can be acquired only by the development of resistant powers within the human host. It is when we consider malaria as an infection of the human host by a parasite, which in the majority of infections lasts for at least three or four months, and in exceptional cases for years; in which the relationship of the parasite to its host is that of enemies at constant war; where for a time first one and then the other may be in the ascendant; and where victory in the end may be to either, that we can understand the apparently contradictory results of quinine.

When from any cause the health of the host is depressed, the parasite increases in numbers and may be found in the peripheral blood. As the struggle continues and the life of the parasite is threatened, in harmony with the rule of nature generally, the parasite produces the sexual forms destined to continue its existence as a species. Thus, from time to time, the human host becomes dangerous to others, if anophelines which form a congenial breeding-place for the sexual forms (*i.e.*, capable of carrying malaria) are present.

When, on the other hand, the health of the host is improved from any cause, the parasites are reduced in numbers and may disappear from the peripheral blood. The parasites may, in the end, die or be killed out by the host. It is not unlikely that two separate immunities are required by the host before the parasite is destroyed. It appears to me to be not uncommon for the host to become immune to the poison causing pyrexia long before it acquires powers to reduce the number of parasites; for cases with numerous parasites and without pyrexia over considerable periods are not uncommon, indeed are recorded by every writer on malaria.* The true action of quinine appears to be to assist the human host in working out for himself the resistant power which will ultimately free him from the disease. It acts either by attenuating the virus within the host, or by increasing the resisting power of the host in some unknown way, or possibly by both. Without quinine in many cases, especially in very unhealthy spots, the human host would die before he had acquired his resistant powers. We thus see that, if quinine in sufficient doses be given, the man will gradually overcome the parasites, and apparently suffer little from them; but at the same time we see that during this period he is capable of infecting others. The man is for a time a "malaria carrier" not unlike the typhoid carrier.

There must be an optimum dose of quinine, possibly it varies with the individual, and, from time to time, in the same individual; but whatever that dose be, it must bear a close resemblance to the ordinary therapeutic dose.

Finally if, as has been shown, the immunity from malaria produced by quinine leaves the patient infective while he is acquiring the immunity, then it will be impossible in the presence of many anophelines, and in the presence of many new arrivals (such as newly born children) ever to eradicate

* Among the causes which predispose to a malaria relapse, menstruation is a powerful one. Menstruation frequently is followed by, and sometimes accompanied by, a malaria attack. I have a record of a European who, when in England, had six attacks of malaria following at once on six regular menstrual periods. On her return to the tropics, and after an interval of many months, she had a return of severe pyrexia within two days of a more than usually severe monthly period. (1920.—On account of these relapses at each period, she had to be invalided permanently from the tropics.)

K

malaria by quinine. It follows, too, that if drainage be an alternative, even although more expensive, drainage must be the method which should be adopted. Even if a community possessed no money for drainage, money might be borrowed with which to carry out the works, and at the end there would be an asset to show for the expenditure. Borrowing, however, would be impossible if the object were to buy quinine, since in the end nothing could be shown for the money, except a people still liable to malaria, and possibly some agriculture which could not be maintained without the constant use of the drug.

OBSERVATIONS ON QUININE ADMINISTRATION.

Time and Form.—When I first began quinine administration systematically to large bodies of coolies, I advised quinine sulphate in solution and in the morning. I advised the solution because in solution its action is more certain, and it would thus be possible to use a smaller quantity of the drug; I advised the morning because the parasites usually sporulate in the forenoon, and consequently would then meet with the quinine in full strength.

In practice it was found that there were serious objections both to the time and the form of administration. In solution the action was so certain, that in 10-grain doses cinchonism was so marked that the coolies could not work in the sun. In addition they were frequently sick after the dose; ultimately it was suspected that they deliberately vomited the dose to avoid the unpleasant after-effects.

Since then it has been given when work is finished for the day—that is about 2.30 P.M.

When I decided to abandon the solution I considered that the compressed forms as usually supplied were too much compressed, and coolies were taught to make quinine pills with bread. They became astonishingly expert at this. The pills were supposed to contain 4 grains of quinine, but after a time it was found they were putting in too large a proportion of bread as the pills were thereby more easily made.

In order to standardise the dose, in 1907 I obtained machines from England, and hoped to make tablets, compressing the drug just enough to keep it in a mass. The machines were not a success, as the rate at which the tablets could be turned out was far below that of the coolie making pills by hand, and quite insufficient to meet the demand. I therefore returned to the pills, but now (1909) have them made by mixing dry quinine sulphate with so much gum solution, that when made the pills can be crushed easily between the finger and thumb. There are at the present moment just over 4000 coolies taking 10 grains daily, with double doses when off work.*

The efficiency with which the drug is administered depends on the manager of the estate. Each year the drug is being given over larger areas and with greater efficiency, as its value is being better recognised. A change of manager is usually followed by less care being taken to give the drug, and this is a serious drawback.

Europeans tell me that it is impossible to continue the use of quinine solution for any length of time. If taken in the morning, they cannot take food and cannot work in the sun. If taken at night, even dry quinine prevents sleep. I hoped at one time that, if taken at night, larger doses could be taken, the effects of which would pass off during sleep. But men are unanimous that taken at this time it prevents proper sleep, and the drug is now rarely taken at night.

Quinine sulphate in powder often fails to have any effect on an attack of malaria if there is gastric disturbance; this even when 20 or 30 grains are given in the course of twenty-four hours, and for a period of a week. In such cases I give quinine hydrochloride with a little morphia in solution. This effectively controls the sickness, and the temperature is usually down in thirty-six hours. I have often wished to try the old native remedy of opium with the quinine, but have never felt quite justified in doing so, on a large enough scale to be of value.

Warburg's tincture I have used both for pyrexial attacks and as a preventive. It appears to have no special advantage over a simple mixture of hydrochloride and morphia. I have also given it over considerable periods, combined with additional quinine, to bring the dose of the latter up to 15 or 10 grains as the case might be. I cannot see that it has any special advantage.

Small children learn to swallow pills very quickly. For

* (1920).—For some years the quinine has been given in gelatine capsules.

infants I find the easiest way to administer quinine, is to give euchinine (quinine ethyl carbonate) broken up in a little sweetened condensed milk.

On estates, where quinine has been much used, it is not uncommon to find coolies ask for solution in preference to pills, when they have fever or suspect an attack is coming on. Kanganies are often found to carry pills in their pockets, and give them out to any coolie who complains or asks for them during the day. On the other hand, I recently found the conductor on an estate, where quinine has been given daily to the coolies for four years with the best results, who had suffered from malaria himself and taken quinine for it, would not give his wife quinine when she was almost dead with malaria, until literally forced to do so. If such happens with a native who reads and writes English, who lives on an estate, where if on any place in the world quinine has shown its power to control malaria, it is impossible to believe that native populations will ever be induced voluntarily to take quinine in such doses as will effect any marked difference on the death rate of the disease.

Although quinine sulphate may not be absorbed when there is gastric disturbance, there can be no question about its being absorbed in the majority of cases. For a week after a coolie or a European begins the daily consumption of quinine powder or pills, quite definite symptoms are felt in the head. After that period no unpleasantness is experienced, unless the dose be increased. Instinctively men have learned to take their total quantity broken up into two or three doses. And my object now on the most intensely malarious places is to have from 10 to 15 grains taken daily without producing symptoms.

After an attack of malaria I advise 20 grains in solution daily for a week, and then reduce the dose to 10 grains in pill form, resuming 20 grains should the person feel unwell, and find his temperature 100° F. or more taken in the mouth.

I prefer the sulphate for continuous use because the more soluble forms are more apt to produce cinchonism. There is reason to believe the sulphate is absorbed not only from the stomach, but from the intestines. Its slower rate of absorption, therefore, leads to less violent fluctuation in the amount circulating in the blood, than where more soluble preparations are used. It has the advantage, too, that a dose will, therefore, have a more continuous action, and be present in the tissues and fluid for a longer period, than where the preparation is more rapidly absorbed and presumably more rapidly eliminated or destroyed.

Nor is it an unimportant advantage where thousands of coolies are receiving comparatively large doses daily, that the price of the sulphate is some 30 to 50 per cent. less than the other common preparations.

(1920).—Towards the end of 1912 I contracted malaria for the first time. It was a severe attack of benign tertian malaria with continuous fever for four days. After the febrile attack was over, the attempt to resume ordinary diet was followed by acute gastritis, and I had an unusually favourable opportunity of observing the effects of several salts of quinine.

Very soon I came to prefer a simple watery solution of quinine bihydrochloride flavoured with orange or ginger. Twenty grains divided into three doses were taken daily with meals. It was my custom to swallow a few mouthfuls of some liquid, such as tea, coffee, or soup; then to take the quinine; and afterwards proceed with the meal. The taste of the quinine lasted only a minute or two. After the first week I was not conscious of any ringing of the ears or other symptoms of cinchonism.

When the quinine was taken half an hour before the meal, cinchonism was pronounced and unpleasant; when taken after the meal, it frequently produced "acidity." Curiously enough tabloids and capsules taken with or after a meal produced the same "acidity" and discomfort.

For six months I took 20 grains daily in solution, and rapidly recovered health. No relapse occurred while I was taking it, or after I stopped it.

In 1914 I contracted what there is good reason to believe was a new infection of benign tertian malaria. For it, I took quinine in the same doses for five months, with the same happy result as in 1912. Since stopping the drug I have had no relapse.

(1909) *Relation of Dose to Intensity of Malaria.*—I think the same dose of quinine may be of more apparent value where the amount of malaria is small, than where it is great. I have long been of the opinion, too, that what is supposed to be a relapse, is often in reality a new infection. It is impossible to decide with absolute certainty; but there is a certain amount of evidence, beyond the few cases where we find different parasites in different attacks.

For example, when in the service of Government, it was one of my duties to visit a place called Jugra at regular intervals. Jugra is intensely malarious. Government servants and their wives and families suffer severely from the disease. The place is consequently very unpopular, and at each visit I was interviewed by one or more applicants for transfer on medical grounds. As long as Government decided to keep Jugra as a district centre, so long must its servants remain ; and I refused to grant certificates on the ground of ill-health, if the complaint was merely of attacks of malaria. I advised daily quinine, and it was given to the police daily by a dresser from the hospital.

Before I gave a certificate I had to be satisfied that some danger of serious damage to health existed. I thus had an opportunity of watching people progressively deteriorate, and when I considered there was any real danger, I recommended transfer. This was, in the case of the police and clerks, often to Klang ; and I was then still able to keep them under observation. It was interesting to observe the steady improvement, with but few relapses in most cases, after transfer to a non-malarious place. Had their almost constant attacks of fever when in Jugra been merely relapses, these would certainly not have ceased so suddenly when the patient came to Klang, nor would the improvement in health have begun so soon, and been so marked; and this, when I am sure they were taking less quinine than when in Jugra, and perhaps none at all.

What appears to bear out the same idea is the severity of the attacks of malaria in Europeans on intensely malarious estates. These patients are constantly going down with malaria, even when on daily doses of 10 grains of the sulphate. A short holiday usually enables them to recover; but attacks recur soon after their return to work, often in the usual period necessary for new infections to manifest themselves. Should they permanently leave the unhealthy place, they rapidly recover, even when their new work and the climatic conditions under which they labour are identical with that of the unhealthy place they have left. An observation on Estate

"RR" has some bearing on this point. This estate is in three divisions, and there is a European bungalow on each. Bungalow I. is situated between the lines marked 100 and those marked 37. It is on a ravine in which I have not been able to find *A. maculatus*, and which I think is probably unsuitable for them. Bungalow II. and Bungalow III. are near to ravines in which *A. maculatus* swarm, and the spleen rate of the lines, if we exclude new arrivals, is practically 100. The history of the bungalows is that while I. is malarious, II. and III. are intensely so.

In Bungalow I. six Europeans, who from time to time have lived there, have had attacks, with the exception of one who took 10 grains of quinine daily for the two years he was there. One of the five attacked had only two attacks, and these at intervals of a year. The others suffered more severely, but soon became free on taking the drug daily; while neglect just as certainly led to new attacks. Ten servants had malaria in 1907, and there was difficulty in keeping servants, until they were compelled to take the drug under supervision. It will thus be seen that the bungalow was malarious, but not intensely so.

Bungalow II. has been more malarious, and the three Europeans who have lived in it have been severely attacked time and again, and have frequently been compelled to go on periods of sick leave.

Now in 1909 it was necessary to rearrange the work of the estate. A and B who had lived in Bungalow I. (A never having had an attack, and B who had suffered from only two attacks) were transferred to Bungalows III. and II. respectively, while C was transferred from II. to I. A and B now suffered very severely from malaria, and both were invalided for a time, and this although they were taking the same amount of quinine as when in Bungalow I. C, on the other hand, ceased to have attacks, and gradually reduced his daily dose, until, when taking only about 5 grains a week, he had a sharp attack, which put him on to his full doses again. That there is no improvement in the health of Bungalow I. is seen from D, who about the same time arrived on the estate, refused to take quinine, and had so severe an attack that he had to be sent on leave for a month.

Now the work on all the divisions is practically the same.

It is impossible to believe that A and B were never infected in Bungalow I. during the two years they lived there, and when the servants and other Europeans suffered frequently from the disease. The only explanation appears to me to be that the dose of quinine which kept them free from symptoms in Bungalow I. was insufficient to do so when they had to overcome larger and more frequent infections.

Again we saw (p. 100) that the quinine which appeared to keep the old coolies in health in 1906, failed to keep the new arrivals in health, but that " from the new it (malaria) spread to the old " and the dose of all had to be increased. From this I concluded that the large number of new coolies had raised the percentage of infected mosquitoes on the estates, and that by old coolies infecting new, and these again infecting the old, a vicious circle was established which could only be broken by the gradual establishment of immunity among both old and new.

The following is another instance of a large dose (the largest I have known taken continuously) giving protection where smaller doses have failed. The individual (a close relative of my own) took 20 grains of quinine sulphate daily for three months. He had previously suffered so severely from malaria on an unhealthy estate, although he had been taking quinine in 10-grain doses, that he had to give up his post as manager. He had twice to go to a hill station to recover his health; ultimately he resigned his post. I was anxiously considering the necessity of invaliding him home. He was so breathless he could walk only a few yards; his weight had fallen to 136 pounds. He was, however, determined not to go to England, and took a post on another, but smaller, intensely malarious estate; one where each of his predecessors had left a wreck.

Its spleen rate has been 100 for some years. He took 20 grains of quinine sulphate in gelatine capsules daily, taking 5 grains at a dose. In two months his weight had gone up from 136 to 164 pounds. He said he had an excellent appetite, and was soon playing in an interstate rugby match. After three months he reduced the dose to 15 grains daily, and he has been on this dose for four months.

I have kept a watch on him, and have critically examined him, not without some anxiety, lest the drug should do harm. But I cannot recommend a reduction to less than 15 grains as long as he is well, and when to take less might spell disaster. The fine bungalow in which he lives is at the top of a ravine, and has been so unhealthy in the past that its abandonment was suggested by the owners. *A. maculatus* breeds freely in the ravine.

The marked contrast between this planter whose health improved, when taking large doses, and the progressive deterioration in his predecessors, who were on smaller doses, is so striking as to be a matter of general comment. And I think we are driven to the conclusion that in this extremely malarious place, larger doses are required than are usually taken in malarious places.

Each year has only strengthened my view that, to keep a European or a labour force in apparent health, the amount of quinine to be given bears a relation to the amount of malaria in the place at the time. The more the malaria the more frequently, and in larger doses, must the drug be given.

This would explain, too, the contradictory results obtained by various observers when quinine has been given as a prophylactic. Not only does it explain and bring these contradictory observations into line, but the observations recorded here help us to understand the cause of the variation of the intensity of malaria in different places, and in the same place from time to time.

From clinical observation, I think we are justified in concluding that the very frequent attacks, from which men suffer when in very malarious places as compared with the few attacks when removed to non-malarious places, are due to fresh infections, and not to relapses. If such an explanation of the more frequent attacks be accepted, then the necessity for the administration of quinine in larger quantities, approaching ordinary therapeutic doses, in the more malarious places, and at times of the greater prevalence of the disease, is easily understood. The human host has larger quantities of malarial parasites injected into him, and thus requires an increased protection by quinine.

Again, on the flat land, we saw that the nearer we were to the breeding-place of the anopheline—that is, the jungle—the greater the malaria: indeed, within the half-mile radius, it bears a definite ratio. We are forced, therefore, to believe that the intensity of malaria bears a definite relation to the number of anophelines in the air, to the number of times a person is bitten, and to the number of infections he receives.

Similarly, on the hilly land, observations from all time have shown that the head of a ravine is the most malarious; it is nearest to the chief breeding-places of the anophelines. The most malarious bungalows in the country are those situated at the head of, or close to, a ravine. The once notorious bungalow on Drummond's Hill, Taiping, had its servants' quarters over a ravine. Now it is obvious that the inhabitants of such a place must be bitten oftener, and infected oftener, than those living at a distance from the breeding-place. They are infected time and again by their own parasites after passing through a mosquito in which, too, by the sexual reproduction that occurs in the mosquito, it is not improbable the parasites have acquired an exalted virulence.

Thus again we are forced to believe that the greater intensity and persistence of malaria in the hilly land is due to the greater number of anophelines, and the greater number of infections which the persons in these regions receive.

Now if the foregoing be true, it would follow that malaria would also be intensified by increasing the percentage of the infected mosquitoes, without increasing the total number, which bite. And we find it to be so in fact, as seen from the infection of old from new coolies. The introduction of many new non-immune coolies, who almost simultaneously contracted malaria from the few still infectious old coolies, soon raised the percentage of persons with parasites in their peripheral blood, and capable of infecting mosquitoes to a higher degree than when there were only old coolies, most of whom had acquired a considerable amount of immunity and control over their parasites. A higher percentage of mosquitoes soon becomes infected, and these, in biting old and new coolies indiscriminately, soon increases the infection of the former and leads to their again suffering from attacks of the disease.

The intensity of malaria therefore depends, in my opinion, on the absolute number of infected mosquitoes in a locality, and anything which increases the number of malaria-carrying anophelines therefore increases the intensity of malaria.*

Many of the factors, which influenced the prevalence and

* [1920. — This subject is discussed in an illuminating manner by Ross in Chapter V. of his *Prevention of Malaria.*—M. W.]

intensity of malaria, were well known to our fathers before us. Such were disturbance of soil, interference with drainage, seasonal variations in temperature and rainfall, etc., etc., and it is extremely interesting to see that although their deductions as to the cause of malaria were incorrect, their observations were marvellously correct. In childhood's language they were "very, very hot" in their search for one of nature's most cunningly hidden secrets; and I desire to pay my humble tribute of respect to their memories.

Finally, if these observations be correct and the deductions be sound, the anopheline is *the factor* in the production of malaria which must be eliminated, if any permanent improvement is to take place.

Ill-Effects of Quinine. — It has been with a due sense of responsibility, and no little anxiety, that I have found myself the instrument in causing large numbers of people to take quinine for prolonged periods in doses which appear excessive to many, and doses which year to year tend to increase in amount. I have watched the effect of its administration with care, and if it is producing any ill-effects, they are of such a nature as not easily to be detected—at any rate I have not detected them—and they are of infinitely less consequence than malaria.

I have rarely given more than 20 grains daily unless on microscopic examination the patient's blood was so full of parasites as to show there was immediate danger to life. In such cases I have given up to 40 grains mostly per rectum, retaining the mouth for the administration of nourishment.

I have never seen a case of quinine blindness,* nor have I had in my practice any patient who complained of deafness or ear symptoms for more than a few days. Occasionally a patient, the subject of malaria who does not take quinine in sufficient doses, complains of "indigestion." If on sulphate, I may order hydrochloride in increased doses, which usually puts him right. Time and again, when a man has complained that he has "not been up to the mark" and thought he has been taking too much of the drug, I have advised increasing instead of reducing the dose with the most satisfactory results;

* [1920.—I saw a case for the first time in 1918. But I have been told it has not been rare in this country when much larger doses have been given.—M. W.]

so, too, when a man who has had malaria says he is feeling
" particularly well."

Miscarriage is often attributed to a dose of quinine. Yet
I could quote instances of patients who have taken quinine
throughout pregnancy and been delivered at full time. On
the other hand an attack of malaria is notorious as producing
abortion; and if the attack comes on within the last two
months of pregnancy, labour will almost certainly follow.
It is true quinine is often given in these cases; but the
futility of quinine in ordinary doses when given to induce,
or accelerate labour, in a healthy woman excludes the theory
that quinine is the active agent in producing the abortion
of the malarious patient.

Occasionally, but very rarely, a cutaneous eruption appears,
when doses of quinine are first given, but the rash disappears
with the continued use of the drug. One man when first
put on 15 grains daily developed a severe nettle-rash which
was intensely irritating. It disappeared within a week.

[1920.—Since the above was written I met a lady in
Scotland who has a real idiosyncrasy for quinine. Her
husband, a medical man, informs me that she develops a
severe dermatitis, with grave constitutional symptoms, even
from 2 grains of the drug; and there is little doubt that
a large dose would kill her.]

Cost of Quinine Administration.—It must not be forgotten,
too, that the administration of quinine in effective doses
in a malarious locality is by no means an inexpensive method
of combating malaria. To give 10 grains daily to 1000 people
without any extra to those who actually have pyrexia for
ten years, would cost about £1900 sterling.* Such a sum,
if lent by a Government to a community at a reasonable
rate of interest, would free a very large area from malaria,
if drainage methods suitable to the local anophelines were
employed. And in ten years the community would have some
years of prosperity and health in which to repay the loan.
In the case of many small villages it would probably be
possible to eradicate the breeding - places of anophelines,
where they were in the midst of the community, at a mere
fraction of the money which would be required to dose the
population effectively with quinine even for a year. While

* [1920.—The cost of quinine is now much greater.—M. W.]

for larger communities the cost of drainage would be relatively much cheaper than in the case of the smaller ones, since the same expenditure would protect a relatively larger number of people.

Relative Values of Quinine Administration and Drainage.— We have seen that quinine at its best, and when administered with a thoroughness, the result of a discipline impossible of attainment in an ordinary population, still leaves a large percentage of the population capable of infecting others. It can, therefore, never eradicate malaria in the presence of new comers, and where there are many anophelines. We have seen, too, that to attain this best result in a malarious place costs a fairly considerable sum. Quinine, therefore, in my opinion, cannot for a moment be ranked with drainage.

It cannot be too strongly urged that efficient land drainage not only is a radical anti-malaria measure, but is of first-class importance in almost all forms of agriculture ; and that malaria is essentially a rural disease. In dry forms of culture, it often makes the difference between good land and bad land, between good crops and poor crops. And in wet culture it is no less important. Cromer insists that in Egypt, the success of irrigation. depends no less on the channels for taking off the water than on the irrigation channels for its supply. It is notorious, too, that badly drained irrigated land is not only of less value agriculturally, but is also more malarious than irrigated land, where by means of an efferent system, the water on the land is more fully under control.

Finally I would urge that when the time comes for unanimity as to what should be done, the malaria problem will still be, as it is, essentially a financial one. In the end the affected community must find the means of combating the disease. To me it appears that any means, which will enrich the population, will enable it to make greater effort to overcome the disease. If, by drainage, we can enrich not only the people and the land, but by the same measure help to reduce the disease, drainage must be the measure of first importance.

Whether quinine be supplied free by a Government or sold at cost price or at a loss to the Government, a price is being paid ; and the people are in reality being assessed an amount, however small, which would still have paid the interest on a loan for a radical drainage work. Perhaps the work would only be a small one, but no matter; for it would definitely and for all time, if upkept, place the inhabitants beyond the reach of the disease.

It is here that I think a Government can help to break the vicious circle which makes the malarious poor and the poor malarious, and can assist a people to initiate drainage works, which from poverty they themselves cannot begin; even if Government cannot pay for drainage works out of revenue, then by pledging its credit, a Government can obtain money on loan. Both capital and interest can be paid by assessment of the land benefited.*

Of course care must be taken that the works will improve the area; to me it appears that in this direction lies the chief hope of eradicating malaria.

Malaria over large areas cannot be eradicated in a day. But from what I have seen of the results of radical measures I feel strongly that by radical measures will the end be attained soonest; that every success will help others; that people will be saved who will never consent to take quinine in sufficient doses, if at all; and that only by radical measures will be stopped the infection from, and the .death of, the vast mass of those who suffer from " malaria *sine* pyrexia," those who fail to recognise they suffer from malaria, who as we saw from the Klang figures account for a very large percentage of the death rate of a malarious community.

(1920).—The experience of the war bears out these conclusions. In Salonica, where infection and re-infection by mosquitoes constantly occurred, quinine failed entirely to protect the troops, just as it had failed in the Malay States.

In France, where re-infection did not take place, two divisions of malaria-stricken troops from Salonica were put in the firing line after two months' thorough administration of quinine, carried out under Lieutenant-Colonel J. Dalrymple, C.M.G. Fifteen grains in solution were given for fourteen

---

* The following is Rule 2, under Section 6 of the Drainage Rate Enactment of Selangor, F.M.S. :

"The annual drainage rate shall ordinarily be an amount calculated to yield 5 per cent. on the original cost to the Government of the drainage works, together with the annual cost to the Government of the maintenance thereof. For the purpose of this rule all necessary sluice gates, and other protective works constructed in connection with the drainage of the whole or any portion of any drainage area, shall be deemed to be drainage works."

days; and for eight weeks 10 grains in solution. The strictest discipline was maintained in the administration.

In England, where re-infection does not occur, the routine treatment of the War Office and Ministry of Pensions is 10 grains of quinine daily in solution for nine to twelve weeks. Sir Ronald Ross,[21] who is consultant to both departments, writes :—

"But can we not cure the cases outright by some *therapia magna sterilisans?* I wish we could.

"Unfortunately, though the War Office made innumerable experiments from early in 1917 onwards, no really satisfactory result was obtained. For details the reader should study the forthcoming War Office publication, *Observations on Malaria,* by medical officers of the Army and others (Stationery Office), *The Annals of Tropical Medicine and Parasitology* (Liverpool) for the last two years, and many papers in the *Lancet* and other journals. We tried intravenous and intramuscular injections, heroic doses, kharsivan, and almost everything we could think of. Not one treatment provided a certain cure ; and the treatments which gave the most promising results required at least a month's stay in hospital, and were, I think, almost more severe than the disease. We still live in hopes ; but up to the present the daily dosage described above remains the best, as it is the oldest used. If I had malaria to-day, I should not dream of allowing any other 'cure' to be practised on me."

CHAPTER XIII

A Grave Problem.—The two previous chapters have been a digression, but not unintentional. From them the reader will have learned how grave a problem confronted estates situated in the coastal hills. They were in the forks of dilemma; if their ravines were left in jungle they got malaria from *A. umbrosus;* if their ravines were cleared, *A. maculatus* replaced *A. umbrosus,* and took up the role of carrier. However scrupulously free from grass and weeds the ravine streams were kept, *A. maculatus* could not be driven out. Quinine given for years in large doses had proved a broken reed. What, then, could be done? Although, at this time, the elimination of malaria by control of mosquitoes was almost universally regarded as impracticable even for small towns, and for rural areas had not been discussed or suggested even in a tentative way, except by Ross himself, the ease with which it had been driven from the coastal plains and mangrove swamps, when the conditions there were made unsuitable for the anopheles, had convinced me that an attack on the ravine anopheles was the right policy.

At that time I knew of no method of oiling or poisoning or polluting the water which promised success in rapid streams; and I could think of nothing as suitable as a scheme of subsoil drainage. By carrying off all the springs and streams of the ravines in underground pipes, no water would be left for *A. maculatus* to breed in; and presumably, if a large enough area were done, malaria would disappear. But what was a large enough area? and how were pipes to be laid in the ravines so that they would drain the springs and streams; yet resist the tremendous scouring action of tropical storms?

The Area to be Drained.—The proposal was that all land within a circle of a certain radius should be drained and freed

from the breeding-places of *A. maculatus;* in the centre of
the circle would be housed the labour force. There was little
evidence of the distance that *A. maculatus* carried malaria from
its breeding-places; certainly nothing comparable with spleen
rates of children in relation to flat land jungle; and these might
mislead, if applied to hill land. The measurements on flat land
were made in places for the most part with jungle on one side;
from one direction only *A. umbrosus* attacked. What would
the malaria and the spleen rates have been had the observations
been made on estates consisting of small circular areas carved
out of, and completely surrounded by, the jungle of the coastal
plains? Into such areas *A. umbrosus* would have flown to the
centre from every point of the compass; and spleen rates would
have been of great value from the standpoint of the scientific
sanitarian. But the information was not available; estates were
not developed so as to produce these conditions.

There were two other considerations to be weighed. Into
the hill land sanitary circle, which it was proposed to create,
A. maculatus would not, fly from all points of the compass.
In hill land part of the circle would be low ground and
ravines, which would breed mosquitoes; but another part
would be high ground, which would be harmless. The proportion between the two would vary, depending on the number
and extent of the ravines within the circle. The mosquito
attack on the centre might be likened to a series of columns
invading along the lines of the ravines, rather than to a diffuse
cloud of insects flowing in from every part of the periphery of
the circle. If this were so, then it would follow that the area
to be drained must be larger, the greater the number and
acreage of the ravines within the circle and on its periphery;
and smaller under the opposite conditions; but no mathematical
formula correlating the two factors could be devised until
practical experience of a completed scheme gave us some
knowledge of a third factor—the malaria-carrying power of
A. maculatus under such conditions.

The information required was not merely how far *A.
maculatus* could fly; what was wanted was a knowledge of how
far it could carry malaria. It was immaterial if some mosquitoes
could fly or be blown one mile or ten miles from their breeding-
place; but it was important to know how far the insect could
fly in such numbers that malaria would remain as an endemic

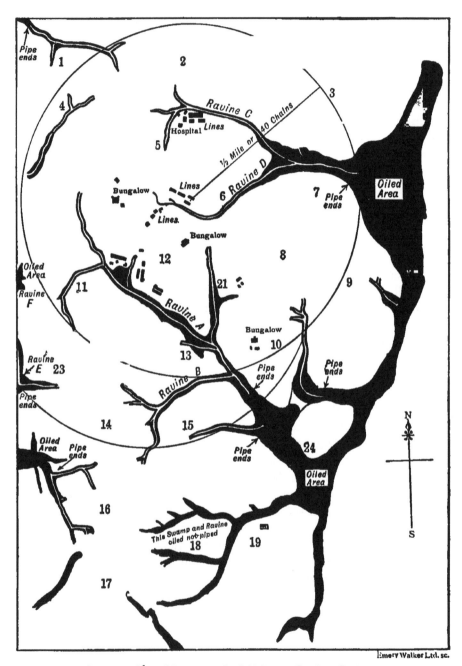

FIG. 31.—Plan of Ravines of Seafield Estate, Southern Division.

disease. On the flat land the spleen rates were found to fall progressively, the further the children were from the jungle home of *A. umbrosus;* until, at a distance of half a mile, the spleen rates were *nil.* Would the circle in the hill land require a radius of half a mile? *A. umbrosus* is a strong flier, and fierce biter; it will attack at any time of the day in heavy shade, either in the jungle or in a house. *A. maculatus* is relatively a delicate mosquito, dying quickly in captivity, and rarely, if ever, attacking during the day. Would it fly as far as *A. umbrosus?* That was a question we could not then definitely answer.

Where so much was uncertain, it was decided to begin with a circle of about 20 to 25 chains, and if that led to improved health we could afterwards enlarge the circle until malaria had entirely disappeared. This procedure would not only be of assistance in determining exactly how large the circle must be; but, on financial grounds, it was sound. To increase the radius of the circle from 20 to 40 chains was to quadruple the area, and would probably more than quadruple the costs; for the farther the ravines run, the larger they become, and the more costly their subsoil drainage would be. Where the cost even of a small experiment was to be considerable, it was important to avoid unnecessary expense; and, since proceeding by stages would give the maximum information with the minimum risk of wasting money, it was the policy I advised.

The Engineering Problem.—Seafield Estate consists of a series of small hills, part of the granite upheaval. The granite outcrops at a number of points in the ravines; but for the most part the rock is covered by deep, rich, friable red soil. In a number of ravines, however, the recently decomposed granite has become exposed; and there the ground consists of a mixture of fine white clay, kaolinite from the felspar of the granite, infiltrated with grains of sand and particles of white gravel, the quartz of the granite. This white clay is practically impervious to water; so springs and seepages are abundant in ravines which contain it; and some Old Seafield ravines are largely like this. Where most of the white clay had been washed away, the sand and gravel were left in a mixture which has about as much stability as "porridge"; that was how Mr Norman Grieve described it.

Down these ravines torrents of tropical rain pour;

frequently one or two inches fall in an hour or less. Twenty inches might fall in a month; there might be twenty wet days in a month. In the steeper parts of the ravines, the once narrow drains had been scoured into wide, deep, un-even channels; in the flatter parts, the drain was obliterated by the silt from above, and the whole ravine converted into a wide swamp. In such ravines, and under such conditions, the new system of subsoil drainage was to be tried. The ancients had employed subsoil drainage in agricultural land; but the method of using it to control mosquitoes in hill streams and ravines, which I now proposed, was, as far as I am aware, new. The idea first came to me when reading Howard's account of malaria in Central Africa, in which he states that the cost of lime is £6 per ton, and of English cement, £17 per ton. On my arrival in England in 1908, I made inquiries into the method of agricultural drainage, and bought some books on the subject. On returning to Klang in October 1908, I discussed the subject with the Chairman of the Klang Sanitary Board, the late Mr J. Scott Mason, and Mr John Gibson, General Manager of the Tremelbye Rubber Company, who was familiar with subsoil drainage in Scotland. It was decided to try it on one of the hill-foot drains in Klang. A Chinese roof tile maker was approached, and after several attempts he succeeded in turning out about fifty very respectable-looking tiles, and agreed to make more at a cost of two cents each. These were the first subsoil agricultural pipes made for anti-malaria work in the F.M.S.

Then appeared Mr Sime's paper in the *Liverpool Annals of Tropical Medicine*, from which it appeared that a system of subsoil drainage had been adopted in Panama with success some two years before. Although it differed in some important points from what I proposed, we decided to take no further action in Klang at the moment, as the special problem in hill land had come into view.

When convinced that *A. maculatus* in hill land could not be controlled by ordinary agricultural methods, I turned to the idea of drying the beds of the ravines by a system of subsoil drainage. It seemed likely, too, that by this drainage silt would be retained in the upper portion of the ravines, and would not cover the outlets of the subsoil drainage system in the lower portions. The ravine soil, consisting of porous silt

FIG. 32.—SEAFIELD ESTATE.
The condition of the upper portion of Ravine " A " before subsoil drainage.

FIG. 33.—SEAFIELD ESTATE.
The Ravine of Fig. 32 when first piped.

[To face page 134.

and gravel, was to cover the pipes to a depth of three or more feet; it would allow seepage water, and some of the storm water to pass through it to the pipes, but would, so to speak, filter out any silt descending from the higher land, and retain it on its surface. The depth of the soil over the pipes would gradually be increased, but that would be no disadvantage. The deeper the soil over the pipes, the deeper the dangerous seepage and springs would be buried, and the less chance would there be of storms scouring out the pipes.

The powerful erosive action of storm water also required consideration. The pipes could be buried under a heavy layer of stone of graduated size with the smallest on the top. But it appeared to me essential, if we were to keep the silt from reaching the pipes in quantity and blocking them, that nothing less than a fine filtering layer composed of silt itself must be the top layer : and if the top layer, which would bear the brunt of the storm waters' action, must be a fine soil, stones under it would not be required from an engineering point of view, and so would be unnecessary and expensive.

It was, therefore, decided not to lay stones over the pipes, but to break the power of the water by widening the storm water channel. This method differs from that employed in Panama, where earth is not put over the stone. " The dirt from the trench must be placed on the down-hill side of the line, to prevent it washing back into the ditch. When the soil uphill from the ditch is covered with vegetation, the space between the cover stones does not fill up "—so Mr W. Prince describes his method. When in Panama, I found that the soil was not friable or sandy like that in the F.M.S. The Panama system, although suited to that country, is quite unsuited to ravines in the F.M.S.; indeed, a modification of it was tried in Kuala Lumpur and proved a failure as we shall see.

A system of open concrete drains in our ravines would have been useless. They would have been scoured out in the steeper portions of the ravines, and silted up in the lower. In Kuala Lumpur they were tried, and failed for these reasons (Fig. 35).

The Scheme approved by the Directors.—From 1905 to 1908 the ravines on Seafield Estate had been kept free from all grass and vegetation with the idea of eliminating *A. maculatus.* Mr H. R. Quartley took the keenest personal interest in the matter; and the failure to eliminate the mosquito was not for lack of care. Nor had quinine been given to the labour force in any perfunctory way. Mr Quartley realised that the success of the estate depended on a healthy labour force, and anything he undertook to do to improve the health was done thoroughly. Quinine was given at the muster, and no coolie received "a name" for his day's work until he had swallowed the quinine. We saw the health improve, and the death rate come down: but a healthy labour force could not be built up. All new comers suffered from malaria; only a small proportion became immune; the others left the estate or died. The failure of quinine to eliminate the disease was definitely established, and accepted by Mr Quartley and myself in 1909; nothing more could be expected from clean weeding the ravines; nor would anything have been gained by abandoning them to revert to jungle. Our only hope appeared to lie in subsoil drainage; we discussed this. It appealed to Mr Quartley; and he placed it before the directors, giving it his strongest support. He pointed out how it had been impossible to build up a healthy labour force; how, despite everything that could be done, the death rate of the labourers was so high that it could not be allowed to continue; how Europeans as well as Asiatics suffered, and proper supervision of estate work was difficult, if not impossible; and that if the estate could be made healthy at any reasonable cost, the expenditure would soon repay itself. Owing to his urgent representations, the directors deputed one of their number, Mr Norman W. Grieve, to visit the estate and decide whether or not to proceed with the scheme. Pending his arrival, Mr I. Irvine, M.I.C.E., in 1910 made a survey of the ravines, and prepared plans and estimates. In 1910, at a meeting held at Seafield Estate, Mr Grieve, on behalf of the Board of Directors,* sanctioned the scheme. Mr Bach, M.I.C.E., was engaged to carry out the work. He arranged for a Chinese roof tile maker to make the pipes; and the first pipes were laid on 1st June 1911 on Old Seafield.

A. maculatus as a Natural Carrier of Malaria confirmed. —The announcement that *A. maculatus* would not disappear without special measures to exterminate it, and that unless

---

* The Board of Directors consisted of H. K. Rutherford, Esq., Chairman; Joseph Fraser, Esq., Norman W. Grieve, Esq., John M'Ewan, Esq.

FIG. 34 —SEAFIELD ESTATE.
The Ravine of Fig. 32 when finished.

FIG. 35.
An open cement channel in Kuala Lumpur which had to be replaced in the steeper portions of the ravine because of the soil erosion. Such a channel as this could be put down in Panama without any such risk.

[To face page 136.

measures were taken hill areas would remain permanently intensely malarious, naturally caused anxiety to the planting community. Hitherto the hills had been regarded as a refuge from malaria whose home was supposed to be swamps and flat land, especially near to the coast. So it was in Italy, from which country most of our ideas of malaria had come. But in Malaya my observations had cut away all ground for hope of improvement in the hill-land estates, and I received numerous letters on the subject.

The Directors of Seafield Estate had decided to proceed with the work on my advice, but I felt it would be more satisfactory to them if my findings were confirmed by a competent scientific observer. Accordingly I asked Dr A. T. Stanton, of the Institute for Medical Research, if he would be good enough to visit Seafield Estate to check my observations; and, if he confirmed them, to give me a letter which I could send to the Directors of Seafield Estate, and to any other companies that might be interested. This Dr Stanton kindly consented to do; he visited the estate, and sent me the following letter:—

"Very many thanks for your courtesy in giving me an opportunity to test the accuracy of your observations with reference to the malaria-carrying mosquitoes of hill estates.

"As I have already written, I was able to confirm the finding of zygotes in the stomach wall of *N. willmori* by the examinations of specimens taken in Kuala Lumpur, and our finding of sporozoites in the salivary glands of specimens taken in the coolie lines of a hill estate proves the accuracy of your original observation that this species is a carrier in nature.

"The number of *N. willmori* taken in the lines, and the readiness with which we were able to demonstrate the parasite in them during a period, when, as the manager informed us, the estate was comparatively free from malaria, is ample evidence of the importance of this species in the spread of malaria in hill areas.

"I was greatly interested in your demonstration of the breeding-places to which you refer in your book. My own more limited experience of the breeding-places of anophelines would have led me to doubt the likelihood of finding larvæ attached to small stones in a stream of considerable volume and current free from grass and other vegetation. The fact , that we did find them in those situations as well as in large numbers in small pools in sand at the side of the streams shows the very great difficulty likely to be experienced in freeing these areas of malaria.

"I hope you will be successful in the measures you have proposed, and I may perhaps be permitted to congratulate you again upon the very important additions you have made to our knowledge of malaria, the most important disease problem, as I believe, which confronts sanitarians in this country.—Yours sincerely,   A. T. STANTON.

"INSTITUTE FOR MEDICAL RESEARCH,
   "KUALA LUMPUR, 27*th June* 1911."

Progress of the Work—Old Seafield, or Southern Division.— The first ravine drained was one of the steepest, and its soil specially friable. What appeared to be an ample storm-water channel was made; and for several months the work remained intact despite considerable rains. But during the very heavy and continuous rains of December scouring occurred, and it was evident that a wider channel was required.

With characteristic thoroughness Mr Quartley decided to provide the maximum security for the pipes; he swept away all rubber trees from, "filled in," and "barrelled" the bottom of the ravine; so that the stream water no longer acted chiefly on the line of the pipes. It was spread over the whole ravine, and rather on the sides than the centre.

By April 1912 such progress had been made that all ravines within 25 to 28 chains of the coolie lines had been drained. It did not, however, include the large ravine, B. The area was not completely free from breeding-places; wherever white clay had been exposed seepage water poured out, until secondary lines of pipes finally cut it off. Some wells also remained in connection with the water-supply. As all the engineering problems had been solved, and already the health of the labour force had improved, it was decided to extend the area to 40 chains from the lines.

(1913).—The new area taken in consisted of the lower and flatter portions of the ravines, and, although an increased sectional area of pipes was laid down, it proved insufficient to discharge the water quickly enough in the wet weather at the end of the year. Water, therefore, appeared on the surface of the upper parts of the ravines, which had been dry in 1912, just as if drains were blocked. One of the disadvantages under which the estate worked was the impossibility

FIG. 36.—SUBSOIL DRAINAGE.

Finishing off the day's work with timber to prevent damage from rain during the night.

FIG. 37.—SUBSOIL DRAINAGE.
A Wash-out.

[To face page 138.

of calculating the sectional area of the pipes required to drain a ravine. No pipes larger than 8 inches in diameter were obtainable; and it was only by observing the results in wet weather that the right number of lines of pipes could be determined.

In 1914 two additional lines of pipes were laid down in Ravines C and D; and in 1915 in Ravines A and B. So that it was the end of 1915 * before Old Seafield had the advantage of drainage area of a 40-chain radius, everywhere except in one direction, namely, in Ravines E and F.

New Seafield, or Northern Division.—In January 1914 work was begun on the New Seafield Division, and by the end of the year had been carried out for 26 chains in one direction and 16 chains in the other. The whole area was completed by the end of 1915. Profiting by the experience gained on Old Seafield, the sectional area of the pipes was ample, and the ravines have been dry since they were drained.

All wells were closed as soon as the pipe water-supply was laid on in 1913; as *A. maculatus* and *A. umbrosus* breed in them. It was necessary, however, to keep the main water-supply, which comes from a reservoir in a branch of the head of ravine A, situated close to the coolie lines and two bungalows on Old Seafield. From time to time larvæ would be taken in this water; but so seldom as to appear negligible. Alga grew on the bottom of the reservoir; in dry weather portions died off and floated to the surface. To ascertain to what extent this reservoir was a breeding-place, about a quarter of the floating debris was skimmed off, placed in a large jar, and treated with a strong solution of copper sulphate. The alga quickly shrivelled and sank to the bottom, leaving only small fragments of twigs and leaves. On searching this carefully, forty-nine larvæ were found, of which thirty-six were *A. sinensis* (which I do not regard as an important carrier of malaria); ten were *A. umbrosus*; and three were so small that they could not be identified with certainty, but were probably *A. umbrosus*.

In view of this observation, it seemed advisable to control the reservoir as a breeding-place. Oil could not be applied; but copper sulphate is added each week, and has greatly diminished, although it has not entirely killed out the sign.

* One ravine still gives trouble (1920).—M. W.

CHAPTER XIV

SEAFIELD ESTATE (*continued*)

The Medical Results from the Drainage.—The drainage was begun in June 1911, and was completed at the end of 1915. The estate, of course, benefited from each acre of breeding-place abolished, but the full benefit from the work was obviously not to be obtained for some time later. How much the health did improve will be seen from the following table :—

Year.	Average Labour Force.	Death Rate per 1000.	Year.	Average Labour Force.	Death Rate per 1000.
1906	175	114	1913	552	110
1907	380	63	1914	658	69
1908	399	30	1915	804	48
1909	345	52	1916	811	43
1910	426	133	1917	770	36
1911*	520	144	1918	693	75†
1912	427	123	1919	825	37

* Drainage begun.   † Influenza.

On 31st December 1919, there were no fewer than 998 workers, and 143 dependants, that is children and old people who do not work. The table shows a fall in death rate, interrupted only by the influenza epidemic of 1918, and its continuation in 1919 (see Chapter XXIX.). From it we can calculate roughly the number of lives saved in the last six years. Before doing so, however, I must point out that a labour force of over 600 coolies could not have been maintained unless the drainage had been carried out. On Seafield Estate, as on others in Malaya, labour is free, no indentured labour is allowed ; no labourer can sign a contract. He comes of his own accord, usually on the recommendation of relatives living on the estate; he is free to leave on giving a month's notice or paying a month's wages. In practice he often leaves after

FIG. 38.—SUBSOIL DRAINAGE.

Water showing on the surface of a ravine when the pipes are blocked.

FIG. 39.—SEAFIELD ESTATE.

Ravine "A" during a tropical shower, after subsoil drainage.

[To face page 140.

pay day, without notice or payment in lieu of notice. When an estate has a reputation for being malarious, it has difficulty in obtaining labour. Were it possible to pour labour into such

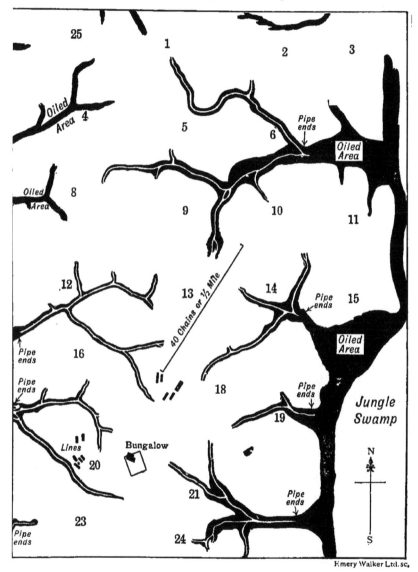

FIG. 40.—Plan of Ravines of Seafield Estate, Northern Division.

a place as Seafield was in 1911, so as to maintain an average labour force of 600 coolies, the death rate would be little short of 300 per mille per annum (see Chapter XI.). In the year 1908 there were in the F.M.S. twenty-one estates (eighteen of them in hill land) death rate of which was over 200 per mille. An adjoining estate, and one not usually regarded as so malarious as Seafield, had death rates between 1906 and 1910 as follows :—146, 157, 176, 111, 152 ; and in 1908 the average death rate of the Batu Tiga District in which Seafield is situated was 140 per mille.

In our calculation of the number of lives saved, we may safely take 144, the death rate for 1911, as the base line ; confident that it is an underestimate. Figures are as follows :—

Year.	No. of Deaths at 144 per mille.	No. of Deaths actually occurred.	No. of Lives Saved.
1914	94	48	46
1915	115	39	76
1916	116	35	81
1917	109	28	81
1918	99	52	47
1919	113	31	82
Total .	646	233	413

This calculation indicates that labourers equivalent to over one half of the present labour force have been saved during the past six years.

The reputation of the estate for health is now such that coolies come to it freely from India ; indeed the year 1919 tested the health conditions severely ; for no fewer than 957 new coolies arrived from India, most of them below the average in health, and large numbers suffering from influenza and its consequences. Not only had the rice famine affected them in India, but on the estate they were on short rice rations, supplemented by other foodstuffs, with the cooking of which they were unfamiliar. To this is attributable the increase of bowel diseases ; for the digestive organs of the Tamil cannot be experimented on with impunity. Influenza, complicated with pneumonia, which apparently had existed since 1915, and reached its zenith in the epidemic of 1918, still haunts the immigrant ships. In the quarantine camp at Port Swettenham in 1919, no less than 5757 cases of influenza occurred ; and there were 839 cases of pneumonia with 356 deaths.

Under these circumstances it is not surprising that in the

FIG. 41.—SEAFIELD ESTATE.

shows how the ravine has been cleared of rubber and covered with grass. On the left of the photograph the end o' Ravine "B" i subsoil pipes.

The lower end of Ravine " " All the water is conveyed where it joins ' A " is seen.

[*To face page* 142.

last four months of the year influenza was epidemic in prevalence on the estate, although not in the severe form of 1918. There was also a slight increase in the incidence of malaria in the last few months of the year, causing three deaths; but for the first time in the history of the estate the great wave of malaria, which begins about April, did not occur on New Seafield. While it is evident malaria is still being propagated, it is satisfactory to note it is decreasing. We can, I think, look forward confidently to still further improvement, and to a death rate not exceeding 10 per mille; for if the death rate of uncontrolled malaria runs up to 300 per mille, there is abundant evidence that, where malaria is absent, the death rate of Indian labour forces in this country need not exceed 10 per mille.

Spleen Rates and the Children.—In the last paragraph of the first edition of this book, I commented on the relation between malaria and the labour problem, and said further: "No estate can ever have an assured labour force where the women wail, 'We cannot have children here, and the children we bring with us die.'" Such is the cry on the unhealthy estates. It is in vain to contend with her "who weeps for her children and will not be comforted."

Seafield was such a place a few years ago. Those who have not seen the barrenness of an intensely malarious estate will find it difficult to picture the conditions. In Chapter XI. Mr Carey tells how in six years no Tamil child was born alive on New Amherst Estate. On 26th October 1909 I noted: "In three years five children have been born on New Seafield, of whom two have died; only three children born on Old Seafield, all died. Three children were conceived on the estate." Pregnant women had come from India; malaria had usually caused miscarriage. But on the estate itself only three children had been conceived.

There is no complete record of all the children who died on the estate in the early years; it would have been sad reading. One of my earliest recollections is of a child being brought to me at Klang with greatly enlarged spleen. He rapidly improved on an ordinary mixture of quinine sulphate; and for months the parents sent to Klang for the medicine, although the identical mixture was made up on the estate. The boy was the only child of M——, the head kangany (or native overseer); he was given the quinine for years, in fact until he left for India in 1911. The story ends in tragedy. All through the malarious years, from 1905 to 1911, M——, his wife, and the child kept alive. These had no other children; but in 1911 the woman became pregnant; great anæmia followed; an attack of malaria brought on labour, perhaps a little premature. Twins were born. They and the mother died within twenty-four hours. It has always seemed to me a cruel fate that, after struggling through all the malarious years, she should have died just when we had begun the measures which were to control the disease. After his wife's death, M—— seemed to lose heart, and went to India, promising to return with more coolies. But he had seen his wife and so many of his friends and relatives buried on the estate that he did not return; and there was reason to suppose he stopped coolies from coming over. If he did, who shall blame him? I believe the boy lived.

To-day the story is very different; although the change came gradually. On 23rd January 1917 on Old Seafield there were fourteen children without enlarged spleen who had been over six months on the estate; on New Seafield there were nineteen. On 18th January 1918 there were eighty-three children, of whom twenty had been born on the estate; not one of the twenty had enlarged spleen. In 1917 thirteen children were born on the estate; in the two succeeding years the numbers were seventeen and twenty-five.

Spleen Rates.

Year.	Old Seafield.		New Seafield.	
	Number Examined.	Spleen Rates.	Number Examined.	Spleen Rates.
1905	16	68	...	...
1906	17	88	...	...
1909	11	81	36	58
1914	20	50	39	76
1915	12	83	30	60
1916	34	85	37	73
1917	32	28	36	47
1918	52	7	31	41
1919	107	21	59	30

In 1918 I recorded that although the spleen rate of New Seafield was still high, in more than half of the children

FIG. 42.—SEAFIELD ESTATE.

The end of the subsoil pipes in Ravine "A." From this point the water continues
in an open drain. Photograph taken in dry weather.

[To face page 144.

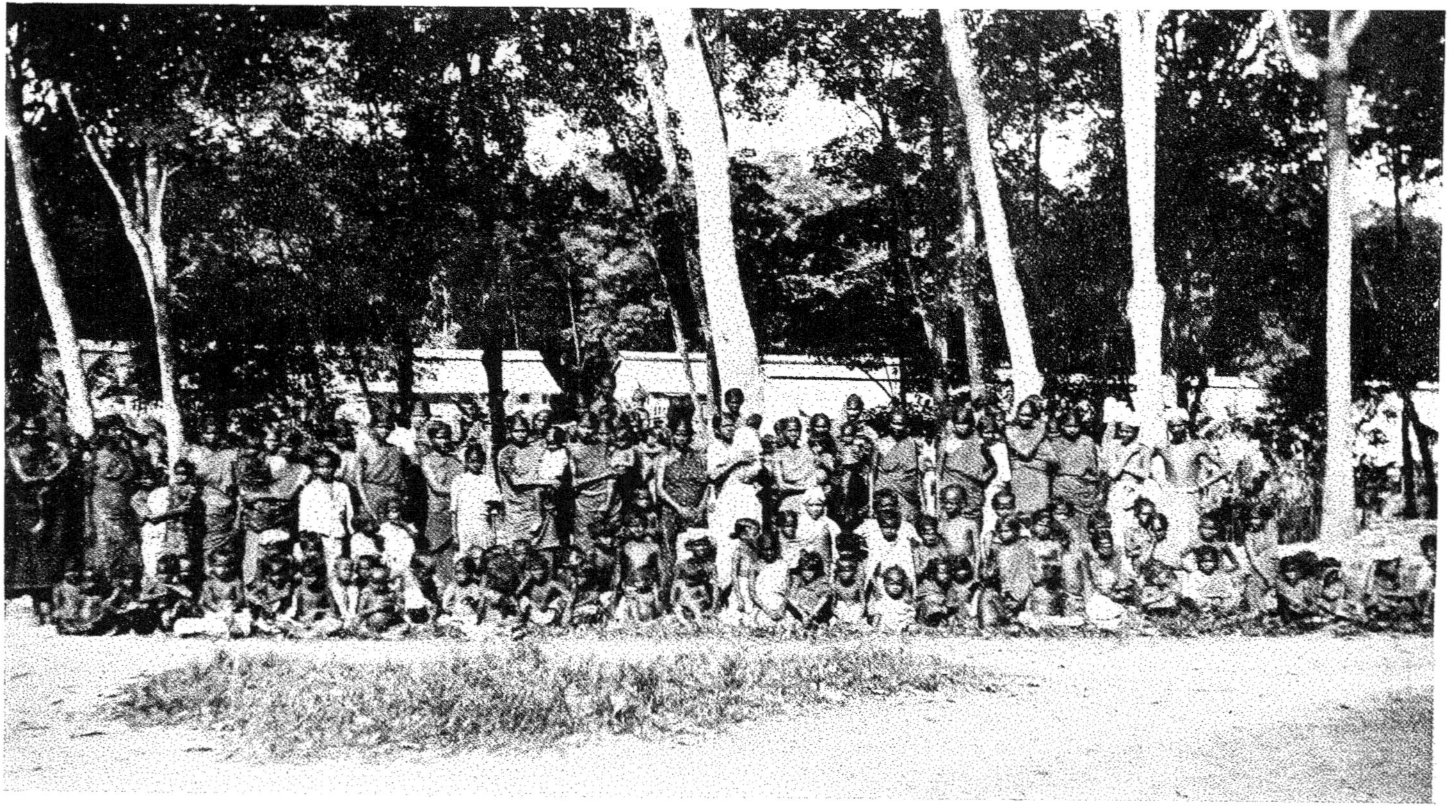

The m i 1920.

[To face page 144.

the enlarged spleen was so small that it was just palpable.
Of course it takes some time for chronically enlarged spleens
to disappear—often three and four years ; so it was of interest
to note the spleen gradually going. I added, " To me the
most gratifying sight of my last inspection of the labour force
was, not so much the large number of healthy coolies, as

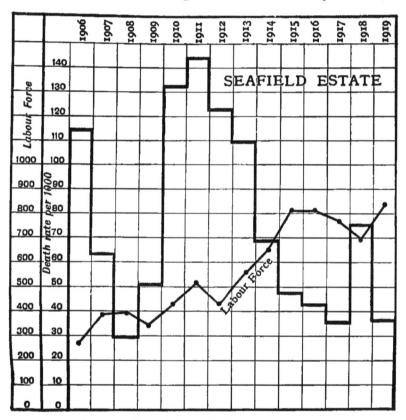

FIG. 44.—Chart of the Death Rate of Seafield Estate.

the number of mothers with the healthiest babies imaginable
in their arms."

In January 1920 on Old Seafield in 18 of the 23 children
with enlarged spleen, the organ was just palpable, and one
child was a healthy infant twenty days old ; 48 children with
normal spleens had been over six months on the estate.

On New Seafield there were five spleens of considerable
size ; the others were just palpable. Of the 41 children with
normal spleens, 24 had been over six months on the estate.

From these figures it is evident malaria is still being contracted on the estate; but it is becoming less intense as it decreases in amount.

To sum up, what was probably as intensely a malarious place as exists on the face of the earth, one which for the Indian labourer was uninhabitable except at an unjustifiable cost of life, is now so free from malaria, although not completely free, that Indians come to it readily, a large and efficient Indian labour force lives on it, and a further reduction in malaria and a further improvement in health may be anticipated with confidence.

CHAPTER XV

The Financial Results of the Drainage.—To determine accurately in dollars and cents the total value to Seafield Estate of the subsoil drainage is a matter of considerable difficulty. Some items can be accurately assessed; on others it is difficult to put a figure. In order that the financial aspect of the work may be understood, it will be necessary to explain the labour problem of estates in this country.

Indian Labour.—In the F.M.S. planters desire to establish on their estates an Indian labour force. In part this is due to tradition; for the pioneer planters of Malaya came from Ceylon, where Indians, and more particularly Tamils from Southern India, were employed on the coffee and tea estates. The habits and customs of Tamils were understood, their language spoken by the planters; so it was natural that when coming to Malaya, where no indigenous labour was available, and some labour foreign to the country must be introduced, Tamils were selected. As a labourer the Tamil is quiet and reliable when justly treated; and from a few hundreds, the Tamil population has increased to tens of thousands.

To the Indian coolie, who comes here, the F.M.S. is an El Dorado in comparison with his native country; there he belongs to the lowest castes or "depressed" classes. In years of a "bad monsoon" and famine, starvation is his lot; years of prosperity give him a bare living. He comes to this country, as a rule, in poor physical condition, penniless, and in rags. A year on a healthy estate, with good wages and good food, improves him and his children beyond recognition. Not only is he well covered with clothes and flesh, and looks healthy; but he becomes relatively wealthy. Until last year he could live well on less than half his earnings, and the balance he could remit to his relatives in India at such a favourable rate of exchange that it often amounted in India to as much in rupees as he could have earned had he remained there. Through the Post Office are sent large sums annually; and even larger amounts are carried over personally. The immigration figures show that the coolie usually returns to India in two years; that means he has saved enough to do so. The employment of Indian labour at the wages earned on estates is, therefore, advantageous both to the Indian and the estate.

The system by which he is introduced to the country is comparatively simple. Some coolie on an estate in Malaya has friends or relatives in India who, he thinks, would come to the estate; so he is given a "licence" to "recruit" by the Labour Department—a department of Government which concerns itself with the welfare of the labourer. Armed with the "recruiting licence" the coolie visits his village, and if successful, brings over a few other coolies. These coolies receive a free passage from a fund raised by assessing all employers of Indian labour, and arrive on the estate free from debt. There is no "indentured labour" in British Malaya; no coolie may sign a contract to labour; he is at liberty to leave on giving a month's notice, or at once on giving a month's pay; in practice, as I have said before, he often leaves without giving either.

By law he must be provided with free housing accommodation, free medical and hospital treatment; and regulations of many kinds for his welfare are strictly enforced by the department referred to above. Where the death rate of an estate is high, the employer may be prohibited from employing Indian labour. In the early years of the industry, this rule was not strictly adhered to; for malaria and ill-health were regarded as inevitable in the opening of a new country and as a passing phase. But as the causes of ill-health have come to be better understood, and its prevention placed on a practical footing, the regulations are now very strictly interpreted and enforced.

So Indian labour is preferred because the coolie and his language are understood by planters, and because it is reliable when healthy. At the same time, there is considerable expense in recruiting it, in transporting it from

India, and for medical treatment on the estate, especially when the estate is unhealthy. Indeed, if the estate be very malarious, the Indian requires higher wages, does poor work, is an indifferent, undesirable labourer, and ceases to be an asset.

Where an estate is very malarious, and the death rate is high, the Indian Government prohibits the employment of the Indian labourer.

Chinese Labour.—His place is taken by the Chinese, to whom Malaya owes so much. Long before the British administration was established in these parts, Chinese were working the rich tin land of the Peninsula. They come from a land where the seasonal variations give a period of comparatively, if not absolutely, cold weather, and are a virile race, full of enterprise and energy, well able to hold their own against any other race in the East; and probably, for that matter, against many in the West. Patient and efficient labourers; yet, for the European, difficult to work. This arises mainly from the fact that the language presents an almost insuperable obstacle to direct communication between the labourer and his Western employer. Language!—it would be more correct to say languages. Although there is one ideographic writing common to the Chinese Empire, the dialects differ so much that Chinese from the several provinces cannot understand each other. In Malaya, the labourers speak many dialects; each one of which requires several years of study before even a smattering is acquired by the average European; and until the European changes his mental equipment or the Chinese his language, there is little chance of direct communication between the planter and the labourer. The difficulty is overcome by the planter engaging and supervising his labour through a " contractor," a Chinese who speaks either English or Malay—the *lingua-franca* of the Archipelago. Through him the employer arranges the terms of the contract; to him the planter gives directions; and he is held responsible for the proper execution of the work.

On an unhealthy estate, Chinese, like Indians, suffer from malaria and its accompanying diseases. He has no natural immunity. On occasions I have seen him as badly stricken by the disease as Indians; Port Swettenham in 1901 is an example. Chinese have little faith in Western medicine, and do not usually seek admission to an estate hospital. When ill, the coolie prefers to leave the estate and go to his friends elsewhere.   There he is treated according to "Chinese fashion": when well, he returns to the estate; if he dies, his friends bury him, and the estate manager probably hears nothing of it. Leaving the estate gives him a better chance of recovery than if he remained there subject to constant re-infection; and we find that a large percentage of Chinese on unhealthy estates have enlarged spleen, showing they have recently acquired or are acquiring a natural immunity.   Two other things are in his favour: he believes in the mosquito net—practically every coolie uses one; and he feeds himself much better than the Indian.   So it comes about that Chinese live and work on places where Indians die off rapidly and where the planter's hope of establishing an Indian labour force—

> " Like Snow upon the Desert's dusty Face,
> Lighting a little hour or two—is gone."

If a Chinese coolie takes the risk of an unhealthy estate, he expects to be well paid for it.   He is no philanthropist; on the contrary, he is fully convinced that the labourer is worthy of his hire—and sees that he gets it.   Centuries of oppression in the Flowery Land have taught him the art of combination.   His Societies and Guilds—practically every Chinese of the lower classes belongs to one—are so highly organised that a Western Trade Union could teach him nothing; and probably could learn a good deal.   He is, therefore, practically in a position to make his own terms; and they are a long way above what the Tamil considers affluence, and flocks from India to obtain.   In short, while with Tamil labour it costs on an average about 7 cents a pound to tap and collect rubber, Chinese tapping costs 14 cents.   So Tamil labour saves, say, 7 cents a pound, and on a crop of 1,000,000 pounds in a year, the gross saving is from $70,000.   This places a high premium on health; and, apart from any other consideration, has been a material stimulus to estate sanitation.

Bark Renewal.—I have said that the Chinese are "patient and efficient labourers." Unfortunately this is often not true; and particularly when labour is scarce.   Good Tamil or Chinese tappers do not remove more than one inch of bark each month, sometimes less. Rubber latex comes from the bark, which thus forms the capital of the estate. The renewal of bark requires time, and systems of tapping are arranged so as to give four or six years' renewal, before the same part of the tree trunk is tapped again. Bad or careless tappers not only remove two or more inches of bark each month, but cut so deeply that the *cambium* is wounded; scars form in the new bark; where there are many scars, tapping over the renewed bark may become almost impossible. There are widespread complaints from estates compelled to employ Chinese of the quantity of bark used and wounds made, and of the inability of the management to effect improvement as long as the only labour possible is Chinese; and there is a shortage even of that. It will be apparent from this that the cost to an estate of Chinese tapping is not merely the 7 or 8 cents a pound that it is over the Tamil cost; the loss of double the amount of bark is of even more consequence, since it may throw an area out of tapping for several years.

Advantages and Disadvantages of Tamil Labour.—Tamil labour, however, is not without certain disadvantages which must be set against the cheap cost of tapping.

As far as Seafield Estate is concerned, the high death rate would have led to an order prohibiting the employment of Indians; even had some Indian labour been allowed, it would probably not have been sufficient in numbers, or reliable enough in "out-turn," to tap the trees; all tapping would have been done by Chinese.

It is now time to detail, if not to assess, the value of the items in the account, and I will begin with the

Disadvantages.—(1) Indian labour has involved heavier medical charges. In 1919 these were $15,061.

(2) The total capital cost of the pipe drainage, 1911-1918, was $68,243.

(3) The upkeep of ravines, including oiling in 1919, was $11,013.

(4) To lay the system many rubber trees were cut out, reducing the rubber crop; this would probably have been an annually diminishing amount, as some of the ravines would probably have become silted up, and the trees would have died out.

(5) Cost of recruiting Indian labour.

(6) Assessment on Indian labour.

(7) Loss on selling rice below cost price.

(8) Loss on Exchange—remitting money to India above the market rate.

Advantages.—(1) The improved health of the Europeans has (*a*) reduced their hospital charges; (*b*) reduced the sick leave; (*c*) improved the supervision of work, particularly of the conservation of the bark—an important item.

(2) Abolished the cost of upkeep of open drains in the ravines—a considerable item on account of silting.

(3) Reduced the cost of tapping by the gradual substitution of Tamil for Chinese labour.

(4) The last of the Chinese left in November 1919; but subsequent to 1914, when the percentage of the total crop harvested by the Tamils had increased from 49 to 89, the improved health of the estate, and the competition from the Tamils, induced the Chinese to work at a rate considerably below the average for unhealthy estates. Before they left, the cost of Chinese tapping on Seafield was 8.31 cents per pound against an average of over 14 on unhealthy estates.

(5) There are certain advantages from the employment of Tamils in estate work generally, particularly in weeding. Under mature rubber, from four years old upwards, the shade is heavy and few weeds grow. But in younger rubber, weeding is probably the most important work. If land is weeded regularly every two or three weeks—that is before the weeds can produce a crop of seed—the cost of weeding may be brought down to well under one dollar an acre per month; but if neglected for three months, it may cost seventy-five dollars or more an acre to clean up, and a heavy monthly expenditure afterwards, as I have explained in a previous chapter.

The best, and in the end cheapest, weeding is done by hand; each weed being picked out of the ground and removed in a bag. This the Chinese will not do; the Tamils will. So during the years when the fields are young, a Tamil labour force is an asset of great value. Even when an estate is unhealthy and Chinese are employed for tapping, every endeavour is made to maintain a small gang of Tamils to weed the younger fields, and do similar estate work.

Cost of Production of Rubber. — After many discussions with those familiar with the subject, it appeared that the only satisfactory way to estimate the value to Seafield Estate of a Tamil labour force would be to compare its f.o.b. cost of production with that of other estates employing Chinese labour, and to ascertain which was the cheaper. Inquiries were therefore made for an estate identical in acreage and yield with Seafield, but unhealthy and employing Chinese labour. As I was unsuccessful in finding one strictly comparable in all respects, I decided to ascertain the average cost on a number of estates employing Tamil labour, and to compare that figure with the average cost of estates with other labour. Messrs Cumberbatch & Co., Ltd., Messrs Harrison & Crossfield, Ltd., Messrs Guthrie & Co., Ltd., Messrs Barlow & Co., Messrs A. C. Harper & Co., Ltd., Messrs Barker & Co., Ltd., and the managers of several estates courteously supplied me with the details of estates with a total of over 71,000 acres in bearing, and from these I have worked out the average yield and cost. All are on hill land; they fall into three groups. For obvious reasons I am not permitted to give further details.

Group A, with 70 per cent. or more of the labour force Tamil. With one or two exceptions, all were intensely malarious, and but for the control of malaria would not now have a Tamil labour force. On several, further improvement in health is to be anticipated.

Group B have a mixed Tamil and Chinese labour force. On some there is a considerable expenditure on anti-malarial work, but a full Tamil labour force has not been built up. The health of this group generally is unsatisfactory, but there are exceptions.

Group C. Estates with 70 per cent. or more of the labour Chinese. Usually so unhealthy that Tamils cannot be employed. As a rule little is spent on anti-malarial work.

The following table shows the total area in tapping in each group; the average yield per acre; and the average f.o.b. cost per pound in cents:—

	Group A.	Group B.	Group C.
	Indians.	Mixed.	Chinese.
Acreage in bearing	29,068	22,120	20,043
Average yield per acre in lbs. . .	431·01	367·40	400·30
Average f.o.b. cost per lb. in cents .	28·25	37·45	36·03

Cost of Production with a Tamil Labour Force.—The average f.o.b. for Group C is 7·78 cents higher than for Group A, or roughly 30 per cent. In 1919 the f.o.b. cost on Seafield was 24·17 cents, or 11·86 cents less than the average f.o.b. cost of Group C, the Chinese worked estates. The saving on the whole of the Seafield crop is, therefore, 11·86 × 1,147,553, or $136,099.

Assuming, however, that Seafield was an average estate in Group A with the average saving of 7·78 cents—then the gross saving still amounts to $89,279, or over £10,000 sterling. The capital cost of the subsoil drainage 1911-18 was $68,243—so that it was more than repaid in one year.

However we look at the matter, it would appear that the whole cost of the subsoil drainage was repaid and probably much more than repaid in the year 1919; and that the gain in previous years, while less in amount, can have been no mean sum. In other words, apart from the saving of human life and conservation of " bark," the cost of the subsoil drainage has probably been repaid several times over in the past five years.

Cost of Production with Mixed Labour Forces.—It is to be noted, and is significant, that on Estate No. 28, the cheapest producer in Class C (f.o.b., 29·78 cents), much is being spent on improving the health both by subsoil drainage and oiling; and its figure of costs may be compared with Estates No. 27 (f.o.b., 30·25 cents) and No. 22 (f.o.b., 26·60 cents) in Group B., on both of which also the health has been greatly improved, although labour forces exclusively Tamil have not yet been established. The higher cost of production of Group B as a whole, and its significant exceptions in comparison with Group C, would appear to indicate that there is a point in descending the scale of health, below which no advantage is to be gained from employing Tamils. It is, indeed, well recognised that, when an estate is unhealthy, Tamils cease to be an asset; and it is not uninteresting that these figures should bear out that opinion.

Cost of Production with Chinese Labour Forces.—Before passing, do not the figures for Estates No. 22, 27, and 28 suggest the thought that Chinese can work better and therefore cheaper where they are healthy; and that it would pay, even where a Tamil labour force is not aimed at, to make the estate healthy for the Chinese or whatever labour is employed? The Chinese, as a race, have keen business instincts. Where there is a choice, not even the most ignorant coolie will elect to go to an unhealthy estate in preference to a healthy one; nor will the headman or contractor under whom he works, for the latter has to live on the unhealthy estate with his coolies. I have already mentioned that the Chinese have no natural immunity to malaria, although they do not die in numbers on the estates. They acquire in time a certain immunity; but during that period there is much sickness, many days when they do not work, many journeys into towns for treatment among their friends and according to their own methods. All this has to be paid for, if the coolie is to live; and he must be paid enough to live, for he is a necessity. It is, in fact, paid for by the higher wages he earns on the days he works. It may be taken as certain—even if the figures of the Estates Nos. 22, 27, and 28 do not prove it—that where an estate is healthy, Chinese can afford to, and do in fact, work at a cheaper rate than where the place is unhealthy.

From the employer's point of view, whether the employer be European or Chinese, there are disadvantages from ill-health on an estate apart from the higher cost of production. It is a disadvantage to have a labour force constantly changing on account of ill-health. At times this leads to an actual shortage of even Chinese labour, which means a direct loss of crop; for the rubber not taken any one day is lost for ever. It means, too, that a succession of tappers have to be trained, for tapping is skilled work; and in the training some damage to the bark, the real capital of the estate, is unavoidable. Finally, where, as in this country, labour is imported at great expense, it is simple common sense to keep that labour at the highest possible state of efficiency. Only a healthy coolie, whether Tamil or Chinese, is efficient; and the higher the efficiency the greater the production. So that, for Chinese no less than for Tamil labour, it would pay to control malaria, and money spent under medical charges would be well spent. I do not, of course, expect that the Chinese will patronise estate hospitals run on Western ideas; but I do think that money spent on subsoil drainage, oiling, removing coolie lines to healthy sites, and screened coolie lines, etc., to control malaria would improve the health and efficiency of the labour, and go far to make the Chinese dislike to hospitals a matter of indifference alike to the employer and employee—for there would be few sick.

The Gross Cost of Disease.—A startling figure is revealed when we consider the gross saving to the estates employing Tamil labour in Group A. The gross crop was 12,528,782 pounds; with the average saving of 7·78 cents a pound we got the sum of \$974,737, or approximately £114,000 sterling in one year—no mean return on the amount spent to improve health.

If this be the saving to these few estates from which I have collected figures, what must be the total sum saved by all the estates in the Peninsula now able to employ Tamil labour forces because they are healthy? It must run into many millions sterling, even on the estates only the careers of which have been traced in these pages; and they are but a selection from the hundreds in the Peninsula.

Finally, we shall see later on, there is some reason to believe that 100,000 lives have been saved in Malaya in the last twenty years by sanitation, and principally through the elimination of malaria. If we estimate the wealth of a country by what its inhabitants produce, the saving of these lives and the value of their work lead our thoughts into figures that stagger us; but only do so, because we rarely count the cost of disease, and have not yet realised the value of medical research and the prevention of disease. As a nation, are we really practical?

CHAPTER XVI

ON THE BORDER OF THE HILL LAND

ON the Coastal Plain and Mangrove belt we saw that malaria was controlled by drainage; or by removing the labourers from the vicinity of jungle; or, in some cases, by opening the jungle so as to push it away from the labourers' houses. On the hill land, the policy has been to concentrate the labourers at the centre of sanitary circles within which all mosquito breeding-places are destroyed.

A number of estates border on the hills; part of the land is flat, and part hilly. In controlling malaria on these, sometimes one method, sometimes another, and sometimes a combination of methods have been employed. In this chapter I propose to give some examples of the problem as it presented itself, and describe what was done in each case.

NORTH HUMMOCK ESTATE.

North Hummock Estate is situated on the border land about four miles north of the town of Klang. From the first it was intensely malarious, Europeans and Indians alike suffering. It consists of three divisions—as will be seen from the plan; each was dealt with differently.

Division A.—The lines on this division were situated on flat land at the end of a spur of the hill. *A. umbrosus* was abundant, and came from the unopened swampy jungle marked 125 acres, part belonging to the estate, and part to a reserve of the Public Works Department of Government.

In 1911 permission was obtained from Government to open its portion (37 acres) of the land; at the same time the estate, on my recommendation, opened the 125 acres which it owned. The result was an immediate improvement in health, as the following spleen rates show.

157

Spleen Rates of Division A.

Year.	Number of Children Examined.	Spleen Rates.
1905. . . .		
1906. . . .		
1909 December .		
1911 November .		
1913 January . .		
1914 February. .		
1914 November .		
1916 November .		
1917 February. .		
1918 January . .		
1918 June . .		
1920 January . .		

The large increase in the child population and decrease in the spleen rate makes comment unnecessary.

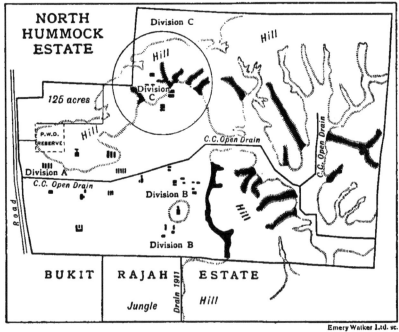

Emery Walker Ltd. sc.

FIG. 45.—Plan of North Hummock.
Areas subsoil drained marked black thus ▬

Division B.—Here the malaria came from swampy jungle about twenty chains away. The problem was complicated ; for that jungle belonged to another estate, and there was no intention of opening it.

The problem was solved in a curious way. In connection with the water-supply of the adjoining estate, I had suggested a large catchment drain at the foot of the hill marked Bukit Rajah on the plan; this was made, and other drains in the jungle were also dry. The result was to dry the jungle so that it no longer provided a breeding-place for *A. umbrosus*. At the same time some breeding-places of *A. maculatus* in the hill near to the lines were drained by subsoil drains. The spleen rate at once fell.

Spleen Rates of Division B.

Year.	Number of Children Examined.	Spleen Rates.
1911 November .	34	50
1913 January . .	72	5
1914 February. .	70	2
1914 November .	122	5
1916 February. .	90	3
1917. .	112	5
1918 January . .	128	6
1920 January . .	128	2

In both 1917 and 1918 two of the children with enlarged spleens arrived ill, the result of malaria contracted in India. In 1920 two of the three children with enlarged spleen had recently suffered from malaria. They had been several years on the estate, where presumably they had contracted it. The third was a recent arrival from a malarious estate.

Division C.—This division is of special interest. The lines were situated on a portion of the spur of hill land that terminates at the lines of Division A. The hills are intersected by a number of quite short ravines, each only about a couple of hundred yards long. They debouch on to the flat land where the soil was somewhat peaty. The ravines, except one, swarmed with *A. maculatus*, which were controlled by subsoil drainage of the ravine streams. As *A. maculatus* is never found in peaty water, it was unnecessary to pipe-drain a complete circle here, so the pipes ended as soon as they reached the peaty water. This knowledge of the habits of *A. maculatus* thus saved the estate much unnecessary expense;

and the very small lengths of ravines to be drained made the cost of the control of malaria only a nominal sum—some $1500.

The malaria had been so intense that even Banjarese, a race of Malayans, who are usually immune to malaria, could not live on the division, and the Tamils were decimated. The spleen rate shows the improvement.

Spleen Rates of Division C.

Year.	Number of Children Examined.	Spleen Rates.
1911	12	91
1913	14	14
1914	77	16
1914	55	16
1916	42	21
1917	44	15
1918	72	8
1919	62	9
1920	55	10

In 1920 three of the six children with enlarged spleen gave history of fever previous to coming to the estate, and another new arrival had a greatly enlarged spleen. Here, as on other healthy estates, there are children who have imported their spleens and malaria. The true spleen rate, therefore, is under 4.

For the whole estate the death rate of 1919 was 9 per mille.

Subsoil drainage proved of advantage to the estate from a point of view other than health; it has been of value in maintaining an efficient drainage system on the flat land. The attached letter from the manager gives an account of what the anti-malarial work has meant to the estate :—

"NORTH HUMMOCK (SELANGOR) RUBBER CO. LTD.,
KLANG, *8th November* 1919.

"DEAR DR WATSON,—With reference to your request for an account of the work done on North Hummock Estate to improve the health, and particularly that done to control malaria, I have much pleasure in sending you these notes.

"I joined this estate in 1910, and have been on it since that date, first as an assistant, and later as manager.* When I

* The manager who carried out this excellent work was Mr R. K. Walker.

first came, the estate was malarious, and all who lived in the bungalow on 'A' Division suffered severely from malaria. After the opening-up of the swampy jungle in that division, the malaria soon disappeared.

"Division 'C,' in which the coolie lines are situated on small hills intersected by small ravines, was intensely malarious, so much so that a satisfactory labour force could not be got together there. The subsoil drainage soon improved the health, and this is now as healthy as any division on the estate. Indeed, there is at the present moment a larger labour force than is actually required.

"On 'B' division subsoil drainage was also laid down in certain ravines adjacent to the lines, and along the foot of the hills. This was done not only to improve health, but because it was an effective way of preventing silt from reaching the open drainage system. We had first noticed this advantage on 'C' division, and by its employment on 'B' division it was possible to prevent the 'CC' drain (the main drain of the estate) from becoming silted up. Many acres of rubber were thus saved from certain destruction, and some acres were reclaimed. The system of subsoil drainage has been systematically extended throughout the estate ravines, quite apart from the health question, far beyond half a mile from any habitation and solely as an agricultural measure.

"The cost of this subsoil drainage has been small. It has been carried out entirely by the estate staff without outside or engineering assistance. In very wet weather the ravines are kept under supervision, as occasionally small places scour, but many of the ravines have not cost a cent in repair, since the pipes were laid down in 1912 and 1913. It has been this long and satisfactory experience of it which has made it the deliberate policy of the estate to deal with ravines by means of subsoil drainage.

"The experience of the last few years has shown the advisability of deepening the drainage generally throughout the flat portion of the estate. This has been done, and led to an increased output of rubber. But it would not have been possible to maintain the increased depth in the drains, had the silt from the hills not been held back. To-day, in spite of a reduction in the amount of their normal food-supply, and in spite of difficulty of recruiting, the estate has become so popular with labour that there are now some 1600 men, women, and children on it. As the figures show, the health is excellent, and the death rate promises to be below 10 per mille for the year.

"To sum up, by clearing and draining jungle, by deepening

the open drains in the flat land, by subsoil drainage of ravine streams, what was once an intensely malarious estate with an inadequate labour force is now one of the healthiest in the country, and possesses a large and contented labour force.

"Finally, the measures taken to improve health have no less proved of the greatest value from an agricultural and financial point of view.—Yours sincerely,

"T. DONALDSON."

BUKIT RAJAH ESTATE.

I have known this estate as malarious since I came to Klang; for, although it had been opened up for a year or two before my arrival, it was not a large estate, and coolies were living close to jungle. To-day it is a large estate, with some 4000 acres opened, part of it hilly and part flat. The coolies are housed on different parts of the estate; they are now almost free from malaria. The following gives a brief account of what was done to make them so.

Triangle Lines.—These were close to the corner of a block of jungle marked 196 acres, through which runs the large drain "AA." In 1911 this jungle was opened and planted on my recommendation: the spleen rates show the improvement.

Year.	Number Examined.	Spleen Rates.
1906	7	14
1909	22	18
1910	42	7
1914	54	2
1917	102	4

Tamils at Sungei Binjai.—The fever in these lines came from the jungle of the 196 acres, and from what are now small native holdings on the south boundary.

The spleen rates show the improvement.

Year.	Number Examined.	Spleen Rates.
1906	8	37
1909	9	22
1914	48	8

Of the four children with enlarged spleen in 1914, three came from a malarious estate.

In 1917 the children were examined along with those

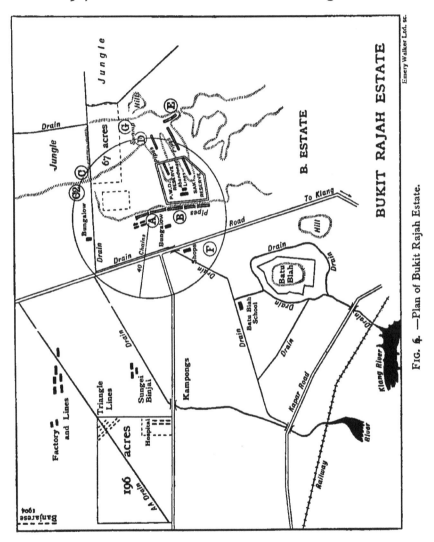

FIG. 4. —Plan of Bukit Rajah Estate.

in the triangle lines—the record of which has been given above.

Banjarese.—At one time a number of these people lived along the edge of the jungle that is now Shelford Estate. They suffered greatly from malaria.

They subsequently removed to native holdings on the road,

Year.	No. Examined.	Parasite Rate.	Spleen Rate.
1904	24	62	50
1905	15	60	60
1906	15	...	13
1910	35	...	23

Tamils at the Factory.—In 1904 the nearest jungle according to the estate plan was 40 chains away; nevertheless the parasite and spleen rates were high. Later, they dropped to normal. In 1917 the rise is owing to the recruiting of labour from an estate known to be intensely malarious. It is, however, easy to make the necessary correction; and I give it as an example of the ease with which the correction can be made, and of how little one is liable to be misled by using spleen rates even on rubber estates where the population moves so freely.

Year.	No. Examined.	Spleen Rate.	Parasite Rate.
1904	42	19	41
1905	34	32	32
1906	7	14	...
1909	72	4	...
1910	51	6	...
1914	11	0	...
1917*	11	18	...
1917†	19	36‡	...

* Malayalams.   † Tamils.   ‡ True rate = 0.

Of the seven Tamils with enlarged spleen in 1917, all had come from a malarious estate; and the same is true of the Malayalams.

Blackwater Fever.—A case of this occurred in a bungalow in field 139 acres, before the jungle on the opposite side of the road belonging to North Hummock Estate was opened.

Boon Hean Division.—In the previous places the problem was simply that of removing and draining jungle on flat land. The Division of which I now write was a pestilential spot, full of difficulties for the sanitarian. The coolie lines were scattered, and mostly close to jungle. Part of the land was hilly, and *A. maculatus*, the dangerous hill-stream mosquito, existed on it. Another difficulty was that 57 acres belonged to Government—

part being a quarry reserve which was of value for road upkeep, and which Government was strongly opposed to selling. The Government land was, however, intensely malarious. About 1902 I chose the top of the hill as a site for coolie lines for the Public Works Department, going on the teaching that in a malarious country a hill ‚was the best site, and that elevation, however slight, was preferable to the heavy clay of flat land. "As high ground as possible is the golden rule for a camp. Against the vertical uprising of malaria, elevation, however small, affords some protection." The lines were built on the site I selected, but the coolies promptly died of malaria ; and until the land was handed over to the estate they remained uninhabited and uninhabitable. On one occasion a man attempted to occupy the overseer's bungalow ; but he, too, had to leave.

To show how intensely malarious the whole area was in 1909, I will give the spleen rates of the various lines. At B, 14 out of 17 or 82 per cent. had enlarged spleen. At F, which is farther from the jungle, there were 9 out of 22 or 40 per cent. with spleen. At C, the lines were within 20 yards of the jungle, and the spleen rate was 10 out of 11 or 90 per cent. ; while at C 2, which is 200 yards from the jungle, it was 8/15 or 53 per cent. In 1912 coolies were put into the lines D, E, and G, but the health was so bad they had to be moved. I have no figures of the spleen rates.

In order to give the estate a healthy labour force, I decided it would be best to "scrap" almost all the existing lines and sites, and to create a new healthy site somewhere in the area. Accordingly, I made the following recommendations, which were adopted, with the happiest results :—

(1) Site A was selected as the future headquarters of the Division—but not because it was healthy ; for it was only a few yards from the Government reserve and site B where the spleen rate was 82. It was chosen because it was possible to abolish all breeding-places within half a mile. Site F would be protected by the same measures.

(2) Sites C, C 2, D, E, and G were abandoned, because they were close to jungle. To make them healthy, it would have been necessary to open up extensive areas of jungle, and probably lay down considerable subsoil

drainage; this was undesirable, since the jungle and hills formed the catchment area of the water-supply.

(3) Part of the jungle marked 67 acres was drained and planted with rubber. The Government reserve was exchanged for a piece of land suitable for a rifle range. The reserve was cleared of jungle, **and** planted up; while the ravines were drained by subsoil pipes.

After these measures were carried out, the health improved, as the spleen rates show :—

Year.	No. Examined.	Spleen Rates.
1909 Lines at Site B .	17	83
1909 Whole division .	65	42
1914 ,, .	63	14
1915 ,, .	49	22
1917 ,, .	62	6

In 1917, there were four children with enlarged spleen; three of these belonged to one family which had recently come from a malarious estate; the fourth child, with a spleen just palpable, came from an estate on which malaria had recently existed. There is now a large healthy labour force on a site which formerly was uninhabitable.

Sungei Rasak Division.—This Division has always been healthy, for the lines have never been less than 30 chains from jungle, and I had advised the manager not to put new lines among the ravines; they are situated at the end of a spur of the hills.

Spleen Rates.

Year.	No. Examined.	Spleen Rates.
1910	12	15
1914	74	14
1915	34	8
1917	46	4

In 1917, one of the two children with enlarged spleen had been on the estate only a week, showing it had brought the enlarged spleen to the estate.

Death Rate of Estate.—The various measures taken to im-

prove health, chiefly the anti-malarial work, have resulted in a
lowering of the death rate. The labour forces and death rates are
taken from the official report of the Labour Department, except
for 1919, which are based on the average monthly population.

Year.	Labour Force.	Death Rate per mille.
1906	950	43
1907	1150	45
1908	1125	63
1909	993	29
1910	1144	33
1911	1143	39
1912	1146	34
1913	1254	39
1914	1146	14
1915	1157	19
1916	1215	7
1917	1269	14
1918	1374	32*
1919	1459	10

* Influenza.

Further comment is hardly necessary.

Batu Blah Drainage.—Close to the Boon Hean Division of
Bukit Rajah Estate are many kampongs or native holdings.
Until 1916, the drainage of the kampongs around Batu Blah
Hill was defective. *A. umbrosus* was to be found in many
drains and in wells around the hill. Consequently, malaria was
prevalent. Two European houses and several of the better
classes of native houses, built here from the spread of the town,
were abandoned on account of their unhealthiness.

In 1914, I represented this to Government; in 1916, about
$3000 were spent on an open drainage system. The spleen
rate of Batu Blah Malay School has steadily fallen since. In
1919, two of the three children with enlarged spleens were old
residents; the third lived $1\frac{1}{2}$ miles away.

Batu Blah School.

Year.	No. Examined.	Spleen Rates.
1909	53	45
1914	60	45
1916	62	30
1917	67	37
1918	54	20
1919	53	5

The abandoned houses have been reoccupied. There is now no complaint from the natives; at first they said they could not get sufficient water; their wells were dried up or closed, and they had to go some distance to the pipe supply. Now they are reconciled, as the improved drainage has given them larger crops—mainly of rubber.

MIDLANDS ESTATE.

When first opened in 1906 this estate was intensely malarious, because the first clearings were on the hills, and the labour force was housed on ravines teeming with *A. maculatus.*

Quinine was given, and the coolies were fed in the morning before going to work, with a certain improvement in health, but not sufficient to enable a healthy Indian labour force to be established.

When more of the estate had been opened, sites on the flat land were available, and the hill land sites were abandoned. The estate is now worked in two divisions. The North Division coolie lines were moved 25 chains or ¼ mile, and the South Division lines 50 chains. In neither case was it possible to move the lines ½ mile from all hills, so additional measures were taken to control the breeding-places of *A. maculatus* within the sanitary circle, namely subsoil drainage and oiling.

There were difficulties with the subsoil drainage in certain places owing to the impervious clay soil, and much of this drainage was pulled up. It is used now as subsidiary to oiling in short lengths round the hills. Open drains round the hills are also oiled for 1 chain from the foot of the hills; special attention is paid to seepage areas. It has not been found necessary to oil the drains in the flat bottom of the valleys, partly because the main drain contains peaty water, which never contains *A. maculatus*, and partly because the oiling of the hill-foot drains pollutes the other drains on the flat.

South or Old Division.—The removal of the lines was commenced in July 1913 and was completed by February 1914.

The effect of this and the other measures is shown in the fall of the spleen rate.

Year.	Number of Children Examined.	Spleen Rates.
1906	61	65
1907	43	83
1909-10	153	45
1914	78	21
1917	48	6
1918	115	2
1920	143	2

In 1920 there were three children with enlarged spleens; two of those were a brother and sister locally recruited three months before; the other was a child many years on the estate, whose spleen was just palpable. The true spleen rate is, therefore, under 1 per cent., and is in keeping with the low death rate.

In December 1914 in a report I made this remark:—

"But marked as this improvement is, an analysis of the figures gives curious and interesting independent evidence of the improvement which is taking place. In 1909-10, in the lines situated on the Government Road, and subsequently abandoned, 21 out of the 22 children had enlarged spleen; the spleen rate of the children who had been over six months on the estate was 81; and out of the total 153 children on this division there were only 4 infants.

"Now I find that among the 57 children who have been longest on the new site (since July 1913) only 8 or 14 per cent. have enlarged spleen, not a single one (except 1 in hospital) is ill, and there are 9 fat, healthy infants. On the other hand, of 21 children removed to the new site in February 1914 still 9 or 42 per cent. have enlarged spleen; but even here only 1 is ill, and there are 3 healthy infants."

This note is interesting, as giving a glimpse of spleen rates during a transition stage from high to low.

North Division.—The same policy was advised for the North Division of the estate. On 3rd August 1910 I wrote to the manager:—

"Sites in proximity to the hills which pretty much follow the cart road, as shown on the plan, are to be regarded as unhealthy. It is, therefore, desirable to put the lines and bungalow as far as possible from them. I, therefore, advise that the new buildings be put close to the pipe line. This will put them close to jungle, which is also unhealthy, but it might

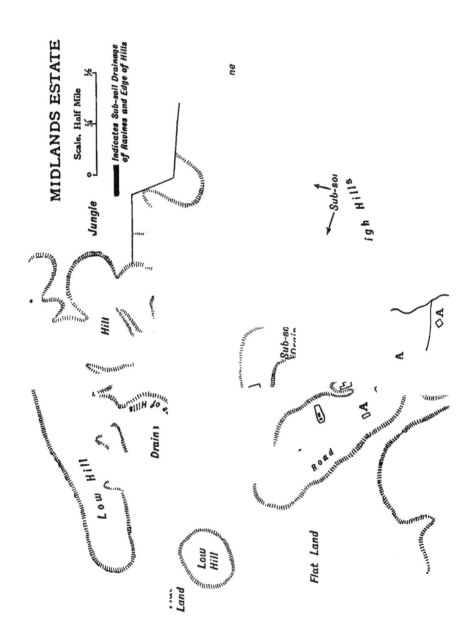

MIDLANDS ESTATE

Scale, Half Mile

Indicates Sub-soil Drainage
of Ravines and Edge of Hills

Jungle

Hill

of Hills

Low Hill

Drains

Low
Hill

Land

Flat Land

Road

Sub-so
Drain

Sub-soi

igh Hills

ne

be possible to make the clearings in the near future along the
pipe line, thereby improving the health of the new buildings."

The buildings were put on the road close to the hills, and
proved unhealthy.   Between January and October 1914 some

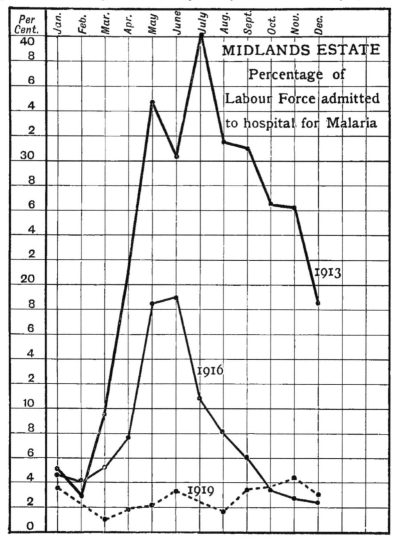

FIG. 48.—Chart of percentage of Admissions for Malaria, Midlands Estate.

ravines were pipe-drained and others oiled, which improved
the health.   In 1915, 1917, and 1918 various blocks of the
flat land beyond the pipe line were opened up, pushing the
jungle some 40 chains from the pipe line, and making it

possible to remove the labour force to the site suggested in 1910; and the whole labour force was removed early in 1918, with satisfactory results, as the figures will show. Not until 1919 was the jungle taken a full half-mile from the lines.

The plan, showing the abandoned sites, gives a better idea of the policy adopted than anything I can write; so I refer the reader to the study of it.

The drainage and oiling were not in force until towards the end of 1914, and so at that date the spleen rate was still high. The labour force was not removed from the hills until March and April of 1918.

Hence the spleen rate of this division fell at a later period than on the South Division.

Year.	Number of Children Examined.	Spleen Rates.
1909-10	21	76
1914	22	63
1918	20	20
1920	29	6

In 1920 there were two children with enlarged spleen; one, born on the estate, had a spleen barely palpable; the other, a local recruit, had been about three months on the estate.

Death Rates.—With the falling spleen rates the death rates came down as the following table shows. In the years 1909 and 1910 large numbers of Telegu coolies were recruited. It was not until the end of 1911, when Mr Harrison became manager, that special measures against *A. maculatus* were commenced.

Year.	Average Population.	Death Rate.
1907	750	
1908	1256	
1909	1369	
1910	1114	
1911	940	
1912	861	
1913	824	
1914	713	
1915	528	
1916	547	
1917	597	
1918	622	
1919	616	

* Influenza.

In the first four months of 1920 only one death has occurred; it was from epilepsy.

The approximate cost of oiling each area of a half-mile radius is \$400 per month.*

This estate is a brilliant example of how intense malaria can be overcome by removal of buildings to the best sites, coupled with subsoil drainage and oiling to breeding-places within the new sanitary area. Quinine is not given to any except the sick.

This work has been carried out entirely by the manager, Mr C. R. Harrison, and reflects the highest credit on him.

DAMANSARA ESTATE.

This estate is situated on the border of the hill and flat land. The measures taken to improve health have been giving quinine, opening swampy jungle, removal of labour from hill to flat land, and oiling. The original Damansara

Parasite Rate.

Year.	Number of Children Examined.	Parasite Rate.
1904	9	22

Spleen Rates.

Year.	Number of Children Examined.	Spleen Rates.
1904	9	11
1909	9	22
1911	10	30
1913	13	23
1914	15	13
1915	20	5
1920	33	3

Estate acquired Telok Batu Estate in 1906, and Labuan Padang Estate in 1907. From a medical point of view, I regard the group of estates as composed of five divisions; as the coolie lines are situated in five groups at some distance apart and under different malarial influences. .

* Owing to the great increase in the cost of oil, additional areas have been subsoil drained.

Some spleen and parasites rates for 1905 and 1906 have been omitted, as the records of Divisions "A" and "B" had unfortunately not been kept separate.

Division "A" is situated on the river. To improve the health quinine was given with the greatest care by Mr H. F. Browell from 1904. In 1910 about six acres of secondary jungle and undergrowth was removed. In 1912 and 1913 150 acres of land belonging to another estate on the opposite side of the river was opened. Some jungle still remains within 40 chains.

The figures on the previous page show the result.

Division "B."—On my recommendation, in 1910, jungle to the extent of 108 acres of flat land was opened. Later on, still more flat jungle belonging to an adjoining estate was opened, and hill-land ravines extensively oiled.

Parasite Rate.

Year.	Number of Children Examined.	Parasite Rate.
1904	32	40

Spleen Rates.

Year.	Number of Children Examined.	Spleen Rates.
1904	32	15
1909	31	51
1911	27	14
1913	22	27
1914	39	20
1915	55	12
1920	39	0

Division "C."—The lines were situated on a low spur of the hills, with streams breeding *A. maculatus* on each side. In 1910 I recommended that the lines be removed to a site on the flat, then under swampy jungle. Part of this jungle belonged to another owner, but it was acquired by the estate, and the whole block comprising 87 acres was drained and planted. Division "C" was removed to it, and on it was built the estate hospital.

Spleen Rates.

Year.	Number of Children Examined.	Spleen Rates.
1909	9	100
1911	1	100*
1913	9	22
1914	22	27
1915	18	16
1920	27	7

* Lines removed to new site in 1911.

In 1920, one of the two children with enlarged spleen was a local recruit from an unhealthy locality. The true spleen rate was 3·5 per cent.

Division "D."—Formerly an intensely malarious spot. Two streams breeding *A. maculatus* were on the sides; in front was a mass of swampy, flat-land jungle. This is the estate to which I refer in Chapter XI. on the effects of malaria in children :—

"Among the children malaria is no less severe. On one occasion I was asked by a manager to advise him what should be done for the children, as fifteen had died in the previous two months out of a total of thirty-three. He told me a native clerk was giving them quinine daily. I examined the blood of the remaining eighteen, and easily found parasites in seventeen. The manager then gave personal attention to the quinine administration of the children, and there were only two deaths in the next three months, these being children who were seriously ill before he took it in hand. The effect of this terrible death rate on the coolies was such, that even although they were living in good lines built less than three months before, and on land opened for ten years, they declared the lines were haunted. The lines had to be pulled down and rebuilt elsewhere."

The new site was on the river about 300 yards from the old one. The health improved when the flat land across the river was planted, and a ravine, part of which is probably not so suitable as it was for *A. maculatus*, on account of shade, was oiled for a time. (See Chapter XXV. on the Mosquitoes of Ravines.)

Parasite Rates.

Year.	Number of Children Examined.	Parasite Rates.
1904	12	100
1905	17	11*
1906	18	94

Spleen Rates.

Year.	Number of Children Examined.	Spleen Rates.
1904	12	75
1909	12	100 old site
1909	30	76 new site
1911	24	66
1913	39	76
1914	44	50
1915	33	66
1920	44	9

* Quinine given carefully.

Division " E."—The lines are situated on the end of a spur of the hills, on one side of which is a ravine, while in front is flat land. The most important ravine has been oiled intermittently since 1914, and regularly since 1918. The ravines farther off are under the shade of heavy rubber and small undergrowth, and so are less suitable for *A. maculatus* than they were previously.

Spleen Rates.

Year.	Number of Children Examined.	Spleen Rates.
1906	26	76
1909	13	100
1911	6	66
1913	11	81
1914	12	83
1915	19	84
1920	33	6*

* True rate, 8.

In 1905, when quinine was being given with great care, the parasite rate of seventeen children was 23.5 per cent.

In 1906, parasites were found in twenty-five out of twenty-six children; the single child without parasites had suffered from "fever" four days before, and was on quinine; its spleen was enlarged.

In 1920, of the two children with enlarged spleen, one was

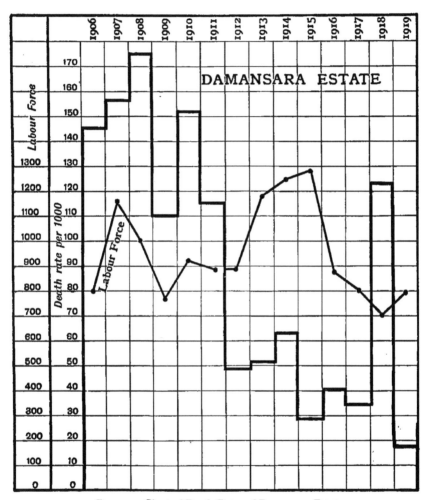

FIG. 49.—Chart of Death Rates of Damansara Estate.

a local recruit only six weeks on the estate; the other child was born on the estate. All the children looked well.

The Death Rates.—With spleen rates so high, one would expect to find high death rates, if many new coolies were employed; and this was so. The estate originally was not uniformly malarious, as will have been noticed from the spleen rates; but the two Divisions last mentioned had at one time an appalling mortality not only among the children but among the adults. For example, in 1906, on Division "E" there were 116 coolies on the 1st January; 170 were recruited from India. Of the 286, 26 deserted, and 60 died; the death rate, worked out on the quarterly labour force, was 300 per mille.

In 1907 the death rate of the 275 coolies on "E" Division was 178 per mille; of 275 coolies on "D" Division it was 200; and of 700 on Divisions "A" and "B" it was 138. These are examples of what malaria can do; and they occurred despite the most careful administration of quinine. On Division "E" the names of the occupants of each room were put on a special check roll, and each person was accounted for and given quinine daily, with extra doses of quinine solution when ill. Euquinine was given to the children.

The European staff suffered no less than the Asiatic, and the manager had to be invalided in 1907. Yet this intense malaria has been slowly overcome, and health has steadily improved since 1910, when radical methods were adopted on Divisions "A" and "B," namely, the opening of swampy jungle and removal of coolie lines. Later, oiling, more or less efficiently carried out on the other Divisions, the opening of some jungle, and probably the heavy and close shade of rubber trees and ferns now growing in some of the ravines, have contributed to reduce the number of stream-breeding mosquitoes.

The death rates show the nature of the change :—

Year.	Labour Force.	Death Rate per mille.
1906	800	146
1907	1155	157
1908	1005	176
1909	772	111
1910	926	152
1911	892	116
1912	887	49
1913	1186	52
1914	1251	63
1915	1295	29
1916	877	41
1917	800	35
1918	703	123*
1919	795	17

* Influenza.

Still further improvement may be anticipated with confidence.

JUGRA HILL.

The estates in the district of Kuala Langat, whose history
is given in Chapter VIII., are on flat land, and the malaria
from which they suffered at one time was carried by *A. umbrosus*.
But in the district rises Jugra Hill, a mass of granite 915 feet
high, isolated from all other hills by some 15 to 20 miles of
flat land. It is not uninteresting, as Dr Leicester[7] remarks,
that the mosquitoes of the hill are not those of the surrounding
flat land, but of hill land. And among the hill mosquitoes is
A. maculatus, the stream breeder. As a result of its presence,
all around Jugra Hill has been extremely malarious, while
only a short distance from it people have enjoyed good health.

What amounts to an experiment took place a few years
ago, when a set of lines belonging to the Public Works Department was removed from the base of the hill to a spot a mile
from it. The result was an immediate and marked improvement
in the health of the coolies, which has ever since been
maintained. The condition of the coolies in 1901 and 1902
can be seen from the following extract from a report dated
15th January 1902, made by me to the Government on the
prevalence of malaria in Jugra.

"Para. (4) . . But I would like to draw attention to some
observations made at the P.W.D. coolie lines at Permatim
Pasir which show that the malaria is not confined merely to
the town, but extends round the foot of the hill, and which
also explains the absolute refusal of many of the coolies to
remain after the term of their agreement had expired, although
they were willing to work at Klang.

"(5) On 5th February 1901, out of nine persons in the
lines one alone was healthy.

Two men and one child had malarial fever.
Two children, two men and one woman had enlarged
spleens, the result of repeated attacks of malaria.

I was informed about fifteen coolies were living there at the time.

"(6) On 10th July 1901, I found of these P.W.D. coolies :—

In the lines :

Two women, one man and three children with malarial
fever.

O

In the hospital:

Seven with fever, and three with enlarged spleens and ulcers.

At this time there were about thirty-four persons living in the lines.

" (7) On 7th January 1902, there were eleven children under ten years present at my visit. All without exception had enlarged spleen. Two women had fever.

" The overseer volunteered the statement that fifteen children had died within the past six months, which is not improbable, as malaria often affects children severely."

As the result of these representations the lines were removed in 1903 from the immediate foot of the hill, and, taking no risk, I advised they should be put a mile from the hill.

The result has been successful in the highest degree. From 1903 onwards I have often gone to the lines, and I have never once found a coolie in them suffering from fever, although doubtless a coolie may occasionally do so.

On 18th January 1910, I examined fourteen children in the lines. Two of them had splenic enlargement, and the overseer told me both had come to the place about a year before from other P.W.D. lines, and that they had not suffered from malaria since their arrival.

The overseer said he had been two years in the lines, and had not suffered from fever. No children had died since he had been in charge; the only death had been that of a coolie who was ill when he arrived from India, and had died shortly after his arrival. No adult or child had fever on the day of my examination.

That no improvement has taken place in the health condition at the foot of the hill, is to be seen from an examination of thirty-five Malay children in the Permatim Pasir School made on 16th May 1909. Of the thirty-five, eleven, or 35 per cent., had enlargement of the spleen. This is in marked contrast to the P.W.D. coolies only a mile from the hill, and from the freedom from malaria on the Estates " KK " and " LL," distant 1½ and 2 miles respectively.

The town of Jugra, situated at the foot of the hill, is the official headquarters of the district; but it has been so persistently malarious since 1896 that in 1917 the Government decided to remove it to a site on flat land about 5 or 6 miles

FIG. 50.—JUGRA TOWN.

Photograph shows two abandoned houses; in the foreground the timbers of a demolished house.

[To face page 180.

from the hill. The new buildings are now in course of erection. The new site is close to Estate "TT," so it should be healthy.

Practically half of the shop houses of the town have been abandoned or pulled down : more than half of one side of the street has disappeared. The place forms a picture of desolation to which the camera fails entirely to do justice.

In passing, I may mention that the story of the malaria of Jugra given in Volume I. of the *Studies from the Institute for Medical Research* is entirely wrong. The coolies came to Jugra to work the quarries in 1898, not in 1896 as stated; and malaria had been rapidly increasing for two years before their arrival, as the table printed in the *Study* shows. The coolies did not introduce the disease; they were its victims.

KARIMON ISLAND.

I will now give an instance where the hill land bordered, not on flat land, but on the sea.

At Malarco, on the Great Karimon, one of the Dutch islands of the Archipelago, some 30 miles from Singapore, a company had started a large factory for the treatment of jelutong, a "wild rubber" found in the Malay Archipelago and Peninsula. A first-class factory, with electricity as its motive power, had been erected. A model village had been built, and a pure water supply had been brought in from a reservoir 3 miles away. The village was on a reclamation, with deep water immediately beyond ; and the latrines were over the sea. Everything that could be thought of to improve health had been done, including the clearing of jungle and undergrowth for some acres round the site. Despite everything, the people were "much troubled with a virulent form of malaria." Mr Galbraith, the General Manager in the East, invited me to visit the island, and advise on what should be done to improve health.

This I did on 22nd July 1912. The factory and village were on the end of the island which rises steeply from the sea, as is seen from the photograph. In front of this is a small island, which thus forms a breakwater to Malarco. Through the Strait a steady breeze blew both night and day during my visit. For the general sanitary conditions, I had nothing but praise. " The buildings in which the coolies are housed are of excellent design, of good construction, maintained in good order, and well laid out," was my note on the housing; and other sanitary arrangements were equally well carried out.

There was a coolie population of between 800 and 900.

Evidence of Malaria.—There being practically no native child population, no spleen rate could be obtained. The death rate was also valueless. When ill, many of the Chinese left for Singapore, where indeed a number died in the hospitals; eight are reported to have died in Singapore hospital in January 1912; but many Chinese refuse European treatment, go to friends, and die unknown to the manager of the place they come from. The hospital statistics showed that in 1911 there had been 811 admissions, of which 72 per cent. were for malaria; from 1st January to 20th July 1912, there had been 389 admissions, malaria being 61 per cent. of them.

The Europeans were suffering no less than the Asiatics, and a number had resigned. Of a total of thirteen former residents, I was informed that eleven had suffered from malaria. At the time of my visit, fourteen of the twenty-two had had malaria; some of the others had been only a short time on the island.

There had been five cases of blackwater fever, three of which had been fatal.

The cause of the malaria was *A. maculatus*, which I found breeding in large numbers in every stream and spring on the hillside except two. The more the hillside was cleared of vegetation to stop the malaria, the more extensive became the mosquitoes' breeding area; and the measures taken to reduce malaria were really causing its increase. Accordingly, among my recommendations, I said: "With regard to the clearing of the jungle, I do not recommend this area be extended. Rather I would advise that all mosquito breeding-places in the already cleared area be abolished."

I also advised that the best way "to eradicate these mosquitoes is to put all the water on the hillside underground." The hillside was a mass of granite boulders, some of large size, and others small; and most of it was very steep. "In the steepest portions of the streams, I noticed the water was already finding its way underground among the boulders, and that the water only appeared where the grade was less

FIG. 51.—MALARCO.
Great Karimon Island.

FIG. 54.—AT MALARCO.
The Line of a Buried Stream.

[To face page 182.

steep." Therefore I advised that this natural subsoil drainage be assisted; subsoil pipes being laid down where the water could not be drained in the natural channels. As a warning " In work of this kind, where everything tiny, spring or trickle of water oozing from the hillside is a danger, the first essential is thoroughness. It is also important to remember that new springs may appear in wet weather, if the whole be done in a dry period."

The same energy and thoroughness with which Mr Galbraith had developed the factory, and created a model village, was brought to the anti-mosquito work. Writing on 19th December 1912, Mr Galbraith said :—

" I had hoped to advise you before Christmas that we had sunk all the streams, but the weather has been so wet that we have been forced to suspend work until January. There are nineteen streams altogether to sink, besides a lot of little streamlets coming out of the foot of the hills along the seashore, and a dozen small outlets in the cutting behind the factory. We have cleared and exposed all the streams from end to end where they run on the surface, and have, so far, buried twelve, leaving seven large streams to finish. We have also done most of the work in the cuttings and cleared the seashore springs, and towards the end of January I hope to advise you we have finished.

" The buried streams are holding fairly well notwithstanding the heavy rains (twice as much has fallen as in Singapore), and so far I don't think we have had to repair 500 feet out of about 11,000 buried."

On 31st December he added :—

" I may say that at first some of our pipes were displaced, but this was partly due to insufficient depth and the incidence of heavy rain immediately after placing them, and they were almost perpendicular. We have since used a light mixture of sand and cement to cap all streams whether in pipes or only under rocks (as per sketch on next page), and any recent trouble we have had is due to silt blocking the stream and the water then bursting out; but this in turn was due to the storm water finding an entry higher up, and in time we expect to get over such accidents entirely

" I cannot say the improving health is yet due to the burying of streams—indeed, I do not think it is to any great extent— the number still open in our more or less restricted area is too large to stop breeding yet awhile. By March, however, I hope to show you the hills as dry as bones two days after the heaviest rain."

On 15th March 1913 I visited the island, and found the hills as dry as had been predicted, and the health greatly improved. Doubtless the heavy rains had helped to scour out the anopheles, for they breed most freely in dry weather.

The work had been done splendidly; the photos show how steep the hillside is, and the difficulties that must have been overcome to make the drainage an engineering and anti-mosquito success. The experiment was promising. While there had been difficulties, owing to the steepness of the

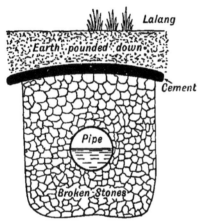

FIG. 52.—Malarco—Subsoil Drain. The Storm Course is divided wherever possible.

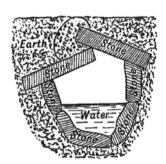

FIG. 53.—Subsoil Channel at Malarco.

hillside, and the complete unfamiliarity with anti-malaria work of those who were responsible for its execution, all the difficulties had been successfully overcome by the splendid energies and intelligent appreciation of the essentials brought to the work by Mr Galbraith, Mr Grant, Mr Day, and others of the staff; and all *A. maculatus* breeding-places had been destroyed. There was in its favour that no danger came from the seaside of the settlement; the jungle-clad hinterland beyond the clearing was steep hill land and probably harmless —for no *A. umbrosus* was taken at my visits. In other words, no dangerous anopheles now existed; or, if present, were so only in small numbers.

So I was hopeful of a great improvement in health by the

end of 1913. But on my return to the East I found that the heavy fall in the price of rubber had practically closed down this jelutong factory, and only some 200 coolies were left. Soon afterwards I heard the factory had been sold, and the place abandoned. Caution must therefore be exercised in accepting an incomplete record; it never was to be completed. Yet for what they are worth, I give the total admissions and total out patients; they eliminate errors of diagnosis, and any anti-malaria success should lead to a reduction of sickness from all causes. They are the last figures I received.

Month.	Labour Force.		Admissions.		Out Patients.	
	1911.	1912.	1911.	1912.	1911.	1912.
July	580	960	27	64	...	693
August	530	860	34	68	...	535
September	600	800	73	41	1761	412
October	760	890	117	33	1647	316
November	850	920	102	34	2348	230
December	690	860	85	22	1540	152

For January and February 1912 and 1913 the figures were :—

Month.	Labour Force.		Admissions.		Out Patients.	
	1912.	1913.	1912.	1913.	1912.	1913.
January	750	800	76	37	1158	249
February	808	840	44	36	751	183

On the day of my visit in 1913 there was only one case of malaria in the hospital out of the whole labour force.

I think the story worth telling, both for the sake of the splendid fight against malaria, and for the guidance it may be to others in similar circumstances. On my last visit one member of the staff, in commenting on the difference in health between the time of speaking and a year before, said: "If ever again I have to do a job in a place like this, I will begin by killing the mosquitoes. The rest of the work will then be quite simple."

CHAPTER XVII

OILING

IN 1901 oiling was employed at Port Swettenham for a few months during the height of the epidemic, and until the new drainage system became effective; then its use was discontinued. On the flat-land estates of the Coastal Plain, malaria was so easily controlled by good drainage that oiling was unnecessary; indeed it would have been impossible to oil the unopened jungle swamps.

The grave problem of persistent malaria in the hill land again raised the question of oiling; but in rapidly running water the prospect of success seemed remote indeed.

" Drainage and eradication of breeding areas is the all-important work in the anti-malaria campaign " was the conclusion reached in Panama; and it confirmed my own views.

During a visit to Panama in 1913, I [22] studied carefully the habits of the anopheles, and the methods of mosquito control. Excellent results were obtained from a mixture of crude mineral oil and a larvacide (the latter a poison made from resin, carbolic acid, and caustic soda), which was used both in pools and streams. The American species of anopheles are, however, different from those of Asia; no Panama species lives in fast-running water like *A. maculatus* or *A. aconitus*. It was, therefore, impossible to be sure that the oiling, which gave good results in Panama would be equally effective in the hill streams of Malaya. Nevertheless, I decided to put aside all preconceived ideas, and investigate the subject *de novo*. If mixtures of mineral oil alone were found, after a careful and thorough trial, to be useless in controlling *A. maculatus* in our ravines, then it seemed me worth going to the expense of manufacturing the larvacide and giving it a trial.

If success was to be obtained, the oil must be got to spread rapidly after spraying, and it must be applied not by drip barrels, but from sprayers which could be carried in the ravines, and from which the oil could be applied to each tiny seepage, spring, and side pool in the ravine, as well as along the edges of the main streams. Ordinary kerosine was too thin; the liquid fuel usually supplied too thick; but by trial, a mixture was obtained that appeared to have the necessary qualities. It now remained to try it on a ravine stream containing *A. maculatus*.

On Sungei Way Estate there is a ravine which I had known to contain *A. maculatus* for many years. It was examined, found to contain the larvæ in large quantity, and then oiled thoroughly. A week later it was free from larvæ; indeed there was a complete absence of all aquatic insect life, even *Chironomus* was dead or absent. On the surface of some of the side pools large numbers of adult insects were found dead; wherever touched by the oil, green vegetation was dead and brown in colour. Mr W. S. Reeve-Tucker, the manager, carried out the oiling with great thoroughness; and on 25th August 1914 I wrote to him :—

"It will be of interest to your Directors to learn that by oiling with the mixture in use on Sungei Way, one of the ravines in the West Division has been kept free from Anopheles for several months. Formerly they bred freely in it. I am encouraged to think that this is not merely due to the physical difficulty the larvæ would have of getting air when oil is on the water, but that some change has actually taken place in the water as a consequence of the oil, and a change which would make it uncongenial to the stream-breeding mosquito. My reason for thinking this is that in the bottom of the ravine a green slime has developed, in the presence of which I have never found dangerous anophelines. It is common enough in flat land.

"The practical point is that it is, in my opinion, additional proof of the value of oiling. And if your Directors decide to oil the ravines, instead of pipe-draining them, they can be satisfied that it will kill out the harmful mosquitoes."

The mixture had been more effective than we had anticipated; no larvacide or other poison had been mixed with the oil; we had got an alternative to subsoil drainage.

Mr Reeve-Tucker was now satisfied of the value of oiling; and placed it under the immediate care of Mr Muir, engineer of the estate, of whose work I cannot speak in too high praise. The result of the oiling was a rapid improvement in the health both of Indians and Europeans.

Death Rates.

Year.	Indian Labour Force.	Death Rate.	Year.	Indian Labour Force.	Death Rate.
1906	400	150	1913	349	63
1907	375	56	1914	381	36
1908	282	223	1915	342	32
1909	260	61	1916	333	20
1910	232	35	1917	305	29
1911	270	121	1918	310	48
1912	320	106	1919	294	26

The oiling on an adjacent estate within the half-mile radius of the Sungei Way lines, has not, until recently, been as efficiently carried out as I desired; otherwise I believe the results would have been better than they are. Yet the health is better than the figures indicate; for not infrequently coolies, who have absconded to unhealthy estates, have returned to Sungei Way to die practically without doing a day's work; for example, in 1919, no fewer than three of the eight deaths were among these "returned bolters."

The manager and his wife have had one attack of malaria since 1913; it was contracted at Morib. His child, aged six and a half years, has not had malaria.

Formerly Mr Muir, his wife, and his two elder children were frequently attacked; one of the children was seriously ill. During the past four years Mr Muir has had one attack of malaria; his wife and three children have been completely free from it. An assistant has been on the estate over three years, another over two years, without being attacked.

Spleen Rates.—These show the improvement that might be expected. In 1906 all the children, thirteen in number, had enlarged spleen; and in 1909, all of four. In 1916 it was fourteen out of thirty-six (38 per cent.); and in 1920 it was seventeen out of sixty, or 28 per cent. An analysis of the 1920 figures is, moreover, of interest. The children are divided into those born on the estate; those from India—small and large; and local recruits.

	Number of Children.	Number with Enlarged Spleen.	Spleen Rates.
Born on Estate	19	1	5
Young children recruited from India	16	3	18
Older children recruited from India .	9	5	55
Local Recruits	16	8	50

In other words, the children with enlarged spleen are mainly the local recruits, who probably brought their spleens to the estate, and the older children, who had been many years on the estate; while few of later arrivals have contracted the disease. Indeed, the children who had been born on the estate were a striking picture of good health, and might well have entered for any baby competition. Eleven children were born in 1919; the only one, who died, did so after going to Malacca.

The success of the mixed oils in controlling *A. maculatus* was so striking that Mr Gilman introduced its use on Rasak Estate and later on Bukit Jelutong Estate; Mr Harrison, on Midlands Estate; Mr Hendrie, on Ebor, S. Neibong, and Tanah Bahru Estates. Now it is widely employed all over the Peninsula, with great advantage to the community.

How Oil Acts.—The action of mineral oil on larvæ is by no means fully understood. The original idea was that, forming a film on the surface of the water, it cut off the larvæ from their air-supply and killed them by suffocation. Another idea is that some oil penetrates their air-tubes, and poisons them directly; while some hold that the oil, or at least some poisonous substances in it, are dissolved in the water, and poison the tissues of the larvæ. Yet another view is that the oil lowers the surface tension of the water, so that larvæ can no longer support themselves at surface.

However the oil acts, anopheles larvæ in this country are highly susceptible to its effects, and die more rapidly after contact with it than any other larvæ.

Apart from any direct action the oil may have on the insect, there is probably an important indirect action. Previously, I mentioned the appearance of a "green slime" on the bottom of the ravine following on the application of the oil. It consists of an alga, the filaments of which are closely "felted" or matted," and attached to the stones or sand forming the bed, of the stream. The filaments are much finer than those of the ordinary alga that one finds in a pool of clear water in a ravine; and the "felting" differs from the "loose floating tangle" of the ordinary alga. When a clear pool containing the ordinary floating alga is "oiled," the alga dies; it becomes a dark green mass, in which the individual filaments are unrecognisable. In its place appears the "felted" alga; and whenever a ravine is thoroughly oiled this alga appears. It is a test by which to know if oiling is properly carried out. Long before I had used oil in ravines I had noticed that the presence of the "felted alga" meant the absence of *A. maculatus*, and I had noticed its association with pollution of the water. For example, on an estate there were four ravines, identical as far as the eye could see. At the head of one there was a well where clothes were washed; that ravine alone contained "felted alga." On no occasion was *A. maculatus* taken in it. In the other three ravines, which were not polluted, and did not contain the "felted alga," the insect flourished. Three bungalows, one on each of these three ravines, were so malarious that they were pulled down; a bungalow on the other ravine was much less malarious, and is still inhabited. This was observed before oiling was used in ravines.

Some ravines are to be found where the "felted alga" is growing freely, although no pollution apparent to the eye takes place, and no oiling has been done. On one occasion I found the "felted alga" in a ravine, and tracked it upwards. The ravine branched, and the alga followed only one branch, in which it could be found as far as a log of a newly-cut timber lying in the water. Beyond that the alga could not be found. I can give no explanation of its appearance; but took possession of a piece of the wood. In ravines where the pollution is extreme, where, for instance, the whole discharge from a rubber factory is poured into a small stream, the aquatic growth will be found to differ in different parts of the stream. Nearest the factory, the growth may consist of dense pendulous fawn-coloured masses, composed of colourless filaments containing no chlorophyl; lower in the ravine this is replaced by the "felted alga."

A full study of the subject[33] is necessary, and may well give us an entirely new method of controlling malaria. It is a part of the subject treated in Chapter XIX., entitled

"On the Possibility of altering the Composition of Water and the Anophelines Breeding in it."

Some Practical Points.—The "Liquid Fuel" used in this country is, I understand, not "crude oil," but a refuse after some of the more volatile oils have been distilled off. Its composition varies greatly. Some consignments, without any admixture with kerosine, can be used in a sprayer, and will give a film which spreads at once on striking the water; other consignments may require the addition of one part of kerosine to eight parts of "Liquid Fuel."

It is best applied through a knapsack sprayer, of which there are several well-known makes, such as the "Four Oaks" and the "Vermorel." The "Four Oaks" is usually supplied with rubber valves, which perish in twenty-four hours after contact with oil; but leather valves are supplied if asked for. In Panama the "Meyer's Sprayer" was considered best. The valves are metal, and give a minimum of trouble. This sprayer has an overhead lever action which is less fatiguing than the side action of some other sprayers; and it has the additional advantage that, by a simple adjustment, the lever may be turned to either side and used by either hand, which gives some relief in the day's work.

The oil is sprayed particularly on to the edge of the streams, and for a foot or two up the banks. This destroys not only larvæ, but all grass and ferns growing on the banks. It saves the costs of weeding these, and the cost is considerable; in addition the brown, discoloured bank shows the oiling has been properly done: the presence of living vegetation indicates lack of oil.

I do not encourage the use of barrels dripping oil on to a stream. Oil so applied fails to reach the side pools springs, and other small but important breeding-places in a ravine. Drip barrels are, by themselves, insufficient, and may lead to a false sense of security; when spraying is properly done, they are unnecessary. I believe there are no drips on the estates under my care.

For each man spraying, two men are employed to carry oil. On a large estate there are usually several depôts to which the drums of oil are carted; this reduces the distance that the coolies have to carry oil to the sprayer.

The cost of oiling an estate varies according to the number

of acres of ravine or swamp in it, the cost of the oil, and the cost of labour. The cost of both oil and labour have increased during the last year; but from $200 to $600 a month is the cost at the present time on different estates.

A Comparison of Subsoil Drainage and Oiling.—Both oiling and subsoil drainage being effective against *A. maculatus* in hill streams, it may be asked which is the better of the two. A simple answer cannot be given; each has certain advantages over the other.

Oiling has two great advantages. The first is that it can be brought into action over a whole estate in a week or less, utterly destroying every anopheles larva in the ravines; and many adult insects that return to their places in the ravines perish also when they alight on the oil. So it comes about that the complete control of mosquitoes on an estate, which is oiled, is rapid, and measured by a period of a few weeks.

The other great advantage is that there is no large capital outlay for oiling, such as is required for subsoil drainage. The cost of oiling is a permanent annual charge, and will not diminish materially, if at all, with the passage of time; but, generally speaking, the weekly, monthly, and annual cost is not heavy when compared with that of subsoil drainage. This is not unimportant, for malaria often causes heavy loss to an estate, and puts it in straightened circumstances.

Subsoil drainage, on the other hand, may involve a heavy capital expenditure. Another disadvantage is that it may take many months to drain the ravines, and during this time the people suffer from malaria, carried by the anopheles breeding in the still undrained ravines. This disadvantage can be overcome by "oiling" the whole estate during the execution of the drainage work.

Drainage has a great advantage over oiling, in that it requires less European supervision. One can see at a glance in walking over a ravine whether or not it is dry; but one cannot check the work of the oiling coolie so easily.

In reality, however, there is no antagonism between drainage and oiling. Oiling should supplement drainage when necessary. In many very steep places on an estate it will be easier to oil than drain; such, for instance, as steep granite slopes. One would choose oil in preference to pipes in a wide ravine full

FIG. 55.—MEYER'S SPRAYER.

FIG. 56.
A well-oiled Ravine, with the sides of the drain free from grass.

[To face page 192.

of good rubber trees. In a narrow ravine one might oil, pipe, or allow jungle to grow up, depending on the particular zone of the country in which the ravine was situated, the amount of silt coming from the hills, and other local circumstances. In all cases, one would begin the control of malaria by oiling ; and oil could be used as a "test solution" to determine the exact area to be drained.

FINALLY, I MUST EMPHASISE, IN THE STRONGEST POSSIBLE MANNER, THE ABSOLUTE NECESSITY OF THE MANAGER, OR ASSISTANT, IN CHARGE OF THE OILING, REGARDING THIS WORK AS NOT SECOND IN IMPORTANCE TO ANY OTHER ON THE ESTATE. THROUGH FAILURE TO DO SO, OILING IS SOMETIMES NEGLECTED, WITH SERIOUS LOSS BOTH OF LABOUR AND OF CROP.

CHAPTER XVIII

IT is impossible, in the space available, to give details of all the hill estates upon which I have been asked to advise, and for which I have suggested health areas. Not all, by any means, have been successful. At the beginning, before I could speak from experience, the area suggested was 20 to 30 chains in radius for pipe drainage. This is not sufficient in most places to eradicate malaria; although it will improve health. It is clear now that in dealing with *A. maculatus*, probably the most efficient carrier of malaria in the Peninsula, and where that mosquito is present in large numbers in much broken hill country, an area of at least 40 chains in radius is required. 'It must either be drained by pipes or oiled.

Another cause of failure was the difficulty some managers evidently had in grasping the right way to lay the pipes, and in learning how to look after the ravines once they were drained. In some places where damage done by storm water was not repaired at once, the whole system became blocked by silt, or it was extensively torn up. The early days had its quantum of scoffers: oiling they sneered at; naturally they took little interest in or care of an engineering system which calls for both intelligence and diligent supervision. Under such, anti-malaria measures made little progress, or were failures.

It was no small disadvantage that after starting a scheme in some distant part of the Peninsula, I could only visit it at long intervals, and so was unable to supplement what was sometimes deficient in the manager.

But ten years have passed since I pointed out the special difficulty of anti-malarial work in hill land; both subsoil drainage and ravine oiling have proved themselves capable of controlling *A. maculatus* and its malaria; each year sees their extended use; indeed, on few malarious estates are anti-malarial measures of some sort not in force; and the result is seen in the general lowering of the death rates of estates throughout Malaya.

In this chapter I propose to give simply the plans of several estates, with, in a few instances, remarks on the reasons which guided the selection of the health area. They may be of use to those called upon to deal with similar conditions.

Glenmarie Estate.—This is one of the oldest estates in

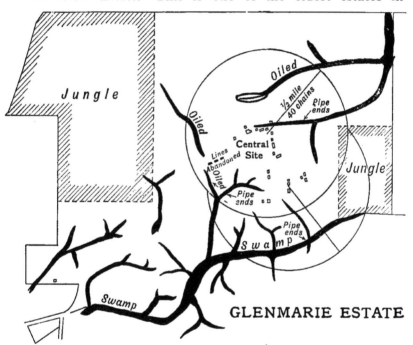

FIG. 57.—Plan of Glenmarie Estate.

the country; it has always been malarious. Indeed, so much did malaria trouble it, that a former proprietor built "Turkish baths" in order to "sweat" fever out of coolies. It was only tried once, as the coolie was brought out dead. The building still remains—as a motor shed.

To improve health, a number of lines were abandoned in 1911, and all were concentrated on a central area. At first some 20 chains were drained by pipes; the work was excellently done by Mr. Solbé. It produced a marked improvement in health, and enabled the estate to establish a force of Malayalees, a tribe of Indians highly susceptible to malaria, and one which cannot live in untreated ravine land. The 20 chain area did not, however, give the required result, so in 1917 the area was extended, partly by piping, partly by oiling ravines. Health still further improved, so that in 1919 the average monthly malaria admission rate was 3 per cent.

The table on page 197 shows the death rates.

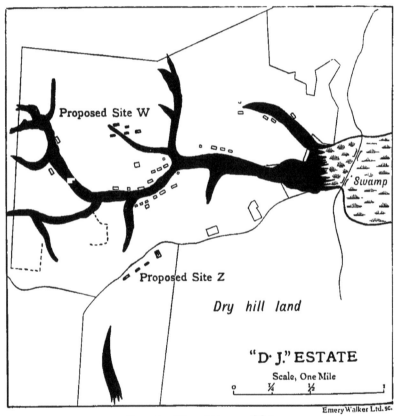

FIG. 58.—Plan of Estate " DJ."

Estate " JM."—The difficulty on this estate was that swampy land, under different ownership, came within the circle. The coolie lines were well built, and I hesitated at the time to condemn them on account of their site. Now I would not hesitate to do so, and would strongly recommend the alternative site proposed.

Estate " JC."—Fig. 60 shows the buildings of the estate widely scattered. The best course would be to concentrate

them about the spot marked "Central Site." The ravines
should be oiled or drained by pipes within the half-mile circle,
and outside the circle at the heads of ravines A, B, and C.
Alternative sites would be found lower down the main ravine.

Year.	Death Rate per mille.	Remarks.
1910	168	
1911	126	Subsoil drainage begun 1911.
1912	103	
1913	51	
1914	59	
1915	51	
1916	40	
1917	65	Area extended.
1918	173	Includes influenza, 47 deaths.
1919	35	

Estate "SC." — The history of this estate "SC" is of
unusual interest. In 1909 I visited it, recommended that the
coolie lines in ravine 4 be abandoned, and selected the site on
the bank of the river, which is heavily polluted by mining silt.

The bank of the river is in places swampy, and there are
numerous abandoned mining holes filled with water. In the
ravine site the mosquito was *A. maculatus*, the most efficient
carrier of malaria in this country; and along the river bank
and in the mining holes the mosquitoes were *A. barbirostris*,
A. sinensis, *A. fuliginosus* var. *nivipes*, and *A. rossi*, which are
poor carriers, if they carry at all. The removal of the lines
led to a great improvement in health; so that in 1913 the
average Indian labour force was 857, no fewer than 816 new
coolies were introduced, yet the death rate was only 18·6 per
mille. This low rate would be impossible with so large a
labour force, if malaria were present to any extent.

The good health continued until August 1914, when malaria
broke out severely; and in January 1915 I again visited the
estate. At this visit, I was unable to determine the cause of
the malaria; but in a subsequent visit in June, *A. maculatus*
was discovered breeding in a branch of ravine 2 coming from
an adjoining estate. The ravines 2 and 3 did not contain
A. maculatus, and were heavily coated with the felted alga *
referred to in the Chapter on Oiling. From 1912, when the
adjoining estate was opened, to 1914, the branch of ravine 2

* This was not due to oiling in this instance; but was a natural growth.

was probably unfit for *A. maculatus* on account of the silt from the clearings; by 1914 the silt decreased, there was less decomposing vegetation, so the water probably became pure enough for *A. maculatus*. Oiling this ravine rapidly improved the health, and it has continued good since.

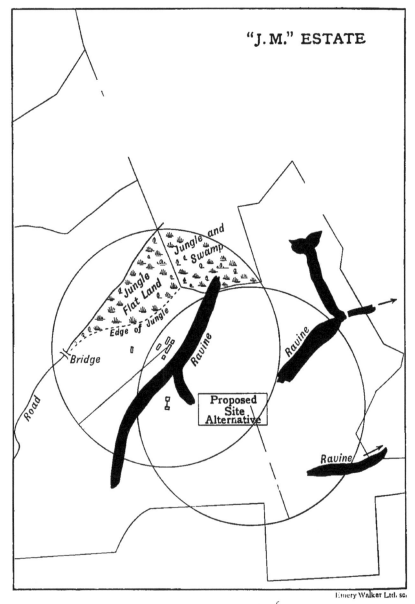

"J. M." ESTATE

Jungle and Swamp

Jungle Flat Land

Edge of Jungle

Bridge

Ravine

Ravine

Road

Proposed Site Alternative

Ravine

Emery Walker Ltd. sc.

FIG. 59.—Plan of Estate "JM."

The following table tells its own tale:—

Year.	Labour Force.	Death Rate.
1913	857	18
1914	561	53
1915	427	74
1916	422	4
1917	512	7
1919	614	11

An examination of forty-one children in 1915 on the river site showed a spleen rate of 43; in 1920 there were 110 children on the same site, with a spleen rate of 5.

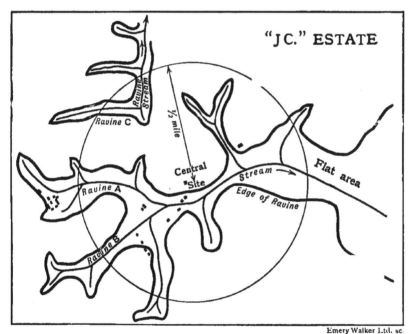

Emery Walker Ltd. sc.

FIG. 60.—Plan of Estate "JC."

A few coolies live in a set of lines in Field XI., on a ravine similar to that from which the labour force was removed in 1909. In 1915 there were twenty-two children, with a spleen rate of 100; in 1920 there were four children, with a spleen rate again of 100. This shows that the ravines in the centre of the estate still remain intensely malarious; in strong contrast to the site on the swamps next the river.

"S.C." ESTATE

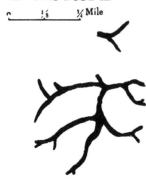

A. aitk

Ravine 3

Ravine 2

NEW
SITE

rbstris-

Pon

Abandoned Mining L

R I

Road

A. fuliginosus

B   Dry land

Emery Walker Ltd. sc.

FIG. 63.—Plan of Estate "SC."

FIG. 61.—ESTATE "SC."

Photograph from point marked "A" on plan looking towards coolie lines, just seen in the distance ; the great mining holes and swampy nature of the site selected are well seen.

FIG. 62.—ESTATE "SC."

Photograph from point marked "B" on the plan. The coolie lines are seen on the flat land. The river runs between the observer and the lines ; one of the numerous abandoned mining holes is seen just across the road. *[To face page* 200.

CHAPTER XIX

ON THE POSSIBILITY OF ALTERING THE COMPOSITION OF WATER AND THE ANOPHELINES BREEDING IN IT

(1920).—This chapter has been reprinted as it appeared in the previous edition, except for some minor alterations in composition and changes in the names of mosquitoes to those now generally in use.

(1909).—It has long been established that mosquitoes, including the anophelines, exercise discrimination in the selection of water in which their larval stage is passed. Each species prefers its own special type or character and quality of water as a breeding-place. Some have a wide range, others are peculiarly selective. *A. maculatus* is one of the latter. In Malaya it is found exclusively in hill streams, and in the springs which feed these. I consider that the eggs are laid in, and that the larvæ prefer, the shallowest waters; indeed they are most numerous in ground with so little water on it that, in order to take the larvæ, it is often necessary to make an excavation in the earth into which the water from the surrounding ground flows, carrying the larvæ with it. As these springs are very common at the head of a ravine, the presence of this mosquito in them probably accounts for the well-recognised danger of living at the head of a ravine. The old explanation for this was that mists were carried up the ravine, and naturally struck with special force those living at its head.

From these springs the larvæ are carried down the streams; but they cannot be entirely washed out, even by the strongest currents or rains. I have found them in a drain after a 2-inch shower. When one attempts to take them they often wriggle completely out of the water on to the damp ground. I have watched them at play in a clear pool at the foot of a rock, down which water was flowing with considerable force, since the rock sloped to the pool at an angle of 45° and its face was a foot long. The current of water was still further increased in strength by the rock being funnel-shaped, and all the water coming down the face was gathered into a solid stream as it entered the pool. The larvæ were playing, not exactly like trout, head to stream, but were floating round in the current, and every now and then one would swim right into the stream, up it for a short distance, and then hang on to the side of the apparently bare rock in the full strength of the current.*

As *A. maculatus* is never found on the flat land, it is obvious that this mosquito requires water of a special character; such as water well aerated and quite free from vegetable decomposition.

In May 1909, having accepted an invitation from the late Mr C. Malcolm Cumming, Chairman of the Planters' Association of Malaya, to visit a Tamil settlement which he had successfully established, I motored into Negri Sembilan and saw the padi swamps, rice-fields, or sawahs† there. These consist of valleys, the whole bottom of which have been rendered flat, so that they can be irrigated by the waters coming down the valleys. They seemed to me ideal breeding-places for anophelines, and I asked if they were unhealthy. I was assured that the inhabitants were extremely healthy, and that malaria was unknown. It occurred to me then that the process of padi cultivation must alter the composition of the waters in some way, so that what I should regard as the normal inhabitant of the valley stream, namely *A. maculatus*, had been driven out.

The following day, when passing an estate, Mr Cumming informed me that the estate had been healthy until Tamils had been introduced, and since then had been extremely unhealthy. I remarked that the valley through which we were passing was very swampy, and he then told me that it originally had been sawah, but that the Malays now were employed on the estate, where they got better wages.

It appeared to me that if there was any truth in the statement that sawahs were healthy, then the abandonment of the sawah, and not the introduction of the Tamil coolie, was responsible for the outbreak of malaria on the estate. The idea was that by abandoning the sawah, the *A. maculatus* had been enabled to return to the valley. It was obvious, too,

---

* Dr Lamborn is publishing an interesting paper on the hooked caudal hairs of larvæ.

† "Padi" and "sawah" are Malay words, meaning rice and rice-field respectively.

FIG. 64.—KRIAN IRRIGATION.
A Main Channel.

FIG. 65.—KRIAN IRRIGATION.
Showing the grassy sides of a subsidiary drain and the flooded, yet healthy, land.

[*To face page* 202.

that it might be a method of treating ravines on rubber estates where the drainage was difficult, or where weeding was so expensive that it might be an economy to abandon the ravine, if this could be done without impairing the health of the labour force on the estate.   The matter appeared to be of importance economically, and called for investigation.

I therefore spent that night on the edge of a sawah.   In the evening three anophelines were taken—one *A. fuliginosus*, one *A. sinensis*, and one *A. rossii*.   Under ordinary circumstances, I should have expected to find at least one *A. maculatus*.   I learned that this sawah was considered healthy.   In the morning I examined fifty Malay children at Kampong Batu Malay School, of whom twenty (or 40 per cent.) had enlarged spleens.

So far these results appeared to bear out my conjecture, but I had no opportunity of further investigation until August, when I went to the Krian Irrigation Padi Fields, and also to those at Bukit Gantang.   I was only able to spend a week on the work at that time, and was unable to return to finish it until November.

The investigation consisted of an examination of the children and of the species of anophelines breeding in the waters, and found in the houses in the two places.   Although both were padi swamps, the most extraordinary difference in the health of the two places was discovered, and a difference in the species of anophelines was also found.

Krian Irrigation Padi Fields. — This irrigation scheme, carried out at the cost of about $1\frac{1}{2}$ million dollars, was completed in 1906, and was at once a financial success.   It enabled the people to reap a good crop in a dry year, when their neighbours, outside the irrigation area, were suffering from want of water.   The area irrigated is about 60,000 acres.

The water-supply is from two rivers, the Sungei Merah and the Sungei Kurau, which are dammed at a pass in the hills, so that by overflowing their banks they spread over ten square miles of jungle.   The effect of the constant water on the jungle has been to kill it out slowly, and in passing along the railway, which crosses the reservoir, one sees comparatively few of the larger trees now alive, while many dead ones are still standing.

These rivers have already traversed considerable distances before they reach the impounding reservoir, but the waters of both have originally come from the hills.

From the impounding reservoir the water is led by the usual

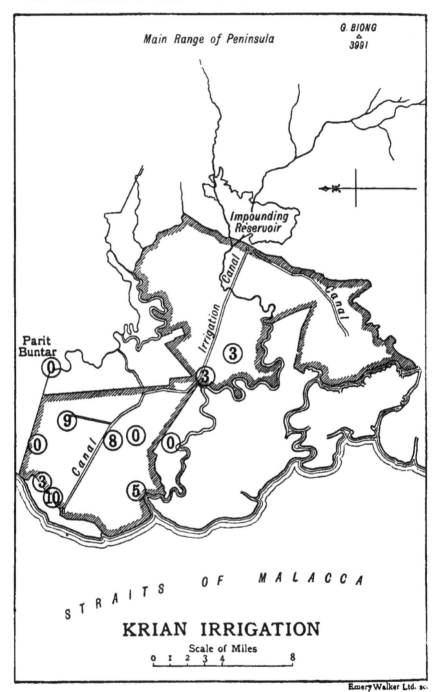

FIG. 66.—Krian Irrigation Map.

canals, and after flowing over the land is led off by drains to
the nearest rivers as will be seen from the map.

Health of Children.—During my two visits I examined
304 Malay or Tamil school children and 47 estate Tamil
children; and the late Dr Delmege, the Government Medical
Officer, kindly furnished me with the figures of 367 school
children whom he examined. Out of the total 718 examined,
only 20 (or 2·7 per cent.) had enlarged spleen.

The details of the examinations are as follows:—

Observer.	Place.	Number Examined.	Number Enlarged.	Per cent. Enlarged.
Dr Delmege	P. Buntar—			
	Malay boys .			0·0
	„ girls .			0·0
	English, mixed .			0·0
	Sungei Star .			0·0
	„			0·0
	Sungei M. Aris			3·3
	„ Labu			10·0
	Titi Serong			8·7
	Jalan Bharu			7·6
Dr Watson	Bagan Serai—			
	Malays .	66	3	4·5
	Tamils .	34	0	0·0
	Telok Maiden	71	2	2·7
	Jin Heng Estate—			
	Tamils .	47	0	0·0
	Sungei Siakap	65	3	4·6
	„ Bharu	68	0	0·0
	Grand total . .	718	20	2·7

A reference to the map will show that these examinations
cover practically the whole district, and can be considered
quite representative of it. They show conclusively that this
irrigation area is to a striking degree free from malaria. This
is the general idea, and Dr Delmege writes me as follows:—
" I quite agree with you that there is very little, if any, malaria
contracted in the padi fields."

The Anophelines of Krian Irrigation.—The anophelines of
the Krian District were found to be—

A. rossii,	A. sinensis,
A. kochii,	A. barbirostris.

The two last-named mosquitoes are found breeding freely in the
irrigation channels and in the padi-fields. They are also found
in the houses, where they feed freely on the inhabitants.

The low percentage of infected children in a place in which adult anophelines are so abundant is strong evidence that these species do not carry malaria; or, if they do, they act as extremely inefficient hosts for the parasite. The fact that the percentage of children with enlarged spleens is practically the same as in Klang, and on the healthy estates, where a history was obtained of the affected children, mostly immigrants, who had suffered from malaria before their arrival, makes it extremely probable that the affected children in the Krian District had contracted their malaria outside its limits.

I was unable to make any investigations into the health of the children on the estates in the Krian District beyond that of the one mentioned, which was on the opposite side of a road from the irrigation area, and where the spleen rate of the forty-seven children was found to be *nil.* An examination, however, of the death rates of the estates on the flat land of Krian is so low that malaria can hardly be a serious consequence. One estate, however, which is shown to be on the edge of a Government forest reserve has a death rate of 100, evidence that malaria is to be found near to the jungle in Krian as in Klang, and that opening of the land gives freedom from malaria there also.

Bukit Gantang Valley Rice-fields.—About 10 miles southeast of the Krian Fields the main range of the Peninsula is cleft by a valley leading to what is locally known as the Bukit Gantang Pass. (Bukit in Malay means a hill or mountain). The valley runs in some 5 miles, and its mouth, 2 miles wide, has Chankat Jering and Bukit Tebok on the north and south sides respectively. From side to side, from end to end, the valley is a sea of padi, in which are studded Malay kampongs, like the "islands" of an archipelago. There is a considerable Malay population among the hills and on the "islands."

An examination of the children living at the foot of the hills showed that they were suffering severely from malaria.

In thinking over the idea of excluding certain species by altering the composition of the water, it occurred to me, that, if an experiment were to be carried out, it would be best to avoid housing the coolies near the foot of the hills and sides of the ravines. Where *A. maculatus* were most likely to breed, would be the places to avoid in housing the coolies; and if an

FIG. 67.—BUKIT GANTANG VALLEY.

The photograph shows the *padi* (rice) fields in the foreground and Malay houses along the foot of the hill on the left. On the right the valley widens out, and the small clump of trees is the beginning of the series of kampongs which I have likened to " Islands " in a sea of *padi*.

[*To face page* 206.

island in the middle of the padi could be made, there the coolies would enjoy the best health.

Having ascertained that the children on the edge of the hills were very unhealthy, I at once realised that in this valley the conditions of the experiment I had thought of were actually to be found on the most magnificent scale. The valley being 2 miles wide, the possibility of mosquitoes flying from the sides to the centre of it in such numbers as to carry malaria was excluded. It remained, therefore, to ascertain the percentage of children infected on both sides of the valley and in the centre, and to determine the species of the anophelines. Starting at Chankat Jering the Malay schools were examined.

At Chankat Jering fifty-one children were examined, of whom twenty-two (or 43 per cent.) had enlarged spleens. Two miles farther up towards the Pass, Jelutong school was examined. Of the thirty-nine children, seventeen (or 43 per cent.) had enlarged spleens, and several others had fever at the time of the examination without having enlargement of the spleen.

Still nearer the Pass, Bukit Gantang school was found to contain fifty children, of whom twenty-five (or 50 per cent.) had enlarged spleens.

Thus out of 140 children living at the foot of the hills and on the edge of the padi, no fewer than sixty-four (or 45·7 per cent.) had enlarged spleen, strong evidence of the prevalence of malaria. While at Simpang, 2 miles from Chankat Jering, out of thirty-three children examined at the school only three (or 9·9 per cent.) had enlarged spleens, showing that as we passed from the hills malaria was less severe. I next examined the Bendang Siam school in the middle of the valley on the road running south towards Bukit Tebok. On this road, in the 2 miles where it runs through the padi swamps, there are no fewer than ten bridges, each indicating a small stream running down the valley. In the school of thirty-one children, nineteen (or 61 per cent.) had enlarged spleens. There were sixty-two on the register, but, as examination was made at the time of the fruit season, the attendance at the school was then about sixteen daily, and three visits had to be paid before the thirty-one children were obtained for examination. In order to broaden the basis of the observation, and at the same time to obviate error due to the attendance of children from the south side of the valley, I examined fifty children in the houses of the "Islands." I was accompanied and assisted in this by Dr Bryce Orme of Taiping, and we spent the best part of a day in going through the valley, which consisted of patches of dry land and of padi swamp irregularly mixed together. On the dry patches the Malay plants his house and his trees, and in the swamp grows his padi. Of the fifty children in the "Islands," eleven, or 22 per cent., had enlarged spleens. Only one case of fever was found among the fifty children, and the inhabitants insisted that fever did not trouble them. The children found in the houses were mostly younger than those at school. It was thus obvious that both at the sides and in the centre of the valley malaria was present in serious amount among the children; but that the adults, presumably from having had the disease during childhood, were now immune, and consequently regarded the locality as healthy.

Apart from the evidence of the children, the history of the making of the railway, which runs over the pass, was one of severe malaria, especially at Ayer Kuning and Bukit Gantang, where large cuttings had been made.

I may remark here that the spleen rates of Malay children in their kampongs is not comparable with that of Tamil immigrants on an estate, since among the latter the non-immune new arrivals of all ages up to ten form a larger proportion of the total population than do the new born of the Malays. While a number of the Malays in the higher ages will already have acquired immunity, and lost the enlargement of the spleen, the Tamils, at all ages, will still be suffering from the disease.

Places newly populated by an immigrant coolie population showing a spleen rate of 100 may really differ considerably in the amount of malaria present.

Anophelines of Bukit Gantang Valley.—During the four days (16th to 19th November, 1909), twenty-six adult anophelines were taken in the houses of the "Islands," or Kampong Paya and Bendang Siam, as the places are locally known. They were the following:—

A. rosii	10
A. aconitus	6
A. barbirostris } A. sinensis }	9
A. umbrosus	1
	26

The larvæ of these mosquitoes were found breeding as follows:—Enormous numbers of *A. barbirostris* and *A. sinensis* were in the padi-fields. *A. rossii* were in pools near to the houses. *A. aconitus* was found breeding in a stream running through the padi swamps and in swampy grass through which

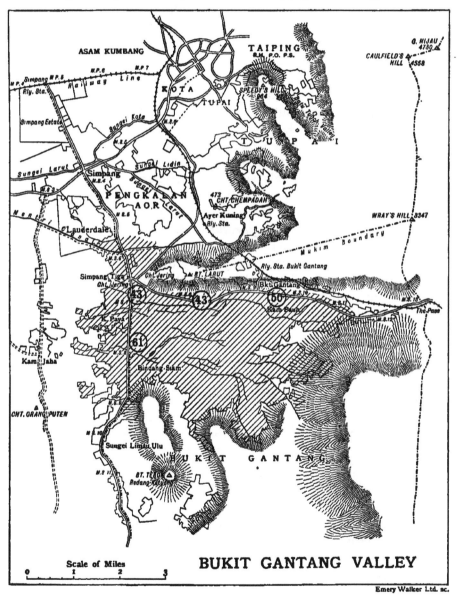

FIG. 68.—Map of Bukit Gantang Valley.

water was flowing slowly.   Larvæ of *A. umbrosus* were not found.

In addition, one specimen of *A. fuliginosus* was hatched from a padi swamp about a mile in from the road.

In a set of coolie lines at Ayer Kuning, on the Chankat Jering side of the valley, three adult *A. maculatus* were caught in a few minutes.   At Bukit Gantang village fifteen adults were taken in houses, of which fourteen were *A. rossii* or *A. sinensis* and one *A. aconitus*.   In a stream flowing down from the railway at Bukit Gantang numerous larvæ with simple unbranched frontal hairs were found in a backwater. These failed to hatch out.

On the Bukit Tebok side of the valley in a house at the 11th mile two adults were taken, one of which was *A. barbirostris* and the other *A. fuliginosus*.   Larvæ were taken in a spring at the edge of a swamp near this, with the characters of *A. maculatus,* but they failed to hatch out.   While in a ravine running towards Bukit Tebok, numerous larvæ belonging to the Myzorhyncus group, possibly either *M. separatus* or *M. umbrosus*, were found among the swampy grass.   They, however, suffered, as did the other larvæ, from the 200-mile journey to Klang, and failed to hatch out.   A few miles further down this road, in the lines of a very unhealthy estate, ten *A. maculatus* were taken in half an hour.   The estate is traversed by hill-streams.

Table comparing the Anophelines taken at Bukit Gantang Valley and at Krian.

At the foot of the Hills forming Bukit Gantang Valley.	In the Rice Fields of Bukit Gantang Valley, "the Islands."	In Krian Irrigation Area.
Much Malaria.	Much Malaria.	No Malaria.
A. maculatus. A. aconitus. A. fuliginosus. A. umbrosus. A. barbirostris. A. sinensis. A. kochii. A. rossii.	... A. aconitus. A. fuliginosus. A. umbrosus. A. barbirostris. A. sinensis. A. kochii. A. rossii.	... A. barbirostris. A. sinensis. A. kochii. A. rossii.

Reviewing these facts, we may conclude that in the hill ravines and springs of Ayer Kuning and of the main range generally *A. maculatus* is acting as an efficient carrier of malaria, but the entire failure to take it in the "Islands," when it was so easily taken at the sides of the valley, warrants the conclusion that it does not spread far from the hills, and does not breed in the padi swamps. It is, however, evident that some of the other anophelines found there are carriers of malaria. *A. rossii* and *A. barbirostris* and *A. sinensis* can be excluded, since their presence in Krian caused no malaria. Suspicion must, therefore, rest on the other three, namely, *A. umbrosus*, *A. fuliginosus* and *A. aconitus.** The first of these is the great carrier of the flat, undrained jungle-land in Klang. It is easily seen and captured, as it is a large mosquito. As only one was taken, it is probably not the important carrier at Bukit Gantang rice-fields. *A. fuliginosus* is closely related to *A. maculatus*, and *A. aconitus* is one of the small black-legged Myzomia group to which *A. funesta* (the African carrier) and *A. culicifacies* (the India carrier) belong. The time at my disposal did not permit me to complete the investigation of this point.

Conclusions from the Observations of the Krian and Bukit Gantang Irrigation Padi-fields.—Incomplete though they be, the investigations have established certain important points. These are :—

(1) That the conversion of ravines into ordinary sawahs would not improve the health of a rubber estate.

(2) That these sawahs or padi swamps at the foot of hills or in ravines are extremely malarious, and that, although the adults appear to enjoy good health, the immunity from malaria which they possess has been acquired through their having suffered from malaria when children.

(3) That the estate in Negri Sembilan, which was supposed to become unhealthy on the introduction of the Tamil coolies, had always been unhealthy; and the adult Tamils had only suffered in the same way as the children of the Malays and other newcomers did.

(4) That vast areas may be put under wet padi or irrigated

* Dr A. T. Stanton has since then proved *A. aconitus* to be a natural carrier of malaria. It is probably the chief carrier in the rice-fields in valleys in the Peninsula.

land without causing malaria was seen from Krian.

(5) That padi land at the foot of hills irrigated by the water from the hills is very malarious.

(6) That different groups of anophelines are found in (*a*) the water of hill-streams; (*b*) the water close to the foot of the hills; (*c*) the water at some distance from the hills.

(7) That on the difference of species of these anophelines depends the presence or absence of malaria.

It is not my purpose to record speculation here, but rather facts regarding malaria which have come to my notice during the past nine years. I cannot, however, pass from this subject without pointing out the great hope which these observations raise of dealing with malaria on new lines.

Hitherto the attitude towards the malaria of rice-fields, and all rice-fields were supposed to be malarious, has been that rice and malaria are inseparably connected. Rice, being the staple food of many millions in the tropics, must be grown. The choice appeared to be starvation or malaria; this is of course really no choice, since people must always run the risk of disease rather than starve.

The only attempts to destroy malaria where it was impossible to remove the breeding-place entirely by destruction of the larvæ, have been by the use of petroleum and by the use of certain poisons put into the water. The Italians favour an aniline dye.

The cost of such applications, on the very large scale which would be required for rice-fields, prohibit their use.

Very powerful larvicides are infusion of tobacco leaves, and the powdered flowers of the Dalmatian chrysanthemum. But here again expense prohibits their use. Daniels experimented with the tuba root—*Derris eliptica*—but even if it could be applied on a very extensive scale, it is doubtful if it is not too comprehensive a poison, since it poisons fish, and as Daniels[28] says, "few forms of animal life are unaffected." Such wholesale poisoning would probably interfere with the equilibrium of life in the padi-fields and produce consequences of an unwished-for character.

But in Krian we have seen that nature has carried out in

FIG. 69.
A Rice-field in the coastal plain, near Malacca, not cultivated—not malarial.

FIG. 70.
A Rice-field in the coastal plain, near Malacca, under cultivation—not malarial.

[To face page 212.

the most successful way a method of altering the composition of the waters of the hills that the carriers of malaria no longer find it suitable for their existence, and malaria practically does not exist. I can imagine few greater benefits which the F.M.S. Government could confer on the Malay inhabitants than the discovery of the alteration which has occurred in the water, and its application to the numerous padi-fields of the Peninsula. It is not inconceivable that an industry might be found which required the maceration of a fibre, which, while changing the composition of the waters, might also provide the inhabitants with work. The culture of flax and hemp in Italy supplies a line upon which to work. A very large Malay population lives on the padi-fields of Perak, Negri Sembilan, and Pahang, who are now suffering from malaria in a severe form, unrecognised, it is true, since the children are the chief sufferers. This malaria must, in the course of generations, have left its stamp on the race, and possibly is responsible for the indolence of the Malay. Perhaps the Malay would become a less likeable character were he to acquire the energy of his Chinese competitor.

In the past the struggle was perhaps no uneven one; for what the Malay lacked in energy and capacity for constant work, he made up for by force of arms. In a sense, peace has disarmed but one of the competitors; and in the struggle for existence the Malay has now, unaided by the weapons of the past, to face an alien foe full of the energy and strength of the colder North.

If he is to survive in the struggle, it is essential that every obstacle be removed, and I can imagine no greater than malaria. Nor can I imagine how the West can more gloriously crown the benefits which it has heaped on the Malay in the past, than by the overthrow of the pestilence which saps the springs of his childhood life, and stamps the happy years of youth with pain and death.

The Effect of Drainage on Different Species of Anophelines.—Now from the observation of species in Malaya and their behaviour to drainage, I would suggest it would be of practical importance to classify the anophelines of each country according to such behaviour.

We have seen that *A. umbrosus* is only to be found in a pool without a current, while a current of water means its destruction and disappearance. It can, however, breed in very weedy and obstructed ravine streams, as there the current is practically *nil*.

A. karwari, on the other hand, is a pool-breeder, which prefers a gentle stream of fresh water flowing through its pool. Such pools are commonly found in the springs at the foot of a hill, and this I consider is the normal habitat of *A. karwari*. A ravine stream, if much obstructed by weeds, has so little current that it closely simulates the normal habitat of *A. karwari*, and so we find this mosquito in weedy ravines. Remove the grass and the mosquito disappears. There is then too much current for it.

A. maculatus appears to prefer clear running water. There may be weeds, but they must not too seriously interfere with the free current of water. When disturbed it can leave the water, and it has powers of attaching itself to objects not possessed by pool-breeding larvæ. These habits it doubtlessly has acquired; and it is perhaps due to evolution that the species of anophelines (both Myzomyia and Nyssorhyncus), which breed in streams, are generally smaller than the pool-breeders, since thereby they offer less surface to the current. We have seen that, since this mosquito prefers a current of water, an open drain is its normal habitat, and open drainage fails to eliminate it and the malaria it carries. Open drainage can only eradicate malaria carried by pool-breeders. Therefore in Malaya, whether a hill stream be clean weeded or grassy, malaria remains, only the species of anophelines carrying it differs.

A. rossii is at the opposite end of the scale from *A. maculatus*, and is a puddle-breeder. Since it is always found near to human habitations, the presumption is, it prefers pools soiled to some extent by human sewage. (*Culex fatigans* can breed in pure sewage, such as is found under a Malay house). On some estates, both on the hill and the flat land, this mosquito cannot be found. It, therefore, does disappear with thorough open drainage, although common enough in Klang town.

We have thus a series of waters differing in quality and rate of current. Each water has its peculiar mosquito inhabitants, which have a limited range of waters in which they can breed.

The Breeding-Places of some common Malayan Anophelines and the Effect of Drainage.

Breeding-Place.	Condition.	Mosquito.	Carrier in Nature.	Effect of Weeding and Drainage on	Effect of Drainage on Malaria.	Remarks.
Hill-stream	Free from grass	A. maculatus	Yes	Nil	Nil	
	Grassy	A. maculatus	"	"	—	Because A. maculatus remains.
	"	A. karwari	"	Disappears	"	
	Choked with grass	A. umbrosus	"	"	"	Because A. umbrosus, which had been driven out, reappears.
Springs and iH-foot swamps	Grassy	A. karwari	Yes	Disappears	Disappears	Upkeep of drainage does not require to be very perfect.
		A. umbrosus	..	...	...	
		A. fuliginosus	?	"	...	Upkeep must be perfect to eliminate these
		A. kochii	No	"	...	
		A. barbirostris	"	"	...	
		A. ; ...	"	"	...	
Pools not ...	Grassy	A. kochii	No	Disappears	...	Surface drain perfect to
		A. barbirostris	"	"	...	
		A. sinensis	"	"	...	Fortunately they do not carry malaria.
		A. separatus	"	"	...	
		A. rossii	"	,	...	
Pool	Polluted	A. rossii	No	Disappears	...	As above.

Note, fuliginosus is not an important carrier of malaria, if it carries at all.

On whether the mosquito carries malaria or not, and on the ease or difficulty of eliminating the insect by drainage, depend the amount of malaria in a country, and the ease or difficulty of combating it.

We see that in Malayan hill land, as long as there is an open system of drainage, malaria must remain, and in these hill lands malaria is as intense as anywhere in Africa.

On the other hand, by good fortune, *A. rossii*—which only perfect surface drainage can abolish—does not carry malaria; and hence, as Daniels points out, Malayan towns do not suffer from malaria so much as African towns, where *A. costalis*, a mosquito with breeding habits similar to *A. rossii*, carries the disease. Consequently, although *A. costalis* can be destroyed by open drainage, to eradicate malaria in Africa would require a more thorough drainage and upkeep of drainage, than is necessary on the flat land of Malaya,* where mosquitoes like *A. karwari* and *A. umbrosus* are the carriers.

Finally, I would urge that our knowledge of the prevention of malaria would be materially advanced if more attention were paid to the places where malaria does not exist. A truer idea of the part played by anophelines will thereby be obtained, and a less pessimistic view be taken than is often the case.

---

* 1920.—*A. ludlowi* is a carrier of malaria in the flat land of the Malay Peninsula and elsewhere in Asia. It has been shown, however, that the thorough open drainage required to eliminate it is well within the range of practical sanitation ; so there is apparently no reason why malaria carried by *A. costalis* could not be controlled ; or if malaria were carried by *A. rossii* in Malaya, why it also could not be controlled.

CHAPTER XX

THE INLAND HILLS

The Need for Research.—The more I thought of the observations recorded in the last chapter, the more necessary it seemed there should be a thorough exploration of the habits and breeding-places of the anophelines; for it was likely that out of such research important methods of controlling mosquitoes and malaria would be evolved. The subject was fascinating; and in a public lecture,[24] given in Kuala Lumpur in 1910, I outlined my hopes:—

"But when we came to work out the anophelines, it was found that different species were found in the middle of the swamp from those on the hills. Nature has, therefore, carried out a great experiment. There were three groups of anophelines: one on the hills, one in the rice-fields close to the hills, and a third lot in Krian far from the hills. Now, why do these vary? Clearly on account of something in the water, and it can easily be imagined that only a small change would bring the Bukit Gantang water to that of the Krian rice-fields, and then malaria would disappear from Bukit Gantang too. I believe that in this way a great anti-malaria method will be evolved, and I can look to the time when we will be able to play with species of anophelines, say to some "go," and to others "come," and abolish malaria with great ease, perhaps, at hardly any expense. Drainage schemes may become methods of the past, and future generations may smile to think of how their ancestors, who thought they were so clever, burned the house to cook the pig."

At all times I was eagerly looking for facts that would not fit in with my theories of malaria in hill and flat land; for exceptions either prove the rule, or throw new light on the whole subject. Above all, I sought a healthy town, village, or estate among the hills.

The last chapter concluded with this remark:—

"Finally, I would urge that our knowledge of the prevention

of malaria would be materially advanced if more attention were paid to places where malaria does not exist. A truer idea of the part played by anophelines will thereby be obtained, and a less pessimistic view of the prevention of malaria will be taken than is often the case."

These two lines of thought dominated my researches in the following years. From 1909 onwards I was alert to discover some place among the hills from which malaria was absent, or even less in amount than would be expected ; for the discovery of a healthy town or village among the hills would at once give a solution of the problem. Although I found, on several occasions, swampy valleys in the hills with comparatively little malaria, I could not discover any place completely free from the disease. The significance of what had happened in Kuala Lumpur in 1906 and 1907, and of the observations of Mr Pratt, Dr Fletcher, and Dr Wellington, I had failed to realise. (See Chapter XXVI.).

It was not, indeed, until Dr C. Strickland had been some time engaged in his research, and visited parts of the Peninsula to which I had never been, that he found the long-sought-for " happy valley."

In May 1912, Dr Strickland arrived in the F.M.S. to take up malaria research, and more particularly to study the biology of the anopheles in relation to malaria. With pleasure, I showed him all that I thought could help him, and we discussed the lines of research indicated above.

In a memorandum to Government I suggested the following as his course of study :—

" (1) Healthy, flat land (coastal belt) ; (2) healthy, wet land (Krian rice-fields) ; and (3) then working up from the coast into the valleys of Negri Sembilan, from what I believe healthy into what is unhealthy. There is much to be learned here, I am sure, for the undrained swamps in valleys are certainly in many places healthier than those that are clean-weeded. Why this should be is clearly an important question? . . . The above seems to me the main line of research he. should pursue."

More and more I had become convinced of the danger of opening ravines in hill land, and in 1913 wrote what represented my ideas at the moment :—

" There is no doubt that an ordinary jungle-covered ravine —harmful though it undoubtedly is—is less harmful than a well-drained swamp which breeds the mosquito *N. willmori* (*A. maculatus*). In the opening of an estate many changes occur in an undrained ravine, one of which—the filling of the ravine with silt from the clearings—is prejudicial to dangerous mosquitoes. Whereas the drainage of a ravine by open drainage is favourable to the more dangerous mosquitoes. I have no doubt that this is the explanation of many severe outbreaks of malaria which are reported as following the drainage of such ravines. In other words it is the real explanation of what used to be explained by 'turning up the soil.' I do not pretend to know all about these swamps yet, but it is certainly best to leave them alone, neither to drain nor fell the jungle, until sub-soil drainage is to be undertaken."

After my experience of the prevalence and danger of *A. umbrosus* in jungle, both in the coastal plain and coastal hills, it is not surprising, perhaps, that I was slow to conceive of the possibility of some jungle-covered ravines farther inland being free from *A. umbrosus*, and so free from malaria. Yet this was to prove the case; and although I had realised the advantage of leaving a ravine under jungle unless subsoil drained when opened, I had not observed the cause for it among the more inland hills.

It was not until 1915 that Dr Strickland told me he had discovered not only a town in the hills which was free from malaria, but also the fact that *A. umbrosus* was not found in much of the hill land of the Peninsula; that it was confined largely to the coastal plains and coastal hills; and that in the jungle covered ravines of the inland hills it was represented only by an occasional *umbrosus*-like larva.

Observations in Kuala Lipis and the Pahang Railway Construction.—These discoveries were of the highest importance; and accompanied by Dr Strickland I crossed the main range of hills to where a railway was being made through virgin jungle. From Tembeling to Kuala Lipis we searched the houses occupied by the construction coolies for adult mosquitoes, and examined numerous swamps and ravines for larvæ. Where the sun was on the stream we often got *A. maculatus;* in the shade *A. aitkeni; A. barbirostris, sinensis, kochii,* and *rossii* were abundant; but never an *A. umbrosus*, either adult or larva.

We then visited the town of Kuala Lipis, which is situated on a promontory at the junction of two considerable rivers.

Everywhere it was surrounded by virgin jungle; its ravines were still almost entirely covered by jungle.

On 7th August 1915, I made a house-to-house visit in the town ; forty children were examined, and only two were found with enlarged spleen. One of the two had arrived in Kuala Lipis from Ulu Jelei only two days before ; the other was two months from Raub—a notoriously malarial spot.

In the Malay school at Kuala Lipis seven children out of seventeen had enlarged spleen ; but enquiry showed only two of the children had been born in the town, the others having come from Raub (one year before), Kuala Medan (two years), Bentong (one year), Bandjar (four years), Pulau Tawa (two years).

In the ravines of Kuala Lipis, only one *umbrosus*-like larva was found.

Since then, I have often discussed the health of Kuala Lipis with people who lived there before the railway came to it. They are unanimous not only in witnessing to its freedom from malaria, but to its freedom from all mosquitoes. So free was it from these pests that people usually slept without mosquito nets, which is not done by Europeans elsewhere in this country that I have heard of.

In travelling along the construction work of the railway, we had found the spleen rates were lower the more the place was closed in by virgin jungle, and the more permanent the class of people examined.

For example, my notes record : " A summary of all living in Tembeling at the time shows that, out of ninety-seven, twenty-one had enlarged spleen; but of the most permanent part of the population, viz., those connected with the workshop and the children in the *kongsis* (workmen's houses), most of whom had been two years and three months in Tembeling, only three out of thirty-six had enlarged spleens, a remarkably low rate when we consider that the cleared area of the town probably does not exceed ten acres, and that it is entirely surrounded by virgin jungle." In contrast to this—

" *Tembeling Estate.*—We found that, among twenty-two Tamil adults on Tembeling Estate, eighteen had enlarged spleens, and of the eight Tamil children, all had enlarged spleens."

Again, " Krambit, like Tembeling, is shut in by virgin

FIG. 71.—THE RIVER AT KUALA LIPIS PAHANG.

FIG. 72.—COOLIE LINES FOR RAILWAY CONSTRUCTION IN PAHANG JUNGLE.
No *Anopheles umbrosus* found.

[To face page 220

jungle, except that towards the west a portion of the land is covered by lalang, intersected by ravines, shaded by secondary growth." Here we found six children, none of whom had an enlarged spleen.

Observations on the Railway Construction at Batu Arang in Selangor.—In view of the absence of *A. umbrosus* from the part of the State of Pahang which we had just visited, I considered it would be of interest to visit some railway construction then being undertaken in the coastal hills of Selangor, where I expected to find *A. umbrosus.* In this we were not disappointed, as the following catches of adults show; only a few minutes were spent in each house.

		Other Anopheles.
12/9/15	Station-master's room	
	Rest house . . .	
	Chinese house	1 *maculatus*
	Clerk's house .	
13/9/15	Station-master's house	
	Chinese coolie lines, 1½ miles	
14/9/15	5th-mile lines abandoned .	
	Railway lines at Kundong .	
	Wood-cutter's house .	4 *barbirostris*
	Railway lines, 1½ miles from Kuang . . . 1	

86

Everywhere, in swamps both open and under jungle, we found the larvæ of *A. umbrosus;* and as this was hill land, the swamps were in the ravines.

The larvæ of *A. aitkeni, barbirostris, rossii* were also taken.

Observations in the State of Pahang from the Gap to Ginting Simpah via *Tras and Bentong.*—In order to exclude the chance that *A. umbrosus* had been absent for some unknown reason during my previous visit to Pahang with Dr Strickland, I again visited it by road. Most of the road is through virgin jungle; here and there dotted along it are P.W.D. coolie lines, a wood-cutter's house, an occasional shop, and maybe a small native holding planted with rubber or fruit trees.

The larvæ of *A. aitkeni, maculatus, barbirostris, aconitus,* and *kochii* were taken, each in its usual breeding-place. "With the exception of the houses in Tras and Bentong, all the houses examined for adult anopheles during this three days' trip were situated in the midst of heavy virgin jungle; but nowhere was *A. umbrosus* taken, in remarkable contrast to my experience in Batu Arang, Batu Tiga, and the flat-land estates of Klang."

.   .   .

Such was Dr Strickland's important discovery. He had found a zone of land—the "Inland Hills" which is not malarial when under virgin jungle, but becomes intensely malarial when the ravines are drained and cleared of jungle. This zone is a complete contrast to the "Coastal Plain," which is malarial when under virgin jungle, and becomes non-malarial when the jungle is felled and the land drained. It differs, too, from the "Coastal Hills," which are malarial, whether the land be under jungle or cleared. The differentiation of these hill zones was possible from the discovery of the peculiar distribution of the mosquito, *A. umbrosus.*

I have called it Dr Strickland's discovery, because to him, more than to any other, our knowledge on this point is due. It is true, as will be found in Dr Wellington's interesting Chapter (XXVI.), on "The Malaria of Kuala Lumpur," that the absence of anopheline larvæ from ravines had been reported as early as 1907 by Mr Pratt, and confirmed by Dr Wellington in 1909. But this had failed to carry conviction; partly because the observations had not been published in detail; partly because they were in flat contradiction with what was known of apparently similar hill land; partly because no explanation of the contradiction was forthcoming; and mainly because no one then suspected the peculiar distribution of *A. umbrosus.*

It was reported that no anophelines were found in the jungle-covered ravine. This was incorrect. For a description of the species of mosquitoes that live in the ravines of the "Inland Hills" see Chapter XXV. "On Mosquitoes." There is no doubt that Messrs Pratt, Fletcher, and Wellington had caught more than a glimpse of the truth; and had there been an earlier investigation of the subject it would have been of the highest advantage to the Malay Peninsula.

CHAPTER XXI

THE MALARIA OF RIVERS

RIVERS differ greatly in different countries; the same river in the same country may pass through different zones of land; and in any zone it may alter its character to become narrow and swift, or broad, swampy, and sluggish. So in considering the malaria of rivers, it may make the subject clearer if I take a river at different points of its course and discuss its relation to malaria.

TIDAL RIVERS.

Tidal and Brackish Rivers.—This is really the zone of the mangrove swamp, and *A. ludlowi* with which I deal in Chapter IX. The river has a muddy bank, fringed with mangrove; while behind the mangrove comes the swampy, coastal plain. Mosquitoes do not breed in the river bank itself, nevertheless, the banks of a river in this land are intensely malarial, unless a thorough system of drainage is constructed. How unhealthy it can be is seen from the early history of Port Swettenham and from the cocoanut estate mentioned in Chapter IX; how healthy it can be made is shown by the estates on Carey Island.

Tidal, Non-brackish Rivers.—With so large a rise and fall of the tide (some 16 feet) as occurs in this part of the Straits of Malacca, the tidal wave passes fully 20 miles up the rivers as they twist and wind through the coastal plain.

In the upper reaches of the river the water is no longer brackish; and here, as in the lower brackish reaches, no larvæ are to be found on the river's bank; but the land through which it passes is malarial from *A. umbrosus*—the inhabitant of the coastal plain. In a previous chapter we saw how healthy this can be made; for example, Estates "OO," "TT," and "HH."

223

NON-TIDAL RIVERS.

Rivers with Swampy Banks in the Umbrosus Zone.—Beyond the tidal, but non-brackish, portion of the river, we reach a part where the character of the land through which the river runs is still the important factor in determining the presence or absence of malaria. Where the river course is not well defined, or the banks are very low, there may be a permanent swamp that will be dangerous from the presence of *A. umbrosus.* These swamps may be of great extent; almost certainly they cannot be efficiently drained; to "fill" them with earth would cost a King's ransom. The simplest way to make a people healthy in such a place is to move them back from the river swamp a distance of half a mile or more. The following is an example of the problem that may be met.

Three Estates, "SA," "HW," and "JS," are situated together on a Government road. Estates "SA" and "HW" are rather above the level of the coastal plain; they are not dead level, yet would not be called undulating land. The drainage is good. *Estate "JS"* is definitely hilly, or rather a hill or island, for it is almost everywhere surrounded by lower land; there are no ravines, and no *A. maculatus.* In 1915 the health was good, the true spleen rate being *nil;* the only death in a labour force of 114 was that of a child.

Estate "SA" had been unhealthy, the spleen rate of twenty-seven children, examined in January 1916, being 59 per cent. The coolie lines were situated about 100 yards or less from the road, on the opposite side of which was a piece of flat land which Javanese had begun to cultivate, but which until a few months before had been under jungle. Thinking it probable that the opening of the Javanese land would improve the health of Estate "SA," without the estate having to do anything, I recommended no action be taken with regard to the site of the lines. The fact that the labour force looked so much healthier than I expected, from the spleen rate of 59, suggested that the improvement had already begun.

Estate "HW" was also unhealthy. The spleen rate in January 1916 was 29 per cent. out of thirty-seven children, which was lower than that of Estate "SA." The reason for the difference was that whereas the lines on "SA" were close to the road and within 5 chains of undrained jungle, the lines

FIG. 73.

A River within tidal influence—brackish.

FIG. 75.

A Stream too large for Pipe Drainage.

[To face page 224.

on " HW " were 20 chains away from the road, and so farther from the breeding-place of *A. umbrosus.*

When, however, I came to consider how to bring down the spleen rate on " HW," the matter was not so simple as on " SA," where my recommendation was to do nothing. The jungle opposite "SA" had been drained, and was being cultivated by the Javanese; the jungle opposite " HW " was undrainable and could not be cultivated, as we found on visiting it.

As the lines were within 20 chains of this swamp, and I advise 40 chains as a minimum, it was necessary to inquire if a better site could be obtained elsewhere.

Behind the estate was jungle; so that the site could not be within 40 chains of the back boundary or south of the line XY; there was swamp across the Government road, so the site must be at least 40 chains in or south of the line AB. The east boundary, being " JS," was harmless, being hill without ravine; the west boundary was "SA," and no dangerous anopheles were found in it. So there was the area ABYX within which the site might be. A local examination led to the selection of a slightly raised portion of the land. In May 1916 I made these recommendations in writing; the report was sent to the Directors in England, who at once cabled their approval, and by September the new lines were finished and all the coolies removed, at a cost of $7000.

On both estates the health improved, as was anticipated. On Estate "SA," where the lines remained in the original spot, the jungle swamp was removed through the Javanese cultivation, the spleen rate was reduced.

Spleen Rates of Estate SA.

Date.	No. Examined.	Spleen Rates.
January 1916 . .	27	59
November 1917 . .	84	2

In 1917, of the two children with enlarged spleen, one was an old resident; the other, a recent local recruit. Out of the whole labour force of 340 mustered for inspection, there was only one case of slight anæmia and one case of fever. The

whole force was in splendid health; and it was apparent that
the health had begun to improve as soon as the land opposite
was opened, and before my inspection in January 1916, as I
had surmised.

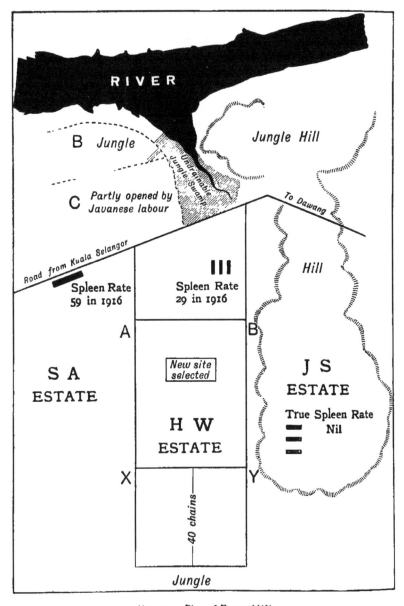

FIG. 74.—Plan of Estate HW.

On estate "HW" the coolies had not been so long removed from the malarious influence as on estate "SA"; for it was September 1916 before they were removed. But even they had improved in health.

Spleen Rates of Estate "HW."

Date.	No. Examined.	Spleen Rates.
January 1916 .	37	29
November 1917 .	46	15
June 1920 . .	44	9
June 1920 . . .	41	4*

* True rate.

RIVERS STILL FARTHER INLAND.

The Batu Road Swamp.—To decide upon the right method of dealing with a river swamp, especially in a large town, is not by any means always a simple matter, as this swamp showed. It was situated in the centre of the town of Kuala Lumpur, the capital town of the F.M.S. It lay between the river and a row of houses, the sewage of which discharged into the swamp; there were no sewers to convey it to the river. For days at a time the swamp was flooded.

The Sanitary Authority rightly decided to take action to abolish this foul swamp; and issued an order to the owner requiring him to "fill" it with earth to such a level that it would not be covered by the majority of floods—the filling to be to over "average flood level." The engineer for the owner estimated this would cost $61,677 (as a matter of fact the level given by the Sanitary Authority was incorrect, and the cost would have been considerably less, as was discovered afterwards). In view of this large expenditure, I was asked to advise on what was necessary to prevent the swamp being a nuisance.

The swamp was not a cause of malaria in my opinion; and Dr Strickland who examined the houses next to the swamp confirmed this. He found "only one child with any enlargement at all (of spleen) out of twenty-five."

Nevertheless, it was a foul spot, which was breeding many mosquitoes.

The level to which I thought the land should be filled was about 1½ feet above swamp level; and I regarded swamp level

R

as fixed by the lowest level at which the sensitive plant, *Mimosa pudica*, would grow.

Part of the ground was dry, covered by *M. pudica*, and not suggestive of swamp; part was frankly swamp, being covered by water; while other parts were dry at the moment, and not covered by *M. pudica*.

All around there was a well-defined line at which *M. pudica* stopped growing, and below which the vegetation consisted of bulrushes and swamp grasses.

I regard the *mimosa* line as the level of the swamp water or permanent ground water, because *M. pudica* cannot grow in a swamp. It is a leguminous plant with nitrogenous nodules on its roots. These nodules absorb nitrogen from the air, and, therefore, must be in what normally is dry soil.

An engineer with a theodolite took levels at widely different parts of the swamp, when I set the staff on the line of the *M. pudica*. The readings (using his own datum) were curiously consistent:

42·51   42·49   42·33   42·12

The river level was found to be on (10/3/15) 40·21.

My advice was that the whole ground should be filled to the level 44, which was fully 1½ feet above the *mimosa* level. The cost of filling to the level 44 was estimated by the engineer at $2324; a difference of over $59,000 from what was required by the Sanitary Authority.

In view of this evidence the Sanitary Authority obtained a report from another engineer, who said :—

" The level of the line between *mimosa* and swamp grass noted by Messrs Mace, Hall, & Co. as being quite distinct, was ascertained in the vicinity of the large patch of low-lying ground in the centre of Lot 11."

The reduced levels from town datum were as follows on 9th May 1915 :—

Reading.

4   .   .   .   .
5
6   .   .   .   .   .
7   .   .   .   .
8   .   .   .   ,

9
10   .   .   .   ____
       Average   .   .   .

It was evident from the readings of the two engineers that the *mimosa* line was something definite, and could be fixed with sufficient accuracy to justify action being taken on it. The line being fixed, and the cause of the line (the depth of dry soil in which the *mimosa* roots would grow being indisputable), the Sanitary Authority adopted my suggestion of basing the amount of " filling " on the *mimosa* line.

I have discussed this question at some length; but not more than it merits. Riverine swamps occur in many places, and in many towns. In Kuala Lumpur there are many acres, part belonging to Government, and part to private owners. To fill them one foot per acre more than is necessary would lead to great waste of money, whether the money be that of a private individual or of Government.

Inland Plains.—It is on the banks of the larger rivers that we find the representative in this country of the " INLAND PLAIN "; for it is on too small a scale to furnish examples of ancient lake beds or plateaux much above sea-level. Still there are some stretches of inland flat land, and they are healthy. As an example I may give the spleen rate of an estate a few miles beyond Kuala Lumpur, on the river of which I have just been writing. The estate, or at least the portion of it next to this river, has had a reputation for its good health for many years, and the spleen rate justified it. On 26th September 1911, I examined twenty-seven children, all of whom were free from enlarged spleen.

It may be said generally of the larger rivers in this country that they are non-malarious; by which I mean that where the banks are well defined, dangerous anopheline larvæ will not be found in any quantity in the vegetation that may grow on the bank. Where the river-bank is not defined, but loses itself in a swamp, the health depends on the zone of land in which the river is situated; if in the *umbrosus* zone, the swamp will be dangerous; if farther inland and *A. umbrosus* is not present, it will be harmless; unless *A. aconitus* is breeding in it. In 1909 I recommended the removal of coolie lines from ravines to the banks of another river with entirely satisfactory results.

The Smaller Rivers.—As one passes still farther towards the source of a river, and before the small ravine streams are reached, one finds a stream perhaps some 20 feet wide and a foot or so deep, pursuing a rather tortuous course down an inland valley. The river is clear, the bottom sandy, the sides grassy.

Along the grassy banks are found the larvæ of *A. maculatus;* they are also present in side pools along the river. In heavy rain, the stream becomes a raging torrent; in dry weather, a sleepy stream; but always too big to be put underground in subsoil pipes. If malaria exists in such a community, how can it be eradicated?

Tarentang Estate.—In 1912 I was asked to advise this estate, as malaria had been severe; and I found there the problem described above; with the complication that many small ravines, breeding *A. maculatus*, ran through the estate and discharged into the river. The banks of a clear stream are attractive sites for coolie lines, and in many places throughout the country have been selected as headquarters for a labour force. If such sites could be made healthy, it would be an advantage to the whole country to know how it could be done. If it were impossible to make them healthy, no less valuable to everyone would be the knowledge; for then these sites could be avoided in the future, or abandoned if already in use.

It appeared to me that the procedure to be adopted should be experimental; and, as such, a portion of the cost might fairly be borne by Government. Accordingly I suggested an experiment both to Government and to the estate; and both agreed to share the expense equally. My idea was to render the ravine streams harmless by subsoil drainage, and to oil the edges of the main stream. Unfortunately there appears to have been a misunderstanding of what I required; and on my next visit to the estate in 1914, I found not only the ravines being "piped," but an entirely new channel being made for the main stream, at, of course, a much heavier expenditure than all the ravine drainage put together. The Government labour employed on the drainage had been decimated by malaria; the engineer in charge had been laid up so frequently that proper supervision had been impossible; and the work was not satisfactorily carried out.

A. maculatus still breeds in side pools in the bed of the main stream in dry weather, and although the health has improved, the unhappy experiment has not been carried far enough to warrant any final conclusions.

The course of a river has now been traced from the sea backwards almost to its source in the hills; probably in some ravine. Of ravines and their malaria I have already written in the chapters on Seafield Estate; so, for the present, shall say no more. But before closing I must reprint Dr Strickland's unpublished paper on "The Mosquitoes of Stream-courses" which sums up the results of his extensive research.

PAPER S.

THE MOSQUITOES OF STREAM-COURSES, BY DR STRICKLAND.

"Of course, at the eye of a stream, exactly where the stream-course resolves itself from out the swamp from which it springs, it is impossible to say. Sometimes, however, especially in the dry weather, the stream commences as a series of pools in a definite well-cut course, and such places I have included here, although there be no semblance of a stream through the pools.

"I do not include flooded land as being in a stream-course. From first to last, the following species have been taken by me from stream-course:—

	Per Mille.		Per Mille
Maculatus	340	*Albirostris*	53
Barbirostris	153	*Umbrosus group*	47
Sinensis	127	*Fuliginosus*	40
Aitkeni	67	*Rossii*	40
Karwari	60	*Leucosphyrus*	13
Kochi-tesselatus	60	*Ludlowi*	0

"This table shows the very marked predominance of *maculatus* over the other species in this respect, and justifies the appellation usually given to it of a stream-breeder, originated by Watson.

"One very common characteristic about a stream-course is the absence of grasses at the edge, probably due to the scour. That may account for the comparative absence of *albirostris* which otherwise would like the swift current.

"We will mention a few types of streams and their mosquito fauna.

"I. *Tidal Rivers and Streams.*—Along these is usually nipah palm and mangrove. The highest spring tides will sometimes leave pools of water among the nipah roots and occasionally one can find *umbrosus* in such pools. If the vegetation is within reach of the lowest range of tide, nothing can be found.

It will be noted in the table that *ludlowi* was never taken from a stream-course.

" 2. *Small Streams running slowly through Jungle.*—At the edge among fallen timber may be found species of the *umbrosus* type.

" 3. *Larger Streams running through Jungle*, like the Batu Pahat river or the Sungei Jembulang. The jungle trees form a dense canopy over the edge of the stream, and the current is strong and deep enough to keep the edges clear of flotsam and jetsam. Consequently, no breeding-places are found.

" 4. *Scouring out Pockets in the Banks.*—This is the home of *maculatus* and *barbirostris*, sometimes *fuliginosus* and *aitkeni*, *e.g.* Jementah Estate, Johore.

" 5. *Small Ravine Streams under Jungle.*—The stream is usually difficult to define; the whole is rather a streaming morass. I have recorded *aitkeni* and species of the *umbrosus* type in such places.

" 6. *Great Streams* like the Kelantan river. Such are nearly all opened up, unless the hills which come to the edge are too steep for Malay kebuns.* In any case, nothing can be found along the banks except in the interesting case of a terrace of the river-bank, showing a seepage swamp. In such a place at Kota Bharu, Kelantan, I obtained *kochi*.

" 7. *Mountain Torrents.*—It may be taken that no mosquito lives actually in the torrent, but only in pools along the course, or in silted-up pools. I have there taken *leucosphyrus* and *rossii*, while in pools among granite boulders I have obtained *maculatus*, *leucosphyrus*, *aitkeni*, or if the jungle covers such places only *aitkeni*.

" 8. *Certain Streams tributary* to great streams like the Kelantan or Pahang, which have reached the base level of erosion, and that a muddy base, have *umbrosus* species growing in them, if under jungle, or *kochi* and *maculatus* if exposed."

* Small estates, or gardens, or native holdings.

FIG. 76A.

FIG. 76B.—THE PERAK RIVER.

[To face page 232.

CHAPTER XXII

THE REAPPEARANCE OF MALARIA

DURING the past twenty years malaria has reappeared in greater or less virulence in several places from which I had seen it disappear. As the causes which led to the disappearance of the disease had been observed, it was possible to study the changes which brought about its reappearance; and by appropriate action to make the places healthy again. Probably an experience of true alterations of health and sickness is comparatively rare; in any case they are of interest and value to the sanitation, so I will record them in some detail.

I.

THE REAPPEARANCE OF MALARIA AT PORT SWETTENHAM.

[1909].—When, in 1901, the Port was opened, in order to obtain exact information of the number of people who were attacked, I caused, as already mentioned, a daily visit to be made to each Government house. This was continued for several years. When it was discontinued, I caused the Deputy Health Officer to inform me when any officer complained of fever, and no officer received sick leave until he had come to Klang, and his blood had been examined. Further, I issued instructions to the Deputy Health Officer, who was also in charge of the Dispensary, that no person living in Government quarters was to be supplied with quinine except on my orders. I had thus a very firm grasp on the Government population at Port Swettenham. Seeing those who, complaining of sickness, sought sick leave, and making blood examinations if there was any complaint of temperature, I am in a position to state that no officer suffered from malaria from 12th July 1904 until December 1906. In that month three officers were found to have malaria, which had evidently been contracted in the Port.

The matter was at once reported to the Chairman of the Sanitary Board, the late Mr J. Scott Mason, afterwards Governor of British North Borneo, and, accompanied by the Executive Engineer, we made a careful survey of the drainage conditions of the Port.

It was, I think, more than a coincidence that, at the very moment of the recrudescence, cement inverts had been put into the road drains at such a level that they effectually blocked all the lateral drains which previously opened into them. The whole of the area marked " C " on the plan (Fig. 9) was, therefore, much less efficiently drained than previously; in fact was now entirely without any drainage, as the photo shows.

We recognised the fact that a larger population than formerly were living entirely outside the bunded area. In 1904 it numbered 548, whereas in 1901 only 127 lived beyond the bunds, and those were housed along the Klang Road on the edge of a deep drain, and on land fairly well drained before the new concrete inverts had been put in.

The spleen rate was affected by the outbreak, as the following table shows :—

Year.	1904.	1905.	1906.	1907.	1909.
Blood examination—					
Number examined . . .	87	76	100	...	...
Number with parasites . .	1	0	5	...	...
Per cent. with parasites . .	1·14	0	5	...	...
Spleen examination—					
Number examined . . .	...	...	100	41	109
Number with enlargement . .	...	...	2	9	9
Per cent. with enlargement. .	...	...	2	21·9	8·9

In 1906, I found evidence in the children of the recrudescence of the disease, simultaneous with its reappearance among the adults, as I shall relate. In 1907, the examinations were made by a dresser. In 1909, I myself made them, and visited, along with the present Medical Officer of Klang, Dr Millard, every house up to the 4th mile on the Klang Road. Practically every child in the town was seen and was examined by both of us.

We also recognised that the drainage system within the bunds was not so efficient as previously, since in some places

FIG. 77.

One of the lateral Drains in Area " C " at Port Swettenham, blocked by a new cement drain in 1906. It was swarming with *Anopheles*.

FIG. 78.

Another of the blocked lateral Drains in Area " C " at Port Swettenham in 1906.

[*To face page* 234.

filling had sunk, and in other places drains have been diverted and lateral drains obstructed by cementing the mains. The Board decided to spend the balance of a vote in 1907 in cutting outlets for area " C," but owing to the great competition for labour at the time, it was absolutely impossible to do so. In 1907, I formally brought these matters to the knowledge of Government.

In 1908, when I was in England on leave, the condition was still further aggravated by the extension of the railway embankment from the point marked " K " to the point marked " H," in order to provide further wharf accommodation. This, of course, completely blocked the outlet of the whole of the drainage from the South bund. I am informed that malaria increased rapidly then, but an outlet was soon made for the water beyond the end of the railway; and as the figures show, the amount of malaria now (1909) in Port Swettenham is not very serious. Government, however, appointed a Commission to make recommendations in 1908; and a sum of $27,000 is being spent in improving the automatic outlet valves, improving and increasing the bunds, and in improving an open sewer system for many of the houses.

I am of the opinion, however, that malaria will not entirely disappear from Port Swettenham until it is recognised that a large proportion is now outside the protected area. The bunded area should be increased to include these.

[1909]—*Criticism of the Original Drainage Scheme at Port Swettenham.*—In 1901, our chief· fear was that mosquitoes would breed in the drains within the bunds. We considered it essential the drains should have such a fall that they would dry during every tide, or at least would have such a current as was calculated would prevent the insect from breeding within them. Accordingly, the level of the outlets made in 1901 was that of about half tide. At such a high outfall level, and with a grade to provide a good current, in many places the drains soon ran out practically on to the surface of the soil, especially at the top of the system. Places where water stood when the drains had been completed were, therefore, " filled in " at great expense. Since then, filling has been continued to provide sites for buildings, etc. It must be clearly understood that expense was not allowed to stand in the way of success, as the whole existence of the Port was at stake.

Experience has shown that our fears were groundless; and that the danger from open drains in flat land is *nil*, if they are kept moderately free from weeds. Any further works will, therefore, be immensely cheaper, since the outlets of the new drains can be put at the level of low water neap tides. *Deepening of the drains is more satisfactory than filling, as the cost is a mere fraction ; this cannot be too strongly insisted upon.*

I am indebted to Government for the figures below and the levels, which show that the general level of Port Swettenham is 2 to 3 feet below that of spring tides.

The levels on the plan range from 50·24 to 54·26, and the highest known tide was 56·36, and the following are the official levels :—

H.M.S. "WATERWITCH" BENCH MARK.

The surface is 14 feet 4 inches above the datum used for the reduction of soundings.

Low-water spring tide   .   .   .   .
B.M. above datum   .   .   .   .   .
High-water spring tide   .   .   .   .
Low-water   ,, ...
High-water ordinary tide   .   .   .   .
Low-water   ,, ...
High-water neap tide   .   .   .   .
Low-water   ,, ...
High-water on 30/10/09   .   .   .   .
Invert of culvert 87   .   .   .   .   .

Invert of flap valves in South bund .   .   .   47·59, 46·67

Invert of flap valve in North bund   .

* Highest known tide.

I make these criticisms in order that others may benefit by the mistakes made in our pioneer work.

The level of the outlet is most important ; and when a sea is tidal, bunding gives enormous powers of drainage. I need only mention how the English Fens have been drained by bunding, and incidentally malaria has disappeared. I think that is more than a coincidence.

[1920]—*Port Swettenham from* 1909 *to* 1920.—In 1909, I was unable to induce the Government to extend the bunded area to include Area " C," and so to protect the large population living outside the area originally protected. But Mr Byrne, the District Engineer of Klang, appreciated my suggestion of

FIG. 79.—CULVERT AT PORT SWETTENHAM.

The photograph shows the old culvert on the left. The small culvert on the right is the low-level culvert put in by Mr Byrne. It is three feet lower than the old culvert, and has enormously improved the drainage of the town. The high tide of October 1909 came over the railway at this point.

[To face page 280.

lowering the drainage level; and he put a small low-level culvert beside Culvert No. 87, only 3 feet lower. This improved the drainage of the land so much that, when a scheme for the whole of the Port came to be discussed in 1914, I insisted on a low-level scheme being put down; and pointed out that the level of the outlets might go still farther down that of the small culvert at No. 87. This was done in the new scheme, to be presently described.

In 1911 the decision to build a quarantine station at Port Swettenham for coolies arriving from India, once more made the malaria a question of importance and urgency. To pour thousands of coolies into a quarantine station where they would contract malaria would have been a disastrous course to pursue; and I advised the Planters' Association of Malaya to insist on the Port being made healthy as a condition of a quarantine station being built there. This they did; and the work was begun. The area required for the building was bunded and drained (being below high-tide level this was necessary before even a start could be made with the buildings); but on Area "C," which was adjacent to the station, the work was not completed for several years after the scheme was sanctioned. The bund was built and a gate of sorts erected; but the tide entered almost unimpeded; no drainage system existed; and the last condition, which was worse than the first, lasted until 1917.

In 1914 a plan for the drainage of the new area, excluding that actually occupied by the quarantine station, was prepared. But it included many of the mistakes which one would expect from an engineer who was not familiar with the previous history of the drainage of the Port. Over $100,000 was to be spent on masonry or glazed earthenware drains, most of which would have been quite unnecessary. But the chief fault lay in the omission to consider the level of the outlets of the drains through the bunds. The total estimate was $149,342.

The plan was rejected; and a small committee appointed to prepare another. I pointed out the history of the drainage of the Port, the advantages of a low-level drainage system; and insisted that masonry drains should only be laid down where sewage had to be carried in addition to the ground water; where the latter only was present, open earth drains had proved to be sufficient on estates in similar land. On these lines a new plan was prepared, the estimate for which was $68,849, a saving of over $60,000 on the first scheme. From a malarial point of view the new plan was infinitely superior ; another illustration of the connection between knowledge, efficiency, and economy. In view of the importance of the matter I give a summary of the two estimates ; so that they may be compared and the lesson more clearly brought out.

Estimate of First Scheme.

Earth drains . . . . .
Masonry drains, 9-inch . . . .
        ,,   12-inch . . . .
Earth drains with glazed inverts . . .
Culverts . . . . . .
Screw-down gates, 9 . . . .

Contingencies, 10 per cent. .
                Total . . .

Estimate of Second Scheme.

Earthwork in drains . . . .
Masonry work in drains and culverts
Subsoil drains . . . . .
New bund at outlet " C " . . . .
Filling low ground, say . . . .
Strengthening bund .
New sluices, including railway culvert at " B "

Contingencies, 10 per cent. . .
                Total . . .

This estimate and plan were approved, and the work will be completed in the course of 1920. Already it is shown how advantageous deep-level drainage is; all the portions already drained have a great depth of dry soil.

The Engineer-in-charge, Mr F. D. Evans, has supplied me with the following data of the levels :—

Mean sea-level is given as 100.

Maximum spring tides range between about level 92·00 and level 108·00.

Minimum neap tides range between about level 98·6 and 101·3.

The highest tide on record is about 109·5.

The sill of outlet "A" is set lower than the level 95, as an experiment; but the drains were not set down to it.   Outlet "E" with its drains is set lower than 96.   The outlets in creeks

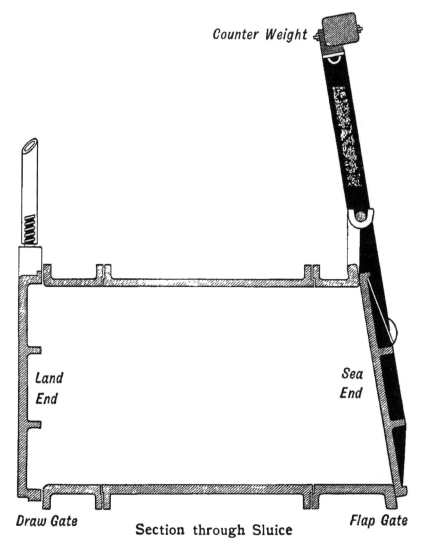

Counter Weight

Land End

Sea End

Draw Gate   Section through Sluice   *Flap Gate*

FIG. 80.—Section through New Sluice Gate at Port Swettenham.

are set higher.   The engineer is satisfied with the lowest outlet; and adds that all the drains could be down to 95, or 5 feet below mean sea-level.

Only on one or two days in the month are the gates kept

closed on account of the neap tides; this has not proved a serious disadvantage, as the gates, which in addition to automatic flaps have screw-down valves, keep the water out effectively. The great depth and capacity of the drains, as well as the large capacity of the well-drained soil to·absorb rain, prevent flooding of the land when heavy rain falls during the period when the gates are shut.

The population of Port Swettenham in 1920 was found from the Rice Controller's forms to be approximately 6000.

The spleen rate of the Malay school children was 7 per cent.; but the true rate was *nil.* At the examination in 1920 there were forty-two children present. Of these, three had enlarged spleens; two were brothers who had come two years before from Port Dickson, and one, a policeman's child, had come from Rawang. All three gave a history of fever before coming to Port Swettenham.

II.

THE REAPPEARANCE OF MALARIA ON AN ESTATE WITHIN TIDAL INFLUENCE.

A few miles from Port Swettenham, there is an Estate "CC" situated on a tidal river, the water of which is practically pure sea water. Most of the estate is above the reach of high tides, but portions are within tidal influence; and so the estate at these portions is enclosed within embankments. The drainage was good; the land well cultivated; and there was a large healthy labour force as free from malaria as any flat-land estate in the district. The death rates were low, 9, 5, and 9 per mille in 1908, 1909, and 1910 respectively; and the spleen rate only 3 per cent. in eighty-two children in 1909; the daily number in hospital out of a labour force of several hundreds, usually between two and four; and the trivial illnesses treated on the estate hardly more.

There were a few more cases of malaria than usual towards the end of 1910; but suddenly in September 1911 malaria became virulent. The death rate jumped from 9 in 1910 to 101 in 1911; the spleen rate rose from 3 in 1909 to 58 in 1911. The hospital could not contain the sick; and in November there was an average of eighty sick on the estate in addition to over thirty daily in the hospital.

The outbreak caused great loss to the estate. Some $5000 were spent on the hospital in new buildings, but that was the least of the loss. The Indian labour force rapidly melted away from about 600 to 300 coolies; the rubber crop could not be collected, and was short of the estimate by 30,000 lb., which at the then price of rubber probably represented a loss of some £6000 sterling.

The Cause of the Outbreak.—The year 1911 was more than usually malarious, and a breakdown in the quarantine arrangements at Penang had a serious effect on the mortality of the year. But the estate had recruited only eighty-four new coolies, and something more than an annual variation seemed necessary to account for the outbreak, which showed itself not merely in attacks on the adults, but also in its effects on the children, many of whom died suddenly.

For a time I was completely at a loss to account for the epidemic. In ten years I had never seen the reappearance of malaria on a flat land estate; none of the lines, as far as I knew, and I thought I knew the estate thoroughly, were within 40 chains of jungle or swamp; and the manager assured me this was so. I was, therefore, seriously alarmed at the outbreak; it looked as if we could not rely on healthy flat land estates remaining healthy; that malaria, on the flat land estates, might become persistent, as in hill land, from the appearance of some malaria-carrying anopheles hitherto not recognised. For the whole rubber industry, indeed for the whole country, the outbreak looked most ominous.

Accordingly, I searched every drain, pool, and puddle close to the coolie lines, and among the rubber trees for some new anopheles; but without discovering any.

In the course of my examination, I decided to tour the whole estate, and then I discovered the cause of the outbreak was a very simple one.

Requiring increased line accommodation for his labour force, in May 1910 the manager built new lines about 20 chains from the jungle, without realising that the jungle was so near, for at two points the boundary of the estate bends inwards, instead of running in a straight line as I had assumed it did. The new sites were responsible for the cases of malaria in 1910, which had quickly disappeared; and it was not until September 1911 that the disease became of serious consequence—that is some fourteen months after the lines had been built.

The outbreak would have been confined to the new lines, but, for estate reasons, the labour force had been redistributed; many of the infected coolies had been moved back to the old lines, and the healthy coolies moved to the new lines. In consequence of these changes, when I came to investigate the outbreak, I found malaria cases in the old lines, and the disease appeared to be spread over the whole estate. It was only after I discovered that the new lines were close to the jungle, and made inquiry about any changes in the distribution of the labour force, that the whole story was elucidated.

The Remedy was obvious. The new lines were at once abandoned; others were built on the old site, and the health at once improved, as the following figures show :—

Year.	Labour Force.	Death Rate.
1907		
1908		
1909		
1910		
1911		
1912		
1913		
1914		
1915		
1916		
1917		

Spleen Rates.

Date.	Number of Children Examined.	Spleen Rates.
1909 December	82	3
1911 October	86	58
1913 January	73	19
1914 March .	112	4
1918 March .	104	0.9

In 1918 the only child with enlarged spleen came from a malarious estate in Johore. The moral is plain. An Estate Medical Officer should know by inspection the whole of an estate, and should, if possible, possess a plan of it.

III.

THE STORY OF A COAST RAILWAY.

In Chapter V. I told the story of a coast road; how the road blocked the drainage of land inland to it; how it appeared to be responsible for a great wave of malaria; and how, as drainage was improved, the malaria gradually disappeared over a wide extent of country. Many years later, history was to repeat itself in the same area; this time the offender was a railway running parallel to the coast. Fortunately, the outbreak was less severe on the whole, although intense enough in places as I shall show. It is of interest, too, that the outbreak did not occur until some considerable time after the construction had been completed; it was not due to the construction coolies and camps to which Major Christophers and Dr Bentley have so clearly traced many outbreaks in India.

The railway, like the road, runs from Klang to Kuala Selangor, a distance of some 28 miles; for the first 12 miles it is on the sea side of the road, but at that point it crosses the road and runs along rubber estates and through native holdings. From the 12th to the 15th mile, it is within a mile or so of the sea; and the land in this section, being close to the mangrove zone, is at a rather lower level than along most of the track. It was here the malaria first showed itself. The railway was opened to traffic in 1914.

Malaria reappears on "PG" Estate.—For a year or so after it was opened in 1906, this estate suffered from malaria; but by 1907 it was healthy, and remained so until 1915, as the death rates show. In January 1913, the spleen rate of 120 children was 4 per cent.

The health continued satisfactory until September 1915; towards the end of that month, and until the end of the year, malaria was present to a considerable extent. In view of the complete freedom from malaria in the past, it seemed at the time impossible to believe the whole of the ill-health was due to malaria; especially as only 3 out of 120 children had enlarged spleen. Accordingly, 150 coolies, who were anæmic, were given a course of chenopodium treatment in order to eliminate ankylostomiasis as a contributing factor in

S

the ill-health (about 99 per cent. of Indian labourers harbour the worm).

Health improved somewhat in the early months of 1916, these being the least malarious months in the year; but, by July, there was no doubt we had to face the fact that, for some reason or other, malaria had taken a firm hold on the estate. Not only had the acting manager suffered from the disease, but so had his servants. Of seventy-two coolies who had arrived from India between 1st November 1915 and 31st July 1916, sixteen had absconded; and of the remaining fifty-four, no fewer than thirty-nine, or 72 per cent., had suffered from malaria since their arrival on the estate. Finally, the spleen rate had jumped from 3/120 (2·5 per cent.) in September 1915 to 35/144 (24·3 per cent.) in July 1916.

The Cause of the Outbreak was difficult to explain. The lines remained on the sites they had occupied for years; the drainage of the estate had been improved year by year. It was therefore necessary to look outside the estate boundary for the cause; some condition that had come into force within the previous two or three years; something that had presumably created mosquito breeding-places, which had not previously existed.

Having this in mind, it occurred to me that, although the railway had not interfered with the estate drainage, it might have done so with that of the native holdings; and, in any case, had probably created a series of borrow pits which would be breeding-places for anopheles. An examina-tion showed this to be the case.

In borrow pits along the railway, the following species of anopheles were found: *A. rossii*, *A. sinensis*, *A. umbrosus*, and in enormous numbers *A. ludlowi*. *A. umbrosus* was a known carrier. Dr Barbour, who kindly dissected some *A. ludlowi*, found in the first he examined the salivary glands "stuffed with sporozoits" (13/8/16).

An interview with the Acting General Manager of Railways found him willing to drain the borrow pits; a cable from the directors of the estate gave the manager a free hand to carry out my recommendations. The borrow pits and native holdings had their drains opened up; oil was freely used and health rapidly improved. To-day the health is excellent again.

Death Rates.

Year.	Labour Force.	Death Rate per 1000.
1907	200	
1908	278	
1909	224	
1910	301	
1911	430	
1912	502	
1913	472	
1914	542	
1915	605	
1916	472	
1917	462	
1918	453	
1919	452	

* Quarantine.   † Influenza.

The spleen rates show a similar rise, and are now coming back to normal.

Year.	No. Examined.	Spleen Rates.
1913 January . .	120	4
1915 September .	120	2
1916 July . . .	144	24
1917 September .	130	28
1918 March .	95	13
1919 November . .	132	8

In 1919, at the examination, ten of the eleven children with enlarged spleen had been several years on the estate; so it is evident the enlarged spleens are evidence of the outbreak of 1916.

In a letter dated November 1919, the manager tells me, " At the present time conditions of health could not very well be better."

Estate A.—The adjoining estate suffered in a similar way; and so did others to a less degree. The cure was similar. It is unnecessary to give these in details.

The wave of malaria spread inland to a considerable distance and affected estates which one expected might have escaped. A number of conditions exist in this district, which call for careful investigation in the light of our present knowledge of malaria; for this outbreak shows the margin of safety of some of these estates is small.

Before closing this section I would appeal to the engineers of this and other countries, not to allow history to keep on repeating itself. Some time ago I was reading a book about the Fens of Lincolnshire in England, and therein noted some things not without bearing on this matter. "The Romans, discovering the remarkable fertility of certain of the dry or drying parts, desired to increase their area, and formed a rude plan for the reclamation by embanking. . . ." "They laid down, too, certain causeways across the Fens, a notable example of which extends from Denver in Norfolk, over the Wash to Chark, and from thence to Marsh and Peterborough, a distance of about 30 miles. The Roman embankments, however, along the coast seem to have had the result of increasing the inundation of the low-lying lands of the Level." Then came some lines, as a quotation, the source of which is not given—"whilst they dammed the salt water out, they also held back the fresh, no provision having been made for improving and deepening the outfalls of the rivers flowing through the Level into the Wash. The Fenlands in winter were thus not only flooded by the rainfall of the Fens themselves, and by the upland waters which flowed from the interior, and also by the daily flux of the tides which drove in from the German Ocean, holding back the fresh waters, and even mixing with them far inland."

So there is precedent for coast roads, if not for coast railways, interfering with drainage; but surely work which "leaves a trail of malaria behind is bad engineering." It is high time to break with the past.

IV.

MALARIA FROM THE DELAYED SPREAD OF
A. MACULATUS.

Klang Town.—The town of Klang is situated at the end of a small range of low hills isolated from other hills belonging to the group of coastal hills. The malaria from which it suffered originally was carried by *A. umbrosus;* and simple open drainage eliminated the mosquito and its malaria. Being isolated from the other hills, which from 1901 to 1907 were still under jungle, the town for long escaped invasion by *A.*

FIG. 81.—WICKEN FEN.
The most interesting relic of the true Fen. " Here we find the peace of the fens unbroken . . . where the reeds grow beautiful along the watersides, guarding from sight the last home of rare and beautiful things, which almost everywhere else have been destroyed by man."—*Camb. Geog.*

FIG. 82.—WINGLAND MARSH, near Sutton Bridge, in Lincolnshire.
Reclaimed from the sea, and under cultivation. (" Marsh," in Lincolnshire, means salt-water swamp ; " Fen," a fresh-water swamp.)

[To face page 246.

maculatus. But with the great opening of land from 1907, due to the growth of the rubber industry, the adjacent hill land was gradually cleared of its jungle; *A. maculatus* became

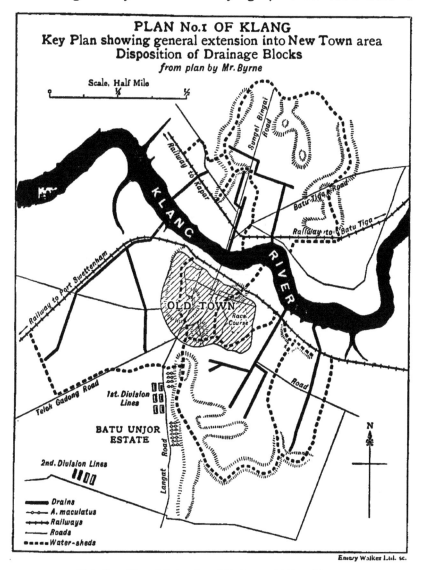

PLAN No.1 OF KLANG
Key Plan showing general extension into New Town area
Disposition of Drainage Blocks
from plan by Mr. Byrne

Scale, Half Mile

Railway to Kapar

KLANG RIVER

Sungei Bingai Road

Batu Tiga Road

Railway to Batu Tiga

Railway to Port Swettenham

OLD TOWN

Race Course

Telok Gadong Road

1st. Division Lines

BATU UNJOR ESTATE

Langat Road

Road

2nd. Division Lines

N

——— Drains
–∘–∘– A. maculatus
+++++ Railways
——— Roads
●●●●● Water-sheds

Emery Walker Ltd. sc.

FIG. 83.—Plan of Extension of Drainage of Klang Town.

widespread in the hills; and in 1913 this mosquito was found in small quantity in some of the hill-foot drains in Klang town. Occasional cases of malaria occurred; but the disease never gained a serious hold on the town; for soon after the discovery of the insect, the open hill-foot drains in which it had been found were converted into subsoil drains.

The town had increased in size ; to-day (1920) the population is over 20,000. To protect them a scheme for improving the drainage of what may be called the "suburbs" was prepared by Mr Harold E. Byrne in 1916, at an estimated cost of $78,400. It drains an area of 1868 acres. The scheme was approved, and has since been carried out except for some of the sluice gates.

Although occasional cases of malaria occur in Klang, particularly from the less well-drained land between the railway and the river, the total amount is small, as the spleen rates show.

Spleen Rates of the Anglo-Chinese School.

Date.	Number of Children Examined.	Number with Enlarged Spleen.	Observer.
1915 December .	125	1	Chief Dresser, Government Hospital.
1916 ,, .	151	1	,, ,,
1917 ,, .	172	2	,, ,,
1918 ,, .	163	1	,,
1919 ,, .	198	1	,, ,,
1920 June . .	135	2	M. Watson.

This school has pupils of all nationalities, Chinese, Tamils, Malays, etc., and is representative of the general population. On 8/6/20 I examined the children only under fourteen years of age. Of the two with enlarged spleen, one had arrived only three months before from an estate where he had suffered from fever; the other was eighteen months from India where he had fever.

Spleen Rates of Malay Schools.

Name of School.	Date.	Number of Children Examined.	Number with Enlarged Spleen.
Bukit Rajah School .	1917 December .	75	3
,, ,, .	1920 March .	93	3
Klang School . .	1920 ,, .	130	5

Of the five children with the enlarged spleen in Klang Malay School in 1920—only one lived within town limits. All these figures show that Klang still retains a fairly complete immunity from malaria.

Batu Unjor Estate.—About a mile from Klang on the Langat Road is what is now called Batu Unjor Estate; and on the opposite side of the road, Tremelbye Estate and some native holdings. At the time this part of Tremelbye was under jungle, it was full of *A. umbrosus*, as I recorded at page 14; and the bungalow of Batu Unjor Estate was malarious.

With the opening of Tremelbye Estate in 1906, *A. umbrosus* and the malaria disappeared; and Batu Unjor became a healthy estate, described as Estate " X " in the earlier part of this volume.

It continued healthy until 1913, when a ravine in a native holding opposite the lines of Division I. was invaded by *A. maculatus.* The native owner at first refused to permit the estate to control the mosquitoes, and a sharp outbreak of malaria occurred, showing the *maculatus* rise in the month of May.

Admissions to Hospital for Malaria.

1913 for the Whole Estate.   1918 for First Division only.

1918.	Admissions.	1918.	Admissions.
January . .		.	
February .		.	
March .		.	
April .		.	
May . .		.	
June . .		.	
July . .		.	
August .		.	
September . .		.	
October . .		.	
November .		.	
December . .		.	

Dr Ansley-Young gives me the spleen rates taken quarterly since 1915. The contrast between Division I. which is close to the hill, and Division II. which is out on the flat land, is striking. Dr Ansley-Young attributes the rise of malaria in 1918 to some breeding-places having been overlooked by the oilers; in fact he found *A. maculatus* breeding close to the lines.

Spleen Rates—Batu Unjor Estate.

Year	31st March				30th June				30th September				31st December			
	Division I		Division II		Division I		Division II		Division I		Division II		Division I		Division II	
	Children Examined.	Enlarged Spleen. Per cent.	Children Examined.	Enlarged Spleen.	Children Examined.	Enlarged Spleen. Per cent.	Children Examined.	Enlarged Spleen.	Children Examined.	Enlarged Spleen. Per cent.	Children Examined.	Enlarged Spleen. Per cent.	Children Examined.	Enlarged Spleen. Per cent.	Children Examined.	Enlarged Spleen.
1915	...	...	...	...	...	...	...	...	15	26·6	23	8·7	10	30·0	19	Nil
1916	38	10·5	25	Nil	30	16·6	24	Nil	43	2·3	27	Nil	39	7·7	31	"
1917	37	Nil	29	'	40	Nil	25	"	48	2·08	28	'	37	Nil	36	"
1918	38	7·9	32	"	32	31·2	29	"	44	11·3	32	"	42	19·0	23	"
1919	62	14·5	41	...	54	9·2	27	'	...	...	...	...	...	...	...	...
1920	...	...	...	...	66	10·6	55	'	...	...	...	...	...	...	...	...

Estate " S."—Haron and Klang Lands Estates are, like Klang town and Estate " X," situated on a small range of hills. They lie about 3 miles from the Klang range, and parallel to it. Most of the range was, until comparatively recently, covered by jungle, and the malaria was caused by *A. umbrosus,* which was abundantly found in the jungle, coolie lines, and bungalows.

In 1912, on my recommendation, close on 200 acres of jungle were opened up, in two places—which pushed the jungle, if not 40 chains from the lines, at least much farther than it had been.

In view of the extension of *A. maculatus* to Klang and Estate " X " in 1913, I was anxious lest a similar event should occur on the hill division of this estate. Klang Lands Division is flat land, and the spleen rate at once fell; the hill division, Haron, contains only one ravine, which I searched time and again for *A. maculatus* without success.

The following figures show the death rates and spleen rates.

Death Rates per 1000.

Year.	Labour Force.	Death Rate.
1908	262	116
1909	373	16
1910	573	54
1911	768	97
1912	1061	10
1913	1065	26
1914	499	30
1915	351	14
1916	432	16
1917	506	26
1918	499	47
1919	477	20

Spleen Rates.

Year.	Haron.		Klang Lands.	
	Number of Children Examined.	Spleen Rates.	Number of Children Examined.	Spleen Rates.
1909	32	31	20	20
1913	84	15	51	7
1915	27	22	25	4
1916	53	16	33	3
1917	70	14	37	0
1920	36	36	46	4

The position, therefore, was that while the health as a whole had greatly improved, and the flat land division had become practically free from malaria, on the hill division the spleen rate refused to fall satisfactorily, and malaria still

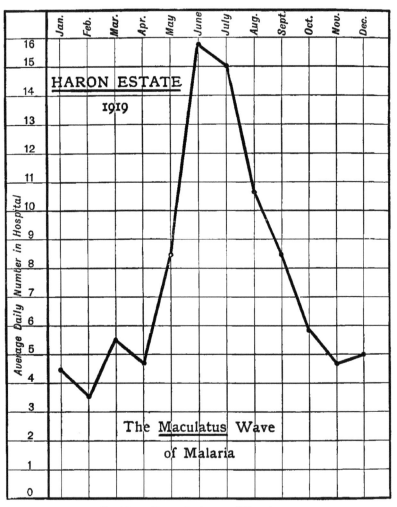

FIG. 84.—Chart of *Maculatus* Wave in 1919.

persisted. It is true jungle swamp existed within 40 chains of the lines, but I was not completely satisfied that it was responsible for all the malaria.

In 1919 I was on leave; and on my return found there had been an outbreak of malaria in the middle months of

the year on the hill division with the characteristic curve of
A. maculatus malaria. No larvæ were, however, found in the
ravine in February and March of 1920. But an examination
of the children showed the spleen rate was higher than it
had ever been: the rate for fourteen children in the lines
nearest to the ravine was no less than 57 per cent.; against
22 per cent. for seventeen children in lines farther off.

I felt pretty certain after this that *A. maculatus* had been
in the ravine in 1919, and would probably return in 1920,
on the cessation of the wet weather. Since the cost of oiling
would be considerable, it appeared to me more satisfactory
to prove definitely the existence of the mosquito before
recommending oiling. Towards the end of May malaria began
to increase, and *A. maculatus* was found in the ravine in great
abundance. Oiling was begun at once, and I have little doubt
will give excellent results; for the manager, Mr Hammond
Smith, has had experience of, and success with, oiling on
Pitchakawa, an estate situated at the other end of this same
small range.

Some years ago I found *A. maculatus* in the ravines of
Pitchakawa, and oiling was begun. The spleen rates show
the results.

Spleen Rates.

Year.	Number of Children Examined.	Number with Enlarged Spleen.	Spleen Rates.
1914	41	18	43
1916	46	26	56
1917	28	13	46
1920	45	6	13

In 1920 all the six children with enlarged spleen had been
over five years on the estate, except one who had been
three years.

Of twenty-seven children transferred from Klang Lands
Divisions about eight months ago, not one had an enlarged
spleen. All the children looked well and healthy. Excellent
work had been done here.

V.

THE REAPPEARANCE OF MALARIA ON A HILLY ESTATE.

The estate, which comprises both hill and flat land, has its coolie lines at the foot of the hills, because there is not sufficient flat land to allow the lines to be built half a mile away from the hills.

As a consequence of the presence of *A. maculatus*, the estate was intensely malarious. Between 1907 and 1910 no fewer than eight Europeans resigned on account of ill-health, one of them died. The coolies suffered equally. In 1912 a subsoil drainage scheme was carried out very thoroughly by one of the staff of the estate, and, although the pipes in places were laid on a steep hillside, they were not disturbed by heavy rain. In my notes of 1912 I find: "The fact that I saw it after four days in which 5·01 inches of rain had fallen, with one shower of 2·44 inches in forty-five minutes, shows how thoroughly the work has been done. Not only had the whole system withstood the heavy rainfall without suffering the least damage, but all the finished portion was completely dry within twenty-four hours of the rain ceasing."

The result of this excellent work was soon seen in the improved health of the children and labourers.

Year.	Number of Children Examined.	Spleen Rates.
1912		50·0
1913	91	42·8
1914	111	29·7
1915	131	10·6

The death rate showed a similar improvement.

Year.	Labour Force.	Death Rate.
1911	373	160
1912	492	68
1913	501	24
1914	520	13
1915	500	10

The births increased from two in 1911 (both children died) to nineteen in 1914; and the European health also improved.

In 1918 I was asked to visit the estate again, as the health had become bad. The two Europeans on the estate were constantly down with fever, and another was on leave on account of it.

The spleen rate showed an increase as follows:—

	Year.	Number of Children Examined.	Spleen Rates.
Children on the old site near the hills	1915 1918	135 100	10.6 43.8
Children farther from the hill (a new site)	1918	18	16.0

Deaths.—There had been twenty-nine deaths for the first eight months of 1918, giving a death rate per annum for working coolies of 64.9 per mille against 10 per mille in 1915. In addition, nineteen children had died. The admission rate to hospital had increased, and additional hospital accommodation had been erected at considerable cost. " *The cause of the recrudescence:* On revisiting the main ravine next the lines, which used to be the chief source of *A. maculatus*, it was evident that the importance of maintaining the anti-malaria work had not been fully realised. A considerable amount of water was still coming from the pipes, which had thus stood the test of six years' use without taking much harm. But probably half of the water from the ravine was coming down an open channel scoured out by the storm water. In some places there were probably pipes blocked by silt, but on the whole, from the amount of water discharging from the pipes, it would appear that blocking is comparatively slight." Oiling was being done with a not very effective hand sprayer; and on my visit, I found the oiling coolie fast asleep in the upper part of the ravine.

The war had thrown special work and responsibility on the manager; and, through shortness of staff, insufficient attention had been given to the anti-malaria work.

On my pointing out these things, the drainage and oiling were again made efficient, and the health rapidly improved. Writing in June 1920, the Estate Medical Officer says, " The work on the main ravines is all in good order," "leads and road drains are now being made thoroughly and systematically oiled." He reports the spleen rates as follows :—

Year.	Number of Children Examined.	Spleen Rates.
1919	133	9·0
1920	171	3·5

From these figures it is evident that the health has become practically normal again.

VI.

Another example of the reappearance of malaria on a hill estate is given in Chapter XVIII. in the notes appended to Fig. 63. Here the malaria came from the ravines of a newly opened estate which adjoined estate " SC."

CHAPTER XXIII

SCREENING

(1909).—In October 1900, a Beri-beri Convalescent Hospital at Jeram was opened. It is on a stretch of sandy shore. But at Jeram, as in Italy, the shifting sand is continually blocking the drains, so much so that one tide will undo a week's work. In fact, the task of keeping them open was abandoned, and the water was led off by a circuitous route. The result was that the patients suffered from malaria. When I took charge in January 1901, I went through all the case sheets of the patients who had contracted the disease and tabulated the results. From 1901 to 1907 the record was kept continuously. The population was under complete control; its number was definitely known, and in many ways it presented a very satisfactory field for observation.

The patients were provided with mosquito nets from the beginning, and yet, in spite of these, they continued to suffer from malaria.

It was then decided to make the hospital mosquito-proof. This appeared in the estimates for 1902 and was actually completed on the 17th November 1902. The gauze was of iron wire; the sea air rusted it, and . on the night of 11th October 1903, a strong wind carried it away. It was never replaced. From 1st January 1905, no malaria case was admitted into the hospital, in order to see to what extent the local admissions of malaria influenced the spread of the disease in hospital. From the beginning of 1906 all the beri-beri patients were on a weekly dose of 10 grains of quinine.

In this way I have tried to gain some idea of the relative importance of some of the factors influencing the epidemic.

The following are the figures obtained :—

Table showing the Number of Beri-beri Patients attacked by Malaria at Jeram. Daily average about 50.

Condition of Hospital.	Mosquito Nets only. Oct. 1900 to Nov. 1902.	Ward Mosquito. Nov. 1902 to Oct. 1903.	Mosquito Nets only. Oct. 1903 to Dec. 1904.	Malaria Cases not admitted. Jan. 1905 to Dec. 1905.
Number of months .	26	11	15	12
Number of patients attacked	75	c	48	20
Average number attacked *per mensem* . . .	2·87	0·45	3·20	1.66

It is to column No. 3 particularly to which I would direct attention. It will be seen that malaria was greatly reduced by the use of the gauze, and increased at once when the gauze was removed. That any malaria occurred is probably due to the purposely lax conditions which prevailed. No restraint was put on the patients to be indoors after sunset. Two double doors permitted entrance and exit after 6 P.M., and the patients often wandered to the native village only about a quarter of a mile away.

I was proposing to prevent the possibility of outside infection by looking the hospital after 6 P.M. when the storm put an end to the experiment.

The value of this experiment in my eyes is that the conditions were lax enough to permit of their being applied to coolies on an estate, or to coolies engaged on Government construction work, such as the making of railways or water works, where malaria is as great a scourge as it is on the worst estate.

With these results I accordingly approached the Government in 1904 with a suggestion for an experiment on the above lines, on the proposed extension of the Klang Water Works. Dr E. A. O. Travers supported the suggestion, and Government instructed the State Engineer to include my requirements in his estimates.

An Estate Experiment.—There was some delay in the preparation of the plans of the new works ; and the Government then, at my suggestion, sanctioned a special vote of

$2000 (about £240) to be spent on mosquito-proofing lines on an estate. I chose the most unhealthy spot I knew. The object of the experiment was, of course, not to test the mosquito theorem, but to discover whether lines could be built which would be sufficiently mosquito proof to reduce malaria, and yet would be acceptable to the ignorant coolie and in which he would be willing to live.

The spot chosen for one of the lines, the only one to be completed, was on a saddle at the head of two ravines, one of which was opened and drained by the estate, but still contained *A. maculatus*, and the other was unopened and undrained jungle. There had been trouble in building the lines originally; two contractors who tried to build the lines died from malaria since they refused to take quinine, and the first gang of coolies who inhabited it were practically exterminated by malaria. All children under the age of fifteen were found to be infected with malaria on blood examination. These coolies were soon removed. Ultimately the lines were finished. No coolies on the estate would inhabit them; and further, it was desirable to put in new coolies who presumably were free from malaria. A gang of coolies was put in during November 1907.

They were not given quinine daily like the other coolies, but were carefully examined by the dresser of the estate, and I paid as many visits to them as possible. Unfortunately my health was not satisfactory at the time, and I had to go on leave. Before going, however, I was able to determine that it was impossible to find anophelines or other mosquitoes within the lines, although my observations, extending over a year, had shown that before proofing it was always possible to take about ten anophelines by looking through all the rooms, and other mosquitoes were much more numerous. The mosquito proofing, therefore, certainly succeeded in reducing the number of anophelines within the lines.

Within a short time the coolies became aware of the character of the lines they were in, and asked to be removed. On one occasion I was told by a coolie that on the previous night a devil had been heard knocking on the walls.

I am unable to give any evidence as to the termination of the experiment. The manager stated that, as long as the coolies were there, they did not suffer from malaria, but that on account of their terror it was impossible to keep them there for long. He strongly suspected they left the lines at night and went to other unprotected lines. He also informed me that the coolies said the lines were very hot, and that at night they would often lie outside in a blanket. The lines had a wooden ceiling, and as they were more enclosed than other lines, it is probable they were hot.

I had unfortunately to leave this experiment, and therefore am unable to draw any conclusions. Doubtless the F.M.S. Government will take an early opportunity of testing the value of mosquito-proof lines on the railway extensions now being carried out towards the Siam States, where malaria will doubtless be as serious an obstacle as it has been in the previous railway and other public works.

(1920).—Although I suggested to the Malaria Advisory Board that it should undertake an experiment with screened lines, nothing has been done.

Screened Houses.—On a malarial estate in Johore where there were difficulties in getting healthy sites, I recommended that a bungalow and servants' quarters be screened. The manager was afraid that it would be uncomfortable, and that he would feel "cribbed, cabined, and confined" in it. However, I advised the whole building should be done; only two doors opening to the outside were to be left. There being no internal screened doors, the occupants could move about in the house as usual.

A year's trial convinced the manager that his fears were without foundation, and that screening was of value; and three other bungalows on the estate were screened. This was in 1914; since then, sixteen bungalows on other estates in the neighbourhood have been screened, which is the most satisfactory proof of the value of screening.

Dr Hickey, the medical officer of these estates, sends me an interesting letter full of details, from which the following are excerpts:—

"As regards screened houses, there has never been any doubt in my mind about their success. Not only on Segamat, but on Labis, Jenang, Genuang, Rubber Estates of Johore, and Johore Rubber Lands, Batu Anam, they have proved a success.

"I know what a difference screening has made to my

Fig. 85.—Mosquito-proof Coolie Lines.

Under the *atap* (palm leaf) roof there was a wooden ceiling. The verandah was closed by weather boarding for about three feet, and to the ceiling by iron wire gauze. There were two doors closed by spring hinges.

[*To face page* 260.

bungalow; in 1912 and 1913 I suffered a good deal from malaria."

Other anti-mosquito measures are employed on the estates, which have improved their health, but Dr Hickey adds :—

" I quite realise that malaria is gradually becoming less prevalent on the estates here, but the improvement in the health of those who occupy screened houses is really wonderful. Men ask for screened houses now."

Screened Hospitals.—On an estate where many anophelines exist, the malaria patients in hospital are a reservoir of parasites which soon infect the anophelines. These infect and reinfect the malaria patients, as well as patients coming in with other diseases; nor do the hospital staff escape. Consequently the administration of the hospital becomes difficult; and patients recover slowly, if, indeed, they do recover.

Protection from the insects is, therefore, a necessity. At first this was attempted by mosquito nets over the beds; but with natives the nets are ineffective, and it is usual to find a number of mosquitoes within them each morning. In fact, these nets are so effective as traps that, when I desire to get specimens of adult insects in a place, I search the nets at daybreak; for I know of no better way of getting a haul.

In view of the failure of the nets, in 1911 I advised an estate to screen its hospital. This was done, proved a success, and now there are screened hospital wards on six hill estates where malaria at one time was severe. Only one door is allowed at each end of the ward in which it is rare to see an insect. If any get in, they are caught in a bottle containing a plug of cotton-wool sprinkled with chloroform.

The plan, kindly supplied by Messrs James Craig, Ltd., who have built several of these hospitals, shows the details of the ward. One or two points call for comment :—

First.—It is important that the screening of the jack roof be by two vertical strips of gauze, and not by a horizontal strip as first suggests itself; for a horizontal strip catches and retains much dust, while vertical strips are relatively self-cleansing.

Secondly.—The doors should open outwards only, so that any mosquitoes resting on them are driven outwards when the door is opened. Double doors have not been found necessary.

Thirdly.—The drain must be inside the ward, as it is not possible with this design to wash the floors, and allow the water to escape under the side walls of the ward.

Fourthly.—Attempts were made to retain a screened space of 6 or 8 inches along the floor of the ward; in some hospitals the screening was on a hinged frame, in others it was fixed. The hinged screening has been most unsatisfactory; the fixed screening rather less so. In future I would have no screening within a foot of the floor; because it is liable to be damaged when the floor is washed.

Fifthly.—In Panama nothing but an almost pure copper, or alloy free from iron, withstood the climate; this was due to the screening being used on the outside of the verandah and exposed to rain and sun. In some hospitals here, the gauze used has been iron; it is placed so as not to avoid rain or sun, and is standing the climate well; indeed, in one hospital the gauze originally supplied in 1911 is still in use, and it has not yet been necessary to renew it in any hospital. The cost of screening a hospital depends on the area and the cost and quality of the gauze.

As a result of my experience of screened hospitals here, and from what I saw in Panama, I am strongly of opinion all native hospitals in this country should be screened instead of being supplied with mosquito nets.

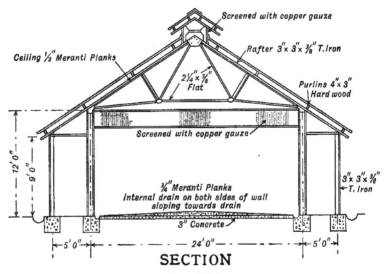

SECTION

Fig. 86 (a).

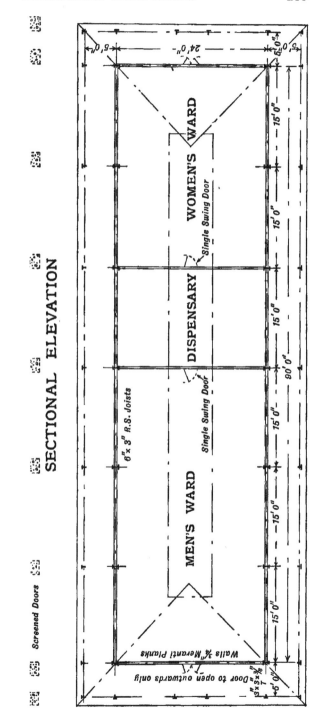

SECTIONAL ELEVATION

24. Gauge Galved: Corrugated Iron Roof

View with Corrugate
Roof removed shoui.
copper gauze sens

Screened Doors

WOMEN'S WARD

DISPENSARY

MEN'S WARD

Single Swing Door

6" × 3" R.S. Joists

Walls 3/4" Mercanti Planks

3"× 3"× 3/8" T

Door to open outwards only

24' 0"

6' 0"

5' 0"

15' 0"

15' 0"

15' 0"

90' 0"

15' 0"

15' 0"

5' 0"

FIG. 86 (b) and (c).

NED HPITAL.

CHAPTER XXIV

FOR the control of mosquitoes and malaria, land drainage in some form or other is so often required that the medical officer should learn at least the principles of this art, just as he learns the entomology of the disease. To most medical men the subject is a closed book; few engineers have studied it in relation to malaria prevention. In the tropics the engineer has responsibilities in connection with roads, water-supplies, electric-lighting, bridge-building, and other branches of a great and highly specialised profession; and it would be unreasonable to expect of him familiarity with the entomological aspects of drainage until these had been demonstrated to him. Yet the co-operation of the engineer and the medical officer is essential for a successful result; and co-operation cannot take place unless each understands something of the other's point of view. The engineer should learn something of entomology; the medical officer something about drainage. So a chapter on drainage as an anti-mosquito measure may be helpful; and, as an American engineer tells us, "There is no mystery connected with the theory and practice of land drainage, as some would have us believe; neither is there an instinct born in men which will relieve them from acquiring knowledge of this work in the old-time way."

The Composition of Soil.—The soil [20] consists of particles of the rocks forming the earth's crust; sometimes it overlies the rocks from which it came; sometimes it is composed of particles which have been carried by water far from their original source, and in ages long gone by. The particles vary in size, weight, and arrangement; between them are air or "pore" spaces; and the weight of the soil depends on all these factors. Sand particles being large and heavy are easily consolidated and contain a smaller amount of "pore" space than clay. Clay particles are relatively small and light, and are not readily consolidated, and have a higher "pore" space than sand. Although a clay soil is commonly called "heavy," it is not really heavier than a sandy soil; the expression "heavy" having reference to the difficulty of drawing a plough through it. The "pore" space in sand comes down to 25 or 30 per cent. of the whole; and in a "stiff clay" rises to over 50 per cent.

In addition to the particles of earth, soil contains water in varying quantity. Some of the water is so closely associated with the particles that it can only be driven off by heating much above the air temperature, and it is reabsorbed from the air, when the temperature is allowed to fall to normal. This is the hygroscopic moisture; it is not available for plant life.

In addition, each particle of soil is usually surrounded by a thin film of water which maintains itself by "surface tension"; that curious condition which allows us to blow soap bubbles, and causes water to climb up the sides of a glass, so that it stands above the general surface level of the fluid. When particles of soil, surrounded by this capillary water, are in touch with each other, the water exercises a powerful binding force. To its presence is due the fact that damp sand can be moulded into shapes which fall to pieces when the sand becomes dry.

The capillary water occupies very little of the "pore" space, for the thickness of the water film is hardly measurable; nor can this water move through the soil. When more water is added to the soil, the film over each particle becomes thicker; this surplus water can move upwards to the surface when there is evaporation, downwards to the subsoil water or "water table" and to drains, if the land be drained.

When still more water is added, the surplus passes downwards until, at a varying depth in the soil, all the "pore" spaces are filled. This is the level of the "water table," a level that varies according to the amount of water in the soil, which again depends on drainage and rainfall.

When the "pore" spaces are filled with water, the thin film round each particle of soil no longer exists, the particles are no longer bound to each other by the "surface tension" of the film, and they may easily move on each other. Hence wet sand is almost fluid; and swampy land is soft.

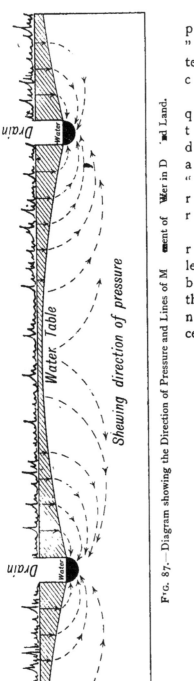

FᵢG. 87.— Diagram showing the Direction of Pressure and Lines of Movement of Water in Drained Land.

wet. In that case another drain may be cut through the centre.

It will be understood that when there is a drain at A and C only, the undrained soil must be highest at B, the point farthest from the drains; but if an additional drain be placed at D, then the highest levels of the water will be found at E and F. The water, as a whole, will then be farther below the surface, and the land better drained. See Fig. 88.

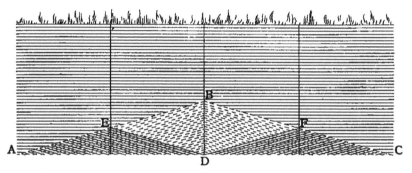

FIG. 88.—Diagram of Influence of Distance between Drains on Depth of Drainage. (After King.)

The Results of Drainage.—The results of draining land are numerous, and need be referred to here only very briefly. Drainage removes an excess of water, which is replaced by air; not permanently, however, for each fall of rain refills the "pore" spaces with water that in its turn again gives place to air. This is the aeration of the soil, so important to the agriculturist. Without it the organisms, which convert the oxygen and nitrogen of the "pore" spaces to the use of plants, cease to work; the plant dies, and is replaced by the swamp grasses and plants with special adaptations to make soil air unnecessary. To the anti-mosquito worker the drying of the soil is no less important; it allows rain to be absorbed, instead of standing in pools, or making the land a swamp.

Drainage sweetens the soil, as the farmer says. In some countries it removes the excess of alkali which makes the land entirely unfit for agriculture; in peaty lands it removes the excess of peaty acids, no less injurious to most plants of value to man. These changes come from the movement of the water; stagnant water allowing excess of acid or alkali to accumulate. Drainage hardens the soil. It allows men, and, it may be, cattle and vehicles to move over the surface without inconvenience or without making deep impressions in the ground, which expose the ground water and form mosquito breeding-places. As we have seen, when a soil is saturated with water, there is little cohesion between the particles, and so they are easily moved; when land is drained, the soil particles are bound together by the thin films of capillary water that surround them and are not easily moved.

Many other changes occur in drained soil, such as an increase in the temperature, which are important to the agriculturist, but need not be considered by the sanitarian at the moment.

Subsoil Drainage.—At first drainage was probably carried out by shallow surface drains; later, these would be converted into trenches. But as land increased in value, and the number of trenches had to be multiplied, subsoil drainage was invented.

Poles and Faggots were laid in the drains, which were then covered over, so that the surface of the land was uninterrupted. Needless to say, the drainage by these was not very permanent, except under special conditions.

Stone Drains were an advance on poles and faggots. Sometimes the drain was simply half filled with small stones; sometimes a flat stone was placed horizontally over the small stones, or larger flat stones were placed on edge in the bottom of the drain, from which was evolved the system of putting down three flat stones to form a triangle with a channel between them. But stone drains were expensive; and in time they were replaced by the tile or pipe drain; for a cartload of pipes went as far as a hundred cartloads of stones.

The Pipe Drain.—The drain pipe itself has undergone various modifications. In its earliest form, the pipe or tile was made singly, and by hand. The clay was rolled out and then pressed over a block into the shape of a horse-shoe (Fig. 89); and in using these horse-shoe tiles it was only deemed necessary to lay them on a hard bottom of clay. It was soon found, however, that this was not enough. The run of the water wore the bottom of the drain and softened the clay, till the tiles were either displaced altogether or sank into the bottom, and the drain became useless. The next improvement was to make the tile with feet, as in Fig. 90, in order to prevent it sinking into the earth or clay on which it rested. An obvious improvement on this, however, was to set the horse-shoe tile upon a flat sole, a little wider than the tile itself, as in Fig. 91. When placed in position the possibility of the tile sinking into the earth was overcome, and at the same time a solid run was provided for the water which flowed through the drain.

"*The Cylindrical Drain Pipe.*—The sole-and-tile was in turn superseded by the machine-made pipe, in which the horse-shoe form, as in Fig. 92, was at first closely adhered to, but this has now been entirely superseded by the cylindrical pipe shown in Fig. 93, which possesses many advantages. It forms a complete conduit in itself; it is stronger than any other form of pipe; its extreme lightness makes it very easy of transport, and owing to its small diameter a less quantity of earth need be excavated in digging a drain for a cylindrical pipe, at a given depth, than for any other drain material."—(SCOTT).

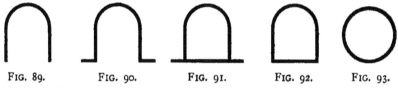

FIG. 89.   FIG. 90.   FIG. 91.   FIG. 92.   FIG. 93.

These Figures show some Stages in the Evolution of the Subsoil Drain Pipe.

Pipe Collars were at first generally used to join the ends of the pipes; these were short lengths of a pipe wide enough to admit the ends of the pipes forming the drain. But they have gone out of use, as an unnecessary expense, except possibly in very peaty soil.

"*How Water enters the Pipes.*—The question [27a] 'How does water enter a drain pipe when it is laid 3 or 4 feet deep in the soil?' is often asked by beginners. From experiments which were carefully carried out by Mr Josiah Parkes, in order to determine this point, it was found that under a pressure of 4 feet of soil the absorbent power of various pipes formed of various soils was equal to the passing of about one five-hundredth part of the quantity of water which enters the conduit through the crevice existing between each pair of pipes. By so much, therefore, the porous nature of the pipe material is useful; practically, this influence is so small that we may regard the whole of the water as entering at the joints, but the greater portion of it enters the drain pipes from below.

"In all soils requiring drainage there exists a water-table

or level of supersaturation, and in a well-drained soil this level corresponds with the level of the drain pipes. When rain falls on the surface, the water finds its way downwards till it reaches this water-table. It then begins to rise, and if the drains are sufficiently active the pipes will carry off this rise of water as fast as it enters them from below. If the water rises above the level of supersaturation faster than the drain can take it off, then of course the pipes become completely swamped, as it were, and the water enters at every part of the joints. When the rain has ceased to fall, however, the continued action of the drain will soon suffice to again reduce the water of supersaturation to its proper level; water will even cease to flow from the drains until more rain falls, and then the same thing will go on as before, the height to which the free subjacent water rises being wholly dependent on the activity of the drain, and the sufficiency of the pipe to carry off the water from it in a given time.

" That the water will be freely admitted to the pipes at the joints is easily shown. With 2-inch pipes, when laid as close end-to-end as possible, the opening between two of them is usually not less than one-tenth of an inch on the whole circumference. This makes six-tenths of a square inch opening for the entrance of water at each joint. In the length of a drain between any two points, say 100 yards distance, with pipes 12 inches long, there will be 300 joints or openings, each six-tenths of a square inch in area, or a total of 180 square inches for admitting water to the drain. The area of the outlet from a 2-inch pipe is, however, only about 3 inches, so that the inlet area is nearly sixty times greater than the outlet area."

The Drainage of Ravines.—In an early chapter (II.) I pointed out how money had been spent needlessly in the town of Klang in "filling in" swamps at the foot of hills, and how these swamps could be dried by intercepting the water coming from the hills by a hill-foot drain. In ravine drainage the same principle is applied. In narrow ravines a pipe along each hill foot may be sufficient, but in the wider ones and longer ones a central line of pipes is also required. The method of laying them so that they are not disturbed by storm water has already been described in the chapter on Seafield Estate.

Roots of rubber trees grow into subsoil pipes, just as the

roots of many water-loving trees grow into pipes in England. To guard against this, the ravine should either be cleared of rubber trees, or the pipes opened at once, if there be evidence of blockage, and the roots removed.

It sometimes happens that a long ravine begins beyond the sanitary circle and runs through it; and that only from the point it enters the circle is subsoil drainage required. So far no really satisfactory way of draining such a ravine by pipes has been discovered. Attempts have been made to pass the water from the upper and open part of the ravine into the subsoil pipes of the lower part through rough stone filters; but silt has blocked them so frequently that they have become usually but not always useless. It has generally been found necessary to carry the stream down in a cement channel, or to oil the whole ravine.

A Demonstration at Klang.—When' the sanitarian begins mosquito control in a town he will find many difficulties in putting the principles of correct drainage into force. Almost at every step he will be tempted to make some compromise; the engineer may not quite grasp what is required; and before he is aware, the sanitarian may find himself saddled with a system of drainage which he can only regard as something considerably below the standard he intended to attain. At least that has been my experience. So when asked in 1911 to advise the Municipality of Singapore on the control of malaria, I suggested that the officers who would carry out the work in Singapore should come to Klang for a demonstration. The points discussed were subsequently embodied in my report, and are republished now in the hope that they may be helpful.

MEMORANDUM ON MALARIA IN THE DISTRICT OF TELOK BLANGA, SINGAPORE.

By MALCOLM WATSON.

A Preliminary Demonstration at Klang.

1. When invited by your Anti-malaria Committee to proceed to Singapore and advise on the anti-malaria measures to be adopted, I at once suggested the advisability of a preliminary visit to Klang of your own officers, who would eventually be

responsible not only for the local investigation of the disease, but also for the necessary engineering works.

2. My object in proposing this visit was that those upon whom would be thrown the duty of recommending and of carrying out remedial measures, should have an opportunity of seeing for themselves the anti-malaria works which have been adopted at Klang and at Port Swettenham, and of becoming acquainted with districts where the malaria conditions have been the subject of study for some years.

3. Malaria in the F.M.S. has been found to disappear from areas of low-lying land where the ground water lies very high, and where there exist what would appear to be dangerous mosquito breeding-places; while on the other hand many hill areas are intensely malarious, although the only water to be seen consists of springs and of clear running streams.

4. It occurred to me that a visit to such areas would be of infinitely greater value than many pages of descriptive writing. I could thus, moreover, take this opportunity of demonstrating the details and essentials of land drainage, and of pointing to some of the errors (which were perhaps unavoidable) in the pioneer work done here, the repetition of which in Singapore I was anxious to prevent.

5. The officers selected for this visit were Drs Middleton and Finlayson and Mr Ball. They spent three days in examining these areas :—

    (i.) *Hill-foot Drains.*—In the town of Klang the system of hill-foot drains was seen, and special attention was called to the importance of draining at as low a level as possible; the higher up the hill the drain is cut, the greater the excavation, and consequently the greater the expense, while the lower the drain and the nearer it is to the edge of the swamp, the more effective it is, both in cutting off from the swamp all water coming from the hill, and also in withdrawing water from the swamp.

Where a spring appears on the side of a hill some distance above the hill-foot drain, the most economical way of dealing with it is by cutting a lateral drain from the hill-foot drain up to the spring.

    (ii.) *Dangerous Swamps drained by Earth Drains.*—In Klang

the dangerous hill-foot swamps were, and still * are, drained only by open earth drains. These have been found sufficient, and are, of course, much less expensive than brick or masonry drains. Originally the whole anti-malaria drainage system at Klang (except the main outlet which took sewage) consisted of earth drains, and it was by means of earth drains that Klang town was freed from malaria. Gradually the system of earth drains is being replaced by brick drains, and as these have too often been constructed with more regard to some ideal "grade" than to the requirements of the ground through which the drain passes, I have no hesitation in saying that the actual land or anti-malarial drainage of Klang is less effective now with its brick drains than it was eight years ago with its earth drains. I would even go further and say that, if a close watch be not kept on the level at which brick drains are laid down in Klang, the hill-foot swamps will reappear (as two now threaten to do), and malaria will recur in the town.

It is important, therefore, constantly to bear in mind that a brick drain is unnecessary in the eradication of malaria on flat land in this country or for draining swamps at the foot of small hills. Not only does a brick drain add greatly to the original cost of the work, but, unless graded with care and due regard to the surrounding land, it may actually hinder effective drainage.

(iii.) *The Grading of Brick Drains :—*

(a) The explanation of the current practice in putting brick drains down with a steeper gradient than the original earth drain is to be found in the necessity of laying a sewer with a stiffer gradient than a drain carrying only clean water from land drainage.

(b) Brick drains are not as a rule laid down in this country except in towns; and then only in places where a considerable population has so polluted an earth drain that it has become a stinking stagnant mass, more akin to a cesspit than a channel carrying off sewage. On the advantages of substituting for such a stagnant channel a self-cleaning brick drain it is unnecessary for me to dwell.

* Subsoil drains were subsequently laid down when *A. maculatus* appeared in Klang in 1913.

(*c*) Experience has shown our engineers that a steep gradient is necessary if such a brick drain is to be satisfactory and self-cleaning, and it has consequently become a rule that such drains 9-inch to 12-inch diameter shall be laid down with a gradient of about 1 in 100, unless they be of abnormal size.

There is no question that this is sound practice for brick drains when they carry sewage.

(*d*) It must not be forgotten that engineers have an additional reason for insisting on a steep grade for sewers in this country. Although we have heavy storms to scour out our sewers, the average composition of sewage in a brick drain in this country is much more concentrated than in England, because the absence of water-closets, of baths, and of house-to-house water-supply reduces the quantity of water employed in a tenement, and the domestic waste water or sewage is thus not diluted to the extent to which it usually is in England.

(*e*) The greater the concentration of sewage, the greater difficulty it has in finding its way along a channel; consequently the gradient of the channel must be the steeper according as it is to be the more self-cleansing; (and all channels carrying sewage should be self-cleansing, whether classed as sewers or brick drains).

(*f*) There are many swampy places in this country where a gradient of 1 per centum, carried up from the outfall, would bring the top end of the drain at such a level that it would be ineffective as a channel for draining the land through which it passes, the invert of the drain coming above the level of the ground.

As an anti-malarial measure, it would be a pure waste of money to lay down a brick drain at such a level and with such a gradient, although it might be quite proper to do so, merely from the point of view of a sewage system.

(*g*) It would appear, therefore, almost as if sewage and land drainage were incompatible. Undoubtedly this is so in many places. It should be the rule wherever possible to combine the two, for it is an advantage to carry off the land drainage water quickly by means of a brick channel, and a further advantage to be able to dilute the sewage by the land water, thereby expediting the flow of the sewage.

(*h*) It sometimes happens that in constructing a brick drain in place of an earth drain, either for the purpose of carrying off storm water, or as part of a sewage system, the level of the invert of the brick drain is the same as that of the original earth drain, and the swampy condition of the surrounding land is overlooked. If the brick drain has been put down at such a level that the swamp cannot be drained into it, and the brick drain is the only outlet for the drainage of the swamp, as is sometimes the case, then the swamp can only be drained by pulling up the brick drain and relaying it at a lower level.

(*i*) I would therefore advise that no anti-malaria drain be constructed other than as an earth drain in the first instance. If such an earth drain be found to be inefficient through being insufficiently deep, then it is an easy matter to deepen it. If, on the other hand, a brick drain be put down and the surrounding land be still found swampy, the deepening of the brick drain involves the heavy expense of reconstructing it at a lower level, and at even greater expense than that of the original drain.

(*j*) Where the sewage must be at a higher level than the land drain, it may be possible, when we have had more experience of underground drainage, to combine the two systems with advantage. A system of underground pipes might very well drain the land at the sides of a brick sewer; the sewer, being laid with a steeper grade than the subsoil drain, would soon reach a level that would enable the subsoil drain to discharge into it. I have mentioned this only as indicating the line in which an advance can be made, and a difficulty overcome. While for anti-malarial drainage a brick drain is not essential, it is nevertheless an advantage to have the land water carried off quickly. And equally is it an advantage in this country to dilute the sewage with land water so that it flows more freely.

(*k*) There is a further advantage in replacing earth drains by some self-cleansing system, either closed pipes or brick drains, namely, that diseases other than malaria are carried by mosquitoes. Not to mention dengue, the mosquito carriage of which may be open to question, the subject of " Filaria " is one of the gravest moment, and it is one which is certain to engage

U

more attention in the future. I will deal with this *infra.*

(*l*) The visit to Port Swettenham showed how land could be freed from malaria by drainage even when it was below the level of high tide. The position and level of outlets protected by tide valves was discussed. There appears no reason why such outlets should not be one or even two feet below the level of half-tide.* The lower the outlet, within limits, the greater the reservoir of dry earth which can absorb rainfall until the outlet is opened by the falling tide.

(iv.) *Filling up a Swamp:*—

(*a*) In Klang attempts were made in more than one place to get rid of the water of a hill-foot swamp by filling it in with earth. They were failures. Filling might be a success if the earth were of a very pervious nature, so that the water from the springs which were the cause of the swamp could freely traverse the "filling," and travelling under it make its way to the nearest drain.

(*b*) But "filling" in this country usually consists of a very impervious reddish clayey earth taken from a hill. To place such an impervious material on the top of the impervious bed of a swamp is merely to raise the level of the impervious layer, and to enable the water descending from the hill to appear at the resulting surface. The springs accordingly appear on the top of the filling, and spreading out on it continue to form important breeding-places for dangerous anopheles.

(*c*) Not only is such filling ineffective, but it is very expensive, costing at least ten times as much as the earth drains which would effectively drain the swamp, and often much more.

(*d*) There is another reason for draining a swamp in preference to "filling" it in. Owing to the expense of "filling," it is unlikely that more will be applied than is just sufficient to obliterate all traces of water from the surface. The ground water will therefore still be within a few inches of the surface.

On the other hand the cutting of an extra depth of drain will lower the subsoil water at a very small cost, as compared with filling.

(*e*) There is an advantage in lowering the level of the

* 1920. They have been placed much lower since then.

subsoil water, namely, that the dry soil above the water forms a reservoir for rainfall. Two feet of soil may very well be able to absorb one-third of their volume of water; in other words, will be able to take up eight inches of rain.

Such drained land will therefore be much less liable to become swampy in very wet weather than the land which has been so "filled in" that the ground water even in dry weather is still only a few inches from the surface.

(*f*) It is an old observation, made long before anything was known of the part played by the mosquito in the propagation of the malaria parasite, that, lowering the level of the subsoil water and the dry cultivation of the soil which then first became practicable, led to a disappearance of malaria. And it is well known that even in non-tropical and non-malarious countries, houses built on land with a low ground water are healthier than those on land where the water stands nearer to the surface of the ground.

(*g*) If houses are to be built at all on the swampy land, I have no hesitation in saying that they will be healthier in every respect if the swamp has been drained, than if it has simply been "filled in."

(*h*) Of course there are times when, and places where, to fill in and raise the level of land will add greatly to its value. And the money spent on such filling may be a sound commercial investment, which may be quickly realised in the market with great profit. Not to "fill in" under these circumstances would be to neglect an opportunity not only of adding to the area of land available for use, but also of making an addition to the revenue which may be employed advantageously in other directions.

(*i*) Or, as in the case of the Tanjong Pagar reclamation, a great area may be added to a city, the occupation of which will relieve prevalent overcrowding of more central portions. Such a work has a sanitary value which can hardly be overestimated.

To reclaim a dangerous swamp, to bring a labouring population near to its work, to house that population in buildings constructed and maintained according to the highest sanitary standard, to add to the revenues not only a large annual sum from rent, but also a great asset of ever-increasing value, all at one stroke, is a conception of sanitary statesmanship of the highest order.

(v.) *Mosquito-borne Diseases other than Malaria :—*

(*a*) There is another point of view from which the anti-malarial drainage of the land must be looked at. I refer to the other diseases which are carried by mosquitoes. The most important of these in this country is Filaria.* We know it occurs among Malayans in all parts of the Archipelago. According to Manson, 10 per centum of Amoy's inhabitants harbour the parasite, and it is present only in a slightly less percentage in the Southern Chinese. Some parts of India are seriously affected, and so are places in Japan. These are countries which send many of their inhabitants to Singapore.

(*b*) The disease is none the less serious because infection by the parasite may show no symptoms for many years. But the condition of the Fiji Islands where Filaria is present in 25 per cent. of the population, and elephantiasis is so terribly prevalent, is a warning that the ever-increasing immigration attracted to Singapore by its prosperity may be drawing unawares to the island and to the city unrecognised carriers of the disease, and a rude awakening may come to a knowledge of the fact that the disease is silently but none the less tragically spreading among the populace.

(*c*) Year by year we see more clearly that along with its benefits Western civilisation, with its free system of communications, is introducing serious dangers in the form of increased liability to disease ; and the greater the populations and the freer the communications with other countries the greater is the danger.

(*d*) Plague was carried to India at the end of last century by ships from the West. But for these, India would in all probability now be free from the disease. Indeed, in vast regions of India any benefits ever given by Western civilisation have been more than balanced by this disease.

(*e*) Sleeping sickness is an example how in a few years a terrible disease can march across a great continent, keeping step with the white man in his progress, and cause such devastation that whole regions have to be abandoned.

(*f*) Throughout the tropical cities of the world, the security

* A worm whose embryos live in the blood.

from fire given by the more substantial house built under Western rule, is being paid for in an alarming increase in *tubercle*.

(g) The great increase of malaria in Singapore is undoubtedly due to the conditions produced by its increasing population and prosperity. It would surely be unwise to wait until a dreadful disease like elephantiasis is upon the city before taking steps to check its course.

(h) I would strongly recommend, therefore, that in such time as he can spare from his malaria work, Dr Finlayson should carry out an investigation into the prevalence of Filaria among the people. This can easily be done by having slides of blood taken from the inmates of the hospitals. For, while the drainage of swamps by means of open earth drains does away with probably 95 per cent. of the mosquito-breeding area, the very drains, especially if neglected, produce a few mosquitoes capable of carrying this disease.

(i) While urging the use of earth drains for the purpose of eradicating malaria, I confess I regard them only as marking a stage in our progress towards the not far distant day when all breeding-places of mosquitoes within a town will be obliterated. In time it may be possible to replace the open earth drains by closed subsoil drains, thereby not only reducing the cost of upkeep, but rendering them impossible as breeding-places.

(j) This, however, must be in the future, and only when from experience we can be sure that the subsoil pipe in this country has a reasonable life of usefulness. So far as I know there do not appear to be any special difficulties in using pipes in this climate. But before launching out on any large scheme it would be wise to give a small area a thorough trial.

(k) If no unforeseen difficulties arise, the drainage of the future will be brick drains where there is sewage, and a system of subsoil drainage for the land; the latter falling into the brick drains. Storm water will be carried off by shallow drains under which are the subsoil drains. Should a definite system of closed sewers be adopted for Singapore* with pumping stations at various places, it would obviously be more economical to deal with storm water separately. The

* 1920. This now exists.

employment of subsoil drainage, connected with the sewers but independent of the shallow storm water drains, would in all probability facilitate the separate treatment of the storm water.

6. I have endeavoured in the foregoing pages to place on record some of the points discussed at Klang and Singapore. It will be seen that the malaria problem, like most other problems, cannot be kept in a water-tight chamber. Measures for its eradication should be considered not only from the malaria aspect alone, but from its bearing on other questions.

7. In dealing with malaria, and especially in spending money on measures for its eradication, every care must be taken that some other problem is not made thereby more acute or more difficult of solution.

8. I would summarise the foregoing demonstration as follows :—

(a) Do not spend money on filling in a swamp unless—

(i.) You cannot drain it (a situation which will rarely be the case) ; or

(ii.) You can see your way clearly to realise within a reasonable period the money so invested at a profitable return in either cash or health.

(b) Don't begin by filling up the natural outlet when a swampy area *must* be filled up. This only aggravates the swamp, and it will be pure luck if an outbreak of malaria does not follow, or if already present, is not increased.

(c) An open drain properly placed at the foot of a hill intercepting the water from the hill, costs a mere fraction of the filling which would be necessary to cover the water of a hill-foot swamp, and renders the ground drier, and less liable to revert to a swampy condition in wet weather, and healthier as a building site.

(d) Only consider the question of filling in a swamp after trying to drain it. After your attempts it will often be found that the filling is unnecessary. Much waste of money will thus be prevented.

(e) If an earth drain when first cut does not efficiently drain the swamp through which it runs, it is often possible to dig it deeper, at a very small additional cost.

(*f*) If a brick drain has been constructed, the cost of deepening it will be probably more than the original cost of the drain.

(*g*) No anti-malaria drain should be piped or bricked *until it has been proved to be thoroughly capable of draining* the swampy land, through which it runs. If it cannot drain the water off as an earth drain, it will certainly be less efficient as a brick or piped drain.

(*h*) An open earth drain will, except in hilly land, eradicate malaria. In the future it may be possible either to brick in, or pipe the drain, so as to render it harmless as a breeding-place for any class of mosquito. In the meantime, it is doing its work in eradicating malaria at a minimum cost, and it forms no obstacle to any system which may be desirable in the future.

CHAPTER XXV

ON MOSQUITOES

ONE of the first difficulties confronting a medical officer who attempts mosquito control is the identification of the local mosquitoes, and even of the anopheles. When, after Ross's discovery that the mosquitoes carry malaria, the importance of the subject came to be recognised, Mr Theobald,[28] of the British Museum, undertook to receive, describe, and classify the insects sent to him ; and he published a series of volumes in the course of the following six or seven years. During the same period, a number of observers in different countries published descriptions of the mosquitoes taken by them ; with the result that few insects have escaped being described under one or more names.

As time went on and new specimens were discovered, the distinctive characters originally employed to separate various genera and species were often seen to be connected by intermediate forms, and shaded off into one another, making classification a matter of difficulty and controversy. It has been confusing in the extreme to the student ; and, for the beginner, has proved an almost insuperable obstacle to progress.

Although considerable progress has now been made, and the synonymity of many species is worked out, it will yet probably be the simplest plan for a new worker to learn only the local species as species—without troubling too much about genera. It will be of the greatest advantage to him, also, if he can obtain some practical demonstrations of the insects from one familiar with the local species. This will save him many a weary hour, much wandering in the wilderness of the unknown, and may prevent him making serious mistakes.

It is not my purpose here to attempt to describe the distinctive features of our local anopheles. The beginner will find the two keys—of larvæ and of adult insects—prepared by Dr C. Strickland helpful. After mastering these, he may proceed to the papers published by Drs Strickland [29] and Stanton,[30] the names of which I give in the list of references. Dr Barbour's [31] paper on the infecting of the local anopheles must also be studied; and the first of a new series of papers by Dr Hacker [32] on local malaria has been published.

Here I purpose merely to make some general observations on the different anopheles and their relationship to malaria. In the course of this volume much has already been said on the subject; but there are some gaps which may with advantage be filled.

In doing so I propose to utilise some of Dr C. Strickland's unpublished observations. During the period of his work in the Malay Peninsula, he carefully recorded his observations in such a form that they admitted of tabulation. He did so in order that, as far as possible, the study of the conditions in which mosquitoes lived, or did not live, might be put on a mathematical basis; he aimed at giving something more than "impressions," and hoped to supply a scientific basis for any conclusions he might draw, and any general statements he might make. His observations deal with 15,165 breeding-places; and as a large number of details of each breeding-place is recorded, and analysed, · it will be realised how laborious the work was, and how valuable it is. General statements, such as that *A. umbrosus* is a pool breeder, or *A. maculatus* is a stream breeder, have been tested mathematically; and it is now possible to see how far they are true or untrue.

I understand Government does not propose to publish the report; but as Dr Strickland has lent me a copy with permission to publish extracts, I gladly do so on account of the value of his observations, and of the important contributions he has made to our knowledge of mosquitoes, and the prevention of malaria in this country.

A. ludlowi.—So much has been said of it in the chapter on "The Malaria of Mangrove Swamps and *Anopheles ludlowi*," that I will content myself with emphasising the one great practical point. At first sight the problem of its eradication seems insoluble. It is a prolific pool breeder; perhaps the most prolific anopheles one meets. It breeds in almost every pool in the zone which it frequents; tufts of grass, bits of stick, and every sort of obstruction are usually found to shelter it in enormous numbers. Cracks in mud, hoof marks, blocked drains are loved by it.

The malaria it causes is shown by the high spleen rate; its zone has acquired a world-wide notoriety for unhealthiness; and it will be strange if there are not well-known local instances of its malignant power. The control of malaria in these circumstances may well daunt the bravest optimist. Yet I must insist that it can be controlled with ease by a simple system of clean, open drains; and this had been demonstrated time and again in the Malay Peninsula.

A. rossii (Giles) is comparatively rare, but does occur. It plays no part in the epidemiology of the disease in the F.M.S., as far as is known; just as it is a negligible factor in India. *A. rossii* var. *indefinita* is the common form here; it, too, is not, I believe, of practical importance.

The Umbrosus Group.

In the original description, *A. umbrosus* was given with only one white spot on the costal vein of the wing; but when I came to work with the insect I found a second spot so common that I designated it *A. umbrosus* var. *x.* There are now known to be several anopheles closely allied to it, although none are found in the profusion of *A. umbrosus*. *A. umbrosus*, as we saw, breeds in the inner Mangrove Zone, the Coastal Plain, the Coastal Hills; rarely, if ever, in the Inland Hills, although further research is required to map the line of its inland limit.

A. separatus is not unlike *A. umbrosus*, but has white bands on its palpi, which at once distinguishes it. It frequents the coastal region like *A. umbrosus*.

A. albotaeniatus also breeds in the inner Mangrove, is very rarely taken in the Coastal Plain, but seems to become commoner in the Coastal Hills, although even here it is rare. The character chiefly distinguishing it from *A. umbrosus* is the broad, white banding of the hind legs. It is not known to be a natural carrier of malaria.

A. albotaeniatus var. *montanus* may be called the *umbrosus* of the Inland Hills; but in comparison with the number of

A. umbrosus found in the Coastal Plains it is a rare mosquito. It is like *A. albotaeniatus*, but has still more white on its legs. It is not known to be a natural carrier of malaria. Like *A. umbrosus* it is a jungle species, and Dr Hacker's observations would indicate that it disappears when the ravine is opened; indeed the whole *Umbrosus* group just named are primarily jungle mosquitoes, living in pools, or very slowly streaming swamps.

In his chapter on "The Mosquitoes of Virgin Jungle," Dr C. Strickland, after describing the dense shade through which "not a sunbeam filters," says :—

"As for mosquitoes of any sort they are very rare; all travellers in the virgin forest testify to it. Travellers will sleep there with impunity and not be bitten by mosquitoes.

"But it is only in certain parts of the virgin forest, those parts which lie on the uplands and on the mountains. If the traveller enter the forest on the flat land he will certainly be attacked by species of the *umbrosus* type, by *Mansonia* species, and *Stegomyia scutellaris*.

"During the rainy season the little pockets among the roots of the trees on the flat forest land become filled with small pools, if the land is not actually under flood from the neighbouring rivers. In such collections of water *umbrosus* will be found breeding. On the hills, of course, no such breeding-grounds form.

"During the dry season the shallow valley beds, on the flat land and between the hills on the low hill-land, become morasses of sodden and wet ground between great gnarled trees and creeper roots. In these little pockets *umbrosus* delights to breed. As also *aitkeni* among the low hills, but not on the flat.

"In this flat land virgin forest I have never found any other species than *umbrosus*, and among the low hills none other than of that type or *aitkeni*.

"In the uplands and mountains *aitkeni* is the common species in the pools among the rocky streams and in the tributary ravines, occasionally specimens of the *umbrosus* type, but probably not *umbrosus* (Theobald), are found.

"It may be recalled that in a paper entitled 'Certain Observations in the Epidemiology of Malarial Fever in the Malay Peninsula,' which was reported to Government, I said that *umbrosus* does not occur in the hill-land jungle. This is, I believe, true, *sensu restricto*, though some of the rare anopheles mentioned in that paper as occurring in the hinterland hill jungle belong to that type.

"As for other species, I have never found any in virgin forests. Still I have found *barbirostris, asiaticus,* and *leucosphyrus* in situations in secondary jungle which would seem to indicate that they too might be found in virgin forest. With regard to *leucosphyrus,* if it does occur in the virgin forest on the flat land, it must be very rare, and of no importance, because Watson, in all his records of flat-land estates, never mentions it. At Batu Arang, one day, Dr Watson and I caught fifty *umbrosus* in a few minutes, but in two days did not see a *leucosphyrus,* although we were working along the edge of virgin jungle all the time."

In contrast to these jungle mosquitoes, I may just quote Dr Strickland's next paragraph :—

"Of the common Malay species, *fuliginosus, albirostris, maculatus, karwari, sinensis, rossii, ludlowi* and *kochii,* I have never found one in situations which cause one to suppose they would be found in virgin jungle. If ever they do it must be so rarely that it does not matter, except as a curiosity."

.   .   .   .

Writing of the Peat belts, Dr Strickland says :—

"I have only found one species of anopheles in the peat deposits, namely, *umbrosus,* and that occurs in some quantity. I have examined peat swamps, and drained peat, and peat under jungle and peat opened up."

It will be remembered how a knowledge that *A. maculatus* did not live in peat reduced the amount of land drained by pipes on North Hummock Estate, and saved much money. (See Chapter XVII.).

Again, in his paper on "The Mosquitoes of Stream Courses," Dr Strickland describes the different kinds of streams and rivers to be found, and says :—

"Small ravine stream under jungle. The stream is usually difficult to define; the whole is rather a streaming morass. I have recorded *aitkeni,* and species of the *umbrosus* in such places."

In the table of occurrence rate Dr Strickland gives the *umbrosus* group as only 47 per mille observations on stream courses; but in the record of wells, *umbrosus* and *sinensis* head the list, both being 241 per mille.

These short extracts will have given some idea of *A. umbrosus.* Called by Mr Theobald *umbrosus* from its dark colour, the name is no less appropriate if we look at its habits and haunts. As an adult it frequents the deep shades of the forest; and although, as a larva, it is often found in wells of pure water at a hill foot even in sunshine, it most frequently lives in stagnant pools of brown peaty water, or in the slowly streaming morasses of the virgin jungle.

It may, however, be found among grass and debris in a drain; but not if there is much current. So it is destroyed when a drain is cut through its breeding-place; as we have seen in studying the opening up of the Coastal Plain. Fortunate it is that it should be so easily overcome, for with it disappears the malaria it carries; and, as Dr Marshall Barbour says: " The evidence obtained in these experiments, both in regard to the artificially and naturally infected insects, would confirm Watson's conclusion that *A. umbrosus* is an important carrier in Malaya."

ON THE MOSQUITOES OF RAVINES.

In the preceding pages on the *Umbrosus* group the reader will have learned that *A. umbrosus* is to be found not only in the "flat land" or Coastal Plain, but in the low hills or Coastal Hills, as I have called them in this volume, when these zones are undrained and under jungle. Further inland, in the "uplands and mountains," or "inland hills," *A. umbrosus* gives place to a closely allied species, *A. albotaeniatus* var. *montanus.*

In the ravines of both of the hill zones, that is of the Coastal and the Inland Hills, another mosquito is found. In almost every respect save two it is the antithesis of *A. umbrosus. A. aitkeni*, for that is its name, lives in mountain streams for preference; at the edges of the torrent where it dashes down the granite mountain-side, the mosquito is found often in considerable quantity. Behind roots and rocks, in little bays of gravel or sand, it can be caught by one with some experience of methods appropriate to stream mosquitoes. Whether the speed of the current be great or little does not concern it much; it is found both in crystal streams on the steepest parts of our mountains, and in slowly running peaty swamps in the Coastal Hills.

But one condition it demands: there must be heavy shade, and, for preference, virgin jungle. The shade of a rubber estate is not sufficient. Yet shade is not the only condition; for it has never been found in the Coastal Plains even when under heavy forest. It is in the strictest sense the stream breeder of our hill land when under virgin forest; and not a pool breeder like *A. umbrosus.* Unlike *A. umbrosus* it rarely, if ever, attacks man; indeed, it rarely enters a house: nor is it like an anopheles in its general appearance, being a little brownish-red, hunchbacked, culex-looking insect. *A. umbrosus* is a fierce biter, a strong flier, and lives well in captivity; *A. aitkeni* is the opposite. While *A. umbrosus* is an important carrier of malaria, *A. aitkeni* has never been infected experimentally; which can be said of few anopheles, even of those known to be harmless under natural conditions.

In two respects it is akin to *A. umbrosus:* one is its presence in virgin jungle; the other its low place in the developmental scale of the anopheles. *A. umbrosus* is covered mainly by hairs; it has not a ventral tuft of scales, like *A. barbirostris* and some others of the *Myzorhynchus* group. *A. aitkeni* has still less scale clothing, and has not even a patch of colour on its wings. Both belong to the group of primitive mosquitoes called by Major Christophers—the Proto-anopheles; and it is not uninteresting that they support his theory of their ancient ancestry by being the sole and original inhabitants of our virgin jungle; for *A. albotaeniatus* var. *montanus* is perhaps an offshoot of the original *umbrosus* stock living in the coastal swamps, which has pushed its way up into the ravine swamps in the hills; at least so I often think of it.

It was the discovery that *A. umbrosus* did not extend beyond the Coastal Hills into the Inland Hills (where only the rarer *umbrosus* types were found), which led Dr Strickland to his theory of the Inland Hills being non-malarious as long as they were under jungle; a discovery which I discuss in the chapter on "Inland Hills" (XX.).

When a Ravine is Opened.—Having described the mosquitoes of the ravines when under forest, it is now time to consider the changes that occur when the jungle is cut down: what happens to the original inhabitants; and what new-comers, if any, appear.

Fig. 94.
The Vegetation in a Ravine destroyed by Silt, and sunlight admitted.

Fig. 95.—Silt Pits.

[To face page 288.

I. If the jungle be felled and burned off, and the bottom of the ravine converted from a slowly streaming morass to a dry bed intersected by clean weeded drains carrying crystal streams sparkling in the sunshine, the conditions are no longer suitable for the original inhabitants. *A. umbrosus, montanus,* and *aitkeni* all disappear: in their place appears the deadly *A. maculatus,* which, alone of all mosquitoes in Malaya, can make its home in fast-running streams free from grass and other vegetation; and which, as we saw, is the cause of the persistence of malaria in the hills (Chapter X.). This mosquito is one of the most important carriers of malaria, an observation which has been confirmed by Stanton, Strickland, and others ; and so readily is it infected artificially that Dr Barbour used it as the "control" when experimenting with other species.

Its liking for streams is shown statistically by Dr Strickland's tables. In streams there is, of course, often a deposit of silt ; and among the species found in silts, *A. maculatus* occurs at the rate of 522 per mille of the observations ; the next, *A. aconitus,* which requires a grassy edge to the stream, being 175. In another table, that of the "Mosquitoes of Stream Courses," even although it includes streams of every description, from great rivers to streaming ravine morasses, many of which are unsuited to the insect, *A. maculatus* still heads the list with a rate of 340 per mille ; while *A. barbirostris* comes next with 153. Commenting on this, Dr Strickland says: "This table shows the very marked predominance of *maculatus* over the other species in this respect, and justifies the appellation usually given to it of a stream breeder, originated by Watson."

Had the table been confined to fast-running streams in sunshine free from weeds, the position of *A. maculatus* would have been even more predominant; if indeed, as I believe, it would not have been the sole representative of these insects.

To the power it has of living in such streams is due the difficulty of eradicating the malaria of hill land by ordinary agricultural "cleanliness"; and the necessity there is for the use of "oiling," "subsoil drainage," or some other special measure.

II. When the jungle in a ravine is felled, the timber is not always burned off; nor is the ravine always drained. The timber may be allowed to rot, and the ravine to remain a swamp. Then *A. maculatus* is no longer the sole and supreme occupant. In the portions of the ravine where the water is clearest and running freest, it will be found. In parts where, the water is more stagnant, vegetable decomposition is going on under water, on the surface are frothy masses, and bubbles rise through the water as one wades in it; one takes *A. sinensis*, a mosquito much less fastidious than *A. maculatus*. At other spots, where there is little current, may be found such mosquitoes as *A. barbirostris*, *A. kochii;* and if the ravine is flat and some grass has grown up, it may be *A. aconitus* and *A. fuliginosus*. *A. rossii* readily appears if there is any pollution from human or animal excrement.

III. Into such a ravine silt may be washed down from the hills. If grass be present, the silt may kill it out, and the decomposition of the grass unfits the ravine for *A. maculatus*, but makes it suitable for *A. sinensis*. On the other hand, silt pouring into an unopened ravine may kill out the jungle and allow the ingress of *A. maculatus*. If it is desired to preserve the jungle in a ravine, then measures must be taken to prevent silt being washed down. The favourite method at present is the " silt pit "; but the end can also be achieved in some places by growing a belt of grass above the ravine.

IV. Another condition of great interest, which may occur in ravines, is that where the ravine is drained, but weeds, and particularly ferns, have almost completely covered the ground. In addition to the close shade of the ferns there is the shade of rubber or secondary jungle. This is a different condition from that of the original ravine when under virgin jungle, and is practically harmless from a malarial point of view. Owing to the drainage there is no great area suitable for *A. umbrosus* to breed in; for the drains, even when obstructed in parts, are not comparable with the wide morass stretching from side to side of the ravine, when undrained and under jungle. Nor is it a favourite spot for *A. maculatus*, since the heavy shade of the ferns and trees is inimical to that insect. Some may be taken in the more open places, but nothing in comparison with the haul got were the ravine clean-weeded and without the shade of the ferns and weeds. This condition represents a stage in the reversion of the ravine to virgin jungle, when it is becoming unfit for *A. maculatus*, and has not yet become extensively suitable for *A. umbrosus*.

V. Yet another condition is sometimes found not favourable

FIG. 96.

The Drain is almost obliterated. The ground is covered by ferns and secondary jungle. This "represents a stage in the reversion of the ravine to virgin jungle, when it is becoming unfit for *A. maculatus*, and has not yet become extensively suitable for *A. umbrosus*."

FIG. 97.

Photograph of a recently-drained "Sendayang Swamp." The Sendayang is seen to be as high as a man, and forms a dense covering over the swamp. In the background is seen the edge of a secondary jungle which is creeping in ultimately to cover the Sendayang, so that once again "the jungle comes into its own."

[*To face page* 290.

to the spread of malaria. The ravine is free from jungle, is swampy and undrained, and covered with "rushes," known locally as "sendayang." This may form a complete cover to the water of the swamp; and where the shade is complete, no larvæ will be taken as a rule; although occasionally *A. sinensis* will be found. Where, however, the shade is not complete, larvæ may be found; the species depending on the quality of the water. As vegetable decomposition is the rule, the commonest species is *A. sinensis;* where the water is a little clearer, *A. barbirostris,* and where clearer still, *A. maculatus.* As the former two are not important carriers of malaria the "sendayang" swamp is not specially dangerous; but one must beware of the open spaces. Where such a condition occurs on an estate and malaria exists, it is safer to drain the swamp and oil the drains, than trust to the cultivation of a complete cover of "sendayang."

.   .   .

The Silent War.—Such are a few of the kaleidoscopic views of malaria and mosquitoes presented in the different zones of this country, and even in one ravine in a single zone. Untouched by the hand of man, this is a country covered by an evergreen jungle, marked off into zones, some of which are malarial, and some non-malarial. When the jungle is rudely swept away, man seems to conquer. In reality a condition of "unstable equilibrium" has been produced; or rather it can be described more correctly as the beginning of a war that can only end in man's defeat, however long it may be prolonged: man with knife and axe and fire; the jungle with its myriads of aerial troops.

Against the intruder, the jungle wages a ceaseless, though silent, warfare. It neither sleeps nor slumbers; and if it is to be kept in check, it requires of man endless effort. Ever vigilant, it sends forward, at every opportunity, its advance battalions. Along the drains creep the water-loving grasses and rushes; on their sides soon appear other grasses and tiny ferns. Grasses, ferns, wild bananas, and bushes grow on the dry ground of the ravines. Gradually leaves, sticks, and silt obliterate the drains; the ravine reverts to its original swamp; the ferns and bushes are replaced by the trees of the original forest. The jungle comes into its own. With all these changes, the insect life of the ravine changes too: at one period the

X

insect inhabitant may carry disease; at another period it may be harmless. And one zone differs from another. It is in the power of man temporarily to arrest these changes at any stage favourable to himself, or to allow them to march to their destined end.

Interesting as these changes are from a scientific point of view, no less important are they to the sanitarian. From their study we have learned to understand why malaria appears, varies in intensity, or disappears; although at first sight there may be little to account for it all. And the knowledge has given us power already to advise what should be done, or left undone, to control the disease. As we learn more, perhaps the time will come when we shall be able to say to one species of anopheles, "Come," and to another, "Go," and shall be able to "abolish malaria with great ease, perhaps at hardly any expense."

FIG. 98.

This photograph of Jugra Town shows

CHAPTER XXVI

THE MALARIA OF KUALA LUMPUR

Measures taken to bring about its Abatement, showing the Failure of Empiricism and the Success of a Scheme based on the Findings of Entomological Research. By Dr A. R. WELLINGTON, M.R.C.S., L.R.C.P., D.P.H., D.T.M. and H. Cantab., Senior Health Officer, F.M.S.

Introduction.

THE town of Kuala Lumpur is situated on the Klang River, near the centre of the State of Selangor. It is a double capital, being the capital of the State and the capital of the Federation, and it is the headquarters of both the State Government and the Federal Government.

The whole township has an area of about twenty square miles.

The town is bounded roughly by a circle, having at its centre the junction of the Klang and Gombak rivers.

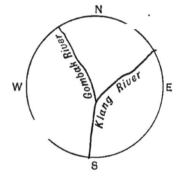

The Klang makes, with the Gombak and its tributary the Batu, the figure of a Y, which divides the town into three approximately equal portions.

The western portion, which is the European residential reserve, is made up of hills and ravines.

The northern portion is flat.

The eastern portion is flat in its northern half, hilly in southern half, except for a strip, 60 chains long and 20 chains wide, by the side of the river. This strip constitutes the business area of the town.

The population which in 1905 was 38,459 is now (1920) 67,930.

In 1905 most of the European officials were housed on the hills in the European residential reserve. The sides of the hills were for the most part covered with jungle, and the inverts of the valleys were jungle-covered swamps. The unofficial Europeans occupied houses on the flat to the east of the Klang River. They were isolated houses in their own compounds.

The business area, in which three-fourths of the total population resided, was closely built upon.

Distribution of Malaria previous to 1906.

Dr Fletcher, in his report dated 30th July 1907, states as follows :—

"Until the end of 1906, malaria among the inmates of the European quarters was almost unknown, except in a few instances, and in these it could generally be proved that the disease had been contracted elsewhere. In those cases in which malaria was thus imported it never spread; no other inmates became infected. From this it may reasonably be inferred that no mosquitoes were present which were capable of carrying the infection. Until September 1906 I had not seen a case of malaria in a European house in which the probability of infection in another district could be excluded. Dr Travers, whose experience in Kuala Lumpur extends over a period of twelve years, states that until this year he had not seen malaria among the European women and children of Kuala Lumpur, though cases have occurred among the men whose duties take them outside the town.

Malaria is endemic amongst that portion of the population which resides along the banks of the river, or near the swamps which border it.

Since 1903 the blood of all patients suffering from fever has, when practicable, been examined. Any figures, therefore, quoted hereafter refer only to cases which have been proved to be malarial by the demonstration of the parasite. During 1906 malaria parasites were found in sixty-six cases from Kuala Lumpur. Nearly all the cases seen came from the endemic area, only three occurring in European houses, and these during the last quarter of the year."

Dr M'Closky, who had had twelve years' experience of Kuala Lumpur, stated in August 1907 : " I saw my first case of malaria in a European, contracted in Kuala Lumpur, only last month."

There can be no doubt that up till 1906 malaria was confined to the areas which bordered on the river, and the hills were free.

Outbreak of Malaria in the Hill Land, West of River.

Early in 1906 the jungle-covered swamp at the foot of Federal Hill was cleared, and an attempt made to dry the area by means of earth drains. The clearing was done by the Public Works Department, in order to improve the amenities of the locality prior to the erection of buildings on the high ground adjacent. About the same time Dr Fletcher had the blukar and scrub cleared from the swampy valley below the General Hospital. This was done to improve the appearance of the place, and to allow for better drainage.

During the year the hospitals in Kuala Lumpur received many bad cases of malaria from the hill estates which were being started in the neighbourhood. The danger of opening up land had long been known to the pioneers of the country who attributed the high malaria incidence and death rate to some miasma set free by disturbance of the soil.

Towards the end of the year cases of malaria began to occur in Kuala Lumpur among the Europeans occupying the bungalows near the clearings, and among the patients and servants in the hospital. Previously both areas had been healthy. The incidence increased, and by the end of 1907 all the houses on Federal Hill and Carcosa Hill had cases of infection. Cases had also occurred in most of the houses near the hospital. The Police Barracks which were on the hill opposite the hospital had many cases.

Dr Fletcher, in July 1907, sent in a report describing the outbreak. By means of a spot map he showed that the cases were coming from the neighbourhood of the clearings. He said :—

"The two main districts affected by the disease are—(a) Those parts near the swamps at the foot of Federal Hill; (b) the General Hospital and surroundings.

"The cause of this outbreak must be some condition favourable to the breeding of the mosquitoes which convey the infection.

"In each of the two neighbourhoods, the Federal Hill and the General Hospital, there is some low-lying swampy ground.

A couple of years ago these swamps were not drained, and in wet weather there was a considerable depth of water, but at that time there was no malaria in either neighbourhood.

"About one and a half years ago these swamps were drained, and subsequently malaria appeared in the houses near. The drains which were made are very irregular, and in places there are small pools and miniature dams which probably make ideal breeding-places for the noxious mosquitoes.

"The remedy for the outbreak is efficient drainage. On that subject I am not qualified to advise, but would venture to suggest that the matter be laid before the Health Officer.

"The following figures show the actual numbers of the cases from the various districts which have come under my personal notice, and I would point out that they are, therefore, merely an indication of the distribution of malaria in Kuala Lumpur, and not the actual number of cases which have occurred. To obtain the latter, the figures given below would need to be multiplied by a factor, in most cases as large as 10, and in some, such as the Police Depot, not larger than 1·50."

	Brickfields Road.	Batu Road.	Ampang Road.	Police Depot.	High Street.	Central Workshops.	Federal District.	General Hospital.	Other Districts.	Monthly Totals.
January .	5	1	1	5	5	1	2	0	2	22
February .	0	1	2	4	2	1	6	3	4	23
March .	2	1	1	3	2	0	8	1	2	20
April . .	1	0	0	1	3	0	3	1	3	12
May . .	3	2	0	4	5	1	2	3	5	25
June . .	6	3	1	4	2	5	4	3	2	30
Total .	17	8	5	21	19	8	25	11	18	132

Dr M'Closky, the Acting State Surgeon, in forwarding the report to Government, wrote :—

"Dr Fletcher rightly attributes this increase of malaria to some condition favourable to the breeding of mosquitoes which convey the infection, but I think there is another factor to be considered, viz., the source of infection of mosquitoes. This has multiplied considerably by the large increase of malarial patients admitted to the General Hospital from the different estates."

The matter was referred to the Health Officer, Dr Thornley, who wrote :—

FIG. 99.—PETALING HILL, KUALA LUMPUR.
The Ravine before drainage.

[To face page 296.

" The method of draining valleys below Federal Hill is far from satisfactory, if not entirely wrong, as far as the attainment of the object of preventing breeding-grounds for mosquitoes is concerned. The herring-bone system adopted leaves the ground between dry, but the drains themselves are grand breeding-places. The drains· below the European Hospital are lined with stones, and these result in the formation of small pools. The drains should be on the lines of Klang. Without money for upkeep it is a case of throwing money into swamps."

At Klang, Malcolm Watson used contour hill-foot drains to intercept the water from the hills.

The Malarial Committee, its Investigations, Discoveries, and Recommendations.

In September 1907, the British Resident appointed a committee for the purpose of (*a*) examining the area complained of; (*b*) inquiring into the results arising from the present condition; (*c*) advising as to the methods to be employed for the improvement of each area, and to make an estimate of the cost in each case. The members of the Committee were —the Chairman of the Sanitary Board, Mr E. S. Hose; the Health Officer, Dr Thornley; the Medical Officer, Dr Fletcher; and the Executive Engineer, Mr J. E. Jackson.

The Committee started work by asking for the services of the Government Entomologist, Mr C. H. Pratt, to make a thorough investigation into the areas complained of, for the purpose of ascertaining (*a*) the actual existence of malarial mosquitoes in the quarters infected, (*b*) the proportionate extent to which each area actually constitutes a breeding-ground, for such mosquitoes.

The entomologist, during his investigations, discovered larvæ of anopheles "present in the streams flowing through the cleared portion of the valleys, but not in those parts where the streams remained covered with a thick growth of bushes. Even in the open portion anopheles were not found where the stream flows swiftly between even banks, but wherever it had been scoured by flood and the stream had broadened out with retarded flow at the sides, there anopheline larvæ were present in large numbers."

Fletcher, who confirmed Pratt's discovery, was quick to

recognise the importance of it, and in his letter to the Chairman he stated: "These facts demonstrate the great danger of clearing jungle, unless it is possible at the same time to convert these streams into regular channels with clearly-cut sides, preferably of cement or brick."

The Executive Engineer, Mr J. E. Jackson, prepared surveys and estimates for a system of drainage in the areas referred to. The plans showed open brick drains running through the centre of the valleys, and subsidiary rubble drains covered with turf discharging into them.

In February 1908 the Committee sent in a detailed report.

The following extract from Para. 2 shows the importance they attached to Pratt and Fletcher's discovery :—

"It is very noteworthy that anopheles were found to be most prevalent in sluggish streams or earth drains where the thick overhanging undergrowth had been cleared away, as is the case, for instance, in the valleys on both sides of Hospital Road below the General Hospital, and at the foot of Federal Hill, and in the low-lying land in the angle between Brickfields Road and Damansara Road. These facts demonstrate the great danger of clearing the jungle covering of streams unless it is possible at the same time to convert such streams into regular channels of a uniform and fairly steep gradient, with clearly-cut sides. The Committee do not, however, wish to underrate the value of clearing jungle, provided that efficient drainage is undertaken at the same time."

Plans of Mr Jackson's drains, viz., open brick and *subsoil rubble*, were put up. $27,585 were asked for.

In asking for upkeep, the Committee said, "We consider that it will be necessary to maintain an upkeep gang of ten men who should be constantly employed in keeping these drains free from obstruction and in good order after they have been made, and with this end in view we recommend an annual expenditure of $1500, to which should be added a further sum of $500 for current repairs to drains."

Criticism of Committee's Findings.

The findings of the Committee came in for a good deal of criticism.

Pratt and Fletcher's discovery and deductions drawn from it were so incompatible with the generally accepted ideas,

FIG. 100.—PETALING HILL, KUALA LUMPUR.

Photograph shows the original central drain and rubble herring-bone lateral drain. Along the side of the ravine is seen the contour or hill-foot drain cut at a later date.

and so contrary to the teaching of the day, that little credence was given to them.

In every country where mosquito control had been attempted, emphasis was laid on the importance of clearing up all scrub, undergrowth, and jungle near to habitations and in towns. Local medical men had always advocated similar measures.

DRAINS RECOMMENDED BY THE COMMITTEE.

2 feet

1 to 1

1 foot

4 ins.

←1 ft.→

Medium Open Concrete Drain.

1 foot

Covered with turf

2 feet

Rubble filling

←9 ins.→

Subsoil Rubble Drain.

In Klang and Port Swettenham jungle clearing had been used with success, and to most there seemed to be no reason why the opposite should be the case in Kuala Lumpur.

That anopheles carried malaria was known to all the local medical men, but the fact that there were a dozen or more species of anophelines in Malaya, and that some were carriers and others were not, was known to two or three only, and their knowledge of the subject was very limited.

Practically nothing was known of the life-history of the different species, and it was not realised that conditions favourable for one might be unfavourable for another.

The anopheline which did the harm at Klang and Port Swettenham was *A. umbrosus*, a jungle breeder on flat lands; that which did the harm in Kuala Lumpur was *A. maculatus,** which breeds in the open on hilly lands.

In due time the report was submitted to the High Commissioner for his consideration. The High Commissioner, who paid a visit of inspection to the areas in question, was not convinced that the clearing had had any connection with the outbreak. He pointed out that there were cleared valleys of a similar nature in Singapore, and that they were free from malaria. He disallowed certain of the open brick or concrete drains and substituted rubble drains.

The sum asked for by the Committee was $27,585, the sum sanctioned was $10,320. Nothing was allowed for upkeep.

First Attempt on part of Public Works Department to exterminate Malaria by Drainage.

The European residential area was on State land, and the task of ridding it of anopheline breeding-grounds was entrusted to the State P.W.D. to carry out in 1908.

It does not seem to have been realised that the problem was chiefly an entomological one, and that the engineering works necessary were only a means to an entomological end. The end aimed at was the rendering of certain areas impossible for mosquito propagation, and no system of drainage, however satisfactory, from an engineering point of view, was of the slightest use if that end were not attained.

Also it seems to have been forgotten that the extermination of any animal from an area where it is prevalent is rarely possible, unless the exterminators possess some knowledge of the animal and its habits, and that the chances of success are infinitesimal when the hunter cannot recognise the animal when he sees it.

Mosquitoes are animals, and the above applies to anti-mosquito schemes.

With only one-third of the sum deemed necessary by the Committee the Public Works Department had no chance of

* *A. maculatus* was then called *A. (Nys) willmori.*

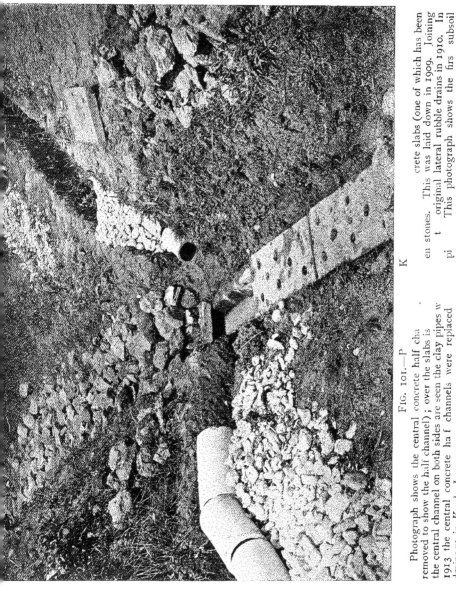

Fig. 101.—P   K

Photograph shows the central concrete half cha
removed to show the half channel); over the slabs is
the central channel on both sides are seen the clay pipes w
1913 the central concrete ha f channels were replaced
drainage in Kuala Lumpur.

crete slabs (one of which has been
en stones. This was laid down in 1909. Joining
t original lateral rubble drains in 1910. In
pi   This photograph shows the firs subsoil

[To face page 300.

success even had they gone to work in the best possible way. They did not, however, attack the problem in the proper manner, and it is probable that, had the full sum been voted, the result would still have been a failure.

The engineers had never made a study of mosquitoes, and they could not spot an anopheline larva when they saw one. Being unfamiliar with the appearance of the larvæ, they were unable to find out for themselves which were the dangerous areas and which were not. They could not tell, therefore, where to begin. The index of success was the absence of larvæ from areas which, before treatment, contained them. They could not check their results, and they therefore did not know where to end.

As they knew nothing of the mosquitoes they wanted to get rid of, it was clearly a case for co-operation with those who did know. Co-operation was not invited.

In direct opposition to the recommendations of the Committee, the valleys were cleared without being efficiently drained.

Dr Thornley had advocated drainage on the Klang system, that is to say contour hill-foot drains, to intercept the water before it got to the swamps. His advice was not followed, and straight tap drains were put in instead. These drains only dried the ground within a few feet of them; the intervening spaces remained wet.

The subsoil rubble drains recommended by the Committee were not put in, open rubble drains were used instead. These soon became choked with silt.

When all the money had been expended, the valleys were only half done.

No provision having been allowed for upkeep, the drains when finished were left to take care of themselves.

Investigations by the Health Officer, and his Findings.

In the middle of 1909, malaria in the European quarter was as bad as ever, if not worse, and it was evident that the measures taken had not been successful.

In an endeavour to arrive at the cause of failure, the writer who had succeeded Dr Thornley as Health Officer made a personal survey of every valley in Kuala Lumpur from top to bottom, through cleared portions as well as through those still covered by jungle.

Every stream, pool, or collection of water met with was searched for anopheline larvæ. Those caught were bred out and identified.

No larvæ were found in the jungle-covered portions of the valleys, though water was plentiful and careful search was made. In the cleared portions they were easily found. There were many cases where larvæ were plentiful right up to the edge of a clearing, but absent from the jungle-covered pools a few feet away. Pratt and Fletcher's observations were thus confirmed.

In the valleys which had been treated by the Public Works Department, larvæ were plentiful. They were particularly numerous in the spring water which trickled over the surface of the rubble drains. Not having been covered with turf (as recommended by the Committee), or otherwise protected, the spaces between the stones had become blocked by mud and silt, and the water which should have percolated through the rubble flowed over the top.

In some valleys where concrete drains had been constructed, the only place where one could walk dry-shod was the top of the drain itself; everywhere else was like a sponge, and among the thousands of pools existing it was not difficult to find larvæ.

A. maculatus and A. karwari were the species most common in the spring water which oozed from the bases of the hills. The smaller the pool the more likely it was to contain larvæ; even the scrapings from the surface of wet sand showed them. Running spring water contained them.

A. rossii* and A. kochi were found in dirty water such as is contained in buffalo wallows, wheel tracks, and drains contaminated by sewage.

A. barbirostris and A. sinensis were met with at the edges of larger pools and ponds, especially where those edges were grassy or grass appeared above the surface. They were also found among floating debris.

A. umbrosus larvæ were not met with.

After the valleys had been done the flats were searched.

A report accompanied by a spot map was submitted to the Principal Medical Officer. On the map fifty Anopheline breeding-places were shown. Attention was drawn to the fact that water in cleared valleys harboured anopheline larvæ, while water in jungle-covered valleys did not.

* A. rossii now called A. vagus.

FI 102.—PETALING HILL, KUALA LUMPUR.
Subsoil Pines ready for laying.

[To face page 302.

Malcolm Watson had demonstrated that *A. umbrosus* and *maculatus* were carriers; nothing was known concerning the carrying properties of the other species. Watson had also shown that *umbrosus* is a jungle breeder, and that it disappears in clearing.

The cause of the fever could not be *A. umbrosus*, for that species was conspicuous by its absence; besides, the clearing of jungle would have lessened the amount of malaria, whereas it seemed certain that it had had the opposite effect.

A. maculatus, the only other carrier known, was found breeding freely in the open valleys but not in those covered by jungle. The houses close to jungle-covered valleys had no fever, those near cleared valleys had. The obvious inference was that the clearing of the valleys had created conditions favourable for the propagation of *maculatus*, that the *maculatus* population had therefore increased, and the increased number of carriers had raised the incidence rate among those living in the neighbourhood.

Pratt and Fletcher's theory was correct, and the warning issued by the Committee was sound.

In the execution of the anti-mosquito works, that warning had been ignored. The valleys were felled and cleared but not efficiently drained, and an increase instead of a decrease in the number of breeding-places resulted.

The following is an extract from the Health Officer's annual report of 1910:—

"It was noted that where the valleys had been cleared of jungle and blukar, larvæ of the malaria-carrying anopheline (*A. maculatus*) were found without difficulty in the clear water which had issued from the springs at the hill-foot. In the valleys covered by blukar or jungle, where the water (of which there was plenty) was coloured with vegetable matter, not a single anopheline larva was found. This experience agrees with that of Pratt and Fletcher in 1907. As malaria-carrying anophelines breed in cleared valleys and shun those covered with blukar, the obvious inference is that the clearing of valleys will be followed by an outbreak of malaria if foci of infection be present and the valleys are left inefficiently drained."

The findings of the Health Officer were not generally accepted, and even the medical officers remained unconvinced of the danger of clearing valleys.

The subject was so important that independent action should have been taken to prove or disprove the theory, but nothing was done.

Experimental Drainage Works on Petaling Hill.

The investigations of the Health Officer commenced about the middle of 1909, and the report on the anopheline survey was delivered to the Principal Medical Officer in April 1910.

During the interval notifications of malaria were constantly being received. Each case was gone into as thoroughly as time permitted. At the end of 1909 a European who lived on Petaling Hill, a new residential area not included in the Committee's report, wrote in complaining that all his household had been down with fever, for which he blamed the ravines in front of his quarters in Belfield Road. The ravines contained scrub and blukar, but there were open spaces in them. The inverts were wet and swampy (Fig. 99). An anopheline survey by the Health Officer showed the presence of the fever-carriers *A. maculatus* in the open areas. The findings were reported to Government and drainage recommended, a concrete drain to run down the centre, and contour

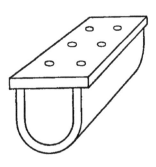

open earth-drains at bottom of slopes to connect at intervals with centre drain.

The State Engineer fixed upon one of these valleys as a suitable place for experimentation in drainage, and trials were begun.

The valley was cleared of scrub, and drainage on the herring-bone system tried. The central drain was an earth channel, having at its invert concrete half-pipes roofed with flat, perforated, concrete slabs; the rest of the channel was filled with broken stone. Except that the pipes were different, the drains were similar to those used with success at Panama.

The subsidiary drains or ribs of the herring-bone were earth channels filled with broken stone (Fig. 100).

The experiment was watched by the Health Officer, who checked the results by frequent mosquito surveys.

The concrete pipes worked well. The rubble drain when

FIG. 103.—PETALING HILL, KUALA LUMPUR.

A general view of the ravine, with the central concrete and rubble drains ; some subsidiary rubble lateral drains ; in the distance some subsoil clay pipes being laid in a contour drain and on the land ready to be laid.

[*To face page* 304.

new dried the soil for a couple of feet on either side; beyond that they had no influence, and the ground remained wet and sloppy, and in the small pools larvæ continued to develop. In a short time the interstices of the rubble drains became choked with mud and silt, and the drains ceased to convey water. The choked drains were taken up and relaid. To dry the spaces between some contour or intercepting drains were constructed at the hill-foot. The contour arrangement was a great improvement on the simple herring-bone, and for a time the valley was dry. In a month, however, the rubble drains had again become choked, and it was decided to abandon them.

In February 1910, Dr Malcolm Watson, at a meeting of the British Medical Association in Kuala Lumpur, read an interesting paper on malaria prevention. He described what had been done in Malaya and the results. He pointed out the difficulties he had encountered in hill lands, and he advocated a system of contour hill-foot drainage by means of clay pipes laid underground. At that time clay pipes were not to be had in Malaya. The local potters made flower-pots and jars, but they had never tried their hands at pipes. Dr Watson pointed out that there was no reason why these pipes could not be turned out very cheaply, and he showed specimens which he had had made locally. He described a system of clay-pipe drainage, which he proposed to use on certain hill estates in the highly malarious Batu Tiga district.

In July, Dr Watson paid a visit to the experimental drain at Petaling Hill, and offered some friendly criticism. He considered that the main drain, the concrete pipe overlaid with stone, was performing its task satisfactorily, but that it was unnecessarily expensive. The rubble drains he condemned. A trial of clay pipes was recommended, and as none could be obtained in Kuala Lumpur he offered to provide a pattern which the local potters could copy. Mr R. D. Jackson, who had newly taken over the anti-malarial drainage of State lands in Kuala Lumpur, took action on the lines suggested and arranged for pipes to be made. The potters, seeing there was money in it, commenced making pipes on their own. This was the beginning of an industry which has so developed that there are now half a dozen potteries which manufacture clay pipes for anti-malarial purposes.

The rubble drains were all taken up and replaced by clay pipes overlaid with broken stone, a system similar to that which had proved successful in Panama (Fig. 101). The valley was dried, and remained dry for a year or more. Upkeep was necessary.

Second Attempt by Public Works Department to exterminate Malaria by Drainage.

Somewhere about the middle of the year 1910, a sum was voted for the purpose of remedying the defects of the 1908 drainage system, and for certain extensions. The work was again entrusted to the Public Works Department to carry out. On this occasion both Federal and State lands were concerned. Operations on Federal land were allotted to a Federal engineer, that on State land to a State engineer. The two worked independently.

Plans for the State land were submitted to the Health Officer, who passed them on condition that they were not to be considered final, but that any deviation found necessary during the progress of the work would be carried out. The Health Officer asked for the drainage of jungle-covered valleys and the felling to proceed side by side. This was rejected as impracticable.

Plans for the Federal land were not submitted.

Work on State land commenced in July. The writer made frequent mosquito surveys during the progress of the work, and communicated the results to the Executive Engineer.

Contour drainage had been repeatedly advocated by the writer, but up to this time no engineer had consented to give it a trial. In this month a trial on a small scale was made, both in Belfield Road experimental area and in Club Road Valley (Fig. 106). An entry in the Health Officer's diary, dated 28th July, says: " Inspected Belfield Road and Club Road. I am glad to see the P.W.D. are trying contour drains at last, though they are not making them deep enough." That they were only half convinced is shown by the following extract from the same diary : " Inspected anti-malarial drains in Club Road. The P.W.D. are putting in straight drains where they ought to put in contour drains. The scheme will be a failure unless the P.W.D. use common sense." Common sense eventually prevailed, for the diary entry of 28th September says :

FIG. 104.—CLUB VALLEY ROAD, KUALA LUMPUR.
The original condition.

FIG. 105.—CLUB VALLEY ROAD, KUALA LUMPUR.
The Pond at the foot "did not furnish carriers.

[To face page 306.

" Inspected Club Road Valley. The contour drains have done the trick and the valley is perfectly dry." Leaving out the experimental one in Belfield Road, this is the first instance of a valley having been drained to the satisfaction of the Health Officer.

Other valleys received attention but the work there was not so thorough, and when operations ceased there still remained sufficient breeding-grounds to supply all the carriers necessary for maintaining the high malarial rate existing in the neighbourhood. Much good work had been done, but it had not gone far enough.

While the State authorities were engaged with the works on State land a Federal engineer was dealing with the Federal area. The Health Officer offered advice but it was not taken. Watch was kept, and the various collections of water were frequently examined for the presence of larvæ.

The concrete blocks intended for the open drains were cast on the spot. Unfortunately, the ground chosen for the casting operations was wet and spongy, and many small pools formed. The pools became populated with *A. maculatus* larvæ. At the end of 1910 so much breeding was going on that an increase of malaria seemed inevitable. Warning was given, but no action was taken and the breeding continued.

Formation of Health Branch of the Medical Department.

In January 1911 the Health Branch of the Medical Department came into existence, and the writer was transferred to Taiping in the State of Perak as Health Officer, Perak North.

Taiping is situated on the flat at the base of the hills. The European quarter is on that side of the town next to the hills. Until the previous year this quarter had been healthy, but it was now malarious. The malaria followed the clearing of the hill land for rubber growing. Investigations were made, and it was found that, as in Kuala Lumpur, the carriers were coming from the cleared valleys. All the valleys were searched. In those covered with jungle no larvæ were found; in those which had been cleared *A. maculatus* breeding-grounds were found in plenty. A mosquito survey of the whole town was made, and a spot map prepared. Only near the bases of the bills were carriers found. The European

Y

area suffered, but there was little malaria in the rest of the town.

Malarious hill estates in the neighbourhood were investigated, and in each case *A. maculatus* breeding-grounds were found in the cleared valleys and not in the jungle-covered ones. Pratt and Fletcher's theory was true for the hill lands of Perak.

Continuance of Malaria in Kuala Lumpur.

Malaria in Kuala Lumpur in 1911, instead of declining, increased.

The conditions of the valleys at the beginning of the year were as follows.

Club Road Valley was dry except at its mouth, where there was a large pond (Fig. 105). The pond did not furnish carriers, and it therefore had no influence on the malaria.

Bluff Road Valley and Hospital Valley had not been completely dried, and there were still *maculatus* breeding-grounds, especially in the upper reaches.

Venning Road Valley was not satisfactory, and breeding-grounds existed.

In the gardens there were still many dangerous places.

A. maculatus larvæ were easily found near the Federal Anti-mosquito Works.

In fairness to the engineers it must be stated that the valleys which had been treated were not the only ones which contained anopheline breeding-grounds.

Owing to the general disbelief in the danger of clearing valleys, no action had been taken to prevent further clearing.

New valleys had been cleared by the Agricultural Department and by others and new breeding-grounds had been created. These furnished their share of mosquitoes.

Every house on Carcosa Hill and Federal Hill had cases. All were within easy flying distance of the Federal Anti-mosquito Works.

Confirmation of Watson's Discovery that Maculatus is a Carrier.

On June the 8th Dr Stanton, the Government Bacteriologist, demonstrated the presence of zygotes in the stomach wall of *A. maculatus* taken in a house in Brickfields Road, close to the Federal Anti-mosquito Works. On June the 28th,

FIG. 106.—LOWER END OF CLUB VALLEY ROAD, KUALA LUMPUR.

Showing the central concrete open channel, and a shallow contour drain in the foreground. In the upper portion of this ravine, the concrete channel had to be replaced by a subsoil clay pipe, as shown in Fig. 35.

in conjunction with Dr Watson, specimens of this mosquito were taken in coolie lines on a hilly estate in the notoriously malarious Batu Tiga district and sporozoites were demonstrated in the salivary glands. Watson's discovery, made in 1906, that *A. maculatus* is a carrier in nature, was thus confirmed. Dr Stanton says:—

"The number of *A. maculatus* taken in the lines and the readiness with which parasites were demonstrated in them at a time when I was informed the estate was comparatively free of malaria, and the absence of parasites in other species of anophelines examined, show the great importance of this mosquito in malaria transmission in hill areas."

It is a pity that Pratt and Fletcher's theory was not tested at this stage. The question, however, was not taken up, and the theory remained discredited until 1915 when Strickland published a paper confirming it.

Clearing went on steadily in Kuala Lumpur.

An extract from Dr Gerrard's health report of 1911 says:—

"During the year much jungle and undergrowth was cleared, and many subsoil drains laid. In spite of this malaria has increased."

A further extract from the same report is of interest:—

"The anophelines of the environs of Kuala Lumpur are being worked out by Dr Stanton of the Institute of Medical Research, and maps showing where larvæ are found are nearing completion."

The fact that there was a recent anopheline survey map of Kuala Lumpur already in existence seems to have been overlooked, at any rate no use was made of it.

Formation of Malaria Advisory Board.

Dr Charles Lane Sansom was appointed Principal Medical Officer, F.M.S., in January 1911.

On his arrival he found that the medical problem which most required attention was malaria and its prevention. The position in Kuala Lumpur was far from satisfactory. The subject had been engaging the attention of the authorities for four years, yet in spite of the efforts made, malaria was on the increase. Dr Sansom made investigations and came to the conclusion that the reasons for failure to reduce malaria lay in division of responsibility, lack of thoroughness, and unsuitable methods resulting in bad drainage. The works had been controlled by various State and Federal authorities, each of whom proceeded independently.

In August Dr Sansom wrote in to Government and pointed out "that the suppression of malaria in these States is not such a simple matter as it is described in the works of Ross and Boyce." Because of the difficulties which had to be overcome he recommended the appointment of a standing Committee to—

(a) Collect information and evidence with regard to the incidence of malaria.

(b) Select the most appropriate schemes which could be used in various parts of the States, and advise Government as to how they should be carried into effect.

(c) Issue instructions as to details, control, and upkeep of anti-malarial works.

(d) Diffuse information.

(e) Undertake any other duties which in the opinion of the Chief Secretary would be likely to prevent malaria.

The Committee recommended was—

The Principal Medical Officer.

Dr Stanton, "to keep members in touch with research work here and elsewhere."

Dr Malcolm Watson "as the medical representative who had had much practical experience."

One or two prominent planters.

A district officer who had had experience in Sanitary Board work.

An engineer skilled in drainage work.

"Such a Committee would inspire public confidence in the first place and therefore there would be less resistance to any measures which might have to be enforced. The Government would be advised as to the best means which could be adopted to control the disease, and if all contemplated schemes are submitted to the Committee not only would uniformity result but expenditure on useless fads and theories be prevented."

Government accepted the recommendations and the Malaria Advisory Board was formed.

The composition of the Board was—E. L. Brockman, Esq., C.M.G., Chief Secretary, President; Dr C. L. Sansom, Principal

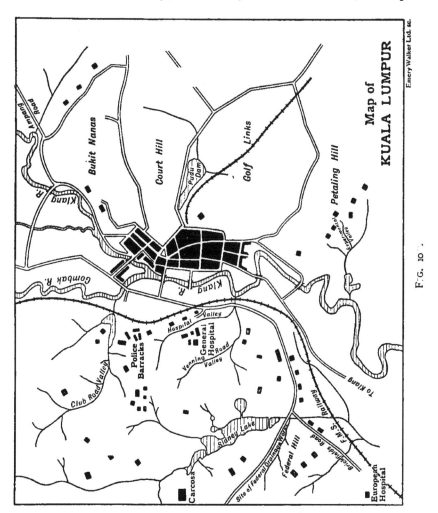

Medical Officer, Vice-President; J. H. M. Robson, Esq.; Dr Malcolm Watson; H. R. Quartley, Esq.; Dr A. T. Stanton; F. D. Evans, Esq., Assistant Engineer, Public Works Department.

The Board met for the first time in November and there was a second meeting in December.

It was decided that the drainage of the European residential area should be completed under the instruction of the Board "to serve as an illustration of what could be done by this means to free an area of malaria."

It was decided to work on the following lines :—

(1) All ravines to be cleared for 6 feet up the hill.

(2) Open earth channels to drain land previous to pipe laying.

(3) Subsoil contour pipe drains (clay pipes) to be placed at the foot of all slopes.

(4) The cement drains already in position to be left for the time as they might prove satisfactory.

(5) Mr F. D. Evans to supervise the work.

Work commences under Malaria Advisory Board.

Mr Evans, who was seconded from the Public Works Department and appointed Executive Engineer to the Board, realising the vital importance of the mosquito side of the problem, early took up the study of the local anophelines. He was the first engineer in the F.M.S. who had ever bothered about them. He was thus able to check results and ensure that each section had been freed from breeding-grounds before another was commenced.

Some idea of the incompleteness of previous works can be got from the minutes of the Board of 12th February 1912: "The Board is informed that every ravine head is left unfinished, thus creating typical mosquito breeding-places for mosquitoes most dangerous to health. Additional drainage on Petaling Hill is approved. Undergrowth along drains in Federal Reserve to be cleared, and *when drainage has been completed*, jungle on both sides of the hill to be cleared. Additional work required in ravines between Club Road and Maxwell Road."

To subsoil the whole of the ravines west of the river was a big job, something like 50 miles of piping being necessary. The work was pushed on rapidly, but of course it took time to complete.

Experiments were made in draining, and it was early found that the rubble filling over pipes was not only unnecessary but harmful—better results could be got by protecting the pipes from silt with a layer of dried palm leaves and covering in the trench with earth. The same system had been used with success on Seafield Estate, which had been drained under the supervision of Dr Watson. The subsoil drains laid in the 1910 campaign were left until they showed signs of blockage, when they were taken up and replaced by others. By the end of 1913 there were practically none of the old type left.

European Residential Area cleared of Malaria.

The results of the drainage was most satisfactory, and in 1913 the European residential area for the first time in seven years was free from malaria, and it has remained free ever since.

For the first time in the history of Kuala Lumpur, anti-mosquito works had been carried out under the authority of a Board containing medical entomologists familiar with the mosquito it was desired to get rid of.

The success was due to the complete eradication of *A. maculatus* breeding-grounds, brought about by a system of drainage specially designed to deal with the problem. Particular mention must be made of the excellent work done by Mr F. D. Evans, the Board's executive engineer. He was keenly interested in the subject, and he carried out the details of the scheme with such thoroughness and skill that no place was left suitable for *A. maculatus* to breed in. Strict attention to detail was absolutely essential, for with so efficient a carrier as *A. maculatus*, even small and insignificant-looking pools of water are sufficient to keep the disease smouldering.

Malaria not being a notifiable disease, the incidence figures are not available. Europeans, however, are never slow in complaining to the Health Officer when a case occurs in their households, and the fact that complaints which had been of almost daily occurrence in 1910 and 1911 ceased to be received after 1912 shows that malaria in the European residential area came to an end about that time.

Influence of Drainage not confined to Residential Area.

The influence of the drainage operation was not confined to the European quarter; the shop house area of the town was within flying distance, and there is no doubt that it benefited. The malaria death rate for the whole town dropped from 9·87 in 1911 to 5·53 in 1912 The report of the Health Officer (A. R. Wellington) for 1913 says :—

" The great drop in the death rate for this disease must be attributed to the extensive drainage operations which were undertaken by the Malaria Advisory Board to get rid of the breeding-places of malaria-carrying mosquitoes. Valleys which were teeming with *maculatus* larvæ are now bone-dry."

The action taken by the Malaria Advisory Board in the area selected for demonstration purposes had been so successful that it was decided to extend operations and deal with other areas in the town where malaria was prevalent.

The following table shows the numbers of deaths among the residential population due to " fevers," in most cases malarial, the fever death rate per mille population, and the general death rate :—

Year.	Population.	Number of Deaths from Fever.	Fever Death Rate.	General Death Rate.
1907	41,331	537		
1908	42,775	423		
1909	43,209	341		
1910	45,642	486		
1911	47,076	465		
1912	48,508	266		
1913	56,487	314		
1914	58,107	361		
1915	59,727	325		
1916	61,443	408		
1917	63,064	293		
1918	64,686	393		
1919	66,308*	311		

* The census in 1921 shows the population to be 70,000.

The figures for the year previous to 1907 are too unreliable to be quoted, for, until that year, the importance of distinguishing between deaths due to diseases contracted in the town and those contracted outside was not generally realised, and the subject did not receive the attention it merited, either at the hands of the hospital authorities or the police, to whom deaths outside hospital were reported. The figures for any year are not strictly accurate, for often a native deliberately gives a fictitious address on entering hospital—they are, however, sufficiently accurate for general comparisons.

In 1918 a severe influenza epidemic spread over the whole country, and probably many of the deaths returned that year as due to fever were really influenza deaths.

Drop in Death Rate not due solely to Malaria Advisory Board.

The great drop in the general death rate from 39·02 in 1911 to 26·36 in 1919, that is 12·66 per mille population, must not be attributed solely to the action of the Malaria Advisory Board. The average fever death rate for 1908 to 1911, the period in which clearing of valleys was not followed by efficient drainage, was 9·57 ; that of 1912 to 1919, the period in which clearing was accompanied by efficient drainage, was 5·53, a drop of 4·04 per mille only. (1918, being the influenza year, is not counted.)

Malaria, of course, has an influence on other diseases, and the drop in the fever death rate does not indicate the total improvement brought about by abatement of the disease. Again, the operations of the Malaria Advisory Board were not the only anti-malarial measures being carried out in the town. The Health Officer's staff and the Sanitary Board staff had not been idle, and a considerable amount of oiling and minor works had been done.

It is not unfair to the Malaria Advisory Board to attribute half the total drop in the death rate to their operations and the other half to the improvement in the health conditions brought about by the Health Department of the Sanitary Board.

Confirmation of Pratt and Fletcher's Theory.

In 1912 Dr C. Strickland came to this country as Medical Entomologist to carry out research in connection with the biology of mosquitoes. In 1915 this officer published a paper giving the results of his research in hilly lands. His experiences coincided with those of Pratt, Fletcher, and Wellington, in that he found wooded valleys practically free of larvæ of malaria-carrying anophelines, while cleared valleys contained them. He said that hilly land, provided the valley were left alone, was not malarious, and that hilly land with cleared valleys was. He advocated the non-clearing of valleys in the vicinity of habitations, and recommended that those cleared should be allowed to revert to their original state. The matter was taken up by the Press and given full publicity. Pratt and Fletcher seem to have been forgotten, for their names were never mentioned. The theory was called "Strickland's Theory," and that is the name by which the public knows it to-day.

Malaria Advisory Board acknowledge Danger of Clearing Valleys.

The Malaria Advisory Board now for the first time give the theory serious attention, and apparently it became convinced of its truth, for in August 1916, in a circular issued from the Federal Secretariat setting forth the aims of the Board, the following statement occurs:—

"4. The Board aims at the extermination of anopheles mosquitoes in all thickly populated centres, and wherever economically possible in rural areas, and wishes to effect a reduction in mosquitoes generally.

"The means to be adopted are—

(*a*)
(*b*)
(*c*)
(*d*)
(*e*) Non-disturbance and encouragement of dense natural growth in ravines and swamps where effective drainage is not carried out, and where the conditions are such that this course will result in preventing the formation of anopheline breeding-places."

This, in other words, is the warning of the Malarial Committee issued in 1907, consequent on Pratt and Fletcher's discovery. Nine years were allowed to elapse before the theory received formal recognition.

Summary of Work done by Malaria Advisory Board.

At the end of 1917 the area maintained by the Malaria Advisory Board was 4500 acres (over 7 square miles). The drainage completed included 65 miles of subsoil piping, $8\frac{1}{2}$ miles of open masonry channels, and 12 miles of open earth channels.

The following figures taken from the Board's report for

1918 show the money expended in anti-malarial works in Kuala Lumpur :—

	Year.	Construction.	Maintenance.	Total.
	1908-1911	$47,705	$6,986	$54,691
Malaria . . {	1912	$37,526	$5,559	...
	1913	68,459	11,118	...
Advisory .	1914	22,314	11,156	...
Board . .	1915	8,988	10,705	...
Expenditure . {	1916	23,054	10,487	...
	1917	23,630	10,205	...
		$183,971	$59,230	$243,201

How much of this would have been necessary had Pratt and Fletcher's theory received due recognition and the valleys been left in jungle, it is difficult to say. One thing, however, is certain, the valleys had either to be left absolutely alone or cleared completely and thoroughly drained, for where so efficient a carrier as *A. maculatus* is concerned partial measures are inadmissible. To keep the valleys in such a town as Kuala Lumpur undisturbed, fencings and an efficient system of patrol are essential. Nothing short of this will prevent the Asiatic citizen from trespassing and interfering with the natural growth. Probably sooner or later clearing would have been found necessary.

Conclusion.

The story of the rise and subsidence of malaria in the hill land of Kuala Lumpur has been told at some length, for it is of much interest.

There is no doubt that the clearing of the valleys started malaria in the European residential area, and increased the incidence and death rate in the town generally.

The findings of Pratt, Fletcher, and Wellington showed the relative harmlessness of jungle-covered ravines, but those findings were disregarded.

From 1906 to 1911 the residential area became progressively more malarious, and the anti-malarial campaigns carried out by the Public Works Department did more harm than good.

In 1912 a suitable system of drainage was laid down at

considerable expense; the malaria disappeared from the hills, and the death rate in the town fell considerably.

Kuala Lumpur stands as an expensive warning against interference with jungle ravines in "Inland Hills," unless provision has been made for draining those ravines bone-dry, and maintaining them in that condition.

The lessons taught by the three anti-malarial campaigns (1908, 1910, and 1912) are:—

(1) That anti-mosquito schemes cannot be a success unless framed and carried out under the supervision of those familiar with the habits and life-history of the species it is intended to get rid of.

(2) That a scheme suitable for the eradication of one species of mosquito is not necessarily suitable for another. The methods found successful in the case of *A. umbrosus* proved worse than useless in the case of *A. maculatus*. Schemes suitable in one country should not be slavishly followed in another where the mosquito fauna is different. A thorough mosquito survey is an essential preliminary to any scheme, and the scheme should be framed according to the mosquito findings.

(3) That a problem full of indeterminate elements is impossible of solution without trials and experiments; unforeseen difficulties are certain to arise in the course of the work, and allowance should be made for any deviation from the scheme which may prove necessary. In many cases the estimate of costs can only be a guess, and a scheme should not be allowed to fail for want of a little extra money.

(4) That in hill land clearing of valleys unless followed by efficient drainage is dangerous, as it promotes facilities for the propagation of the dangerous carrier *A. maculatus*.

NOTE ON KUALA LUMPUR BY MALCOLM WATSON.

To the interesting chapter written by Dr Wellington, there is little to add, except on two points. By 1910, over three years had passed since the inception of the anti-malarial work in Kuala Lumpur; yet malaria was becoming more and more severe; mosquito-control and malaria-control had proved a complete failure. It was even said that a place once particularly free from malaria had become intensely malarious as a consequence of the anti-malarial campaign. Money had been spent on open drains, on rubble drains, on concrete drains, and subsoil drains—without success. Government now appeared to be disinclined to spend more money; possibly because it seemed like throwing good money after bad. In June 1910, at Dr Travers' suggestion, I gave a public lecture in Kuala Lumpur, and explained the problem. I urged the need for research, the creation of a Sanitary branch, and co-operation between all branches of the Department of Medicine, namely hospitals, research, and sanitation.

Throughout the remainder of 1910 and most of 1911 practically nothing was done in Kuala Lumpur. To me it was a period of anxiety. I had advised some estates to lay down a system of subsoil drainage to overcome *A. maculatus*, and some had agreed to do so. But it was hopeless to expect much progress throughout the country, when the Federal Capital was notorious as an anti-malaria failure. Indeed I feared that the failure in Kuala Lumpur might be to the Malay States what Mian Mir was to India. At Mian Mir the Imperial Government of India and the Royal Society of England joined forces to eradicate malaria from the Cantonment. It is unnecessary here to go into details; but the experiment was a failure. Sir Ronald Ross [2] says of it: " In fact the whole affair was conducted on unpractical and unscientific lines. It proved nothing at all, and its only effect was to retard anti-malaria work in that and other countries for years."

For anything like that to occur in the Malay States, where so promising a start had been made ten years before, would indeed have been a disaster. Government, however, did not move for over a year; but on the formation of the Malaria Advisory Board at the end of 1911, I urged the importance of clearing away the malaria of Kuala Lumpur, as the first duty of the Government. The system I had devised for Seafield Estate was adopted, as is described in the Annual Medical Report for 1911; and its success is due to the careful way in which it was carried out by Mr Evans, the Board's engineer.

The only other point I propose to mention is the importance of continuous and ample malaria research. Our ignorance of the distribution of *A. umbrosus* has cost this country heavily both in money and in lives. I was familiar with the Coastal Plains and Coastal Hills, with jungle and the jungle-loving *A. umbrosus* and *A. aitkeni.* Dr Leicester had caught *A. umbrosus* in Kuala Lumpur; and some specimens of the mosquito had been taken by a gentleman in his house in Kuala Lumpur and given to me. I had known many curious instances of the appearance and disappearance of the insect. Sometimes enormous numbers would disappear in a few days. At times it is easily got: at other times not. Therefore I attached little or no importance to Mr Pratt's, Dr Fletcher's, and Dr Wellington's failure to find the insect in ravines. These gentlemen, on the other hand, had no knowledge of the Coastal Plains and Coastal Hills, in which *A. umbrosus* abounds. Thus no one realised that the distribution of *A. umbrosus* was so peculiarly limited; and that Kuala Lumpur and Batu Tiga, which are only some ten miles apart, and apparently in similar hilly land, were in different zones; the ravines of one harbouring *A. umbrosus*, those of the other not; from a malarial point of view, a difference of first importance. Not suspecting the truth, I was greatly puzzled by many places, as I have described in the chapter on "Inland Hills"; and it was not until Dr Strickland informed me of his discovery of the absence of *A. umbrosus* from certain hills, and after my visits to Pahang and Batu Arang, that the truth seemed to be found; namely, that *A. umbrosus* was limited to the Coastal Hills, and did not spread to what may be called the "Inland Hills." Had there been more research, in 1909, as Dr Wellington suggests, the truth would have been discovered sooner: and in the extensive clearings subsequent to the Rubber Boom in 1910 many a ravine would have been left in jungle, to the great advantage of the public health. As it was, the importance of what had been discovered by Messrs Pratt, Fletcher, and Wellington was not appreciated; the truth had to be rediscovered by Dr Strickland. Even then Government was slow to believe it; and the treatment meted out to Dr Strickland is a blot on the name of the administration of this country.

To sum it up, the administration in the past has not provided sufficient malarial research nor encouraged it; and for lack of knowledge large sums have been wasted on badly designed or unnecessary work, progress has been spasmodic, and an enormous number of lives have been lost.

CHAPTER XXVII

ANTI-MALARIAL WORK IN SINGAPORE

By P. S. HUNTER, M.A., M.B., D.P.H., Deputy Health Officer, Singapore.

PRIOR to 1911 only temporary measures such as oiling of swamps, filling of pools and the clearing and training of streams and ditches had been carried out, and nothing very permanent had been attempted. In that year, however, in the pandemic of malaria, Singapore suffered fairly severely, and it was felt that something more radical must be done to combat the disease.

In his annual report for 1910, Dr Middleton, the Health Officer, had suggested that a wise course would be to institute "a systematic examination of school children for signs of present and past malaria, ascertain the locality of their present or recent abodes, and make an inspection of these localities for conditions contributing to the disease." This actually was done in 1911 by Dr Middleton himself and Dr Finlayson; and they found that the most malarious district in Singapore was the Telok Blangah area. In August 1911, in the two Malay Vernacular Schools of that district, Telok Blangah School and Kampong Jago School, 46 per cent. and 29·5 per cent. respectively of the children were found to have enlarged spleens.

The district extends from the General Hospital to Morse Road and forms a strip of land a half to one mile wide along the harbour. Consisting as it did of large swampy low-lying areas at its eastern end, and hilly ground with its accompanying ravines and streams at its western end, it was felt that it was an extremely suitable area with which to experiment. It was known to be malarious and was not too large to make supervision difficult. Accordingly Dr Malcolm Watson, whose anti-malarial measures had been so successful at Port Swettenham and Klang, was asked to advise as to the best method of dealing with the problem.

Dr Watson first confirmed the findings of the spleen rates in the schools; and, further, to get more children and to determine more exactly the foci of malaria, made a house-to-house examination. In all, 571 children were examined, and 21 per cent. were found to have enlarged spleens. In the course of the examination, too, it was found that the hilly part of the district with its ravines and streams was much more malarious than the low-lying flat lands.

Thereafter a detailed examination of the whole district was made to determine the varieties of anophelines breeding in the different localities.

Depending on the conditions existing at each area, spleen rates, species of anophelines, and the variety of swamp or stream, Dr Watson made his recommendations—filling (though he was not in favour of this generally) earth drains, hill-foot drains, brick drains and subsoil pipes.

To the newly-formed Anti-malarial Committee the task of carrying out these recommendations was entrusted, and under the supervision of Dr Finlayson, the work was immediately put in hand. During the period of construction quinine was distributed free in the district, and an effort made toward the education of the people in the habits of mosquitoes by the exhibition of illustrative cards in the markets, schools, and public places generally.

School.	Date.	Total Examined.	Total showing Spleen Enlargement.	Percentage.
Telok Blangah .	1911 August . .		18	46·1
	1911 November .		18	48·6
	1912 April . .		26	50·0
	1913 January . .		12	20·7
	1913 May . .		7	11·0*
	1914 January . .		7	13·0
	1914 September .		4	8·1
	1914 November .			3·7
Kampong Jago .	1911 August . .		13	29·5
	1912 April . .		8	17·7
	1913 January . .		8	15·7
	1913 May .		3	7·5
	1914 January . .		0	0·0
	1914 September .		3	6·5

* Almost.

The work was completed early in 1914. Whilst it was going on, and just after completion, Dr Finlayson made several exhaustive house-to-house examinations of the children in the district. The figures are instructive. In April 1912, 508 were examined and 11·4 per cent. were found to have enlarged spleen. In April 1913, out of 485 examined, not quite 4 per cent. were similarly affected. The figures for the two schools during the period are shown in the table on the previous page.

A review of these figures shows that there was a progressive decrease of the spleen rate to practically zero.

During the war the regular examination of these children could not be carried out as frequently as one would have wished; but I visited the schools at intervals and never found any indication that the spleen rates were rising. My last examination was a few days ago, when I found at Telok Blangah School two children with spleens just palpable, out of a total of fifty-two, and at Kampong Jago School, one child out of thirty-one.

All these figures speak for themselves, and I feel I cannot do better than to sum up in the words used by Dr Watson in his second report of December 1914 :—

" Three years ago it was decided to attempt to control malaria in the area of Telok Blangah by abolishing breeding-places of the mosquitoes which carry the disease : the spleen rate was used as the test of the amount of malaria in the district, and by that test has been shown to have decreased to what for all practical purposes may be called zero. Similar measures carried out in other places have had similar results, and the Anti-malarial Committee of Singapore may, with confidence, look on the reduction of malaria in the Telok Blangah district, not as a mere accident, but as the direct result of the work done."

If there should have been any doubt as to the truth of these words in 1914, there can certainly be none now after the lapse of another five years.

The actual expenditure on the works was under $50,000, and a certain amount of that was spent on anti-malarial measures outside the area—a wonderfully small figure in consideration of the great results achieved.

From 1914 onwards it has been part of my duties to keep

z

watch on these areas and to look out for defects. The experience gained has been invaluable in enabling me to come to a decision as to the best method of dealing with anopheline breeding-grounds in other parts of the municipal area.

Regarding the low-lying eastern part of the area, there is nothing much to say. It was originally swamp and was drained by open-earth drains. These open ditches are much the same as when first cut. They certainly dried up the ground, but they are too many and are a source of danger in themselves. But this point I shall refer to more fully later. Occasionally anophelines are found breeding in them, usually *A. rossii*, sometimes *A. karwari*, and rarely *A. maculatus*. By constant cleaning by the maintenance gangs and oiling where necessary, this breeding is kept down, but I am afraid that this part will never be successfully drained until the Singapore Harbour Board take steps to permanently lower the level of the subsoil water in their reclamation, through which the drainage of this whole area ultimately passes. It is purely an engineering problem. With some system of tidal valves it should not be impossible.

Turning to the hilly western end of the area it is interesting to note that sooner or later, as Dr Watson had forecasted, *A. maculatus* was found breeding in all the ravines—very often in the open-earth foot-hill drains that we ourselves had cut. The Radin Mas area is one of the best examples of this. It is a large wide ravine about half a mile long, with a stream winding down the centre. Off the larger ravine five smaller ones, each several hundred yards long, open. In the original scheme it was recommended that the two top ravines only be piped, which was done. Then *A. maculatus* appeared in the spillways, necessitating the concreting of these spillways right down to the main stream. Later, all the other three ravines in which we had cut open drains began to show *A. maculatus*, so that these in turn have been subsoil-piped down to the main stream in the middle of the valley. On my last visit to this area in December 1919, I examined about twenty children in the Malay village there, and found none with enlarged spleen. The older inhabitants, too, assured me that there was no fewer now in the kampong.

I have followed the same policy over the whole of this

area. Roughly, wherever *A. maculatus* has appeared, I have dealt with the breeding-ground by subsoil piping. Open earth drains are all right at first, but they require constant supervision; and with the repeated cutting and cleaning that they are subjected to, they ultimately become too wide and deep, so that water stagnates in them.

And this brings me to a point which I wish to emphasise with regard to the habits of *A. maculatus*. In my experience the dry weather is the time to be on one's guard against this mosquito. In the very dry spell from August to October 1914, when we had practically no rain for three months, I found more *A. maculatus* breeding-grounds both in the experimental district and in the municipal area generally than in the several years since. The reason is not far to seek. In wet weather the larvæ are being constantly flushed out from the smaller drains and never get a chance to develop. But I emphasise the point, because I found that in many places by cutting open drains breeding-grounds for *A. maculatus* had been created. After a little dry weather there is no water in the ditches except that coming from the springs, the outlets of which have been exposed by the cutting of the ditch itself—such a spring is an ideal breeding-ground for *A. maculatus*.

The danger of this is well illustrated in the following. A certain bungalow in the residential area stood on the high ground adjoining a large stretch of flat land. This low-lying flat land was originally a swamp, but had been drained by the cutting of several large, open ditches through it. At the time of which I speak, the weather had been very dry, and these open ditches, which usually stood half full, were empty and dry in their upper reaches. Two Europeans in the bungalow were suffering from malaria, while among the native servants and their children there were other six acute cases. The only anopheline breeding-ground found was in one of these aforesaid dry ditches close to the house, where a small spring oozed from the side of the ditch, ran for a few feet, and finally disappeared in its floor. About half a dozen *A. maculatus* larvæ were found in the whole spring. It was piped at the cost of a few dollars—and there were no further fresh cases of malaria.

In the experimental area I had much the same experience with two private reservoirs. Both these had been formed by the simple process of bunding across a ravine. The sides of the reservoirs were formed by the grassy banks, and the floor by the natural slope of the ravine. Under the scheme the springs in the ravine-collecting area above each reservoir had been dealt with by pipes, the outlet of which delivered over a spill-way directly into the reservoir. All that was necessary was thought to have been done. But in a dry spell the water-level of the reservoir fell, and a large expanse of sloping floor was exposed. In this exposed part were numerous springs which showed themselves as trickles of water running down to the water-level. My attention was first drawn to the danger by the occurrence of several cases of malaria in houses over-looking one of these reservoirs. I found *A. maculatus* breeding in these springs. A similar condition of affairs existed in the other reservoir. The fault was remedied by a little rough concreting and excavation of the floors.

From these and similar experiences, I concluded that the best way is to put down subsoil pipes wherever possible. The pipes in the area, some of which have been down for over six years, are still working perfectly, and there need never be any fear in employing this method of drainage. All that is necessary is to see that the pipes are of good strong material and that due allowance is made for storm-water, *i.e.*, the pipes must be many times bigger than those capable of taking the ordinary dry weather flow.

Once pipes have been put down in a ravine all that is necessary is that the maintenance gangs should visit the area at regular, short intervals to cut down the blukar and other secondary growth which soon springs up. If this is religiously done for eighteen months to two years, it is my experience to find that these coarser growths tend to die out, and are replaced by a firm, springy turf which no amount of storm-water will dislodge, and which requires a minimum of supervision and expenditure in upkeep.

With regard to the maintenance of these anti-malarial areas after completion, there is one difficulty we have had in Singapore to which I feel I must make reference—and that is the trouble we have had to keep Chinese squatters from settling in the area—or to evict them once they have settled. Dr Watson, in his 1914 Report, wrote very strongly on the subject. Just recently I found that one of the Radin Mas ravines had been converted into a huge vegetable garden. Wells had been dug over the pipes, and the area was slowly reverting into a worse condition than ever before. I say worse, advisedly, because the squatter, in addition to breeding mosquitoes, by keeping night-soil pits and using night-soil in his gardens, directly encourages the spread of diseases like typhoid, cholera, and dysentery. I feel that I cannot emphasise too strongly that no cultivation of any kind should be permitted in these areas.

Turning now to areas with which I am more familiar, because I have supervised them from the start, I have tried to put in practice the various lessons learned from the Telok Blangah area. During the past six years new works have been constructed all over the town, but mostly in the residential districts. This residential area is essentially a hilly area, and roughly it is a system of small ravines, with the houses built on the sides. In the ravine was a swamp or a winding over-grown stream, with wet, muddy banks and springs oozing out at the foot-hills—all ideal breeding-grounds for *A. maculatus;* and sure enough *A. maculatus* was found sooner or later in all of them. To enable me to find the foci of malaria more quickly, I made arrangements with the medical practitioners to notify me whenever they attended a patient with a first attack of malaria. I found this very useful as, whenever I received notice of several cases in one locality, I visited the spot and found the anopheline breeding-grounds long before I should have done in my routine search of the whole district.

Scattered over the Municipality, there were several low-lying areas which had originally been swamps and which were drained by having open earth drains cut through them. And this brings me to a point to which I promised to refer later. My experience is that these swamps have had far too many ditches cut in them. These have certainly fulfilled their purpose in drying up the swamp. But as soon as the ground is freed from its water-logged condition these ditches which become deeper and wider from the attentions of the maintenance gangs, stand half full of water, which is almost stagnant and breeds all sorts of mosquitoes. Further, as I have already pointed out, there is the danger that in a dry spell the level of the subsoil water falls, and springs are exposed in the

ditches themselves.   And in these springs *A. maculatus* breeds.
And even without waiting for a dry spell we may find we
have created *A. maculatus* breeding-grounds, as it frequently
happens that with the drying up of a swamp the springs at
the surrounding foot-hills are exposed.   This was the condition
of things in many flat areas in Singapore—and, as already
pointed out, is the condition found in the eastern end of the
Telok Blangah area itself.   So far as possible with these areas,
I have tried to eradicate the *A. maculatus* breeding-grounds by
subsoil piping all the springs at the foot-hills down to a main
drain.

A swamp prior to being touched may, of anophelines, be
breeding only *A. sinensis ;* and, if by draining it, we are simply to
create a suitable breeding-ground for a more dangerous species,
it had much better be left alone.   So that it is obvious that,
if we must drain, it must be very carefully done.   Remembering
these things, I undertook the drainage of a large swamp some
60 acres in extent lying behind Tanglin Barracks and extending
from there to the Singapore River at Alexandra Road.

The natural drainage of the swamp was by way of the river.
The swamp itself was knee-deep in water practically all over,
and almost anywhere one could find *A. sinensis* larvæ.   The
river was first cleared of silt in its lower part.   In the process of
clearing the river, about four dams, put in by Chinese squatters
for the purpose of diverting water to their pig and duck ponds,
were demolished.   The course of the river, too, in its part
adjoining the swamp, was cleared and straightened.

These simple measures in a month's time did much to do
away with the swamp.   The removal of the dams lowered the
river between two and three feet and permitted the water from
the swamp to drain away.   Large areas of it became quite dry
as the level of the subsoil water fell.

Thereafter one main drain was cut through the centre, with
two smaller ones joining this and draining two ravines, which
formed the head of the swamp.   These, after a little time, were
sufficient to completely dry the area until one can, to-day, walk
over it in the wettest weather and find no water showing
anywhere.   But, and herein lies the danger, springs began to
show at the foot-hills.   As the area was well outside the
residential part and there were no houses near, these springs
were treated by being drained into the main drains by small

FIG. 108.—SINGAPORE.
Open Ditch into which the subsoil drains discharge.

[To face page 323.

open ditches. The big ditches I never find breed anophelines ; but the small ones especially, if allowed to become grassed over, most certainly do. Now the ideal to aim at, in my opinion, is that all these springs should be subsoil piped to the nearest main drains. In this case, it would have been done but for lack of money. But already, with the demand for houses, construction is progressing on the sides of one of the ravines, and knowing the danger, I have advised that we immediately replace the main open drain in the ravine by a cement channel, and the small ditches tapping the springs by subsoil pipes discharging into this channel. And the work will be commenced at once and completed before the houses are occupied.

This brings me back to the method followed in the more purely residential areas with its system of narrow ravines. It is essentially the same as that for the swamp but more advanced. Originally I drained the marshy ground in the floor of a ravine by one open earth drain, or by clearing and straightening the existing stream. Then all springs were led by contour or foot-hill subsoil pipes to discharge over a concrete spillway into this. The main drain was left as an open ditch, and, practically without exception, I have never found them breeding when they are kept reasonably clear of obstructions, and pools are not allowed to form. But, with the rapid extension of the town, the more rigid insistence that houses should have a proper drainage scheme, and the care required to keep these open ditches from silting up, I have lately come to the conclusion that they must be replaced by a more permanent type of drains. One that our engineers have found very successful and not too expensive is a V-shaped open concrete channel with concrete slab revetments and turfed sides—the idea being that the ordinary dry weather flow is conveyed within the concrete area, flood water only reaching as far as the turf. After a time with reasonable supervision these turfed sides become firm and no amount of storm water will break them down. Into these drains the house drains will discharge. What is more important is that many people, despairing of ever seeing a proper water carriage sewage system installed, are putting in their own septic tanks and contact beds. The effluent from these in many cases must go by way of the ravines ; and I, personally, have no objection to its being discharged into the main drains—provided the septic tanks are properly supervised and the main drain is concreted.

I made the experiment in one locality of combining the ordinary house drainage with the subsoil pipes. The house drains, which carry rain and bath water and kitchen washings only, were made to discharge over a sump. I would further advise that when this is done a grid should be interposed in the house drain to intercept refuse like egg-shells, etc.—which the cook insists on putting down the drain.

Further, this grid should be placed well inside the compound where it will catch the householder's eye. He certainly won't look for it.

Though this experiment was quite successful, I don't generally advise it. It is preferable to have house drains discharging into an open channel. I simply mention it because a case might easily arise where, to reach a main drain, the house drains might have to be prolonged for hundreds of yards, and a combination such as I have described would prove much less costly.

With regard to the flat lands in the municipal area with its many pig and duck ponds and the other varied collections of water, so dear to the heart of the Chinese vegetable gardener, nothing much has been done. Indeed, during the war nothing was allowed to be done. All that was possible was to keep a close watch on the larvæ inhabitants of these ponds. Of anophelines only *A. sinensis* is ever found, though of course many other mosquitoes find a breeding-place there.

Difficulty was experienced with three flat areas, all tidal, in that *A. ludlowi* periodically bred out in enormous numbers. Two of these were dealt with by filling, as they were simply a series of pools into which the sea water reached at high tides. The third was in the Telok Blangah area in the reclamation adjoining Nelson Road.

Here all the open ditches occasionally bred *A. ludlowi* literally in millions. The only possible course was to deal with it by oiling, which is now regularly done. A point of interest in connection with this last is, that in his 1911 report Dr Watson was at a loss to account for the fact that at Spottiswoode, the cleaner end of this area, there was so little malaria compared with what was found at Nelson Road, its fouler end. He suggested as a reason that some other anophelines might be

FIG. 109.—SINGAPORE.

The new type of permanent Drain into which the subsoil drains discharge.

[To face page 330.

breeding in the Nelson Road district.   I have no doubt in my
own mind that *M. ludlowi* was the culprit.

Just recently a new Anti-mosquito Ordinance, has been
passed by the Legislative Council, though it has not yet been
out in operation. Under it there are ample powers to deal
effectively with all these low-lying areas.

Practically all these works described above have been done
at municipal expense. I found very early that, if one had to
wait for the owner of a property to carry out the drainage,
one might wait for ever. And, apart from that, it is almost
impossible to assess the cost for each owner or to estimate how
much his property benefits. The following will illustrate what
I mean. In 1914, certain houses, under different ownership,
built on high ground surrounding a ravine, were rendered
untenable on account of malaria. In the floor of the ravine
was a small cocoanut plantation. The water from the high
ground showed as springs only in this plantation, and were all
breeding *A. maculatus.* These were subsoil piped in the usual
way with the result that malaria disappeared. Now it would
obviously have been unfair to make the owner of the plantation
pay. In any case he was a poor man and to pay would have
meant bankruptcy. It was equally difficult to estimate the
amount that each owner of the houses should pay, and there
was no machinery for enforcing payment without endless
litigation. Consequently the only thing to do was, what was
done—to pipe the area at municipal expense. In my subsequent works this is pretty well the policy I always followed.
But with the passing of the Anti-mosquito Ordinance and the
likelihood, one hopes, of things being done on a much wider
basis all over the island and money being spent on a lavish
scale, it will be unfair any longer to put the whole burden on
the taxpayer and the big property owners must be made to
pay, at least in part.

Regarding the cost of these works it is not of much use my
quoting figures. The prices of to-day bear no resemblance to
those of a year ago, I had almost said yesterday; the upward
rise in the price of materials being so rapid. But this I will
say, that in carrying out anti-malarial—as against anti-mosquito
works—I have often found that for a little judicious expenditure
wonderful results may be obtained.

I should now like to describe my experience of what may

be done in the way of controlling malaria in, say, a small self-contained district like a small island.

During the war I was mobilised with the local volunteers, and late in 1915 was sent as medical officer in charge on Blakan Mati.

This island has a European population—mostly Garrison Artillery, of about 500. It is situated at the western entrance of the harbour, is about 3 miles long by a half to three quarters broad, and consists of high ground running its whole length with fairly steep slopes to the sea on either side. The northern side is fringed with mangrove, while the southern slope ends in cliff and sandy beach. The high ground on which the forts are situated is intersected with ravines which are full of tiny streams and innumerable springs.

I had known, prior to my going to live on the island, that malaria was rife amongst the troops; but until I saw my morning sick parade, I did not realise how bad it really was. And, if that were not enough, I was forcibly reminded that something must be done by finding several *A. maculatus* adults on my verandah in the first week of my occupation of the bungalow.

An anopheline survey of the whole island was immediately undertaken. About twenty anopheline breeding-grounds were found. *A. umbrosus* and *A. karwari* were found in one or two places; in all the others our old friend *A. maculatus*.

Prior to 1915 very little in the way of permanent works had been done. A few pipes had been put down in places; but these were not acting as the undergrowth had been allowed to grow down into them. Mostly there were open earth drains with oil-drips. I may say that these drips, in a place like this at any rate, where the person responsible for their upkeep is continually being changed, are useless, and may even be dangerous from the false sense of security which they may give.

From my experience in Singapore, I determined that the only method to ensure success was to put down subsoil pipes; and this work was accordingly put in hand immediately. While the work was going on, temporary measures, as oil spraying regularly applied, were carried out.

Several difficulties were encountered in the course of the work. At one place just below the barracks, a series of springs were found below the level of high tide, but protected from

FIG. 110.—SINGAPORE.

Both subsoil drainage and the effluent from the small septic tank seen in the photograph,
discharge into this permanent concrete drain.

[*To face page* 332.

the sea by a sand bar. The difficulty was overcome by the subsoil pipes being brought to discharge below high-tide level—a system which was found to be quite satisfactory. Then again difficulty was experienced at a wet area artificially created by the raising of the natural subsoil level to supply water for the Dhoby ponds. In wet weather there was formed a large swamp several acres in extent, on the confines of which *maculatus, karwari*, and *umbrosus* were found breeding. As it was insisted that the Dhoby ponds must have an adequate supply of water, the drainage of this area was rendered rather difficult. The problem was cleverly solved, however, by the engineer who tapped two springs outcropping at a higher level some quarter of a mile away. These were led by an open concrete channel to the Dhoby ponds, and proved to give a sufficient supply. The swamp was then drained by very deeply-laid subsoil pipes, and the whole area became dry and remained so, even in the wettest weather.

On the very steep slopes of Serapong, the highest part of the island, we had trouble in the ravines with storm water. It came down so forcibly that it washed out the newly-made ground covering the pipes in the floor of the ravines. This was overcome by cutting a temporary channel in the side of the ravine, well clear of the subsoil pipes. After a time, when the floor of the ravines developed a strong firm turf, the storm water could do no harm.

Except for these and several minor difficulties, the work was easy. Roughly, the same principles were followed as in Singapore, except that on Blakan Mati the subsoil pipes were brought right down to the sea in most cases, instead of discharging into main open channels.

The drainage was completed in two years, that is by the end of 1917. In a report of April 1917, by the Engineer-in-charge of these works, I find that during 1916 a sum of £576 was spent, and that a further sum of £500, which, it was estimated, would easily complete the programme, was granted for 1917. It was further estimated that a sum of £200 would be required annually to keep the 60 acres occupied by these drains clear of vegetation. Personally, I think this sum rather high, as I feel certain that the coarse, thick vegetation will die out in two years, to be replaced by short turf, that will require a minimum of expenditure and supervision. Naturally, at the present day, these figures are valueless—and possibly they are not exact, in that a good deal of money seems to have been spent on the areas in previous years in clearing jungle, cutting open drains (and incidentally creating *maculatus* breeding-grounds), oiling, etc., some of which money might have been required to be spent on the permanent works. But I only mention the figures because the engineer assured me on the completion of the work that the actual cost was only three times as much as was being spent in any one year on purely temporary measures.

In the following list of admissions for malaria, I have excluded those for Asiatic troops, as it would not be fair to include these. On the island there was always a detachment of the Johore military forces. They suffered a good deal from malaria, but as they were relieved every fortnight, their malaria was obviously contracted elsewhere. So, too, with the Indian gunners stationed on the island. It may be that during the war medical examination was less strict. At anyrate, within a day of their arrival on the island, I have found recruits with enlarged spleens. Prior to 1914, the average number of European troops was in the neighbourhood of 350, and after that date about 260. During my stay on the island, many of the men belonged to B category and were suitable subjects for the depredations of the malarial parasite. The figures, so far as I could collect them from the hospital records available, were:—

Year.						Admissions for Malaria.
1912	.	.	.	.	.	. 163
1913		.	.	.	.	. 94
1914	.	.	.	.	.	. 48
1915	.	.	.	.	.	. 87
1916	.	.	.	.	.	. 23
1917	.	.	.	.	.	. 26

In 1916 and 1917 there were only sixteen and fourteen fresh cases respectively, the others being readmissions. I was unable to find the corresponding figures for previous years. On my return from home in 1919, I was assured that there had been no fresh cases of malaria in 1918, and to the best of my knowledge there were none in 1919.

At the risk of appearing tedious I wish in conclusion to reiterate one or two points. It may be argued that the system of drainage I have advocated is expensive, as it certainly would be on, say, a rubber estate. But I do not pretend to advise for other than a thickly populated area such as Singapore.

The anopheline we have to fear in Singapore is *A. maculatus*, and it is more likely to give trouble in dry weather than in wet. Whenever it appears, I believe the only sure way is to put its breeding-place underground.

Dealing with a ravine, subsoil pipe the foot-hill springs into, if possible, one main open channel. This channel may be of the open-earth variety at first, if in a sparsely populated district; but as the town expands, it should be replaced by a drain of more permanent type.

In draining a swamp, don't hurry. Try if anything can be done in the way of lowering the outlet, or clearing it of obstruction. Wait a little and then cut as few open ditches through it as possible. Having done so, and the ground having dried up, be on the lookout for springs at the foot-hills and surrounding ravines. Don't wait for these to breed, but subsoil pipe them immediately into the nearest main ditch.

Where filling is absolutely necessary, consider always the advisability of first putting down subsoil pipes to take the drainage of the adjoining higher ground.

Having constructed anti-malarial drains, see that the areas are frequently visited and carefully tended for two years, and permit no cultivation of any kind. On this last point there should be no compromise.

Results.—As regards results, I do not intend to quote any figures of the reduction of the death rates of malaria. I am afraid that, with our present antiquated system of death registration, whereby 50 per cent. of those who die are never seen in life by a medical man, but are certified (many of them as malaria) from an inspection of the body only, any figures one might quote would be valueless. But I personally feel sure, and I speak, too, for one of our leading practitioners, that in the town and its immediate surroundings there is now very little malaria contracted. And in any case the results obtained in Telok Blangah itself, and on Blakan Mati, are enough to convince me that we are working along the best lines to finally eradicate the disease.

There are, however, certain figures which give unequivocal evidence of the improved health of the town, namely the reduction in the total death rates. These show that, despite the influenza epidemic, there has been a saving of over 16,000 lives in the eight years (1912-1919). The remarkable reduction in the annual malaria curve shows that no small part of this saving of life must be attributed to the anti-malaria work. The subject is dealt with in more detail by Dr Watson in the section on Singapore in Chapter XXIX., and will be better understood after a perusal of Chapter XXVIII., which deals with Statistics and the Seasonal Variations of Malaria.

CHAPTER XXVIII

ON STATISTICS

WITHOUT statistics no clear idea of the health of a community can be formed; to the sanitarian they are as important as his accounts to the merchant. Before he can make out a case for the expenditure of money, he must show in statistical form the prevalence of the disease he desires to control. From a business point of view, statistics are necessary in order to determine if the results obtained are worth the money spent.

The next question that presents itself to the tropical worker is, What statistics should be compiled? To that there can only be one answer. Every figure that bears on the disease should be collected. At the time some figures may not appear of much value; but, if compiled and filed, they may prove of extraordinary value at a later period; such, for example, are routine spleen rates. Changes in health may be occurring of which the observer is not conscious at the moment; later he will realise them, and can then refer to the old spleen rates.

The statistical departments, which exist in most countries in Europe, are practically non-existent in many places in the tropics. To a large extent, the worker must compile and collate whatever statistics he requires. Generally speaking, he works in a narrow field; and this, apart from the personal equation, may lead to error and false conclusions. In this chapter I wish to put the beginner on his guard against some fallacies; at the same time show how valuable figures may be when local conditions are known.

Hospital Statistics.—Admissions for malaria, checked by the microscope, form series of facts of great value. Unfortunately they do not include all cases of malaria, as some may have had quinine shortly before admission, or for other reasons the parasites may not be found. This error may generally be considered as a constant and so be disregarded; and the figures are of great value.

Out-patients treated for malaria are less likely to have their blood examined, and the records are less exact. Both out-patients and in-patients may reappear time and again for treatment, and it is usually impossible to say if the patients are suffering from new infections or relapses.

Nevertheless the number of admissions and the number of out-patients run an almost parallel course in the ordinary native hospital, and the gross figures of each, even admitting they contain many errors in diagnosis, throw much light on the health of a place, and should not be discarded.

When there is much malaria on an estate, some cases are admitted to hospital; but many are not. For where malaria is severe, and the cases are numerous, the hospital accommodation is generally insufficient; this is particularly so when a seasonal wave is severe, and 30 to 40 per cent. of the labour force is incapacitated. When, however, the malaria has been controlled and reduced in amount, it is possible to admit every case with an abnormal temperature. The admissions for malaria may, therefore, show no great fall, and the observer might be misled if he considers merely the admissions; the error can be detected by examining the number of out-patients. In the F.M.S. this frequently happens; no cases of malaria are treated as out-patients on some estates.

If some care be taken in ascertaining the exact residence of cases admitted to hospital, the observer can add considerably to the value of his figures. Having done this for some years, when in charge of the Government hospital at Klang, I can say that this correction is much less difficult than might be imagined; it demands, however, from the inquirer a fairly accurate knowledge of the local details of the country-side from which the patients come. When the exact residence is known, it is possible to make a " spot map " of the disease.

On large estates, conditions may vary widely on different divisions; there may be only half a mile between the best and the worst health, so the admissions and the daily number in hospital from each division should be recorded separately.

The great fallacy of admission rates for malaria as an indication of the health of a place is its variation with the number of non-immune new arrivals. Many new arrivals will raise the admission rate with great rapidity. This is seen when a batch of new coolies arrives on a malarial estate. If no others come, the admission rate gradually falls, until it is so low that the observer may imagine the place has become healthy; but it is not so. Other new arrivals will again send up the admission rate. A fall in the admission rate by itself cannot, therefore, be regarded as proof of the control of malaria. As I will show, the observer can guard himself from mistake by ascertaining the spleen rate.

The observer is liable to be misled by a fall in the admission rate (and as will be seen by the death rate), chiefly when the labour force is under 400. Above that number there is less chance of mistake; for, to maintain a labour force in the F.M.S. at a steady figure something like 30 to 50 per cent. of the force must be recruited yearly; and this means there are sufficient new non-immune labourers to keep the disease in full flame. While referring to the admission rates for malaria, I would remind the reader that, when malaria is controlled, or when labour becomes immune and new arrivals stop coming in, not only do the admissions for malaria fall, but so do the admissions for all other diseases. Diarrhœa and dysentery are so frequently merely the terminal symptoms of chronic malaria, that the control of malaria has a notable effect on the admissions (and deaths) from these two diseases.

Deaths.—All towns tend to attract the sick and dying from the surrounding district; we saw it in the town of Klang in 1901; it occurs daily on a large scale in larger towns like Singapore, as Dr Finlayson showed from a careful analysis of the malaria cases in hospital. While it is generally easy to make the required correction for residence, when a patient is admitted to a hospital, it is more difficult to obtain correct information from those furnishing a death report.

What has been said of the admissions for malaria and other diseases applies largely to the deaths both from malaria and other diseases. Many new arrivals lead to a rise in the admission rates and death rates of malaria, of diarrhœa and dysentery, and generally of other diseases. Similarly, when the new-comers have become immune, the death rate drops, and may deceive the observer. The death rates, like the admission rates, must be read in the light of the spleen rates.

Sometimes I think of the two, the death rates and the spleen rates, as "cross bearings" which fix the health with greater accuracy than any other figures. In this book, I have used them more largely than any other figures, not because many other figures are not available, but because some selection must be made in a work of limited size; and these two sets of figures, in my opinion, give the most accurate information.

Apart from "rates" worked out on the population, the gross number of deaths varies with the seasonal prevalence of malaria, and presents a striking picture, to which I shall refer presently.

Spleen Rates.—Of any single set of figures, the spleen rates appear to me to give, in practice, the most accurate idea of the amount of malaria in a place. The parasite rate makes so heavy a call on time, which in itself limits the number of observations the isolated tropical worker can make, that the spleen rate, based on a larger number of observations, is probably more accurate as a figure indicating the amount of malaria in a given population and locality.

It is usual to examine the children under ten years of age; but as few native children know their ages, the observer soon adopts a height and appearance standard which he almost unconsciously applies before beginning his examination. With a little practice, it is possible to examine the children almost as fast as they can walk past. My custom is to make the children pass from left to right; I use both hands; the left hand is placed below the ribs behind, and the right hand in front. The spleen, if enlarged, is then caught between the fingers of the two hands. This bimanual examination of the organ gives greater accuracy than an examination by one hand alone; for even quite small spleens can be pressed forward by the left hand fingers against the fingers of the right hand, which, with practice, become expert at detecting any abnormal resistance in the splenic region. Only rarely is it necessary to lay a child on his back, in order to relax the abdominal muscles. With adults it is almost essential to make the examination with the patient lying flat.

In making the examination in a country where a kala-azar does not exist, it must not be forgotten :—(1) That an enlarged spleen may persist for several years after a place has become non-malarial; (2) that healthy children may have come quite recently to a malarial place and diluted the spleen rate; (3) that children with enlarged spleen may come to a healthy place, the spleen rate of which is zero; and (4) that healthy infants often have a palpable spleen.

In practice these corrections are easily made; and many instances have been given in previous chapters. Only a very unobservant observer will be misled. On one occasion I had separated the children with enlarged spleens from those with normal spleens, when I overheard a small boy among those with enlarged spleens say in Tamil, "We are the old ones—they are the new." He was mightily pleased with his discovery, which was, as I found, correct.

In several places I have shown how quickly new children acquire enlarged spleen in very malarial localities, even when they are receiving quinine; within two months quite a high percentage may have enlargement of the organ. It will be found, too, that those who have not spleens are those most likely to have "fever" at the time of the examination. For example, there may be ten children who have been four months on the estate ; seven will have enlarged spleen, and three will be suffering from "fever"; as a matter of fact, these are the figures of an observation.

Enlargement of the spleen indicates a certain degree of immunity to the "pyrexia" or "fever-producing toxin"; for, although these children are not suffering from "fever," in a high percentage their blood contains parasites. Where the malaria, as indicated by the spleen rate, is only moderate in amount, say from 20 to 40 per cent., it is mainly among the children with enlarged spleen that parasites are found.

It was a planter, Mr Stevens of Pilmoor Estate, who first made me realise that enlarged spleen meant an approaching immunity. One day I was examining the children on his estate, and had picked out those with enlarged spleen, when he remarked that they were the children who were recovering from their malaria, and the others were still sick; some indeed had "fever" at the time I saw them. Having had this pointed out to me, observations on other estates soon confirmed it. Later on, I found it had been known for the last 300 years. The manner of my rediscovering it was as follows :—

When a medical student in 1894 I purchased a copy, in fair preservation, of

THE

WHOLE WORKS

of that excellent Practical Physician

DR. THOMAS SYDENHAM

WHEREIN

Not only the HISTORY and CURES of accute Difeafes are treated of, after a new and accurate Method : and also the fhorteft way of curing most Chronical Difeafes.

THE TENTH EDITION
Corrected from the original Latin by

JOHN PECHEY, M.D.
Of the College of Phyficians in London.

LONDON

Printed for W. Feales, at Rowe's Head the Corner of Effex-ftreet in the Strand ; R. Wellington, at the Dolphin and Crown without Temple-Bar ; J. Wellington ; A. Bettefworth and F. Clay, in truft for B. Wellington. 1734.

The book is, of course, of fascinating interest. At the time I made an index, in which I find "Giving of Peruvian Bark, the best method"; from which it would appear that 300 years ago there was a quinine controversy. There are also items "Dropsy at the end of Ague," and "Hard belly in children." But I had, however, forgotten all these things; nor were they recalled until, sometime after Mr Stevens had made his remark on the spleens in children, I referred to the book, or at least to Chapter V. "Of the AGUES in the years 1661, '62, '63, '64."

Quinine, or rather Cinchona, Peruvian bark, or Jesuit's powder, had come into use in Europe about 1640 ; and although widely used, there was still doubt about the best method and time to give it. Sydenham appears to have had no certain cure for malaria. Speaking of the Agues in the Fall he says :—

"But if there be any Man who knows how to ftop the Career of thefe Agues, either by a Method or a Spefick, he is certainly obliged to difcover a thing fo beneficial to Mankind ; but if he refufe to do it, he is neither a good citizen, nor a prudent Man ; for it does not become a good

Citizen to referve that for himfelf, which may be advantageous to Mankind; neither is it the part of a prudent Man to deprive himfelf of that Bleffing he may reasonably expect from Heaven, if he makes it his bufinefs to promote the Good of the Publick; and truly, Virtue and Wifdom are more valu'd by good Men, than either Riches or Honour."

"But tho it is hard to cure Agues in the Fall, yet I will mention what I have found moft fuccefsful in the management of them."

He warns against purging and bleeding, but recommends sweating; then he goes on:—

"As to the Cure of Quartans, I fuppofe every who is but little converfant in this Art, knows how unfuccefsful all the Methods have hitherto been, which are defigned for the Cure of them, except the *Peruvian Bark*, which indeed oftener ftops it than conquers it: for after it has ceafed a Fortnight or three Weeks, to the great advantage of the Patient, who having been feverely handled by it, has a little breathing time, it begins again afrefh, tormenting him as bad as ever; and for the moft part, how often foever the Medicine be repeated, it requires a long time before it can be vanquifhed; yet I will mention what I have obferv'd concerning the Method of giving it.

"But you muft take care not to give the Jesuits Powder too foon, before the difeafe has a little wafted itfelf, unlefs the weaknefs of the Patient requires it fhould be given fooner: . . . I think it better to tincture the Blood leifurely with the aforefaid Medicine, and a good while before the Fit, than to endeavour at once to hinder the Fit juft approaching, for by this means the Remedy has more time to perform its bufinefs thorowly, and then the Patient is freed from the danger that might happen by a fudden unfeafonable Stop, whereby we endeavour to fupprefs the Fit that is now about to exert it-felf with all its Might. Lastly, the Powder muft be repeated at fuch fhort diftances of Time, that the Virtue of the former Dofe be not quite fpent before the other be given: for by the frequent Repetition a good Habit of Body will be recover'd, and the difeafe wholly vanquifh'd."

For the very young suffering from the spring and autumnal tertians, he says that bark may be used with good success, but he prefers to leave the whole business to Nature. He does not recommend either change of air or diet: "for I never found hitherto any ill from thence, if the Bufinefs be wholly left to

Nature, which I often observ'd with admiration efpecially in Infants." For the old he recommends a change of air to a warmer country, and cordials strengthening diet.

In all probability malignant subtertian malaria did not exist in England and London in Sydenham's time, so he was able to withhold the powders from infants, and it was possible for patients to go on with their fevers for months on end. This gave him the opportunity of observing the natural course of the disease in more favourable conditions, from certain points of view, than obtains in the tropics. Anyhow he did observe the disease closely, and we find the following on prognosis:—

"It is worth noting, That when thofe Autumnal Agues have a long time molefted Children, there is no hope of recovery till the Region of the Belly, efpecially about the Spleen begins to be harden'd and to fwell; for the Ague goes gradually off as this Symptom comes on; nor perhaps can you any other way better prognofticate the going off of the Difeafe in a fhort time, than by obferving this Symptom, and the fwelling of the Legs, which are fometimes feen in grown people."

That describes pretty accurately what Mr Stevens discovered for himself and told me; which reminds me that I am writing a chapter "On Statistics," and this is the section on Spleen Rates.

In malarial places where the spleen rate is 50 or over, the systematic use of quinine does not appear to affect the rate appreciably; but when malaria is less severe, or where the malarial season lasts only a few months, quinine does lower the spleen rate, as my old friend Major J. D. Graham, I.M.S., showed in 1914.[35]

The Seasonal Variation of Malaria.

In Malaya, where the conditions are apparently so favourable to mosquitoes throughout the whole year, one would hardly expect any marked seasonal variation in the malaria. Yet it is not so. It is true that the introduction of many non-immune people into a malarious place, at any time of the year, will forthwith be followed by a severe outbreak of malaria, showing, as we know, that there is usually a considerable number of active insects present (Fig. 111). But apart from such accidental outbursts, there are definite seasonal variations, which form curves or waves varying with the species carrying

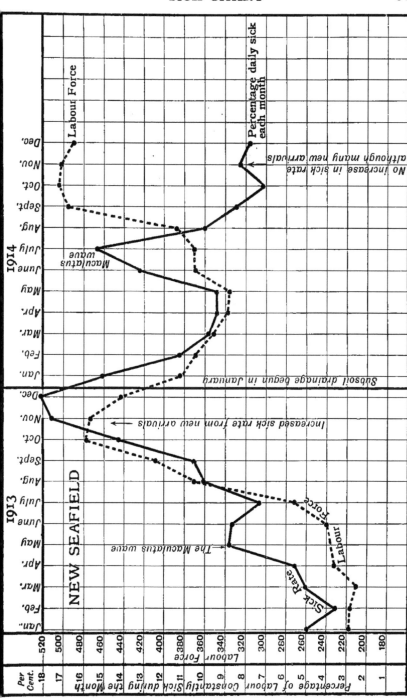

FIG. III.—New Seafield Estate. Chart showing the percentage of the Labour Force constantly sick each month in 1913 and 1914.

the disease. The subject has not been as fully worked out as it might have been, owing to the defective system of death registration in this country. We have, however, learned something.

When, at the end of 1901, the figures of malaria from the

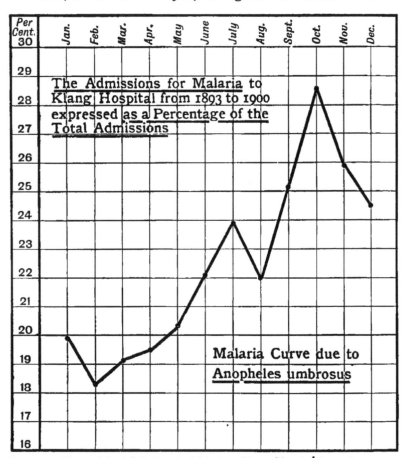

FIG. 112.—Chart of the Admissions for Malaria to Klang Hospital from 1893 to 1900, expressed as a Percentage of the Total Admissions. The *umbrosus* Wave.

hospitals of the three coast districts of Selangor were charted; they showed notable differences. Whereas the malaria wave in Kuala Selangor district had reached its maximum in 1899, that in Klang still rose for two more years, and doubtless would have continued to rise but for the anti-malaria work done, for the population was rapidly increasing.

But there was another difference: this time between the

Klang and Kuala Selangor charts on the one hand, and the Kuala Langat chart on the other. In the Klang chart there was generally a steady increase of malaria throughout the year from the minimum in February to the maximum in October, with slight pause in August. Fig. 112 chart represents the average of the percentages of malaria treated each month from 1893 to 1900. (The percentages are averaged so that the larger totals of the later years may not dominate the results unduly). The Kuala Langat chart, which in reality represented only the sickness of the inhabitants near to Jugra Hill, showed a sharp rise about April or May, when the maximum might be reached, and the epidemic as sharply subsiding in August, September, or October; which was quite a different figure from that of Klang District.

It was not until later that the significance of these differences came to be understood; and this is the explanation.

The curve with the maximum in November—the Klang chart—is due to malaria caused by *A. umbrosus*, and possibly other pool breeders. It is unlikely that *A. maculatus* affected it in these years. The other curve with the wave in the centre months of the year—from April to September—is the malaria of *A. maculatus* in hill land. The larvæ of *A. maculatus* are greatly reduced in number by the heavy rains of November, December, and January; but in the two drier months, February and March, they appear in enormous numbers. Shortly afterwards the malaria wave appears. Fig. 113 shows the monthly admissions for malaria of three hill land estates situated a few miles apart; the general similarity of the waves is striking; and I may add that the rise of the wave took place not merely in the month of April, but almost in the same week of the month, as the following table shows:—

Weekly Admissions for Malaria.

1916.	Estate "A."	Estate "B."	Estate "C."
Week ending 25th March	13	10	5
„ 1st April	16	4	7
„ 8th April	21	12	6
„ 15th April	25	38	36
„ 23rd April	43	39	22

An attempt is now made to abort this wave by special

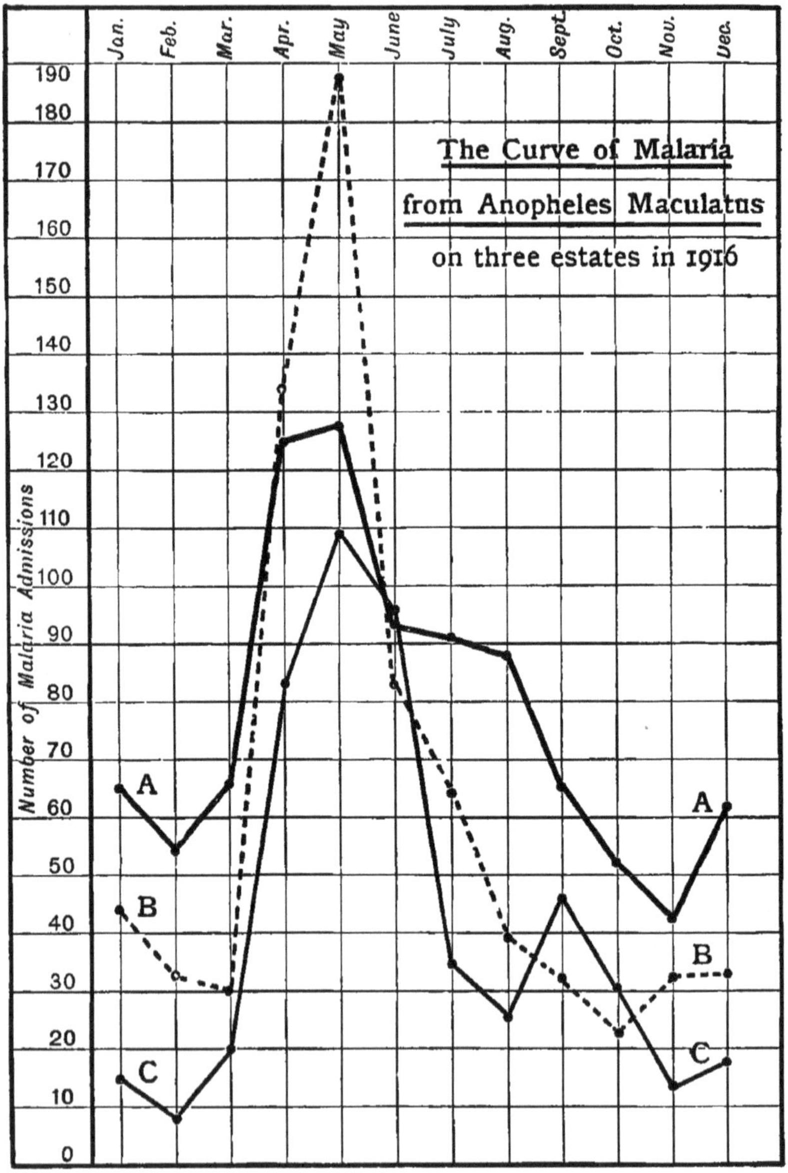
Jan.
Feb.
Mar.
Apr.
May
June
July
Aug.
Sept.
Oct.
Nov.
Dec.
The Curve of Malaria
from Anopheles Maculatus
on three estates in 1916
Number of Malaria Admissions
190
180
170
160
150
140
130
120
110
100
90
80
70
60
50
40
30
20
10
0
A
B
C
A
B
C

FIG. 113.

attention to oiling between February and June, and particularly in the drier periods of these months. Good results appear to be obtained.

Where part of the area is flat and part hilly, the annual statistical curve is, of course, a combination of the two waves.

CHAPTER XXIX

RESULTS

IN the preceding pages many instances of the control or partial control of malaria have been given; and it has been possible to associate directly the improved health with its cause, namely, some form of anti-malarial measure; it may have been open drainage, subsoil drainage, oiling, removal of people from the vicinity of jungle, or of jungle from people, or only the preservation of jungle. The number of people affected by any single operation has usually been small—perhaps only a few hundreds, although in places it has been greater. The sum total of the people is, however, considerable; so it may be worth gathering together the threads to see what manner of pattern they make.

TOWNS OF KLANG AND PORT SWETTENHAM.

The only figures in my possession are those already given in the earlier part of the book.

Table showing Deaths in the two Towns corrected for Deaths occurring in the Hospital.

Year.					Deaths.
1900	.	.	.		474
1901	.	.	.	.	582
1902	.	.	.		144
1903	.	.	.	.	115
1904	.	.	.	.	122
1905	.	.	.	.	113

The anti-malarial work was begun in 1901; and the figures indicate that from 1902 onwards, several hundred lives have been saved annually. In 1901 the population was only 3576 for the two towns; but they have never ceased to expand. To-day, as determined by the recent food control census, the population of the town of Klang is over 20,000 people, and that of Port Swettenham nearly 6000. Can anyone doubt that had the anti-malarial work not been done originally in 1901, and subsequently extended to cover the new population in the enlarged towns, many lives would have been lost annually, which, in fact, have been saved. In the eighteen years many thousands of lives must have been saved in the two towns.

ESTATES UNDER THE AUTHOR'S CARE.

Figures are available of the health of the labour forces under my care. The estate hospital system was started in 1908; but my connection with the estates and researches into the causes of their ill-health began before that—at a time, indeed, when a healthy estate was practically unknown.

The following figures are taken from the Official Returns printed in the Annual Indian Immigration Reports, except for the year 1919, which are compiled from the monthly returns sent to the Health Department. The Immigration Report for 1919 has not yet been published.

Year.	Labour Force.	No. of Deaths.	Death Rates per 1000.
1906	9,939	528	53·1
1907	13,676	707	51·7
1908	15,898	1053	66·2
1909	16,982	527	31·3
1910	23,295	1155	49·5
1911	29,567	1924	65·1
1912	32,394	1017	31·4
1913	38,248	975	25·4
1914	34,040	882	25·9
1915	30,456	572	19·0
1916	31,877	666	20·8
1917	28,954	664	22·9
1918	28,227	1269	44·9
1919	27,030	478	17·9

The figures and the chart show an almost continuous improvement in health: and further improvement may be expected if the recommendations made are efficiently carried out, and the work already done maintained and extended.*

The improvement was checked, however, on several notable occasions. In 1911 about 30 per cent. of the deaths were probably due to the breakdown in the Penang Quarantine Station; of some 10,000 coolies in it many suffered from

* The death rate for 1920 was 17·5 per mille.

cholera, dysentery, and malaria; many died in the station; and many others died soon after their arrival on the estates, and so raised the death rate. In 1916-1917 a severe local outbreak of malaria almost doubled the death rate of the Kapar District. It was mainly due to the new railway—as I have described in the section entitled The Story of a Coast Railway—in Chapter XXII.

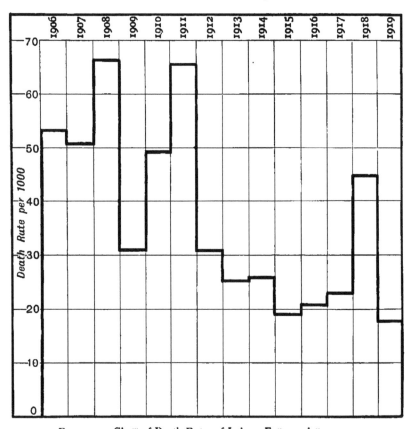

FIG. 114.—Chart of Death Rates of Labour Force under my care.

In 1918 the world-wide epidemic of influenza affected the estates. In 1919 the disease was still haunting the coolie ships, and affected many coolies both in the quarantine station and on the estates. Despite this and the shortage of rice, the death rate for 1919 is the lowest on record.

Had the death rate remained at 66·2—the figures for the year 1908—the number of deaths occurring annually would have been as shown in the following table. The table also shows the number of lives presumably saved.

Year.	Labour Force.	No. of Deaths that occurred.	No. of Deaths at the rate of 66·2 per mille.	Estimated No. of Lives Saved.
1908	15,898	1053	...	...
1909	16,982	527	1221	694
1910	23,295	1155	1537	372
1911	29,567	1920	1951	31
1912	32,394	1017	2137	1120
1913	38,248	975	2524	1549
1914	34,040	882	2246	1364
1915	30,456	572	2010	1438
1916	31,877	666	2103	1437
1917	28,954	664	1910	1246
1918	28,227	1269	1862	393
1919	27,030	478	1783	1305
Total .	...	...	...	10,949

Large as the saving of life has been according to this calculation, there is reason to believe that it is an under-estimate; for we have seen that to increase the number of non-immune people in a malarial area increases the death rate at an ever-accelerating rate until it reaches 300 per mille * or over. The large increase of the population since 1908 would, therefore, have led to a death rate far in excess of the rate 66·2 on which the calculation is based; and the saving of 10,949 may be regarded as well within the truth.

The years have shown how even in a country notorious for its ill-health and high death rates, large, healthy, and prosperous labour forces can be built up out of very un-promising material: for the Indians who come here are usually poverty-stricken, often half-starved, and possess little resistance to disease.

THE ESTATE LABOUR FORCE OF THE F.M.S.

Although ten years ago the control of malaria in rural districts was not considered practicable, and even to-day one hears talk of the almost insuperable difficulty and extravagant cost hardly making "the game worth the candle," that has

---

* General Gorgas claims that 71,370 lives were saved by sanitary work in Panama during the construction of the Canal, and calculated this from the French death rate of 200 per mille.

not been the attitude generally adopted in the F.M.S. On the flat land, the cost was often nothing; for a healthy site was selected instead of an unhealthy one, and the choice cost nothing. To quote the report of the Senior Health Officer for the year 1915:—

"Upon estates situated in the alluvial flats of the Coast Districts of Krian, Lower Perak, and Selangor, the health of the labourers is excellent, the only cause for anxiety is lack of good water in times of drought. . . ."

Of hill land he says:—

"Anti-malarial measures of various sorts are universal upon most up-country estates, the most common is the prophylactic administration of quinine, many estates now spray with oil all swamps and ravines adjacent to the coolie lines, and a few have expended large sums on subsoil drainage.

"Labourers are now generally housed in well-constructed lines built upon open clearings which afford good drainage; these have replaced the dark palm-leaf hovels on the edges of swamps or ravines, and closely surrounded by jungle or rubber which were formerly so common."

Death Rate per Mille of Estate Labourers in the Federated Malay States.

Year.	All Nationalities.		Indian Labourers.	
	Number.	Death Rate.	Number.	Death Rate.
1906	...			
1907	...	...		
1908	...	...		
1909	...	...		
1910	...	...		
1911	143,614	62.9		
1912	171,968	41.0		
1913	188,937	29.6		
1914	176,226	26.3		
1915	169,100	16.7		
1916	187,030	17.6		
1917	214,972	18.1		
1918	213,423	42.5		
1919	237,128	14.6		

Improved water-supplies, increased and improved hospital accommodation, etc., have been provided for labourers, all of which have contributed to the lowering of the death rate; and it is impossible, from the data available, to disentangle the part due solely to the anti-malaria work, important though it must be. So I have contented myself with giving simply the death rate of the labour force in the F.M.S. since 1911. Each year measures to improve health become more efficient, and without doubt further improvement will take place.

From 1906 to 1910, the figures for the Indian labourers include the indentured labour. There are no official statistics of estate labour other than Indian prior to 1911.

Taking the death rate of 62·9 per mille, and calculating as in the previous table, the number of lives saved from 1911 to 1919 is 58,102.

In this calculation no account is taken of the lives saved before 1911 in the F.M.S.; nor have I reckoned the saving of life by similar work elsewhere in the Peninsula; in the Settlements of Malacca, Province Wellesley, The Dindings; or in the Unfederated Malay States, like Johore and Kedah. In these areas there are many thousands of estate labourers; on many occasions I have visited estates to advise on sanitary measures; and to my knowledge much excellent work is being done, and many lives saved. Of the work done in the city of Singapore, the chief city of Malaya, I will speak presently.

These results have been achieved not in a specially selected body of recruits, but among the poorest classes of India and China. The Indians, in particular, often arrive in the last stages of destitution, with hardly a rag of clothing for the adults, and none at all for even large children. The famines, which for ages have swept that land, have left their mark in the poor physique of the Tamils of Southern India; and even to-day famine drives whole families, of two or three generations, to Malaya. Many of the very old people are on the labour rolls, for occasionally they do a little light work; among these, as well as the infants, malaria has a deadly effect.

Great as the improvement in health has been, much still remains to be done; more estates can be made fit for Indian labour than now employ it; and the death rate of all can, I believe, be brought below 10 per mille.

SINGAPORE.

The City of Singapore, placed by the foresight of Raffles one hundred years ago on the great highway to the East, has a population to-day of over 300,000 people. Even twenty years ago, as reckoned by the tonnage of the shipping, it was the seventh largest port in the world.

The entrepôt of the Great Archipelago and the neighbouring lands, it contains a curiously mixed population from East and West, from North and South; the main constituents of which are Chinese, Indians, and Malays. Arriving yearly by thousands, or passing through on their several ways to work in the surrounding countries and islands, such a population places peculiar responsibilities on the Health Department, and has made its work specially arduous. Back lanes, insanitary houses, food and markets, lodging-houses, slaughter-houses, offensive trades, hawkers, and many other things demanding the activities associated with a Health Department in a large city had kept the staff busy; vast improvements had been affected; yet the death rate remained obstinately high. Great waves of malaria from time to time swept the city, reaching in June 1911 a maximum of 85·83 per mille. They defied every effort of the Department, and seemed to render fruitless almost all its work.

In 1911, malaria control was a much discussed subject. Many authorities were far from optimistic about the result of anti-mosquito work. In an able report the Health Officer, Dr W. R. C. Middleton, reviewed the whole subject; and subsequently, at his suggestion, and on the invitation of the Anti-malaria Committee, I visited Singapore and made recommendations for dealing with the most malarial district.

The work was admirably executed; it led to a rapid and permanent fall in the spleen rate; and since then it has been widely extended, although some areas remain to be done.

In such a shifting population, where, from inquiry, 30 to 50 per cent. of the hospital malaria admissions have been shown to be imported from beyond the city limits, the unravelling of death rates and an estimate of the effect of the anti-malaria work may appear a mere juggling with figures. Yet I think it is not so; for much information can be gained by a study of the monthly and annual variation of the death rates, which I have printed in the appendix.

The outstanding fact is a great fall in the death rates since the anti-malarial work was begun in 1911, when compared with those of the previous twenty years.

Death Rates of Singapore.

	Per mille.
1892 to 1911 average death rate	. 42·33
1912 to 1919 „ „ . . .	. 34·78
Difference . . .	7·55

If the average population between 1912 and 1919 be taken roughly as 280,000, the number of lives saved by all sanitary measures in Singapore in these eight years is 2100 × 8 or 16,800. What share of this is to be credited to the malaria control work?

Another outstanding fact, when we consider the figures, is the great rise in the death rates in the middle months of the year, usually beginning in May. Between 1901 and 1911 it occurs every year, with the exception of 1906; and in most years forms the curve, with which the reader must now be familiar, of malaria caused by *A. maculatus*, a mosquito, as Dr Hunter proves, prevalent and of importance in Singapore. To show how serious these waves were, the following table shows the highest monthly rise between 1901 and 1911 (cholera and smallpox are excluded).

Of the eleven years:—

In 11 the monthly rate rose above 40 per mille.
„ 10   „   „   45   „
„ 9   „   50
„ 5   „   55   „
„ 3   60   „
„ 2   „   70   „
„ 1   „   „   80   „

Now if malaria control played any important part in the lowering of the general death rate, it would be reasonable to expect a reduction, if not the obliteration, of the annual malarial wave. The anti-malarial work was begun in 1911, and subsequently we do find a reduction in the magnitude of the malaria wave (cholera and smallpox are included).

In 1912 the wave rose to 56 per mille.
„ 1913   „   „   42   „
„ 1914   „   42
„ 1915   „   „   28   „
„ 1916   „   36
„ 1917   „   „   39   „
„ 1918   „   „   68   „*
„ 1919   „   „   38   „

* Influenza.

To sum up: whereas prior to 1911 it was almost normal for the wave of malaria to sweep the death rate above, and often far above, 45 per mille, the wave has only reached that figure once—the influenza year is excepted—since the anti-malarial work was begun. As long as anopheles breeding-places exist in Singapore, and men who contract malaria elsewhere come into the city when ill, so long will the mortality rates show an upward curve in the malarial season. But when we recall the evidence given in the preceding chapters

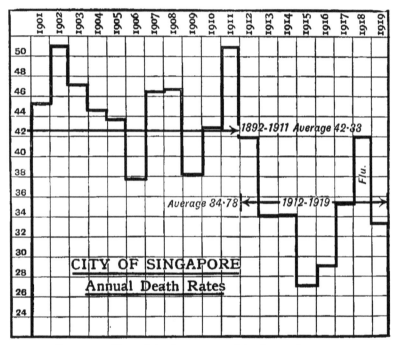

FIG. 115.—Chart of the Death Rates of the City of Singapore.

of this book—of malaria control, its seasonal waves, its effects on special and general death rates, the relationship of death rates and spleen rates—and then consider the lowering of the general death rate, the flattening of the mortality curve, and the fall in the spleen rate of Singapore, it seems to me we are irresistibly drawn to the conclusion that, more than any other factor, the anti-malarial work of the past eight years has led to the improved health of the city, and contributed to the saving of over 16,000 lives.

Yet, whatever the cause or complex of causes may be,

which has lowered the death rate, the saving of thousands of lives is a fact beyond dispute, and one in which the Health Officers of Singapore may take a legitimate pride. It is, indeed, a splendid example of Preventive Medicine in the Tropics, and an inspiration for the great and difficult tasks that still lie before them.

There is a considerable mass of evidence to show that in the past twenty years, sanitary work generally, and particularly the control of malaria in conjunction with other measures, has saved 100,000 lives in the Malay Peninsula, and an enormous, but incalculable, amount of money.

.   .   .

PANAMA.

Critics of the work done by the Americans in Panama sometimes say that what was accomplished there would be impossible under less special conditions. They contend that the canal was built primarily as a war measure to safeguard the interests of Americans; cost was of minor importance, and the work was backed by the whole assets of the United States Treasury. They point out that the area dealt with was only 50 square miles, and declare that the population was under an iron discipline not attainable in other countries.

These criticisms may, or may not, be strictly true; but, if true, they are answered, I think, by the work done in the Malay Peninsula. Here the work has been done by Government in the ordinary course of its sanitary administration; and by the Estates, which are commercial undertakings, whose policy is influenced by price of the produce they sell. The area of the operations extends to thousands of square miles; indeed the area over which the estates under my supervision are scattered is more than 1000 square miles. The population of the estates is under a certain amount of discipline; but, the labour being free and not indentured, the discipline is far from being of the military variety.

In Malaya, the control of malaria has been attempted successfully under many different conditions; from small rural populations of two or three hundred people on estates, and in small towns of three or four thousand inhabitants like Klang, to a city like Singapore, with over a quarter of a million people; the complexity of the entomological aspect of the problem, from the number of species carrying malaria under different conditions, has no parallel in Panama; the number of lives already saved by the work annually is greater in Malaya than in the Isthmus; and I might add that the work was begun here some years before it was started there.

The work in Panama is, in my opinion, without question the most brilliant achievement in Preventive Medicine which the tropics, and for that matter the whole world, has seen; but such a statement in no wise detracts from the value of what has been accomplished in Malaya. The work in the two places may be compared to the advantage or disadvantage of either, as the critic may be biassed. In truth, they are to be regarded as complementary; each developing on the lines best calculated to achieve its object in its own peculiar circumstances. They represent different phases or stages in progress towards the time when man shall conquer the tropics by stamping out its diseases; and these rich lands, many of the most fertile on the face of the earth, shall pour out, in unstinted measure, of their abundance for the welfare of the human race.

CHAPTER XXX

CONCLUSIONS

THE conclusions I draw from these observations are :—

Mosquito Reduction.

(1) From a malarial standpoint, the Malay Peninsula can be divided into several zones which may conveniently be distinguished as, the Mangrove Zone, the Coastal Plain, the Coastal Hills, the Inland Plain, and the Inland Hills.

(2) These zones may be malarial naturally, or may become so through the operations of man.

(3) The part of the Mangrove Zone covered daily by the tide contains no anopheles and is non-malarial. When the forest is felled and the tidal flow obstructed, it may become intensely malarial from the appearance of *A. ludlowi*, which has been proved to be a natural carrier of malaria and is probably the most important carrier in the Mangrove Zones.

(4) The part of the Mangrove Zone covered only by the spring tides is naturally malarial from the presence of *A. umbrosus*, which has been proved to be a natural carrier of malaria. Clearing the forest allows *A. ludlowi* to enter this portion of the zone also.

(5) Both *A. ludlowi* and *A. umbrosus* are eliminated by clean weeded drains and good drainage ; and many examples of how good agriculture abolished these mosquitoes and their malaria from the Mangrove Zone can be given.

(6) The Coastal Plain is malarial from the presence of *A. umbrosus* in its virgin jungle.

(7) Hundreds of square miles of flat land in the Coastal Plain of Malaya have been freed from malaria by simply draining and felling the jungle, and cultivating the land.

361

(8) The disappearance of malaria from the Coastal Plain coincides with the disappearance of *A. umbrosus*, which breeds in pools in undrained jungle, but cannot breed in open earth drains when kept free from weeds, and with a current of water. There are probably other reasons connected with the quality of the water in well-drained land.

(9) Ten years ago the cost of these rural anti-malaria measures in Malaya was about £3 sterling an acre, being £2 to drain, and £1 to fell the heavy virgin jungle. This expenditure is, at the same time, the first step in agriculture, and the land has then acquired a considerably increased value. To-day the cost of draining and felling is about 70 per cent. higher. When an estate is newly opened, it is possible for the Medical Officer to select non-malarial sites, and the cost of controlling malaria is, of course—*nil*.

(10) In the low Coastal Hills next to the Coastal Plain, malaria is prevalent when the ravines are under jungle owing to the presence of *A. umbrosus* in large numbers.

(11) Clearing and draining of these ravines frees them from *A. umbrosus*, but does not free the land from malaria.

(12) Malaria persists in the Coastal Hills after the ravines have been cleared and drained and after *A. umbrosus* has disappeared, from the appearance of *A. maculatus*.

(13) *A. maculatus* does not live in ravines covered by heavy jungle; but appears only after the shade has been removed. The cleaner the water, and the better drained the ravine, the more suitable the ravine becomes for *A. maculatus*.

(14) The utmost care and cleanliness from an agricultural point of view continued over a period of years, fails to eliminate *A. maculatus* and its malaria.

(15) *A. maculatus* can be completely abolished from ravines by subsoil drainage, or spraying with suitable oils: and its malaria disappears with it.

(16) The Inland Plains are poorly represented in Malaya. They are healthy like the Coastal Plains when opened; but *A. aconitus*, if present in streams of running water, must be controlled.

(17) The Inland Hills are non-malarial when under virgin jungle, because *A. umbrosus* does not exist in the ravines. They differ in this respect from the Coastal Hills.

(18) The Inland Hills become intensely malarial when the ravines are opened, because *A. maculatus* appears. In this respect they are like the Coastal Hills.

(19) Subsoil drainage, and oiling which control *A. maculatus* in the Coastal Hills are equally suitable in the Inland Hills. In the future it will probably be found more economical in many places to allow the ravines to revert to jungle. In opening land in this zone in the future, malaria can be avoided by refraining from felling the jungle in the ravines. This will cost nothing.

Rice Fields.

(20) Rice fields on the Coastal Plain are practically free from malaria. The anopheles found are *A. rossi*, *A. kochi*, *A. sinensis*, *A. barbirostris*, and maybe *A. fuliginosus*.

(21) Rice fields in narrow valleys are usually, in my experience, malarial. The anopheles found are *A. rossi*, *A. kochi*, *A. sinensis*, *A. barbirostris*, *A. fuliginosus*, and *A. aconitus* has been proved a natural carrier of malaria.

(22) Further research will almost certainly show how the malaria of rice fields in valleys can be controlled by altering the composition of the water—by polluting it; which will be a great boon not only to the Malays, who cultivate the rice, but to others, by increasing the food production of the country.

Quinine.

(23) Quinine given regularly reduces the sick rate and death rate of those exposed to malaria.

(24) Doses of less than 6 grains daily are of little value where malaria is intense—say where the spleen rate is over 60.

(25) Where malaria is intense, and the population consists of immigrants, take 10-grain doses on six days out of the seven, and 20-grain doses when suffering from pyrexia or not at work on account of ill-health, between 20 and 30 per cent. of those taking the drug will be found with parasites in their peripheral blood.

(26) The use of quinine can, therefore, never result in the abolition of malaria, nor make any material reduction in the liability to infection in an intensely malarial locality.

(27) In twenty years' experience I have seen quinine given systematically for long periods in many intensely malarial places; but in no place have I seen any material reduction in liability to infection due to quinine alone; most newcomers have become infected, and have died or become immune.

(28) Quinine systematically given probably assists the infected to acquire a natural immunity. Where there is no re-infection ten to twenty grains in solution for three months is an almost certain cure for the people of most races— Malayalees appear to be an exception. Rest in bed on four successive Sundays assists quinine to stop relapses. In women there is a special necessity for quinine at menstrual periods. Abortion and the very fatal malarial anæmia of pregnancy can often be prevented by the continuous use of quinine in doses of from ten to twenty grains daily throughout pregnancy. Abortion is produced, not by the quinine, but by the malaria.

Screening.

(29) The attempt to discover a satisfactory screened coolie line ended in an inconclusive experiment, as I was unable to supervise it to its termination.

(30) Screened bungalows for Europeans have proved of great value.

(31) Screened hospitals give a real protection in patients; mosquito curtains in hospitals for Asiatics are practically value-less, and are more expensive than screening.

The Labour Problem.

Much is said about the difficulty there will be in the future of obtaining labour for F.M.S. It is stated that the F.M.S. will never be able to attract from India all the coolies required, and that the estates will have to depend on Chinese labourers.

I confess I am an optimist on this subject, and have no fear for the future, if a wise medical policy be adopted by this country. For a number of years now, I have watched many estates; and as a result have come to these conclusions.

(32) Until the recent difficulties with shortage of rice and adverse Indian exchange, few healthy estates have failed to obtain all the coolies required; some years there may be

shortage, but in most years more are recruited than are required. This applies not only to old estates, but also to new estates like "EE," which in its third year imported more labour from India than any other estate in the F.M.S. The chief difficulty of healthy estates is the prevention of crimping; that is, having their coolies enticed away by unhealthy estates.

(33) Unhealthy estates are perfectly well known to the coolies both here and in India, and are generally avoided; not only have these estates difficulty in obtaining labour, but the annual loss of labour through death, discharge, etc., is 30 to 50 per cent. greater that on the healthy estates.

(34) Chinese labour, being originally non-immune to malaria, suffers almost as much as Indian labour, when living permanently on the estate like Indian labour. It is only when the Chinese labourer can leave the estate when ill, that he survives to resume his work another day; he gradually acquires a natural immunity

(35) Chinese know which estates are unhealthy; and the wages paid on unhealthy estates to Chinese are much higher than those paid to Tamils on healthy estates.

(36) Healthy estates are not without interest in all others becoming healthy, since the unhealthy estates, by their attraction of higher wages, unsettle the coolies of the healthy estates and often attract their skilled tappers.

(37) Were all estates healthy, more Indian labour would be attracted; it would be more efficient; and there would be more inducement for the coolies to make the F.M.S. their home.

(38) Were the country inhabited by the Malays, and more particularly the rice-fields of valleys, made healthy, the Malay infantile death rate would be greatly reduced, and an abundant healthy Malay population supported by their rice-fields would come into being. Java is a wonderful example of how a Malay race can expand.

(39) In this way, even apart from the Chinese, this naturally rich country would obtain the labour force without which its development is impossible, "and I believe," as I wrote ten years ago, "that the labour problem is nothing but the malaria problem, and that the solution of the malaria problem will also be the solution of the labour problem. No estate can ever

have an assured labour force where the women wail, 'We cannot have children here, and the children we bring with us die.' Such is the cry on the unhealthy estates : ' It is vain to contend with the instinct of her who weeps for her children and will not be comforted.' It is because I believe we do now know how to save the children that I am an optimist for Malaya. This volume has shown how malaria has been driven from great tracts of country, and how the development of the country under the British has been a boon, not only to the native but to the foreigner also. Already irrigation and drainage have not only assured them of their crops, and given them wealth beyond anything they had known, but have given them freedom from their most deadly disease over wide areas. It remains but to extend these benefits. And although some details have still to be learned, I think that working on Ross's discovery, and on the method advocated by him, we may confidently hope to drive the disease completely from the land."

REFERENCES.

1. BELFIELD. *Handbook of the Federated Malay States.*
2. ROSS. *The Prevention of Malaria.*
3. MANSON. *Brit. Med. Journ.,* 29th Sept. 1900.
4. GRASSI. *Brit. Med. Journ.,* Oct. 1900, p. 1051.
5. KOCH. "German Malaria Commission," *Brit. Med. Journ.,* Sept. 1900.
6. *Reports to the Malaria Committee of the Royal Society.*
7. LEICESTER. *Studies from the Institute for Medical Research,* vol. iii.
8. WATSON. *Journ. of Tropical Med.,* Nov. and Dec. 1903.
9. WATSON. "Report on Drainage of Country Roads," *Selangor Government Gazette,* 1904.
10. WATSON. "Some Clinical Features of Quartan Malaria," *Journ. Malaya Br. of B.M.A. and I.M. Gazette,* 1905.
11. LUDLOW. (a) *The Mosquitoes of the Philippine Islands; the Distribution of Certain Species, and their Occurrence in Relation to the Incidence of Certain Diseases,* 1908.
    (b) *Disease-bearing Mosquitoes of North and Central America, the West Indies, and the Philippine Islands,* 1914.
12. LUDLOW. *Ibid.* (a).
13. DE VOGEL. *Myzomyia rossii as a Malaria Carrier,* Semarang, 1909.
    DE VOGEL. "Anophelines dans l'eau de mer," *Soc. Stud. d. malaria,* 1906.
14. MANGKOEWINOTO. "Anophelines of West Java," *Meded. Burgerlijken Geneesk. Dienst in Ned. Indie.,* Deel ii., 1919.
15. CHRISTOPHERS. "Malaria in the Andamans," *Scien. Memoirs,* New Series, No. 56, 1912.
16. DE VOGEL. "Report of the Investigations carried out with Regard to the Sanitary Condition of the Port Sibolga," *Meded. Burgerlijken Geneesk. Dienst in Ned. Indie.,* Deel iv., 1915.
17. SWELLENGREBEL and OTHERS. "The Susceptibility of Anophelines to Malaria Infections in Netherlands Indie" and "On the Biology of *M. ludlowi* in Sumatra," *Meded. Burgerlijken Geneesk. Dienst in Ned. Indie.,* Deel iii., 1919.
18. WATSON. "The Effect of Drainage and other Measures on the Malaria of Klang, F.M.S.," *Journ. Trop. Med.,* 1903.
19. CHRISTOPHERS and BENTLEY. *Trans. Bombay Medical Congress,* 1908.

368 REFERENCES

20. DANIELS. *Brit. Med. Journ.*, 18th Sept. 1909.
21. ROSS. *Brit. Med. Journ.*, Jan. 1920.
22. GORGAS. *Sanitation in Panama.*

    LE PRINCE and ORENSTEIN. *Mosquito Control in Panama.*

    WATSON. *Rural Sanitation in the Tropics.*
23. DANIELS. *Journ. Malaya Br. B.M.A.*, 1905.
24. WATSON. *Malay Mail*, 21st June 1910.
25. STRICKLAND. *Certain Observations on the Epidemiology of Malarial Fever in the Malay Peninsula* (see p. 29).
26. HALL. *The Soil.*
27. The reader may consult the following works for further information :—
    (*a*) SCOTT. *Draining and Embanking.*
    (*b*) KING. *Irrigation and Drainage.*
    (*c*) WHEELER. *The Drainage of Fens and Low Lands.*
    (*d*) DAVIS and WILSON. *Irrigation Engineering.*
28. THEOBALD. "A Monograph of the Culicidæ or Mosquitoes."

    HOWARD, DYER, and KNAB. *The Mosquitoes of North and Central America and the West Indies.*

    ALCOCK. *Entomology for Medical Officers.*

    SWELLENGREBEL. *De Anophelinen van Nederlandsch Oost-Indie. Kol. Inst-te Amsterdam.*
29. STRICKLAND.
    1913. (*a*) "Revision of the List of Malayan Anophelines," *Ind. Journ. of Med. Res.*
          (*b*) "The Myzorhynchus Group of Anopheline Mosquitoes in Malaya," *Bull. Ento. Research.*
          (*c*) "Short Key to the Anopheline Mosquitoes of Malaya, F.M.S.," Govt. Printing Dept.
    1914. (*d*) "Description of the Larva of *Lophoscelomyia asiatica*," *Parasitology.*
          (*e*) "Comparative Morphology of the *A. ludlowi* and *rossi*," *Bull. Ento. Research.*
          (*f*) "Notes on *A. brevipalpis*, Roper," *Ind. Journ. of Med. Research.*
          (*g*) "Short Key to the Larvæ of the Common Anophelines of Malaya," F.M.S. Survey Office.
    1916. (*h*) "An Outbreak of Malarial Fever at Morib," *Parasitology*, January.
          (*i*) "The Epidemiology of Malarial Fever in the Malay Peninsula," *Proc. of Federal Council*, Nov. 1916.
          (*j*) "Description of a New Protanopheline Myzorhynchus hunteri," *Ind. Journ. of Med. Research.*
          (*k*) "Description of a New Species of Anopheline—*novumbrosus*," *Ind. Journ. of Med. Research.*
          (*m*) "Note on a New Species of Anopheline—*Myzorhynchus similis*," *Ind. Journ. of Med. Research.*

30. STANTON. (*a*) "The Larva of Malayan Anopheles," *Bull. Ento. Research*, Sept. 1915.

(*b*) "Notes on Sumatra Culicidæ," *Ind. Journ. of Med. Research*, Oct. 1915.

(*c*) "A New Anopheline Mosquito from Sumatra," *Bull. Ento. Research*, March 1915.

31. BARBOUR. "Some Observations and Experiments on Malayan Anopheles, with Special Reference to the Transmission of Malaria," *Phil. Journ. of Science*, 1918.

32. HACKER. *Malaria Bureau Reports*, F.M.S., vol. i., 1919.

33. The following works may be consulted :—

WEST. *Algæ.*

ANNANDALE. *Fauna of the Inle Lake*—in Records of the Indian Museum, vol. xiv., 1918.

ANNANDALE. *The Fauna of British India—Fresh-water Sponges, Hydroids, and Polyzoa.*

MIALL. *Aquatic Insects.*

HARRISON and AIYER. *The Gases of Swamp Rice Soils in Mem. of Dept. of Agriculture in India.*

34. SIMM. "Sub-drainage as Applied to the Anti-malarial Campaign on the Isthmus of Panama," *Ann. Trop. Med. and Hyg.*, vol. ii., No. 4.

35. *Progress Report on School Quininisation*, Allahabad, 1914, by J. D. Graham, I.M.S., Special Malaria Officer, United Provinces.

APPENDIX

Year.	January.	February.	March.	April.	May.
1892	34.36	3	27.64		
1893	38.08	3	33.99		
1894	33.70	28	28.90		
1895	32.35	26	31.43		
1896	46.8	44	44.4		
1897	41.9		38.8		
1898	30.78	26	26.01		
1899	37.58	29			
1900	34.83	29			
1901	44.54				49.00
1902	46.25				
1903	45.33				
1904	36.59				
1905	43.32				
1906	36.86				
1907	34.85			42.49	
1908	33.77			42.06	
1909	43.03			36.61	
1910	37.04				
1911	40.07				
1912	40.26				
1913	33.41				
1914	33.65				
1915	35.74				
1916	24.32			31.07	
1917	30.78			34.28	
1918	39.68			37.49	
1919	32.32			27.77	

NGAPORE.

ath Rates, 1892—1919.

June.	July.	August.	September.	October.	November.	December.
30.27	33.98	32.13	27.14	32.34	30.84	35.48
44.10	38.08	34.75	31.36		28.16	34.74
32.62	38.47	30.40	28.38		31.55	33.36
72.54	50.71	43.20			36.99	44.50
54.3	48.19	.51			40.12	37.26
46.3	49.1	.5			34.7	32.0
39.76	44.43	.94			34.97	
40.53	37.04	56			34.42	
46.41	44.43				52.22	
50.33	50.50				50.10	
61.82	53.89	40.42			48.00	
51.74	48.59	44.50			42.62	
48.77	53.26	53.30				
51.54	51.16	41.51				
36.86	40.65	32.54				
54.00	53.75	68.68				
51.06	50.31	49.46				
39.31	37.79	36.81				
43.68	55.56					
85.83	60.27					
55.96	50.23					
38.30	38.26					
40.62	36.37				33.35	
26.20	25.95				24.13	
34.55	33.42				27.64	
38.73	38.50				33.81	
44.55	51.33		30.36		50.72	34.35
35.79	38.44		36.17	35.53	35.61	35.79

2 C

INDEX

PRINTED BY

OLIVER AND BOYD

EDINBURGH, SCOTLAND

Rural Sanitation in the Tropics

BEING NOTES AND OBSERVATIONS IN THE MALAY
ARCHIPELAGO, PANAMA, AND OTHER LANDS

With Illustrations.

SOME PRESS OPINIONS:—

Journal of Tropical Medicine.—"The author is so well known to practitioners of tropical medicine that little need be said to them on the utility of this work. With regard to the laity, particularly employers of labour, both Native and European, and Government Officials, it is impossible to conceive a more practical book, or one more conducive to good health, the utilisation of labour, and likely to yield satisfactory financial results. . . . Considering the interest that is now displayed in rubber and other companies situated in the Tropics, it is desirous that all having tropical interests should study this work. They will then know the difficulties that have been overcome and the problems yet to be solved."

The Times.—"Dr Watson has spent many years in the practical work of combating Malaria in the Malay States, and he gives a valuable detailed account of the work accomplished there. He has, however, travelled extensively in order to gain a wider view of the problem. . . . The book contains an abundance of matter of much importance to the student, well put together, and based on first-hand study."

British Medical Journal.—"Will be read with interest by sanitarians everywhere. . . . It is a pioneer work, excellently written, and should prove of the greatest value to future sanitarians in all parts of the Tropics. Dr Watson's practical work in Malaya is well known, and his book will undoubtedly add to his reputation."

Journal of the Royal Sanitary Institute.—"A valuable contribution to our knowledge of tropical diseases and their prevention. . . . We commend this work to those who have to reside in tropical countries. It is a most interesting narrative of one who is deeply interested in his work, and he has done a real service to tropical medicine by giving us the results of his investigations."—J. L. N.

Works on Tropical Medicine and Sanitation

THE PREVENTION OF MALARIA

By Sir RONALD ROSS, K.C.B., K.C.M.G., F.R.S., etc. With contributions by twenty leading experts. With Illustrations. 24s. net.

" A thoroughly sound and comprehensive treatise ; Colonel Ross and his colleagues have turned out work worthy of their high reputations. The student of malaria in all respects will find in this work the most complete exposition of the subject in medical literature." Lancet.

A SUMMARY OF FACTS REGARDING MALARIA.

Being Chapter II. of the above work, giving practical directions for the prevention of the spread of the disease. Issued for Public Instruction. 2d. net.

PRACTICAL TROPICAL SANITATION

A Manual for Sanitary Inspectors and others interested in the Prevention of Disease in Tropical and Sub-Tropical countries. By W. ALEX. MUIRHEAD, Staff-Sergeant R.A.M.C. ; formerly on the Staff of the Sanitary Officer, West African Command. With Illustrations. 15s. net.

This concisely written book covers the whole field of tropical sanitary effort. It is copiously illustrated, and ideal for the instruction of subordinates, and will also be found an invaluable book of reference in the office of a municipality, an estate manager, mine owner, or trader. Especially it meets the needs of candidates for sanitary appointments.

RURAL SANITATION IN THE TROPICS

Being notes and observations in the Malay Archipelago, Panama and other lands. By MALCOLM WATSON, M.D., C.M., D.P.H. With Illustrations. 12s. net.

" The author is so well known to practitioners of tropical medicine that little need be said to them on the utility of this work. With regard to the laity, it is impossible to conceive a more practical book, or one more conducive to good health, the utilization of labour, and likely to yield satisfactory financial results." Journal of Tropical Medicine.

OUTLINES OF COMPARATIVE ANATOMY OF VERTEBRATES

By J. S. KINGSLEY, Professor of Zoology in the University of Illinois. Second Edition, Revised. With over 400 Illustrations, largely from original sources.

Works by Sir Rubert Boyce

MOSQUITO OR MAN ?

The Conquest of the Tropical World. By Sir RUBERT W. BOYCE, M.B., F.R.S., Formerly Holt Professor of Pathology, University of Liverpool, and Dean of the Liverpool School of Tropical Medicine. Third Edition. Revised and Enlarged. With Illustrations. 10s. 6d. net.

YELLOW FEVER AND ITS PREVENTION

A Manual for Medical Students and Practitioners. With numerous Plans and Illustrations. 10s. 6d. net.

HEALTH PROGRESS AND ADMINISTRATION IN THE WEST INDIES

Second Edition. With Illustrations. 10s. 6d. net.

Works by E. H. Ross

M.R.C.S. (Eng.), L.R.C.P. (Lond.), sometime Health Officer, Port Said, the Suez Canal District and Cairo.

THE REDUCTION OF DOMESTIC MOSQUITOS

Instructions for the use of Municipalities, Town Councils, Health Officers, Sanitary Inspectors, and Residents in Warm Climates. 5s. net.

THE REDUCTION OF DOMESTIC FLIES

With Illustrations. 5s. net.

THE STORY OF THE HOUSE-FLY.
Being Chapter XI. of the above book. 2d. net.

Lightning Source UK Ltd.
Milton Keynes UK
UKHW01f1308210918
329297UK00007B/816/P

9 781334 7